To Maureen, all
the best Tony Blair

Magda's Daughter

Oct 6 '04

D0823893

Magda's Daughter

A HIDDEN CHILD'S JOURNEY HOME

Evi Blaikie

Introduction by Bella Brodzki

THE HELEN ROSE SCHEUER
JEWISH WOMEN'S SERIES

THE FEMINIST PRESS
AT THE CITY UNIVERSITY OF NEW YORK

Published by the Feminist Press at the City University of New York
The Graduate Center, 365 Fifth Avenue, Suite 5406, New York, NY 10016
feministpress.org

Copyright © 2003 by Evelyne Blaikie
Introduction copyright © 2003 by Bella Brodzki

All rights reserved.
The author has changed the names of certain individuals in this book.

No part of this book may be reproduced or used, stored in any information retrieval system, or transmitted in any form or by any means, electronic, mechanical, photocopying, recording, or otherwise without prior written permission from the Feminist Press at the City University of New York, except in the case of brief quotations embodied in critical articles and reviews.

Library of Congress Cataloging-in-Publication Data

Blaikie, Evi, 1939–
    Magda's daughter : a hidden child's journey home / Evi Blaikie ; introduction by Bella Brodzki.
    p. cm. — (The Helen Rose Scheuer Jewish women's series)
    Includes bibliographical references.
    ISBN 1–55861–443–5 (alk. paper)
        1. Blaikie, Evi, 1939—Childhood and youth. 2. Jewish children in the Holocaust—Hungary—Biography.
        3. Jews—Hungary—Biography. 4. Hidden children (Holocaust)—Hungary—Biography. 5. Holocaust,
        Jewish (1939–1945)—Hungary—Personal narratives. 6. Refugees, Jewish—Biography. 7. Holocaust survivors—United States—Biography. I. Title. II. Series.
DS135.H93B57 2003
940.53'18'092—dc21   2003005051

NYSCA

Steven H. Scheuer, in memory of his mother and in celebration of her life and the hundredth anniversary of her birth (1995), has been pleased to endow the Helen Rose Scheuer Jewish Women's Series. *Magda's Daughter* is the ninth named book in the series.

Text design by Dayna Navaro
Printed in Canada on acid-free paper by Transcontinental Printing

09 08 07 06 05 04   5 4 3 2

To Magda's line:
Her grandchildren, Jennifer, Nicholas, and Peter
And her great-grandchildren, Magda (Maggie),
Sophie, Henry, Joseph, Bailey,
and those yet unborn.

Her courage, determination, and indomitable will granted them life.

Contents

Grateful thanks to:

My family and friends for their infinite patience with me during
the writing of this memoir

To Jocelyn Burrell for her sensitive editing

To my friends Cynthia Conigliaro, who encouraged me to publish,
and Dayna Navaro, who made it possible

To my new friend, Bella Brodzki

To Tomi for his love, unwavering support, and encouragement

Introduction

I have always thought of myself as a Perpetual Refugee, rather than a Holocaust Survivor. This might offend other Holocaust survivors. However, since the age of two I have been a refugee. I did not consider myself a Holocaust survivor until fifty years later.

—from the prologue

More and more, Holocaust survivor testimonies—autobiographical accounts by victims of their experiences under Nazi persecution—have come to shape our understanding of that monstrous era in German history called the Third Reich, whose destructive agenda regarding Europe's Jews was named by the perpetrators themselves the "Final Solution." Recasting the Holocaust library shelf, alongside the volumes of historical documentation, analysis, and interpretation, are the stories told by people who suffered monumental losses—of home, family, of every familiar thing—but who somehow escaped death while millions of others did not. They mourn and immortalize loved ones who would otherwise be forever forgotten and provide us with precious insights into a now-extinct cultural universe. Because the perspectives of these stories are subjective and personal, they serve as a distinctive source of historical knowledge, highlighting the texture of daily life before, during, and, to varying degrees, after the war as well. Holocaust testimonies, both oral and written, describe the complex machinery of mass murder that Hitler created, the enormity of Nazi crimes as they affected people, one by one.

The memoirs and oral testimonies of Holocaust survivors—literally—have singular value, because the Nazis sought, with systematic precision and efficacy, to destroy individual experience, human particularity, personal identity. As if in protest, these narratives recount how individuals, in concert with others or not, across a range of tragic, incomprehensible circumstances, assumed agency and made all kinds of choices, or didn't—how they survived by chance and luck against insuperable odds, as singular accidents of history. Even as these narratives are marked by a distinctive sense of mission—an imperative to remember, bear witness, tell the story despite the awesome difficulty of that enterprise—a disturbing combination of guilt and wonder at the very fact of survival propels them. These narratives are not, simply speaking, life-affirming. Though each act of witnessing is charged by the compulsion to speak, to bring the story forth, each one also struggles to resist the imprint of death while being true to its overwhelming force. All Holocaust narratives, whatever their differences from one another, wrestle with the limits and the excesses of language, with what writing can and cannot redeem, resurrect or restore.

The first accounts of Holocaust survival emerged immediately after the war, as early as 1946; since then, they have come out in fits and starts and then in clusters, especially in the 1980s and 1990s, from diverse places of origin, in numerous languages and styles.[1] Many describe the intricate anatomy of the ghettos, as well as deportations, labor camps, and death factories, fateful encounters, and acts of courage and generosity, betrayal and barbarity. All of them, whether explicitly or implicitly, render the ongoing battle to overcome despair and seek a renewed sense of life after such destruction. Remarkably, Holocaust memoirs are still being written today, more than fifty years after "liberation," demonstrating how extensive and disfiguring the effects of the Holocaust have been and, not incidentally, how dynamic the conditions that constrain and enable the expression and reception of traumatic experience are.

Specific historical proximity to the Holocaust informs each of these narratives differently, of course, and as perspectives inevitably change with the passing of time, so must we fine-tune the instruments by which we calibrate the effects of the Holocaust on those who came after. Arguably, some of the reverberations of the Holocaust have been almost cataclysmic: not only has the geopolitical landscape of postwar Europe, and consequently, the world, been permanently altered as a result of Hitler's Aryan fantasy and genocidal campaign, but our psychic terrain has been dramatically reconfigured, too. Certain categories of limit-experience and understanding previously considered so extreme as to be unimaginable are now at the forefront of our consciousness, even as we refer to them as "unspeakable" and "unrepresentable." One of the primary legacies of Auschwitz, Hiroshima, and other catastrophes of the last century is our obsession with (the imperative of) memory and memorialization—how to remember as well as what to remember—and the transmission of collective memory to subsequent generations, to those who were not there. Intimately linked to this preoccupation with memory is trauma, an umbrella term referring to the psychic wounding and shattering of individuals and groups that has become an elemental part of our vocabulary and frame of reference.² More than fifty years after the Holocaust, there are fewer and fewer survivors left in the world, so their videotaped and written testimonies and memoirs, all of which attest to the magnitude of suffering caused by Hitler's war, now constitute a part of a worldwide cultural inheritance.

What complicates and perturbs even further our capacity to absorb on a human scale the depth of this destruction is that the latest—and final—phase of writing to emerge from the Holocaust is being produced now by the last living remnants of survivorship, by the youngest victims of the war, its children. This demographic phenomenon must be understood within the larger context of the six million Jews who were exterminated in the Holocaust and considered in the light of another crushing statistic: of the approximately 1.7 million European Jewish children under the age of sixteen alive in 1939, only 11 percent survived the war. In order to have survived all the threats to their existence, they had to have been almost by definition "Hidden Children" (only a miraculous few made it through slave labor, concentration, or death camps). As situations became evermore dire, with the Nazis and their local surrogates implementing increasingly drastic measures to root them out, parents sought by all means possible to find refuge and protection for their children. Living under false papers or on the run with no papers, their true identities disguised, Hidden Children often lived among strangers who out of kindness, for money, or sometimes in total ignorance harbored them. They hid in convents, orphanages, haylofts, forests, caves, attics, closets, cellars, and sewers for months and years, sometimes with their families, usually separated from them.³

Evi Blaikie, author of *Magda's Daughter,* is one of those children. She was born in January 1939 to a prospering Hungarian family in Paris, characterized as "a mecca for poor Jewish immigrants . . . between the two world wars" (7). Against a backdrop of impending chaos, Blaikie asserts, the fear and anxiety that pervaded Europe was "absorbed with [her] mother's milk" (7). This was her first emotional imprint, and its effects live with her still. Because she didn't know life before the war, had no conscious understanding of what constituted "normal" existence, no means of comparison, no nostalgic reserves to fall back on for strength or solace, she also lacked the capacity for envisioning a different world, another future. This fact is crucial to understanding the distinctive features of narratives written by survivors who were very young children during the war. Not only was their notion of childhood warped as they lived it and their memories from that time in their lives jagged and disjointed or missing altogether, but their sense of what makes up their identity, once so severely tested, tends to remain insecure and unstable even decades later. This is seen emblematically through the many names these children had to assume and discard so as not to be discovered or recognized as Jews. Blaikie's first experience with lifesaving impersonation (though she does not remember it) took place at the age of two, when after fleeing occupied France with her aunt, she crossed the Austrian border back into Hungary, passing as her male cousin Claude Pollak. In Blaikie's memoir the frequent changing of names, made necessary every time she crossed a border, spoke a new language, or even changed schools, is a dominant motif, a trope for the contingent, arbitrary, fugitive nature of her identity. That she is "Magda's daughter," despite every other nominal variant, may be the only constant in her life.

And yet, we note that this primal connection was invoked more as an ideal than it was experienced as a reality for the author; Magda and Evi's relationship was repeatedly disrupted and increasingly attenuated throughout Blaikie's life, until just before Magda's early death at fifty-two. The surprised reader is impelled to assess the ironic implications of this event. Though "premature," as all deaths are, Magda's passing had a belated quality to it, as if mother and daughter had already played out this final disruption countless times before. At the age of twenty-six months, Evi was crucially separated from her mother, who was rounded up off the streets of Paris by a Nazi dragnet and sent to a forced labor camp. Magda, writes Blaikie, was "my Mother, that mythical creature whom I did not remember. . . . [O]nly the family kept her alive in my head" (8–9). When Magda reappeared at the family doorstep in Budapest at the end of 1943, Evi was nearly five years old. A "pathetic, ragged creature, barely able to stand," Magda had escaped from a death march and survived on snow and tree bark for three weeks (14). She weighed seventy-five pounds, was ill with rheumatic fever, and had no papers. Both narratively and symbolically, for Blaikie, her mother's distressing and disappointing reappearance coincided "with the war encroaching on our lives" (14). This may strike the reader as strange, since the war had ravaged their household long before, when her father, as a Communist, a Jew and a foreigner, had fled underground, never to be seen again. But his absence was not conspicuous to his young daughter at this point; indeed, she didn't even know he was gone, didn't "miss" him until years later. Indeed, although their lives were irreparably "rent apart . . . sometime at the beginning of 1941, a few months after the defeat of the French by the Germans" (8), one could argue that, on a conscious level at least, Blaikie's war story begins with her mother's return and the family's fear that they would now be exposed.

In as much as each Holocaust survivor's story has distinctive traits, and this is no less true of each child survivor's story, grouped together they do exhibit common modes of constructing experience and identifiable literary patterns and themes. Having said that, *Magda's Daughter* shows us that we must be careful not to essentialize or conflate what was a wide range of disparate and diffused experiences—Blaikie herself says, "I was never in a concentration camp," for example—nor should we compare or set different ordeals against each other (1). Though atrocity is but a shadowy presence in this narrative, trauma is written all over it. Indeed, the author's explicit references to readers' expectations and other Holocaust survivors' reactions speaks volumes about how sensitive an issue acknowledgment of their experience is for child survivors across the spectrum. It would seem, as it is expressed in their memoirs, that Hidden Children never really recover from their losses. Moreover, their trauma may have been compounded by the diminishing of their suffering by well-meaning adults, who were also often survivors desperately seeking their own coping strategies and unable to acknowledge the pain that children had suffered. In the years immediately following the war, survivors in general were treated callously, indifferently, or uncomprehendingly by the world-at-large and thus were in no position, psychologically or materially, to help the youngest victims whom they wanted to believe had been spared the worst or would soon enough forget what they had endured. In another vein, there are numerous accounts of deportees who returned at the end of the war to find that their saved children no longer recognized them or wanted to reclaim them as parents. Though the world was invested in getting on with things, brutal ruptures of all kinds, forced abandonments and separations, even under the best of circumstances, wrought havoc on these families, and bonds were forever damaged as a result.

If recently, the perspective of the child has received more concentrated attention by historians and clinicians than in the past, it is surely due to the raised awareness regarding children in distress and increased knowledge about early trauma and its effects upon adult development.[4] This point has important implications for reading testimonies of trauma because the West's cultural bias tends toward survivor narratives that have strong redemption plots, that have at their center "protagonists" who are resilient and come out basically intact in the end, no matter what horrors they may have witnessed or endured. If not in literature, at least in the "real world," the general public has little patience with trauma's discomfiting lingering effects, especially when they are ambiguous or insidious. The "survivor syndrome" is a pathology with curious but unpleasant connotations, the kind that induces shame or fear in others. Clearly, this is one of the reasons why Holocaust survivor narratives, characteristically, have closed with the end of the war, as if making it out of the war alive was all that was supposed to matter, or at least all that the world was interested in hearing about. Blaikie's story of survival, by contrast, is much less about the Holocaust itself than it is about its aftermath. A quick glance at the table of contents confirms this: only about an eighth of the entire narrative is devoted to the war per se. This is, of course, in large part a function of the author's age when the war formally ended. The temporality of consciousness does not conform to any date or treaty; official declarations are performative, even legislative, but they are clearly not determinative. As Blaikie writes at the conclusion of her memoir, "a war does not end till the last survivor has died" (270).

Magda's Daughter also widens the arc of survivor narratives by dramatizing the impact of the Holocaust on several members of one vibrant, close-knit, wealthy, assimilated Hungarian Jewish family. Blaikie focuses especially on three larger-than-life sisters—Klari, Kati, and Magda—who served as "interchangeable mothers" for Evi, her enterprising uncle Denes, and her much-adored cousin Peter, all of whom survived. Her memoir is implicitly dedicated to their unwavering spirit and resilience as well as to her father, uncles, and grandmother who did not survive. This rich genealogical and social tapestry traces the destinies of the sisters and their loved ones, through multiple migrations, across multiply changing frontiers, nations, regimes, and allegiances, all the way to the end of the twentieth century. Blaikie's extended view of survivorship is welcome and necessary. A family saga of damaged psyches and wrecked lives, like so many others, *Magda's Daughter* is a story of exile and displacement that could not be told except from a great distance, not because time heals all wounds but precisely because it doesn't. It shows us that the drama of survival is ongoing, that it is played out over the course of a lifetime, notwithstanding the compensations, successes, or achievements, the external signs of security or gratification that one might attain or regain along the way. Blaikie's narrative stance is self-reflective, psychologically attuned, and wonderfully expressive. In great novelistic detail, with compelling characterizations and stylistic nuance, the author powerfully illustrates the various trajectories taken under extreme duress, the economic and moral decisions made because there were no other choices, the ironic reversals of fortune and possibility, and the long-range, devastating material and psychic consequences of being refugees no matter where they went.

Because Blaikie's perspective on the war itself is refracted through her personal experiences as a young child, the reader may sometimes forget the larger and distinctive context in which her family's destiny unfolds. Beginning in 1941, Jews across Europe were being systematically annihilated. However, it wasn't until the spring of 1944, late by comparison to the rest of German-controlled Europe, that Hungary's estimated 825,000 Jews lost their somewhat protected status and the massive deportations to Auschwitz began (under the direction of Adolf Eichmann). In June the Allies landed in Normandy; although Hitler was in the process of losing the war, he remained determined to pursue the Final

Solution to the Jewish question with all the concentrated and ruthless force he still had at his command. Evi was a precocious five year old at this point, first hidden, as was her cousin Peter, in a countryside children's home outside Budapest. Then, as the SS and the Arrow Cross (Hungarian fascists) closed in, Magda, Peter, Evi, and Magda's friend Juliska hid as Protestants in a remote village on a farm in Trans-Danubia in northwest Hungary. Their forged papers identified Evi as "Iluska Toth" and Magda as her aunt. Though Blaikie describes some precarious situations in which the peasants nearly discovered that they were Jews, she explains, in retrospect, that she was insulated from the gravest dangers, the worst terrors, by her mother's ingenuity and courage and by the limits of her own understanding. Peter, eleven years old and quite aware, was not so fortunate. And yet, when called upon to overcome her visceral fear of black spiders in the face of greater peril, Blaikie reveals how, at the tender age of six, she developed the coping mechanism that has served her ever since: "I knew that something very important was happening and that I had to play my part. The fear had to be conquered. For the first time I retreated to a mental state that I would use for the rest of my life whenever I found myself in a threatening or painful situation. I simply suspended feeling" (34). By late 1944 all of Hungary, with the exception of Budapest, had been made *judenrein* (free of Jews), the Soviet forces were fast approaching the capital, and most Hungarians realized that an Allied victory was imminent. Blaikie renders the confusion, fear, and chaos of the last weeks of the war, as the front kept shifting between Soviet and German control. Finally, in March 1945 the war ended; Evi and her family were among the over one hundred thousand Hungarian Jews alive, liberated (though sometimes in dubious fashion) by the Red Army.[5]

Evi's next ordeal began when her partially reconstituted family in Budapest assessed its situation and strived to regain normalcy amidst the terrible turmoil of postwar Hungary. Their response, like that of the decimated Jewish community in general to the trauma of the war, to the wholesale slaughter of their relatives and neighbors, to the acts of deception and self-deception, was an orchestrated and somewhat complicitous silence. The victims' shame and guilt converged with the perpetrators' suppression of their crimes. Blaikie's memories of this period and the well-meaning but counterproductive messages she received proved to have a determining effect on her emotional development and on the eventual writing of this memoir: "'You don't know how fortunate you are. Thank God you don't understand. Soon you'll forget even this whole episode. Children are so lucky!'" (50). Despite the haunting reminders of the murdered millions, the "unimaginable suffering" experienced by concentration camp deportees who returned "from the dead" "lifeless shells with barely human forms," her family attempted to bury what was still unacknowledged, "to forget, to renew, to go on" (51).

As her narrative makes quite explicit, Blaikie's early bewilderment about her childhood war experiences gradually turned to unmitigated sorrow and rage. What could "going on" mean to a child when there seemed to be no particular direction and the points of reference were constantly changing? Blaikie's topographical memoir poses this question over and over again. By the age of seven, Evi and her mother had left Budapest, never to live there again. The demands imposed by her nomadic life, usually apart from her mother, precluded digging too far below the surface. If *Magda's Daughter* is ultimately an account of the author's lifelong struggle for survival in the existential sense, it is staged primarily within the framework of an ongoing search for identity as a kind of destination, a final refuge where the shuttling stops and all the terms match up: "home." The table of contents is Blaikie's autobiographical map; its chapter titles reflecting a jagged itinerary of places and locations, with dates attached to them, beginning with Evi's birth in Paris 1939 and ending in New York City in 1991. Between those fixed points are the names of cities and countries, châteaux, convents, orphanages and schools, as if it were impossible for Blaikie to resolve the enigma of "Who am I?" without first establishing its correlative "Where am I?" For example, Blaikie's disconsolate refugee mentality is very poignantly and symbolically reflected in the chapter title "An American Marriage, 1961–1978." Her marriage doesn't last, but she finally settles in the most cosmopolitan city in the world, New York. Throughout *Magda's Daughter,* the author's tremendous capacity to perform in different languages, adapt to different lifestyles, adopt arbitrarily imposed names, conform to different class codes (that often excluded her), forge new relationships, and endure radical loneliness and premature independence is impressive; but those skills were acquired at great psychic cost.

Although the table of contents tells the reader a good deal about the spatial dimensions of this migratory memoir, what is perhaps most striking is what it reveals—by indirection—about the temporality of consciousness. Put otherwise, in the narrative of one's life, the symbolic significance attributed to a place, an event or an experience is not contingent on the actual length of time spent there, the duration of the experience. *Magda's Daughter,* the survivor narrative of a Hidden Child, designates only one year—1944 to 1945—when the author was (actually) in hiding, and yet, Blaikie deems it to be the emblematic marker of her identity. The word *hidden* in Hidden Child refers not only to a physical condition or situation, one which can suggest protection or refuge from danger by virtue of being out of sight, but also to a secondary, metaphorical meaning. Blaikie's memoir makes a strong case for the necessity of bringing to light what has been concealed in the discourse of the Holocaust until a relatively short time ago: the lost perspectives and experiences of those who survived Nazi persecution on the periphery or under the surface, in the cracks, those omitted from consideration, not recognized by the dominant perceptual categories and explanatory frameworks. The Holocaust, it turns out, is not only an intergenerational tragedy; it is an intragenerational tragedy as well. Thus, the Nazi victimization of children, though an ineluctable part of the tragedy of the Holocaust, was either subsumed under the broader category of Jewish persecution or not recognized at all. As Blaikie's narrative demonstrates so evocatively, Evi came of age as a child survivor, a Hidden Child—but she didn't know it. So her story of survival, which is truly a story of exile, of nostalgia and betrayal, links her personal trauma to that of other members of her generation. It is part of a larger story, a collective project that situates the "coming to consciousness" of a group of adults now in their sixties and early seventies who quite belatedly began to understand their shared history and its inescapable implications for them and for us.

It would be impossible to stress enough the social role of language in this complex process of "coming to consciousness" and identity formation, whose intimate agonies have such broad cultural resonance. The reader may be wondering: What really is the crucial difference between being a Perpetual Refugee and being a Hidden Child or child survivor of the Holocaust? What do these terms signify and why does it matter? What did Blaikie, as a grown woman, discover about herself that she didn't know before she was able to apply these terms to herself and her past? How does language define us? What is the relation between language and experience? Blaikie's memoir invites us to plumb these depths, enter into these debates, and consider the ways history, memory, and autobiography intersect to transform our understanding of how we construct and reconstruct the past, depending on our particular investments, our conscious and unconscious agendas. As Blaikie testifies, *Magda's Daughter* is, on many levels, an act of translation and transmission—it enacts the painful passage from nightmare to text, from the repressed to the remembered, the unspoken to the articulated, the hidden to the visible, the private to the public. And yet, it must be repeated: though empowering, even sometimes cathartic, writing cannot cure. No less is this narrative of remembrance an act of unresolved mourning for what is irrevocably lost, for what will never be available, cannot be conveyed—not in Blaikie's mother tongue, not in the American English of this testimony, not in any language we know. And yet . . .

Thanks to the Feminist Press, Evi Blaikie's powerful voice and unforgettable story will now be heard. Despite her obvious literary gifts, she did not choose writing as a profession but came to it rather late in life. I have the feeling that this first book might not be her last. Recently, I had the pleasure of meeting Evi. She invited me for lunch to her lovely, book-lined, art- and flower-filled Manhattan apartment, where we spent an entire afternoon talking and looking at photographs. I confess that while I certainly expected Evi to be a woman of special intelligence, vitality, and sensitivity—qualities the reader finds in abundance in her memoir—upon meeting her I was surprised by her appearance, by how young she is. Perhaps I should correct myself: by how close in age we are. There she was, born in 1939, a carrier of Holocaust bodily memory, supposedly positioned "in-between" the survivor generation and the second generation. As the child of survivors myself, born in 1951 (indeed, my mother is also a child survivor—but twelve years older than Evi!), I have always felt that the gulf that separated "them" from "us" was immense. Although we have been unmistakably affected by their trauma, the generational divide was clear, the result of both chronology and historical experience. But looking at Evi, I realized that child survivors and children of survivors are also separated by an abyss (the 1.5 generational divide notwithstanding), that experience trumps chronology, that a generation is defined by specific referents not necessarily contingent upon the calendar. Although Evi and I are not so distant in years, the psychosocial effects of her personal Holocaust history, her "deprived childhood," have made all the difference in the world. In her youthful and energetic presence, I knew that the war was far from over.

Bella Brodzki
Larchmont, New York
October 2002

Notes

My gratitude to Evi Blaikie for her generosity of spirit and support in the writing of this article and to Jocelyn Burrell for her expert assistance throughout this process.

1. For a dramatic and diverse collection of Holocaust survivor testimonies by both women and men, gathered by a psychologist right after the war, see Niewyk's *Fresh Wounds*.

2. For a general overview of how an understanding of trauma and its history aids in the reading of Holocaust literature and testimony, see my "Teaching Trauma and Transmission." For an analysis of a mother/daughter child survivor narrative that focuses on intergenerational transmission of trauma, see my "Trauma Inherited, Trauma Reclaimed."

3. See Dwork's groundbreaking work on the daily life of children under the Third Reich. The child survivor narratives by Friedlander, Kalib, Kisliuk, Kuper, Morhange-Bégué, Nir, Perec, and Tec, for example, describe a range of experiences, including fighting with the partisans (Nir) and imprisonment in Auschwitz (Kalib).

4. See Bergmann and Jucovy, Dasberg, and Kestenberg and Brenner. The self-identification of child survivors as a group as well as a subset of survivors followed by many years the labeling of individuals who were treated in therapeutic settings. Kestenberg and Brenner's work over the last twenty years has contributed significantly to a broader recognition of the specificity of children's suffering and its sequelae.

5. As this introduction was being written, Hungarian child survivor Imre Kertész, author of the Holocaust memoir *Fateless*, won the Nobel Prize in Literature. Other narratives by Hungarian child survivors include Magda Denes's *Castles Burning* and Susan Varga's *Heddy and Me*.

Works Cited

Bergmann, Martin S., and Milton F. Jucovy, eds. *Generations of the Holocaust.* New York: Basic, 1982.

Brodzki, Bella. "Teaching Trauma and Transmission." *Approaches to Teaching Representations of the Holocaust.* Ed. Marianne Hirsch and Irene Kacandes. New York: MLA, forthcoming 2003.

———. "Trauma Inherited, Trauma Reclaimed: *Chamberet: Recollections from an Ordinary Childhood.*" *Yale Journal of Criticism* 14.1 (2001): 155–167.

Dasberg, Haim. "Psychiatric Expertise on 'Deprived Childhood' of Child Survivors of the Holocaust: A Contribution to the Substantiation of a Concept." Unpublished report. Jerusalem, Israel, 1999.

Denes, Magda. *Castles Burning: A Child's Life in War.* New York: Norton, 1997.

Dwork, Deborah. *Children with a Star: Jewish Youth in Nazi Europe.* New Haven: Yale UP, 1991.

Friedlander, Saul. *When Memory Comes.* Trans. Helen R. Lane. New York: Farrar, 1979.

Kalib, Goldie Szachter, with Sylvan Kalib, and Ken Wachsberger. *The Last Selection: A Child's Journey Through the Holocaust*. Amherst: U of Mass P, 1991.

Kertész, Imre. *Fateless*. Trans. Christopher C. Wilson and Katherina M. Wilson. Ann Arbor: U of Michigan P, 1992.

Kestenberg, Judith, and Ira Brenner, eds. *The Last Witness: The Child Survivor of the Holocaust*. Washington: American Psychiatric, 1996.

Kisliuk, Ingrid. *Unveiled Shadows: The Witness of a Child*. Newton, Mass.: Nanomir, 1998.

Kuper, Jack. *Child of the Holocaust*. New York: Berkley, 1967.

Morhange-Bégué, Claude. *Recollections from an Ordinary Childhood*. Trans. Austryn Wainhouse. Evanston, Ill.: Marlboro/Northwestern UP, 2000.

Miller, Judith. *One, by One, by One: Facing the Holocaust*. New York: Simon, 1990.

Nir, Yehuda. *The Lost Childhood: A Memoir*. San Diego: Harcourt, 1989. Reprint, New York: Berkley, 1991.

Niewyk, Donald L., ed. *Fresh Wounds: Early Narratives of Holocaust Survival*. Chapel Hill: U of North Carolina P, 1998.

Perec, Georges. *W, or, the Memory of Childhood*. Trans. David Bellos. Boston: Godine, 1988.

Tec, Nechama. *Dry Tears: The Story of a Lost Childhood*. Westport, Conn.: Wildcat, 1982. Reprint, New York: Oxford UP, 1984.

Varga, Susan. *Heddy and Me*. Victoria: Penguin Australia, 1994.

Miksa Friend —— Lenke Stein

Rozsa Friend ————————————————————
b. Simontornya, Hungary, 1879
d. Auschwitz, 1944

Katalin
b. Rakospalota, Hung., 1901
d. New York City, 1995

1) **Sandor Weisz**
b. Hungary, 1898
d. forced labor camp,
   Hungary, 1944

2) **Andreas Gedeon (Bandi)**
b. Hungary, 1898
d. Vienna, Austria, 1977

Miklos
b. Rakospalota, 1903
d. Auschwitz, 1944

1) **Erzsebet Elbert**
b. Hungary, 1901?
d. Budapest, 1993?

2) **Zsuzsanna?**
b. Miskoc, Hungary?
d. Auschwitz, 1944

Istvan Lengyel
b. Budapest, 1932

Klara
b. Rakospalota, 1908
d. London, Eng., 2002

1) **Imre Oszmann**
b. Budapest, 1897
d. Ujpest, 1940

2) **Laszlo Spitzer**
b. Kassa, Slovakia, 1907
d. Budapest, 1995

Peter Oszmann
b. Ujpest, 1934

Magda Pollak —— **Hermann Weisz**

Evelyne Juliette Weisz ————————————
b. Paris, 1939

Jennifer M.
b. New York City, 1962

Married   1) **Richard Mortner** ——
            2) **Lawrence Robbins**

Magda (Maggie)   **Sophie**
b. 1990   b. 1992

Ferencz Pollak ——┬——Lencsi Engel

Miksa Pollak
b. Palfalva, Hungary, 1871
d. Budapest, 1961

Denes
b. Rakospalota, 1909
d. New York City, 1974

Magda
b. Rakospalota, 1912
d. London, Eng., 1964

1) Eszter Spitzer
b. Poland, 1902?
d. Paris, 1990?

Herman Weisz
b. Somus, Transylvania, 1900
d. Auschwitz, 1945

2) Rebecca Basulto
b. Cuba, 1917?
d. ?

Claude Palmer
b. Paris, 1936

Evelyne Juliette Weisz
b. Paris, 1939

Magda Basulto
b. Cuba, 1948

Robert B. Blaikie ——┬——Matilda Hoyer

Donald Blair Blaikie
b. New York City, 1936

D. Nicholas
b. New York City, 1964

D. Peter
b. New York City, 1970

Married   Emily Lefkowitz

Henry
b. 1997

Joseph
b. 1999

Bailey
b. 2001

Prologue

I have always thought of myself as a Perpetual Refugee, rather than a Holocaust Survivor. This might offend other Holocaust Survivors. However, since the age of two I *have* been a refugee. I did not consider myself a Holocaust Survivor until fifty years later.

I was a Hidden Child.

In order to save my life, I was given another identity and stashed away on a remote farm in Trans-Danubia. There I waited out the end of the persecution that, among millions of others, claimed my father, both my grandmothers, uncles and aunts, and wrecked the lives of those who survived.

So yes, I survived the Holocaust, but a Holocaust Survivor? After all, I was safe on that farm—as long as no one figured out who and what I was. I was never in a concentration camp. I was a child who really didn't understand all that was going on around her and, according to those who did, would soon forget it all. Hence the experience of the war would have absolutely no effect.

I want to scream in protest! What were they thinking? How can a child not be affected by the loss of a murdered father, grandmothers, extended family, of home and identity—or the return of a damaged mother? As a child I was angry not with the perpetrators of the horror but with its victims. They had let me down, those adults. They were not capable of restoring order to my life. They allowed me to become a nomad with no home, no language, no culture to call my own.

Later, I look into the eyes of those same adults, the Survivors. What had I been thinking? I realize that they will never lose the look of shame and degradation that those years left with them: the rage at their fellow citizens, neighbors, and colleagues who had joined Satan's hordes and turned them in to recoup their worldly goods from the Nazis and to legitimize their subsequent plunder; the suffering of losing their loved ones long before their time; the burden of guilt for surviving when others had not. They *wanted* me not to remember, not to be affected. But try as they might, they could not will it so.

But if I forget, who will bear witness for those members of my family whose gassed bodies ended up in mass graves or in the crematorium? Who will remember their names and light the memorial candles on Yom Kippur? I want my father's name written out and remembered. I want my grandmother's name said out loud. I want my uncles, my aunts, and all of my blood to remain in conscious memory for as long as any of our line continues to walk this earth. This book is a tombstone for those family members who don't have one and a memorial to those who do. It is the one place where the family is together, as they never were again after the Holocaust. It is their resting place. The place where I can visit and rummage around in those memories that they said I would never have. They are themselves in this book, warts and all, because while some were martyrs, none were saints. They were human and they deserve to be remembered as such. This family and these circumstances shaped my life. I knew them; I remember them. I am still here: I, the Perpetual Refugee, the Wandering Jew, the Survivor.

If there were a scale to measure suffering, my family would not be counted among those who suffered the most during the Holocaust, nor the least. Perhaps we were an ordinary family in extraordinary circumstances, perhaps not. Are there, were there, ordinary families? Who can tell? All deserve to be remembered. The fabric of my family's life was torn, left with gaping holes. I tried to repair, to reweave it. But memory is fickle, especially that of a child. And more especially the memory of a traumatized child. Children are often selective in their memories, choosing to discard some, while occasionally giving undue importance to something that seems trivial, usually to those adults who fear revisiting the burial ground of an emotionally painful childhood. I am sure that some lapses occurred while I wrote this book. And though I have checked all the important "facts" of the narrative—names, places, dates—surely there exist minor slips in my recollection of certain events. But these are *my* memories, even if they differ from someone else's. What follows is the story of our lives, my family's and my own, seen through my eyes, remembered through my experience, and felt through my emotions.

On Memorial Day weekend, 1991, an international conference was organized under the aegis of the Anti-Defamation League for former Hidden Children, those of us who had survived the Holocaust by hiding. That weekend was for me the most painful and disturbing two days I have ever lived through. It was recognizing who I was, who I had become. It meant facing the past and recognizing how it had affected the rest of my life, finally understanding the person I had become. My emotions overwhelmed me. Like a dam bursting, fifty years of pain, rage, tears, and sorrow came crashing through all my defenses, devastating the landscape of my being and permanently transforming it. The only outlet for this maelstrom was writing, and the result was reams of paper filled with scrawls about my ruined childhood.

Still, there was something wrong with what I had written, something awry, something . . . not quite right. I had written what I remembered, what I felt, yet the words, the expressions had an odd quality to them that somehow missed what my real feelings were and had been. It sounded like someone else's voice. And then I realized: everything I had written about had happened at a time when I spoke only Hungarian. Yet I had written my story in English. I had composed a translation of my early life. But how does one translate feelings from one language to another? As a child I probably would not have been able to describe what I was feeling inside; I wouldn't have had the linguistic skills. And now, my Hungarian is not adequate—never was, since my vocabulary was not an adult's—to write about the child that is buried deep inside me. But English is not the language of that place, that time. So how can I give that child a real voice? I'm writing as though crippled, struggling to do the impossible, trying to find release through words and frustrated by the confines of a dictionary. But are there words to describe the events that happened in Europe between 1933 and 1945, in any language? *Holocaust:* nine letters to describe the indescribable. How many letters, how many words for each life destroyed are we allowed? Words for pain and anguish are but the inadequate substitute for primeval screams, and even our screams would not be adequate anymore. Our barbarism has developed beyond our ability to describe it. I feel that by writing, in English, about the Holocaust and its fallout, I am guilty of deception.

Writing this book was difficult. It didn't start out as a memoir, but as a safety valve. But instead of a catharsis, depression set in. The unhappy child inside me was still there, reawakened. She never learned how to experience joy, to feel carefree. These are feelings that one learns during childhood, and she was never a child. She became an instant, fearful, scheming, desperate adult. She learned that hope is an illusion: a trick to keep her alive, only to feel more pain.

So she stands on the sidelines like an unseen spirit, observing, mourning while the others laugh, and dance, and joke. They are enjoying this thing called Life. She is right beside them, prettily dressed with a sad smile on her face. But she's not really there, and the sadness never goes away. She wonders, How can they be so happy? Don't they know about this life? Don't they know the dangers? The pain? The struggle? Once you've felt all of that, how can you laugh again? It seems like a black shadow raises itself ominously whenever she feels a desire to join them, to laugh, to be happy. It speaks to her and says, "You know that there is no peace or happiness in this world. They are fools. They don't know. Don't you remember?"

She tries to banish the shadow, but it's too late. She's afraid again. How can a child start all over again?

But I am not a child. I don't want to be afraid anymore. I have children and grandchildren, and they have a right to exist, to thrive, to know where they belong, to arm themselves against this persistent Evil that keeps encroaching on our world. Their power will lie in their knowledge of what was and what must never be again. So I will tell them what I know, warn them of the dangers, tell them that I believe that the Righteous exist, and that contrary to all evidence, the struggle is worth it . . . and then I will cry, because I am not certain that I truly believe it.

Part One

Magda and Evi. London, 1950.

Paris~Budapest, 1939~1944

For me it all began on a cold January morning, in Paris, in an atmosphere of dreaded anticipation. Many already knew that before the year was out, Europe would be plunged into a deadly conflict that would unalterably affect everyone's life.

My parents were Hungarian immigrants. My father had come from Transylvania around 1919. He followed his oldest brother, Marci, who helped him get an education, and eventually he opened a small salon where he made custom-tailored suits. My mother arrived in 1931 from Budapest. She also followed an older brother, my uncle Denes, who had brought her to Paris to keep house for him. Both came from very modest, if not poor families. My paternal grandmother had seven children and was left a widow when her youngest child was an infant. I know very little about her or, indeed, about that side of my family. But my mother's family, on the other hand, I know everything about—even the things I shouldn't and that they often deny.

My mother was the youngest of five surviving children. She had two sisters and two brothers. That close-knit, temperamental, explosive group of relatives dominated my early life. Their characters were often intensified by the turbulent times that followed my birth. They fought and they bickered and desperately tried to help one another survive the horror and insanity that we call the Holocaust.

Paris was a mecca for poor Jewish immigrants in the period between the two world wars. They were tolerated and left alone to strive for a better life and they prospered. There was an active social life among the small Hungarian Jewish community. Young men and women were introduced, encouraged to marry, and were helped along by the energetic and pioneer-spirited little circle.

My parents' marriage was a love match. My father was a quiet, thoughtful, and gentle man, with thick black curly hair and a pleasant face, who adored his tiny, vivacious, sloe-eyed bride. When I made my appearance in January 1939, my father's happiness was complete. But it was not a good time to be born. The prevailing atmosphere in Europe at the time was fear and anxiety, which I absorbed with my mother's milk.

Our lives were rent apart and never again put together sometime at the beginning of 1941, a few months after the defeat of the French by the Germans. My father reluctantly fled Paris and went underground. Besides being a Jew, he was a Communist. My mother and I joined the long line of citizens fleeing south toward unoccupied France, where my parents had arranged to meet. The roads leading from Paris were swarming with fleeing refugees, and the Germans were bombing all strategic arteries, including the bridge that we were about to cross. It was a direct hit. We were stranded. With bombs falling on all sides and a screaming toddler in her arms, my mother decided to take her chances and return to Paris. Apparently the blasts had so frightened me that I couldn't stop screaming, even to be fed, and only calmed down when I was finally back in my own crib in our home. A few days later, she left me with her sister-in-law, my aunt Eszter, to go shopping for food. While on the street, she was caught in a dragnet, put on a truck, and shipped off somewhere within the bowels of the Third Reich. My aunt was left alone with me. Her husband Denes, my mother's brother, had been mobilized by the French and sent south. Her son, my cousin Claude, was in Hungary with the family, out of danger. Fearing the worst regarding my mother and the situation in France, my aunt decided that the best place for me was also Hungary, in safekeeping with my mother's family.

Aunt Eszter had been preparing to travel to Budapest to visit her son. She had a passport issued in his name and was taking it with her. He had not needed one to leave Paris but now, with the Germans in charge of the checkpoints, he couldn't get home without one should Aunt Eszter wish to bring him back.

We got as far as Vienna, where Aunt Eszter was told that I could go no further as I had no papers. Aunt Eszter took me to a barber, had my hair cut, dressed me as a little boy. I entered Hungary as her son, my cousin, Claude Pollak.

All of the above was related to me. My own earliest memories are of the apartment in Budapest. I see myself standing in the foyer, surrounded by the shiny white laminated doors of the closets, complaining loudly while my aunt Klari brushes back my hair so hard that it hurts. She weaves in a ribbon, making a bow so big that I could easily take flight. I see my aunt Kati charging through the front door, coming home from business, heading straight for the bathroom to wash her hands, before she kisses me. I remember hiding under the shelf of the kitchen table among various jars and utensils believing that Klari really didn't know where I was. I remember playing with my older boy cousins Peter and Pista in the Szent Istvan Park; gleefully jumping up and down on Uncle Sanyi's stomach when he saved me from my daily well-deserved spanking. I remember visits to Nagyi, my grandmother. And I remember waiting for my mother. My

Mother, that mythical creature whom I did not remember. I was twenty-six months old when I was separated from her: only the family kept her alive in my head. "Magda" was a constant topic of concern and conversation among the adults, and I was always reassured that she soon would come to claim me. My cousin Peter, five years older than I, remembered her. He told me that she was beautiful and kind and loving. To me, my real mother was just a fairy-tale character, as opposed to Klari, whom I called Anyu. I didn't miss her presence. I thought of her as a fairy godmother somewhere "up there," wishing her to appear only when I was in real trouble. I imagined this beautiful angel of mercy floating through the front door and defending me against Klari's wrath for having knocked down a jar of preserves or peeing in my pants.

It was 1942, and though war was raging throughout Europe, we in Budapest still enjoyed a relatively peaceful existence. The adults may have been worried, but my cousins and I lived the privileged life of children of the wealthy Jewish merchant class. Meanwhile, Hungary had allied itself with Germany and joined the Axis. Despite a heavy dose of anti-Semitism, Admiral Miklós Horthy did not seem anxious to rid himself of the country's roughly eight hundred thousand Jewish residents—yet.

My aunt Kati, my mother's oldest sister, and her husband Sanyi owned a beautiful apartment in a ritzy section of Budapest. They had no children. Kati owned a company that manufactured and wholesaled camping equipment; Uncle Sanyi owned a separate wholesale haberdashery. My aunt Klari, the second-born sister, and her son, Peter, were also living there. As soon as she had lost her husband, Klari had appeared on the doorstep and announced that she was moving in. Aunt Klari, Peter, and I were fortunate indeed. Kati's sense of family responsibility and Uncle Sanyi's love of children knew no bounds. There was never a question: we were a family. But it was Klari who became the "Mother." She cooked, kept house, raised the children, and looked after all our needs. Kati and Uncle Sanyi were the breadwinners, Peter and I, the little prince and princess. I had the added bonus of a worshiping, protective older brother. Life was good and predictable for us children.

The apartment was spacious, full of light, and elegant. Kati never forgot the miserable abject poverty of her childhood, and made sure to surround herself with beauty and luxury. Everything was of the finest. The furniture, the paintings, the porcelain, the crystal, the rugs. Oh yes, the rugs. Those beautiful, expensive Persian rugs were the bane of my existence. They all had fringes that had to be combed straight on the polished parquet floors. I couldn't walk through the apartment without somehow kicking the fringes out of line. As predictably as the seasons follow one another, Kati immediately would notice and scold, "Evi, straighten out the fringes!" Reluctantly, I would stop playing, get the little brush that we used only for that purpose, and undo the damage. At the time, this was one of the biggest problems of my young life. Another hardship was standing still while the dressmaker fitted me with new clothes. No store-bought clothes for us! Heaven forbid that I should be seen without a three-inch-wide silk ribbon in my hair or that Peter should appear in company without his jacket, his shoes polished to a high gloss, his hair slicked down, every strand in place. He learned to bow from the waist and I to curtsy while the grown-ups smiled and exclaimed, "Oh, how darling!"

A fräulein would come regularly to teach us German and take us to the park. There were always outings: the zoo, the amusement park, the hills (we called them "mountains") around Budapest. During the summer, Margaret Island, which floats in the middle of the river Danube, was our favorite treat, with its beautiful rose gardens, playgrounds, and the still intact Roman baths, Palatinus, where one could choose among five different bathing and swimming pools. There was a shallow, warm pool, with built-in stone seats that the children climbed over and where the nannies sat and scolded, soaking themselves and keeping an eye on their charges. There was the deep diving pool, for the athletically inclined. The sulfur pool, where the old women dangled their arthritic feet, and the big pool, where, when the gong went off, large waves came, delighting the young men who pretended to save the young ladies who squealed and pretended to be scared. The children played, swam, and guzzled ice cream. The grown-ups drank espresso, gossiped, and played rummy at the café on the grassy perimeter of the pools. On the way home, Uncle Sanyi took us to the pastry shop or the toy shop. He held my hand in his and Peter's in his other. He doted on us and indulged our every whim.

My maternal grandmother, Nagyi, a tiny, round, motherly woman, lived on the outskirts of the city in a modest apartment. Hers was an old building with a courtyard. The apartment doors all opened onto a covered railed passageway that ran all around the three sides of the building; this way, neighbors living on opposite sides of the courtyard could stand in front of their doors, lean on the railing, and loudly converse with one another across the width of the courtyard. In front of Nagyi's door and on the windowsill were pots of flowering red geraniums. They were "Nagyi flowers." They still are. The sight and smell of red geraniums always brings a nostalgic smile to my face as I remember my Nagyi. Under the geranium-laden windowsill was a table covered with a white damask cloth, where Nagyi dried her homemade golden noodles. Cut thin, dusted with flour, Peter and I found them irresistible and would steal them, strand by strand, and eat them raw.

Sundays were reserved for Nagyi. Her grandchildren were the joy of her life. Nagyi always cooked our favorite dishes for us. Chicken soup, the best anyone ever made! And her golden noodles! Peter's mixed with fried cabbage and lots of pepper, mine with ground poppy seeds and sugar. She put the plates in front of us, stood by the stove with her arms folded across her ample bosom, and watched us eat, love written on her face. On occasion there would be bread-baking. Nagyi would knead the dough, let it rise, then place it in special baskets. Our job was to take it to the ovens. We trotted down to the bakery, each of us carrying our baskets. As children, it was a most fascinating place to us: cavernous, dark, and very hot. The aroma of fresh bread permeated everything. Three huge brick-vaulted ovens with enormous iron doors lined one wall. When the doors of the ovens were opened we felt the heat of the red and yellow flames that danced deep within them. Several men stripped to the waist, their bodies shiny with sweat and soot, were feeding them. We stood on line with other bread-bakers. When it was our turn, one of the men took our baskets, stuck a number on each loaf, and gave us the corresponding ticket. He then opened the oven door, emptied the contents of the basket onto a large wooden paddle with a very long handle, and slid the dough into the inferno. We were then told when to come back and warned not to lose our numbers. We always hung around a few extra minutes and tried to catch another glimpse of the fire deep inside the oven, of the men looking like black paper cutouts of devils, silhouetted against the flames, and shuddered, utterly mesmerized.

Nagyi rarely came to the apartment in Budapest. She kept a kosher house. We did not. Kati, Klari, and Uncle Sanyi felt that it was not healthy to advertise one's Jewishness, and their large, attractive circle of friends felt the same way. All were assimilated Jews. Their active social life consisted of theater, opera, large and noisy card parties, and multifamily outings to elegant mountain resorts.

Kati was like an empress, the leader of her social circle, and the undisputed boss of the family. Always immaculately dressed, her golden blond hair coiffed to perfection, she cut an impressive figure. She was decisive, always in control, and always controlling. But Peter and I were her weakness; she couldn't have children of her own. Klari sometimes stood in the doorway of the bedroom, undetected, watching her "sophisticated" older sister with amusement: Kati stretched out on the bed next to me, her high heels kicked off, reading *Snow White* to me. But it was Klari, my beautiful, auburn-haired aunt Klari who was in every sense my mother. I loved and resented her as every small child loves and resents a mother. She fed me, dressed me, cuddled and scolded me. I knew that she loved me even when I felt a stinging slap on my bottom. As the corners of my mouth turned down and I tried not to cry, she did her best to hide a smile. I knew that she thought that I looked cute when I was angry, so I'd turn my back on her and mumble crossly.

"I'm going to tell Sanyi Bacsi on you!"

"What did you say?" she'd ask with mock anger.

"Nothing," I'd reply, vowing revenge.

The next minute she'd feed me my favorite sweet. Discipline was very erratic in our house. The family considered Klari a featherbrain, but she had a streak of slyness that frightened them. She could get away with murder and charm people into doing whatever she wanted them to do; in me, she saw a kindred spirit. I always felt that she favored me over her own son. Nagyi would often shake her head and say, "The wrong child ended up with the wrong sister." There was something to it. My mother and Peter always had a particularly close relationship. But both of us were loved. All three sisters became our interchangeable mothers.

Uncle Sanyi was a gentle, unassuming man with a quiet manner about him. He seemed to go along placidly with everything his wife demanded. He escorted her to the opera, the theater, the parties. But we, the children were the important part of his life. He was in all ways my father. He played with me as only a father plays with his little girl. I remember he had a little nodule on the bridge of his nose, right between his eyebrows. When I asked him what it was, he told me that it was a bell. I pressed it and a bell sounded! I did it again and again. The bell always rang. I sat on his hands to make sure that he couldn't trick me, but the bell always sounded and he always laughed! I was already an adult and Uncle Sanyi long gone when Peter revealed the secret of the bell to me. (Either Peter or Klari were close by, pushing the bell built into the door frame for summoning the maid.)

One evening, I must have been very sassy, and Klari lost her patience. She threatened to put me in a sack and take me down to the cellar. But I didn't care. I knew that my Sanyi Bacsi would never allow it! I nonchalantly climbed into the sack and dared her to do her worst. She picked me up and started to take me out. Uncle Sanyi saw her.

"What's in the sack?" he asked.

"Evi. She's being so naughty I'm taking her to the cellar."

"Are you crazy?!" he bellowed.

Klari, always a little melodramatic, and feigning unsteady nerves, jumped and dropped the bag. I howled as my head hit the floor. Uncle Sanyi was beside himself.

"How could you do such a thing to a child?" he demanded furiously, a man who never raised his voice, and chased Klari out. She fled, frightened and confused by her gentle brother-in-law's anger.

He picked me up lovingly and tried to put me back to bed. But I would have none of it. I was going to play this for all it was worth!

"I want to sleep in your bed," I said with the pout I knew he couldn't resist. "I'm afraid that Klari is going to spank me again!"

He let me, and I kept him up half the night reading fairy tales to me. The rest of the night I twisted and turned and punched and kicked in my sleep. He enjoyed no sympathy from the women the following morning.

There were two other men whose laps were also familiar to me: Uncle Miklos's and my grandfather's. Uncle Miklos was second in line to Kati. A journalist, playwright, and author of strange, arcane poetry, he was the intellectual of the family. Tall, dark, and very handsome, he bore a slight limp and a stiffness on his right side that betrayed an earlier stroke. The family loved his pretty, dark-eyed wife Zsuzsika, who pampered and spoiled him, while they gossiped about and maligned my aunt Erzsi, his first wife and mother of my cousin Pista.

Miklos and Klari had been the enfants terribles that Nagyi couldn't tell enough stories about. Whenever they were together, they reverted to childish behavior, teasing each other, telling jokes, and giggling, much to Peter's, Pista's, and my delight—and to Kati's great annoyance. She admonished them for setting a bad example. But, young as we were, we sensed that Kati felt left out and retaliated by scolding her younger siblings and acting stuffy. They, in turn, laughed at her, which annoyed her all the more. A sense of humor was not Kati's strong suit, and this set her apart from the rest of the family.

My grandfather and Nagyi had lived together for only a very short time. Nagyi had brought up her children alone, in great poverty and under very difficult circumstances. Grandfather's only contribution was a visit home now and again for just enough time to father another child. Somehow I never associated him with my grandmother, only with his numerous brothers and sisters, my great-uncles and great-aunts whom he occasionally took us to visit.

This odd assortment of adults was my world, a place in which I felt totally comfortable and secure.

The non-Jews whom we associated with were, for the most part, employees, business and household. Klari kept up a friendship from her married days with Teri, whom we affectionately called aunt, and her son. They were of Bohemian descent and would later play an important role in our survival. Peter's father, a doctor and Freemason, had owned an ambulance station in the same little town where my grandmother lived. Through his employees, patients, and personal philosophy he associated with anyone, regardless of faith. In fact, foreseeing the troubles ahead, he had not allowed Peter to be circumcised.

As children, we had no idea that we were Jews—or anything else, for that matter. The adults worked hard, played hard, and worried about us and the future. For us, however, life was smooth and predictable. We were protected from the reality of the world around us. Even when the Allied bombing started, we were not frightened. In the beginning, I would gather my dolls and other playthings and Klari would place me on the rug in the living room, in front of the radio. When the regular program was interrupted with an air-raid alert, I was to go and tell her. Usually the telephone rang at the same time; it was Kati calling home to make sure we had heard. We then quickly grabbed our already packed bags and ran down to the cellar, which was our designated air-raid shelter. Peter was away during this time. He had a heart murmur, and our pediatrician felt that he would be better off in a sanitarium in the mountains. At a time when things were worsening rapidly, Peter was among strangers, and I, nearly five by this time, struggled without his unconditional love, his reassurance and protection. We missed each other terribly.

The ring of the doorbell startled everybody. It was late in the evening, sometime near the end of 1943; I was being coaxed to get ready for bed. Klari went to open the door, and we heard a scream. We all ran toward her. Amid gasps of shock and surprise I saw . . . black. An indistinct, disturbing form stood there. As I gradually raised my eyes, the black form took the shape of two people. In front, a small, thin young woman with enormous black, feverishly bright eyes and black hair, wearing a long, black, man's overcoat. Behind her, a shabby looking youth—a peasant's black hat in his hands. The grown-ups cried "Magda!" in unison, and I instantly, shockingly realized that this pathetic, ragged creature, barely able to stand, was my mother. Fear, anxiety, disappointment took over, and I started to cry.

My mother's reappearance seemed to me to coincide with the war encroaching on our lives. The grown-ups became frightened and furtive. There was a lot of hushed arguing. The gaiety stopped. My mother was very sick, having spent the two-and-a-half years that she had been missing in a forced labor camp that produced Nazi ammunition. She had been caught sabotaging, been severely beaten, and placed in solitary confinement for fourteen months. At the end of that ordeal, she along with all the other Jews was ordered to join a march leading to a concentration camp. Assuming that she was going to die anyhow, she left the slowly advancing column and walked into the woods. The guard obviously thought that a bullet would be a waste. Three weeks later she stumbled upon a farmhouse on the Hungarian border. She had survived on snow and tree bark. When she rang our doorbell she weighed seventy-five pounds and was suffering from rheumatic fever. Now she required proper care and medical attention. Without identification papers, admission to a hospital was impossible. A trustworthy doctor had to be found. And she could not stay in our apartment. How could we explain her presence to the maid, the laundress, the concierge? The concierge was responsible for checking identity papers. Everyone had to be registered with the police. Address, date of birth, line of work, religion, political affiliations: everything had to be accounted for. My mother was a fugitive, and there was no shortage of informers. For a short time, she was hidden in a friend's apartment across the street, our Jewish pediatrician attended to her and me at the same time, since, to everyone's distress, during this time I came down with every imaginable child-hood disease. Measles, mumps, chicken pox, and constant ear infections. Meanwhile, there were constant air-raid alarms that made us rush to the cellar. The Allied planes that were bombing Germany often flew over Hungary, and everyone was expecting them to drop more bombs on us. We were, of course, unaware that Admiral Horthy's secret negotiations with the Allies were saving us from that fate—for the moment.

We were not always able go to the shelter. Often, as soon as the air-raid alarm sounded, I had to go to the bathroom. Every alarm—and, later, every bombing raid—brought on an attack of diarrhea, and I wouldn't or couldn't budge out of the bathroom. Klari took the radio out of the living room and put it in the kitchen, closer to the stairway leading to the cellar. The next day Kati frantically burst into the apartment, just as Klari was getting ready to run down the six sto-ries to the cellar, with me in tow.

"Are you crazy?" she screamed at her sister. "How can you gossip on the tele-phone for hours when, for all we know, the bombs are minutes away from here? I've been trying to call for an hour. Sanyi is frantic!"

"I haven't been near the phone. Something must be wrong."

Upon examination, they found the receiver off the hook, hidden behind the fancy pillows of the cut-velvet covered sofa. It was a mystery. But not for long. It happened every day. Kati was not able to call. She had to come home to make sure that we were safe! They confronted me.

"Evike, please don't hide the telephone. It's very important to keep the line open. Please don't do it again!" they pleaded.

"I didn't do it. It wasn't me," I protested.

"Evike, it has to be you. There's no one else here but you and Klari."

"I don't care. I still didn't do it!"

No amount of pleading or threats made me stop hiding the telephone receiver, until my mother took over. She was starting to regain her strength, and Kati had procured forged identity papers for her.

"I'll take care of this," she said.

"No," protested my aunts. "You don't know Evi anymore. She's afraid of you. She's got to be handled delicately."

My mother ignored them. She took my hand, marched me into the next room, and closed the door. We sat facing each other, my legs dangling halfway to the floor. My feet, shod in polished, high-button shoes, idly kicked and scuffed the crossbar of the expensive, black lacquered chair.

"Evi, you know that I'm your mother, right?"

"Yes. But so is Klari."

She sighed.

"No. Klari is your aunt. She is my sister. Children only have one mother. Kati and Klari love you very much and looked after you while I wasn't able to. But now I'm here and from now on I'm your mother. Do you understand?"

"Yes," I said unhappily. I knew there was more to come.

"All right," she said. "Now listen to me. Taking the telephone receiver off the hook is a very dangerous thing. If anyone in the family is in danger, they have to be able to call for help. You are not a baby anymore. We have to be able to count on you too if we need to. Do you understand?"

"Yes."

"Good. Then we understand each other. The phone will never be off the hook again. Right?"

I didn't answer. If I said "right," I would be acknowledging that I was the culprit, and I wasn't quite ready to do that. But she didn't wait for an answer.

"I knew I could count on you," she said.

We stood up and left the room together. Both aunts were standing outside the door straining to hear what was going on.

"It's all settled," announced my mother. "The phone will not be touched again."

And it wasn't.

The rivalry between my mother and her sisters over where and to whom I belonged continued. Kati and Uncle Sanyi had adopted me the previous year. (Coincidentally we had the same last name.) Kati fought dirty.

"How do you expect to protect this child? You couldn't even protect yourself! This is her home now. She knows us as her family. Besides, you can have more. I can't."

"She's my child and my responsibility. Don't think you can bully me as you do the rest of the family. I didn't go through the horror that I did in order to give up my child. Anyway, what makes you think any of us will survive this war? Wait till the Germans arrive."

"Why would the Germans come here? Hungary is their ally!"

"Don't be a fool. You know what is going on better than anybody. By the end of the year we could all be dead!"

My mother had voiced everyone's fear. Though Admiral Horthy, Hungary's regent, had allied the country with the Axis, he was not Nazi. It was more his fear of Bolshevism that led him into Hitler's camp. He was an Old World conservative, not overly fond of Jews, but not interested in annihilating the eight hundred thousand living in Hungary. He "even played cards with them." There were no concentration camps in Hungary. There was, however, a particularly Hungarian way of dealing with the Jews. All Jewish males twenty-one and over had to report to work camp, as though it were military service. It was in fact called *Munkaszolgálat* (literally, "work service"). This was generally under the aegis of the army and, as such, generally given to hard labor and menial tasks. Treatment of the workers depended largely on the military personnel in charge of each detail—until the rise of the Arrow Cross, when it became universally cruel, with many instances of torture. Under the Arrow Cross, few came back alive.

To the Jews of Budapest, some of the most assimilated in Europe, it was absolute degradation. They had always believed themselves to be Hungarian first and Jewish a very distant second. Rumors had been filtering back from Poland about concentration and death camps for Jews, but many refused to believe that such things were possible in the twentieth century.

In actuality, two Czech Jews—Rudolf Vrba, who went on to write *I Escaped Auschwitz,* and Alfred Wetzler—managed in the late spring of 1944 to escape from Auschwitz and wrote a report that was sent to the Hungarian Jewish Rescue Committee (as well as to the Vatican) to warn the Jews of Hungary about their impending fate. At that time, however, the committee was negotiating with Adolf Eichmann himself for Jewish lives in return for goods and decided not to pass on the information, fearing that the negotiations would collapse. (Years later in Israel, this became the basis of a suit against Rudolf Kasztner alleging collaboration with the Nazis.)

Meanwhile, the Arrow Cross, the virulently anti-Semitic opposition party led by Ferene Szálasi, was laying the groundwork for their eventual takeover.

My mother did not believe for a moment that Hungarian Jews would be spared the fate that other Jews throughout Europe were sharing. She did not know how or when the ax would fall, but she wasn't deluding herself. She knew that it would.

Of course, we were not privy to the political machinations that were going on behind the scenes. We didn't know that Admiral Horthy was making secret overtures to the Allies—or that Hitler caught wind of the premier's double-dealing.

The fighting in the family went on and on. Nerves were frayed. One morning after a particularly cruel attack from her sister my mother was crying quietly. She picked me up and stood me on my bed to dress me. It was her sixth wedding anniversary, and she was telling me about my father, vainly trying to revive some memory of him within me. The door opened, and Kati came in. My mother did not turn around. Kati stood in the doorway for a moment: for once she seemed uncertain what to do. Then she said, very quietly, "The Germans have crossed the border."

My mother froze, her arms dropped from my body, her eyes shut tight. A low, painful sound came from her throat. Then she turned and faced her older sister. They stood there for a moment, looking at each other, then simultaneously flew into each other's arms and sobbed uncontrollably. It was March 19, 1944. I was five years old.

Hiding, 1944–1945

By the beginning of April, the new Jewish Laws went into effect and the Allied bombing started.

Several yards of bright yellow fabric were laid out on the dining room table. Klari and my mother were cutting out six pointed stars. I asked them what they were doing.

"We're going to sew these on our clothing. We all have to wear them when we go out."

"I don't want one," I said.

Kati came in, putting on her coat, getting ready to go out. On it was sewn a yellow star.

"I don't want you to have that on!" I cried, lunging at her, clawing at the star, ripping it off.

There was a hush. I was expecting a swift slap to my bottom. But nothing happened. They just sat in stunned silence.

Finally, Kati said, "The child is right. I'm not going out with this. Listen, you two. From now on, if anyone asks, I'm Apuka's daughter from his first marriage."

"So what?" chirped Klari. "Apuka was only married once."

My mother and Kati rolled their eyes.

"Klari, don't be stupid," admonished my mother. "Kati's blond. She doesn't look Jewish. Maybe she can get away with it. Katika, what are you going to do about papers?"

"I'm going to see the Anglican priest. I think I can buy baptismal certificates. Klari, get in touch with Teri Schmutzler. I'm sure she'll help us." Aunt Teri was that close Bohemian Christian friend of Klari's from her married days.

In the countryside, deportation of Jews started immediately after the Germans' arrival. In Budapest, a curfew was established for Jews. We could go out for half an hour around six o'clock in the evening to shop for food. By then, of course, most of the shops were empty of anything fresh; from then on we subsisted mostly on the dishes that Klari concocted out of dry beans, split peas, dry bread, and whatever was left of the canned vegetables and fruits that had always been plentiful in our pantry but that now were being slowly depleted.

The adults were irritable and frightened, terrified whenever the doorbell rang unexpectedly. There were constant hushed conversations, always interspersed with the warning "Ssh! Nicht vor dem Kindern!" ("Hush! Not in front of the children!"). The bombs continued to fall. Some people didn't bother to go to the cellars anymore. We learned new words with new meanings: *ghetto, Jewish House, forced labor camp, safe house, Swedish house, shell shock,* and always, always *papers.* Papers, always in the plural, were the things that everyone was seeking, that were difficult and expensive to get and very, very important. The adults would occasionally mention the name of an acquaintance, shake their heads, sigh, and say, "They didn't have papers."

I was awakened very early one morning by a kiss on my cheek and gentle touch on my head. I opened my eyes and saw Uncle Sanyi wearing an old khaki uniform and a soldier's hat on his head. Kati was standing in the doorway looking very upset. I immediately felt that something was wrong.

Uncle Sanyi whispered, "I'm going away for a while. I need a kiss and a hug to take with me."

I felt panic rising in me.

"No," I cried. "Please don't go. I'll be good. Don't go!" I started sobbing and clung to him.

"I have to go. Don't worry. I'll be back soon."

Kati came over and whispered to him, "She's right. You don't have to go. I'll get the papers. It's just a matter of days. We'll get you away somehow."

"No, Kati. Don't bother. It's not so terrible. They just want us to dig a few ditches. I'll be home in no time at all. Just watch the children."

I would hear none of it. I clung to him, begging him not to leave. I saw the tears in his eyes. He hugged me tightly, kissed me, and while Kati pried me away from him, he dashed out the front door. It was the last time I ever saw him.

Now the bombing raids became relentless; and the cellar, our second home. Often, Klari and I were given an isolated corner because I was sporting one or another kind of red rash, and the other parents did not want their children to become infected.

There was always a crackling radio in the cellar that the men were constantly monitoring, trying to ascertain where the bombs were falling. We could hear the explosions, and depending on the loudness, the adults tried to judge how far they were and whether the targets were hit.

"That sounds like it's in Buda. There goes the Royal Palace."

"Hey, that's close. I think they're aiming for the South Railway Station."

"No. I think that must be the brick factory."

Their heads were close together over the radio, turning the knobs, trying to get information. From the weird shadows cast by a couple of flashlights, I could see that the older women were praying. The smaller children were whimpering. Klari, trying to stifle her panic, held me close and tucked a blanket ever tighter around me. Sometimes she would explode at the men. "Will you all shut up! Who cares where they are, as long as they're not here!"

When the "all clear" sounded, we trudged back upstairs and immediately headed for the balcony, looking to see where there were new fires and what had been hit. We never knew whether we would be next.

The women were constantly plotting and planning, and we children were always in the way. One sunny early spring morning, Peter and I were sent out to play on the balcony. We lived on the fifth floor. The balcony was quite secure as Aunt Kati had flower boxes built in between the bottom of the railing and the floor of the balcony. The sun was quite strong and the blinds were lowered behind us, leaving the balcony doors open. As we were playing, we suddenly became aware that the music on the radio, in the living room, had stopped. We listened and heard the expected air-raid warning. As we tried to get back into the apartment, we realized that someone from inside would have to raise the blinds to let us back in. They were made of heavy wooden slats bound together with thickly woven ribbon and had to be raised and lowered by a pulley system built into the wall. Since the balcony doors were wide, the slats were long and very heavy, needing an adult's strength to raise and lower them. We shouted to be let in, and we soon heard Klari tugging at the pulley cord. The blinds were rolled up halfway, and I started to cross the threshold when the cord snapped and the heavy roll of wooden slats fell on me. The top half of my body was in the living room while my legs were pinned under the wooden roll. I started screaming and was joined by Klari, who was certain that my legs had been severed. Kati and my mother came running and joined efforts to pry me out from under the heavy load. Although it weighed too much for them to lift, they managed to pull me into the living room, where they found that not only were my legs still attached to the rest of my body, but miraculously they were not even broken, just very badly bruised.

Peter, however, was still outside, unable to get in, and the planes were getting closer. He was terrified of bombs and was in a panic. Our balcony was attached to the one next door and separated by a partition that ran floor to ceiling. The only possible way to go from one to the other was to climb over the railing, out toward the street, bypass the partition, and then climb back on the other side. My mother explained to Peter what he had to do. Klari was totally useless and speechless, hugging me on her lap. Neither of us were being paid any attention anymore. Everybody focused on Peter. He balked. "Magda, I can't do that. What if I fall?"

"Why should you fall? You're as agile as a monkey. You're always doing things to show off. Now do it for real!"

The planes were getting closer. We could hear on the radio the names of the cities that they were flying over being listed. We knew the list by heart. We all went next door to the neighbors' balcony while my mother coaxed Peter to step over the railing. The windows on the opposite side of the street were filled with people watching the little drama and shouting encouragement, while people still on the street were staring upward. My mother, totally in control, was giving Peter instructions.

"All right, you've got one leg over. Now hold on tight to the railing and put the other foot over. No! Don't look down! Concentrate on what you're doing!"

Everybody held their breath while Peter straddled the railing, preparing to swing himself past the partition. Just as he was ready to grasp the railing on the other side, his foot slipped—now he was hanging on the outside of the building. His eyes closed tightly, and he was sweating. The radio was droning on. The planes were closing in on the city. We heard a thud; Klari had fainted. Nobody paid any mind. My mother was trying to reach Peter's hands and couldn't.

"Peter," she said firmly. "Stop fooling around! Now pull your left foot up and pull yourself up!"

Automatically, he did as he was told. His hand followed his foot. My mother grabbed one wrist, Kati the other, and they pulled him over the railing so hard that they all fell in a pile into our neighbors' living room just as the first planes appeared in the sky. Klari was resuscitated, none too delicately, with a couple of sharp slaps to her face, and we all dashed down to the cellar.

After this episode, the three sisters decided to keep us children out of danger, away from the bombs, the Nazis, and the increasingly aggressive members of the Arrow Cross. We were taken to a children's home in the nearby mountains. I didn't want to stay and held Peter's hand tightly while the grown-ups made the necessary arrangements. Peter was whispering to me. "Don't worry. We'll be together. I'll look after you."

To my horror, as soon as the Kati and Klari had left, Peter and I were separated. He had to go with the boys, and I, with the girls. The next day I kept looking for him but couldn't find him. I was close to panic. Finally, at mealtime, I spotted him on the boys' side of the enormous dining room, which was divided in the middle by a moveable wooden barrier. I screamed his name and ran toward him. He heard me and came running. A supervisor jumped up and caught me.

"You can't go to the boys' side," she said, restraining me.

"I want Peter! I want Peter!" I cried, struggling to get out of her grasp. But she was holding me tight.

Peter ran up. "Let her go!" he shouted, but he was caught—though not before he managed to kick my tormentor in the shin. There was pandemonium in the dining room while the two of us were being dragged away, kicking and screaming, from each other. I was sent to my room for the rest of the day and deprived of my midafternoon snack. The following day, Peter and I managed to meet on the grounds.

"I want to go home," I said resolutely. "So you have to take me!"

"Evi, it's not so bad here. We can see each other here in the garden, and don't forget the bombs in Budapest."

"I don't care about the bombs. I'm going home. If you're scared you can stay. But I'm going!"

"I'm coming, I'm coming," he said, resigning himself.

We walked out, hand in hand, through the front gate, along the driveway, and down the curving mountain road. It was several miles to the city, but I was never going to admit to being tired and just kept walking. Fortunately, at one point we managed to sneak onto a tram going in the right direction.

The entire household was in an uproar by the time we rang the front doorbell. The home had called as soon as they had noticed our absence. The sisters were frantic. This was no time to notify the police about two missing Jewish children. Peter was called to task.

"How could you do such a thing? Didn't you know how dangerous it was?"

He gave the only excuse he could: "Evi wanted it!"

A large painted yellow star soon appeared on the wall of our apartment building, next to the front door. Ours had become a designated "Jewish House." Jewish families were moved in, one family to a room. The kitchen was a room, the tiny maid's room was a room. Five families were to move in with us.

It was a confusing time for us. People were coming and going, bringing pieces of furniture, clothing, and other personal effects. Peter no longer went to school, nor I to kindergarten. Strangers were living in our home.

A few days later, Peter and I were ushered into the living room. The door was locked, and we were seated side by side at the big, black lacquered dining room table. The three sisters, Kati, Klari, and my mother, were facing us. They looked very solemn. My mother took charge.

"Children, we are going away. You two and I. But before we go, we have to change our names. My name is going to be Emma Zbrinyi, and you, Peter, will be my son, Janos Schmutzler, from my first marriage. Evi, your name will be Iluska Toth, and you will be my niece. Your birthdays will also change. You must never use your old names anymore, not even amongst yourselves."

Peter looked frightened. Even these conspicuously non-Jewish names did not reassure him.

"What if I forget? What if Evi forgets?"

"You can't. Ever. All of our lives depend on it!"

"Magda, don't say things like that to them. They're only children," Klari wailed.

"They have to know. This is not a game. We don't have time for them to grow up if we want them to grow up at all. Besides, don't worry. They'll be fine. These are bright children. Probably smarter than you," she added pointedly.

"God help us if they're not," muttered Kati under her breath.

The names that we were assuming were those of Klari's friend Aunt Teri, her son, and, I believe, her niece. Forged duplications were made of their identity papers, so we had to "match." Since Mrs. Zbrinyi had only a son, I couldn't be her child. From then on, my mother became my "aunt Emma."

For a large sum of money and some of Kati's fashionable clothing, Mrs. Nardely, our concierge, opened the front door of our building for us and did not report us to the authorities. Kati and Klari accompanied us to the railroad station, their clothing devoid of the yellow star.

To everyone's astonishment, my mother introduced us to a friend of hers, Juliska, and told us that she was coming with us. Kati, her face a picture of irritation and anger, roughly pulled my mother aside and told her in no uncertain terms that she had lost her mind.

"Did they beat your senses out of your head at that camp? Have you looked at this woman? Can't you see that she couldn't look more Jewish if she were a cartoon in one those Nazi propaganda papers? She can't possibly go with you!"

My mother looked at her sister in mock disbelief.

"Jewish? She looks Jewish? To me she looks like an Armenian Catholic, which, by the way, is what her papers say she is. And yes, she is coming with us. One, because she is alone and has nowhere else to go. And two, because she speaks perfect German, is well educated, and the children will keep up with their lessons."

Nothing could change my mother's mind. Jewish-looking or not, Juliska was very attractive. She had milky white skin, thick long red hair, and a very curvaceous body. I noticed that Peter was eyeing her in a strange way. A smart and precocious eleven year old, Peter had started noticing women. And Juliska was the kind of woman a boy noticed!

In the late spring of 1944, we arrived at the remote village of Lovászpatona in the northwestern part of Hungary, known as Trans-Danubia. Nothing in our comfortable middle-class upbringing had prepared us for the culture shock that we were about to experience.

We found our way to a tiny ramshackle farmhouse that belonged to the family of our maid. Margit was very close to our family. She had left Lovaszpatona as a young girl in disgrace for having borne a child out of wedlock. Klari had taken her in, and Margit had cared for Peter throughout his babyhood. Later, Denes had taken her to Paris, and she had been my cousin Claude's nanny. She was always with us in some capacity or other. Now she had arranged for us to stay in her family's one-room farmhouse. The floor was dirt, mildew ran down the walls, and the wind whistled through the dilapidated frame of the single tiny window. There were a few sticks of furniture lying about that my mother, aided unwillingly by Juliska, cleaned up and organized in a way that would prove most comfortable. But it seemed as though winter had returned. There was a cold spell, and we shivered in the mildewed shack. My mother kept water boiling on top of the little iron stove, but the draft just sucked all the warmth out of the place, and the mud floor remained icy. The dampness of the place proved too much for Peter's delicate health. He developed a terrible cough and was wheezing. There was no doctor in the area and getting sick could prove fatal.

My mother realized that she had to find better accommodations or Peter's health might seriously suffer. He had spent the previous winter in a sanitarium on account of his heart murmur and what was called "a weak constitution." Margit, unable to bear Peter's slightest discomfort, took it upon herself to look for an alternative. She found a family of peasants who were willing to rent a room. Margit introduced us as Christians, Protestants. Mother, son, niece, and governess who had been bombed out of their home in Budapest. My mother's (aunt's!) husband was supposed to be fighting in the army—on "the right side."

The Csiszars' farmhouse was a palace compared to the one we had just left. The main door opened into a central area with a huge, floor-to-ceiling, tiled stove. This area served as kitchen, living room and general meeting place for man, woman, and beast. Chickens, ducks, geese, goats, and an occasional piglet would wander in without anyone raising an eyebrow. Each end of that area opened onto another room. The larger one was the bedroom of the entire Csiszar family: Mr. and Mrs., four sons, and Mrs. Csiszar's father, an old mustachioed peasant who spent his time sitting by the stove, smoking his pipe, and frightening children. The smaller room, which faced the road, became ours. The house was considered modern since the floors were tiled. There was no running water. The outhouse was on the other side of the yard. In winter we availed ourselves of chamber pots, and melted snow for washing. In the summer the stench and various monstrous-looking beetles in the outhouse kept me away as long as possible and contributed to my chronic constipation. After my bouts of diarrhea in Budapest, it seemed as if my bowels were in constant revolt.

Attached to the house alongside the Csiszars' bedroom was the stable that accommodated their horse and cow and hundreds of enormous black hairy spiders. These spiders terrified me more than anything else there. Spiders had always been my particular bugaboo. They evoked in me a totally irrational fear, a terror so powerful, a panic so overwhelming that I would become paralyzed and could not control the piercing screams that would emerge from me whenever I saw one.

Our cramped room had a large double bed that my mother, Juliska, and I shared. Peter slept on a little cot in the corner. There was a huge, heavily carved armoire that had been part of Mrs. Csiszar's dowry and a small table with two rickety chairs at the foot of the double bed. My mother found an old iron stand with a cracked washbowl in the corner of the yard, which she asked for and was readily given, the peasants having no idea as to its use. This allowed us to wash ourselves in the privacy of our own room rather than at the pump outside by the dung heap.

There was very little room to move, and whenever possible we were sent outside. Soon after our arrival, Peter and I were exploring our new surroundings when a bicycle pulled up to the gate and a uniformed officer of the law approached us. *Csendör* were ruthless, petty dictators, mostly Arrow Cross members, feared by all. Jews and gypsies were their special targets. Peter knew this. The man faced Peter.

"You kids aren't from around here. What's your name?" he demanded.

Peter froze. After a moment the man became impatient.

"What's the matter? You lost your tongue? I asked you what your name is."

Peter looked desperate. I immediately understood what was going on and piped up.

"His name is Janos Schmutzler. And mine is Iluska Toth."

"So what's wrong with him? Can't he talk?"

"He's shell-shocked. We've just come from Budapest. We were bombed out."

"Oh," he said, taken aback. "Well, watch him and keep him out of the way." With that, he got back on his machine and rode away. Peter looked at me in wonder.

"How the hell did you come up with that one?" he asked.

"I don't know. But you better remember your name. I might not always be around, you know!"

Peter was old enough to understand the danger and spent the war fighting his own personal terror. But I, a precocious five year old, felt totally protected. My mother was there, and so was Peter. Nothing bad was going to happen as long as I remembered our new names and alternate family affiliations.

The Csiszars seemed to be ordinary Hungarian peasants. Mrs. Csiszar was a big, handsome woman with a booming voice and weather-beaten face. She worked from sunup till sundown, easily matching the men in strength. Her sons had to mind her or swiftly feel the back of her hand. She was brusk and rough, but she had a good heart and it was obvious that she felt sorry for us. We were thin and pale, and she was going to do something about that! Her husband was a taciturn man with a huge handlebar mustache. That's about all I remember of him except that he always wore highly polished black boots and that I kept out of his way. The four boys were the ones who concerned Peter and me. They ranged in age from seven to eleven. Brawny, well-fed, healthy peasant kids whose heads were shaven from April to October, they wore tattered hand-me-down clothes and went barefoot except in the dead of winter.

The first day we eyed one another warily in the farmyard. The boys were tittering. "She's wearing knickers under her dress," we heard one of them snicker.

Finally, the oldest boy, Feri, approached Peter. "Bet I can piss further than you!" he challenged.

What Peter knew he lacked in physical aptitude, he could make up with city smarts. "So what?" he countered. "I can hit anything better with a slingshot than you can!"

"Oh yeah?"

"Yeah!"

Peter had been the unofficial slingshot champion in his school in Budapest. Slingshots were found, targets put in place. The contestants took their positions. It was going to be the best of three shots. The boys were good, but God had heard our prayers and was with us that day. Peter won, hands down, and the hierarchy was immediately established. Those poor little sparrows in the Szent Istvan Park in Budapest had not suffered in vain from Peter's dubious talents. He had the good sense to be a gracious winner and cuffed me one as I was about to crow on his behalf. He was accepted into their midst, and I was allowed to tag along. My mother was greatly relieved and encouraged us to play with the boys. The less we stood out, the better. Though we were encouraged to blend in, one area of farm life never ceased to shock. The peasants swore constantly, and the language was very graphic and often downright blasphemous. Animal feces, grandmother's private parts, the saints' and God's names were used regularly with total nonchalance, while at the same time the peasants were constantly crossing themselves in a show of Christian piety. Juliska's sensibilities were shattered. She blanched every time Peter and I opened our mouths and a newly learned obscenity popped out. My mother was more philosophical about it.

"I think this is the least of our problems," she told Juliska, who protested constantly. We had to watch our language, however, in the privacy of our room.

While we children were establishing our relationships, my mother was busy cementing hers. She knew very well that having forged papers and paying well for our room did not necessarily ensure our safety. The Csiszars seemed like decent people, but one never knew. And there were plenty of neighbors. We had to make ourselves useful and liked. She insisted that we all share in the farm-work. She helped Mrs. Csiszar with the canning and bottling. Peter did the same chores as the boys, and I fed the chickens and the geese. Juliska balked at the thought of any physical labor. Brought up in a very sheltered, refined, and intel-lectual atmosphere, she had great difficulty in adapting to our circumstances, and this occasioned challenges, one of which was often recalled by the women after the war. My mother broke her comb one day and automatically picked up Juliska's, who indignantly protested. "One does not borrow someone else's comb or toothbrush," she admonished primly.

My mother looked at her in astonishment, shook her head, and laughed bit-terly, then whispered fiercely, "Juliska, the entire might of Hitler's legions are determined to destroy us, not to mention our homegrown anti-Semites. I spent two years in hell already. We have given up our homes, our identities in order to try to survive and Heaven only knows whether we will. And you are worried about a damned comb?"

"What's the point if we even have to give up our human dignity?" demanded Juliska sternly.

There was no arguing with her on certain points. But she pulled her weight in other ways. She made us do our lessons diligently. Whenever not otherwise busy, the Csiszar boys were invited join us. Though they were less than keen on the idea, a cuff on the side of the head, courtesy of their mother, persuaded them otherwise. It gave her status to have her boys instructed by "the lady governess from Budapest."

Spring on a farm is always an interesting time, and our first spring with the Csiszars was no exception. The farmyard was alive with chicks, ducklings, goslings, and piglets. The swallows, darting back and forth, were building their mud nests under the eaves of the stables, and one morning we woke up to the arrival of the storks. Back from their winter sojourn in Egypt, they busily gath-ered twigs and stacked them on top of the chimney, braiding them together in time to have their summer home ready for the arrival of their young.

Whenever these fascinating occurrences of nature's orderly pace tempted us to relax our guard, we were quickly jerked back to reality, as when the new calf was born.

The children were waiting excitedly outside the closed barn door while the adults were assisting the cow, who seemed to be in great difficulty. We heard her painful lowing and the swearing of the men inside. Finally there was quiet, and we were let in. The baby calf was lying next to its mother, who was licking it gen-tly with her large tongue.

Fascinated, I turned to my mother to ask loudly, "Did you lick me too when I was born?"

A warning sign appeared in my mother's eyes. I heard Peter stop breathing. The peasants were staring at us. I had slipped.

My mother recovered instantly and casually answered, "No. But maybe your mother did!"

The peasants burst into laughter. Mrs. Csiszar slapped her thighs. "That was a good one! Fancy ladies licking their young! That's telling her!"

It never happened again. From then on I was constantly on alert.

We were sitting down to eat one evening, my mother ladling out the soup, when there was a knock on our door. Surprised, she called out, "Come in."

The door opened and two immaculately dressed German officers stood in the doorway. The ladle crashed to the floor. Juliska sprang up from the bed. Peter's spoon stopped in midair. One of the officers bent down and handed the ladle back to my mother.

"Zum Entschuldigung!" ("Beg your pardon!"), he said and clicked his highly polished heels. Nobody moved. "Spricht Jemand hier Deutsch?" ("Does anyone here speak German?"), he asked. Juliska took over.

"Ja, natürlich wir sprechen Deutsch" ("Yes, of course we speak German!").

A smile of relief passed over the officers' faces. They introduced themselves.

"Oberleutnant Robert . . . und Hauptman Ludwig."

They were friendly. They had not come to arrest us! They approached the table and sniffed the soup.

"Ahh, Kartoffel Suppe!" ("Potato soup! Homemade!"). They inhaled deeply.

My mother offered to share our supper. After some polite hesitation, they eagerly accepted and sat down on the edge of Peter's cot. Meanwhile Peter was trying to catch Juliska's eye. She saw and looked at him questioningly. His eyes moved to the windowsill on Juliska's side of the room, where she saw with horror Peter's homemade radio negligently left in full sight. The little radio that Peter had cleverly built in an old cigar box with bits and pieces of wire and crystal was our link with the outside world. Late at night, after the blankets had been pulled over the windows for "blackout," everybody would get under the covers and Peter would twist his knobs until the crackle of strange voices could be heard. Some nights were successful, some nights, not. On occasion he was able to reach the BBC, which he and Juliska were able to decipher. Listening to the BBC was strictly verboten and carried the death penalty.

Juliska slowly backed up toward the window. Without turning around, she reached behind, grabbed the radio, and with a casual movement slipped it under the bed. My mother meanwhile was serving soup to the Germans. They ate with gusto and, in between spoonfuls, made conversation. Robert was tall, very handsome with dark hair, stiff and proper. Ludwig was fair and shorter, readier with a smile, especially for us children. They were stationed nearby and had heard that there were two attractive and educated young women refugees in the village who spoke German, and they had decided to investigate. They were delighted to make our acquaintance, they said. Would my mother and Juliska please allow them to visit again? They were most proper. From the depth of their pockets some sweets appeared that were offered to Peter and me and which we eagerly accepted.

That first visit over, Juliska and my mother discussed the situation. There was really very little choice. It certainly would not be wise to tell the Germans not to come again. The Csiszars were delighted with their presence and made good-natured but lewd insinuations regarding future relationships between the German officers and the two young women. The visits continued. The Germans' behavior remained *korrekt,* though Robert liked to take Juliska for walks alone.

Now we would have to be more vigilant than ever. The radio had to go. Peter protested. "Bury it!" ordered my mother. We did. In the back of the stable under the straw, where he snuck in and listened to it when all the occupants of the farmhouse were out working in the fields. That's how we knew that in June 1944 the Allies landed in Normandy. But Normandy was a thousand miles away. It could be a long time, if ever, till they reached us!

The summer was hot. The unpaved roads that had been a sea of mud just a few weeks before turned to dry dust. A large wooden tub normally used for soaking laundry was filled with water from the pump outside, and we took turns, along with the farmyard fowl, wading around in it to get the grit out from between our toes. The smell from the dung heap, the stable, the outhouse, and the animals all mingled together in a heavy, hot, and pungent stench that enveloped us day and night and became synonymous with the farm. The farmers would laugh at our fastidiousness as we screwed up our noses when we ran past the outhouse, where hundreds of enormous bluebottles were crazily zooming and buzzing.

We shed our city clothes that we had rapidly outgrown and donned home-made shorts that Juliska and my mother fashioned out of the old useless ones. This created one of our most threatening incidents.

Peter had a birthmark on his thigh. It was a light brown, large amoeba shape that looked as though he had spilled coffee on himself and the stain had stayed there. One of the csendörs noticed Peter's bare leg, and it jogged his memory.

"Hey, wait a minute. Aren't you the little Jew bastard who came here one summer and stayed with that whore Margit? You have the same birthmark. What's your name?" he demanded.

This time Peter staunchly denied his identity. He was Janos Schmutzler. His mother was here, and the csendör could go check our papers.

"That's exactly what I'm going to do, you little shit," he warned.

We raced home. Peter was ready to pack up and run. Not so my mother.

"There are times when you run, and there are times when you stay. Today we stay and we attack," she said determinedly.

She marched us down to the local police station, walked up to the csendör's desk, and brought her fist down on it.

"You stupid son of a whore. Don't you know who we are? How dare you frighten my son and call him a Jew bastard? I'll make sure that my husband takes care of you, you idiotic little bureaucrat," she shouted at him, seemingly trembling with rage. "You so much as look at my son again and I'll have your balls cut off!" She thrust her body forward over his desk in face-to-face confrontation. He receded in his chair, looking smaller and smaller. He looked terrified. My mother's words may have been vulgar, but her accent was definitely upper class. In the pre-war, stratified society of Hungary, country policemen definitely ranked below ladies. My mother turned on her heels and marched out, while the csendör was mumbling and stuttering apologies. Peter and I ran out after her, not daring to utter a word, although for different reasons. Peter thought that my mother had lost her mind. I was still astonished at my mother's language. We walked briskly back to the farm. At the gate, my mother stopped and looked at us. "There's a time and place for everything. Now let's hope that this was the right time and place!"

As the weather turned hazy and sultry, we took to going into the woods a little way from the farm to play in the cooling shade. Peter had made friends with a little boy who was ostracized by the local children, partly because he had a club foot and partly because he was "illegitimate." They called him by cruel names and threw sticks and stones if he, and the geese he took to the fields, came too close to the farmyard's gate. Marci was shy and bright. Peter and he would act out stories of knights and dragons, cowboys and Indians, while I was usually the damsel in distress who had to be rescued.

One day, the two boys went off without me while Juliska was teaching me the traditionally feminine arts of sewing, embroidery, and knitting, which became a daily occupation when there was no other work on the farm. We were interrupted by Peter's early return. He was flushed and very disturbed. He lay down on his cot and refused to talk, and we saw him trembling. My mother asked him if he felt sick. He shook his head, but soon he was running a fever and vomiting. By evening he was delirious, and my mother was frantic. What could have happened? Peter was not able tell us. My mother sought out Marci to see whether he had any idea as to what was causing Peter's distress. The little boy was terribly frightened but blurted out the story of a horrifying scene they had witnessed while playing in the woods.

The boys had gone further into the woods than they had been permitted to and had come upon some kind of a camp surrounded by a barbed-wire fence. A German soldier was keeping watch at the entrance. The boys had started to retreat very quietly when they heard several Germans coming out through the gate. They had hidden to let them pass, but the Germans, escorting a few youths naked to the waist, had stopped a few hundred feet outside the gate by a large hole in the ground. While the boys watched in horror, the young men were lined up at the edge of the excavation, told to put their hands on the nape of their necks, and then systematically shot in the back of the head, falling into the hole one after the other. The soldiers threw several spadefuls of dirt over the bodies, then left. Peter and Marci had not dared to move and probably could not have if they had wanted to. They stayed there long after the soldiers had gone back through the gate, terrified of being discovered. Finally, without saying a word to each other, they had fled home. Peter was sick for several days. My mother spent most of that time cradling him like a baby, speaking to him softly, trying to get him to talk, and, finally, he did.

During Robert and Ludwig's next visit, my mother casually asked the German officers where their camp was. They told her.

"Oh?" she said casually, feigning nonchalance. "I thought it might be the garrison on the other side of the woods that one of the peasants told us about."

"No," answered Ludwig. "That's a garrison with some work-service men and prisoners. Criminals," he added.

"Jews," added Robert.

I don't know how my mother arranged it, but it was agreed that two boys from the camp were to be "loaned" to the farm as day laborers in exchange for good farm-fresh food for the German soldiers.

Two young men, about seventeen or eighteen years old, were brought to the farm. Astonishment and hope briefly lit their eyes as an instant recognition took place. They immediately knew who and what we were. My mother stared at them hard, warning them: Don't give it away! They understood. The hopeful look disappeared. Their heads bent down. Where were they going to run to? The soldiers were coming back for them at the end of the day.

It was a deal that was good for everybody. The harvesting season was upon us, and work was plentiful. The Csiszars could certainly use an extra pair of hands. The Germans were happy to get fresh food. Laci and Vili had a reprieve, perhaps more. They looked weak, emaciated, and older than their years; they told us where they were from, how they had been separated from their families and sent to the work camp. Since my mother had made the deal it was understood that she had unofficial charge of them on the farm. She was careful not to show her concern for them and scrupulously sent them out to do the work that the Csiszars needed, but not before stuffing them with more food than they could healthily digest. And there were rest periods, during which time Peter would always huddle with Vili, who was an artist and was helping Peter with his drawing.

As the early fall progressed, everyone became anxious and edgy. How long was this war going to go on? We were no longer receiving any communications from Budapest, and we had no idea what was happening to the family. In early June the Allies had landed in France; Ludwig and Robert had boasted that the Wehrmacht was going to throw them back into the sea in no time. But they weren't talking much that way anymore. Apparently things were not going that well for the Reich. The "barbaric" Russians were advancing from the east while the Allies were coming ever closer from the west. Robert still believed staunchly in his Führer, in the might of the German army, in the logic of Nazi philosophy, but Ludwig began to have doubts on all three counts. During their visits, he often took out pictures of his wife and children from his wallet and would stare at them while stroking my hair, sighing heavily.

Toward the end of the harvesting season, Laci and Vili confided to us that things were getting much worse at the camp. Prisoners were disappearing daily and those that became sick were shot. They asked my mother if there was any-thing she could do to help them. That's all she needed. Over Juliska's half-hearted objections, she devised a plan to help the boys escape. On a day that they were not coming to the farm, we would go into the woods. Peter and I would distract the guard; my mother and Juliska would slip some peasant women's clothing through the fence at some prearranged spot. The boys then hoped to be able to sneak out with a group of local women who worked at the camp on a per diem basis.

We set out for the woods soon after, with Peter and I leading the way. Already near the garrison, I was jauntily skipping in front when I suddenly found myself nose-to-nose with a huge black spider in the middle of its web. I immediately felt the panic rising, but before I could open my mouth, I was thrown to the ground. Peter was on top of me, his hand over my mouth, begging me, "Evi, don't scream. Please, please, it's all right."

I couldn't hear him. I felt myself choking. My body was in a spasm. I needed to scream, but his hand was like a vice. His terror was at least as strong as mine. I was near fainting when my mother's voice came through.

"Evi, the spider is dead. I killed it. You mustn't scream. We're near the garri-son. Take some deep breaths. Evi, do you hear me?"

Peter's grip had not relaxed. He wasn't taking any chances. My panic subsided, and I nodded. He let me go. A violent shaking overtook me, and I vomited. My mother cleaned me up, while Peter looked on with concern.

"I'm sorry, Nyunyus," Peter said, using his pet name for me. "I couldn't let you scream. Please forgive me."

"She's all right. Let's go and get this over with." My mother was there when we needed her, but excessive coddling was not her style.

We separated near the entrance to the garrison. Peter and I came out to the clearing, playing with a big ball in front of the guard. He greeted us, and when Peter kicked the ball over to him, he kicked it back. Soon we had a spirited game going. Nobody saw my mother and Juliska slink out of the woods and around the perimeter of the fence.

Peter and I made our way back to the farm, where my mother told us to ask the Csiszar boys to join us that night in sleeping in the stable loft, just for fun. She showed us the place in the loft where she wanted us to spend the night. The boys were eager, but all I could think of was lying in the straw with spiders running over me.

"No. I'm not sleeping in the stable. Let the boys go without me," I said.

"Why?" asked my mother. "You always want to be with the boys. It will be fun. You'll see."

"No!"

"Anyu, it's the spiders," Peter explained.

My mother thought for a moment, then took me by the hand and led me outside.

"Ili, I know that you are only six years old. But today you have to be a grown-up. You have to forget about being afraid of anything. You have to go with the boys. Peter will look after you."

The tone of her voice was sad, but urgent, and I knew that I had no choice. I felt my stomach shrink inside me. I wanted to cry but couldn't. I knew that something very important was happening and that I had to play my part. The fear had to be conquered. For the first time I retreated to a mental state that I would use for the rest of my life whenever I found myself in a threatening or painful situation. I simply suspended feeling. Nothing could touch me or hurt me. I didn't think of anything. I kept my mind blank. I did everything mechanically.

That night we all climbed up into the stable loft. We laid down on a large horse blanket on top of the fresh straw that had been stored for the winter. Eventually we fell asleep, only to be woken up by flashlights and loud German voices. It was a search party. They were looking for Laci and Vili, who had escaped. The Csiszars stood by sleepily and watched the Germans bayoneting through the straw. Up in the loft, I whispered to Peter.

"What are they doing?"

"I don't know. Go to sleep."

"But I have to go to the bathroom! I'm going down."

"No!" He grabbed me and whispered fiercely. "Don't move. If you have to go then just go in your pants. But don't move."

His voice had the urgency to it that I had learned to associate with danger and doing as I was told without question. The Germans climbed up to the loft and saw us. The Csiszar boys were truly asleep, and Peter and I closed our eyes and huddled together. The soldiers bayoneted the straw around us, but finding nothing, they left.

Laci and Vili stayed hidden in the hayloft for two days and then snuck out one night dressed as peasant women. We never heard from them again.

Back in our little room, Juliska shook her head.

"Magda, this isn't fair. Putting the children in such danger!"

"No, it isn't. War just isn't fair to anybody, is it?"

With that the subject was closed.

Peter's little radio kept us somewhat abreast of certain political events, though no one ever knew what was true and what was propaganda. In October, Admiral Horthy was deposed, and the feared Szálasi and his Arrow Cross party took over. Though we did not know it at the time, my mother's fears had become a reality. The Jews of Budapest were now being mercilessly hunted. Columns of them, including children, were marched to the Danube and shot into the river until it ran red. Any man suspected of being a Jew could be ordered on the street to pull his pants down, and if found to be circumcised, be shot on the spot. The international community set up Safe Houses, where several hundred Jews found refuge. Several diplomats, most notably the Swedes Raoul Wallenberg and Per Anger, and the Swiss Carl Lutz, saved thousands by handing out safe passes, with the names hastily filled in, and, at the very last minute, by pulling Jews off the trains bound for the concentration camps. The rest of the desperate Jewish population ran from hiding place to hiding place, dodging bombs and bullets. They hid in cellars, bombed-out buildings, sewers, and occasionally found sanctuary in convents and church catacombs, watched over by a few brave and morally incorruptible women and men of the cloth. These intrepid individuals, along with others who also risked their lives to save Jews, became known as the "Righteous." But no one could keep up with the Germans' and the Arrow Cross's lust for murder.

Toward the end of autumn the bombing became very heavy. A bunker was built, dug out in the farmyard, where everybody rushed to as soon as the alarms sounded. The local police made their nightly rounds to make sure that everyone observed the total blackout by pulling blankets over their windows. No light was to escape into the darkness of the night. A lit cigarette could be a signal to a plane, designating a target. Anyone caught smoking outside at night, innocently or not, could be shot on sight. As soon as the adults covered the windows, we ran outside to check that no sliver of light was escaping.

Winter arrived early and bitterly. The little radio under the straw informed us that the Russians were closing in on Budapest. Robert and Ludwig were agonizing. Their visits became less frequent, but other Germans came. They commandeered food and fuel and ignored the peasants' complaints. Food became scarce, fuel even more so. We were cold most of the time. When I tried to put my shoes back on after a barefoot summer, I found that my feet had grown and that I had to curl up my toes. My mother cut the fronts out, and we covered the holes with rags. But the snow got in anyway, and soon my toes were red and painful and itchy, as were my fingers. Some days we stayed in bed, all huddled together to stave off the cold. Then Peter got sick. His chest hurt. He couldn't breathe without a lot of pain, and he ran a temperature. My mother agonized over what to do and finally asked the Csiszars whether she could borrow the dray. She was going to take Peter to the German field hospital. Mr. Csiszar hesitated about lending the horse. The road was treacherous, and a horse could easily slip and break a leg. Mrs. Csiszar, however, took a look at Peter and told her husband to hitch the wagon.

We were all bundled up in as many blankets as we could find and with our eyes barely showing we headed to the hospital. Peter was lying down in a pile of straw, his eyes feverish, his chest painful. Silently my mother thanked her dead brother-in-law for having had the foresight not to have Peter circumcised. We arrived at the hospital, and my mother asked an orderly to help her bring Peter inside.

"I'm sorry, madame," he said. "This is not a civilian hospital. It is only for the soldiers of the Reich. We can't help your son."

She pushed past the guards and demanded to see the doctor in charge. She marched into his office, and with the bravura that she was now relying on to get her through any situation, she faced him and demanded his help.

"My husband is fighting for the Reich. If he is willing to give his life, is it right for you to refuse help to his child? What are we fighting for if not for the future of our Aryan youth? You simply cannot let me leave here without at least looking at him!"

"Bring the boy in," he ordered.

He examined Peter and determined that he had pleurisy.

"I cannot keep him here," he said. "But I'll give you some medication and a course of treatment."

While he was talking he looked at my hands and took off my shoes.

"This," he said, "is much more serious. She's in danger of developing gangrene. Her extremities should be amputated."

"Amputated?" asked my mother weakly. "No, never!"

He shrugged his shoulders. "If she develops gangrene, she'll die."

"I'd rather she die," murmured my mother.

The doctor got up. The consultation was over. At the door he bowed, clicked his heels sharply, and said, "Auf wiedersehen, gnädige Frau. Ich wünsche Ihnen alles Gutes" ("Good-bye, madame. I wish you well").

"Danke viel mals, Herr Doktor" ("Thank you very much, Doctor"), my mother answered. Then under her breath she added, in Hungarian, "Dögöljetek meg!" ("Drop dead!").

Slowly and silently the horse plodded through the snow and took us home. My mother kept looking at my hands. Mrs. Csiszar was waiting for us with hot soup. She snorted at the death sentence that the doctor had passed on me and offered her homegrown remedy. She took out two basins. In one she put ice water and in the other boiling hot water. I had to keep my hands and feet in each one for as long as I could bear it, then change to the other bowl, repeating the procedure for fifteen minutes several times a day. My hands and feet continued to swell painfully. The skin split and I bled, but I never got gangrene, and though it took years, my hands eventually healed. Peter also got better. Mrs. Csiszar had at least as much to do with our recoveries as had the German doctor.

The war was on our doorstep. There was constant shelling. The closest town to us, Gyor, an industrial center just a few miles away, was bombed to the ground. When there was a lull in the fighting, we went out for some fresh air and to collect spent shells that we played with. We learned to identify which shells came from which type of weapon. When we found some very large unknown ones, we knew that the Russians were very close.

By January 1945 we heard that, after a two-month siege, the Russians had entered Budapest. We were further west. The front had not yet reached us. We waited for the onslaught.

The winter dragged on. Mrs. Csiszar took special care of me. She understood that my mother needed her for me. The doctor's words had been so devastating that she could not allow herself to fully absorb their meaning. It would have been too much. We all made light of my death sentence: "The doctor didn't know what he was talking about, that's all." The two women became close. The big, brown, loud-mouthed peasant woman and my tiny, delicate-looking mother shared something that Juliska was totally excluded from. They both had a toughness of spirit and empathy for those who were weaker than they.

We were awakened at dawn by the local authorities. We had one hour to evacuate the village. Why and where we were to go, no one knew. Bundles were made up of the most necessary items. The women and children got into the horse-drawn drays while the men walked beside them, and the long line of carriages of various shapes and sizes plodded out of the village. We ended up a few miles away, in the waiting room of a railroad station, with no other buildings around us. We were all crowded in, each family assigned to a certain space.

For three days we listened to gunfire, not daring to poke our noses out. We ate dried sausage and dry bread, and I slept wrapped in our bundle of clothing and a pillow that my mother had tied together. Finally there was silence. We waited. No one came. No one told us whether we were to stay or leave. People looked at one another perplexed. What do we do now? My mother stood up.

"I'm going back to the village to see what's going on," she said. "I'll be back as soon as I can. Juliska, watch the children!" And without another word, she left us. The men looked at one another, but stayed put. A day passed. Juliska took us outside for some air. The countryside was deserted. In the distance there were occasional spurts of gunfire, too far away for us to be concerned. We scanned the road for a sign of my mother. An old peasant was trudging toward us. We approached him and, describing my mother, asked if he had seen any sign of her.

"There's been a lot of shooting around here," he said. "I saw a small, dark-haired woman shot and fall in the ditch on the outskirts of the village. Sounds like the one that you're looking for."

His nonchalant statement was so shocking that we didn't know how to react. We were stunned, speechless. We all had the same thought. We couldn't be without her. I was the first to recover.

"She's not dead!" I cried. "You'll see, she'll be back soon."

Peter hugged me without a word. He looked lifeless. Juliska walked us back into the building and told the peasants what we had heard. There was general consternation, but Mrs. Csiszar echoed my words.

"No, not her! She's not dead. Don't worry," she consoled. "Your mother will come back."

I looked at her, frightened.

"She's not my mother!" I said, a little too loudly.

"Oh, of course not. But she'll come back, you'll see!"

Juliska, Peter, and I exchanged confused looks. Without my mother, we didn't know what to do.

At that moment my mother walked in. We looked up at her, astounded. No one said a word.

"What's the matter?" she asked. "Didn't you expect me back?" Tears of relief followed and question after question.

Yes, there had been some shooting, but she had jumped into a ditch and had waited there until it was safe. She reported that the village was deserted, though it was obvious that there had been fighting there. She said that it was safe to go back.

The little caravan retraced its steps and trudged back home.

From left to right: Miklos, Rozsa, (standing) Kati, Magda, Denes, (front) Klari. Ujpest, Hungary, 1914.

Wedding photo, Kati and Sandor (Uncle Sanyi). 1930.

Miklos, 1933.

Klari, Magda, and Kati. 1937.

From left: (top) Denes, Herman, (bottom) Olga (Herman's younger sister who perished at Auschwitz), Magda, Eszter, unknown. 1937?

Wedding photo, Magda and Herman. 1938.

Rozsa, July 1940. Inscription on back: "To all three of you with the most sincere motherly love as a birthday present: and especially to my adored little Evi."

At one and a half with Herman, May 1940. Last photo together.

Magda, 1939.

Kati, 1947?

Klari, 1947.

Eszter. South of France, 1947?

Just before leaving Paris for
Hungary, 1941.

From left: (top) Claude, Evi, Peter, (front) Pista. Budapest, 1942.

The Csiszar farmhouse, Lovászpatona.

Liberation

We returned from the abandoned railroad station to an eerily silent village. I don't even remember the sound of animals. The front doors of the farmhouses were swinging on their hinges. All the locks had been broken, the houses ransacked, the peasants' buried treasures found and looted. Broken furniture and dead livestock littered the farmyard. The peasants stood, stonily surveying the damage. For them, the enemy had arrived. Everybody stood around uncertainly, wondering what to do. Was the war over? Was it safe for us to return to Budapest? Where were the soldiers? Who was in charge? Nobody had answers. Rumors kept filtering back throughout the day. The Russians were coming. The Germans were regrouping. The war was over. The war wasn't over. We were warned against picking up any foreign objects off the ground, opening closed doors or drawers. The Germans were supposed to have left explosives and booby traps upon retreating. There was nothing to do but wait. We ate a meager supper of potatoes and onions, retired to our little room and went to sleep.

I was awakened in the middle of the night by the door flying open violently, a babble of menacing-sounding foreign words, and light rays ricocheting rapidly off the walls. Simultaneously, we heard the rat-ta-tat-tat of a machine gun outside. I screamed as my mother and Juliska leapt out of bed. Peter was sitting bolt upright on his cot, his white face blending into the wall behind him. Three or four men had burst into our room. One was holding an enormous, elaborately decorated church candle. Two of them held rifles at the ready. The candle illuminated the room enough to make the men out. In the flickering light their features looked strange and alien to me. They were unshaven, dirty, ragged, and they looked fierce. I later learned that these were Soviet soldiers from the Central Asian provinces of the Soviet Union. The Hungarians called them "Mongols." The Russian soldiers started shouting orders at us, but we couldn't understand them. With their guns they were pointing us toward the door. One of them stumbled across the room toward Juliska, who was pulling a blanket around herself. She was crying with terror and was begging the soldier not to hurt her. He seemed to be telling her to be quiet, but she was in a panic, sobbing hysterically. Finally he unslung his rifle, spun it around, and hit her with the butt. He caught her on the hip, and we all heard the thud of wood against flesh. It electrified us into silence. Juliska slumped to the floor, whimpering. The other soldier had my mother by the arm, ready to lead her out of the room. I was hanging onto her nightgown, holding her back. She lifted her hand and in a determined voice said, "Just a minute!" The soldier, surprised, let her go. She picked me up, carried me over to Peter's cot.

"Peter, watch Evi. Don't leave this room, no matter what you hear, and try not to be afraid. These are Russians. They are here to liberate us."

She didn't sound too convinced, and we knew that she was trying to reassure us. Outside we could hear rough male voices, women screaming and begging, and what sounded like furniture being thrown about. The two soldiers took the two women out, Juliska limping badly and in pain. The third one threw back the covers of the bed, making sure that there was no one else. He then came over to us and threw our covers back, too. He said something in a reassuring tone, tousled Peter's hair, and left the room. I don't know how long Peter and I cowered under the covers, occasionally peeping out, listening to scuffling, crying, screams, cursing, and occasional shots. Strange shadows formed on the frosted glass of our door, the outer chamber illuminated only by the enormous, flickering stolen church candles. It was a though we were watching a violent theater of shadows being played out in the other room for our benefit.

Suddenly we heard my mother's voice, screaming something outside. We forgot her admonitions and ran to the door. The action had moved from the front room to the yard. As we crossed the room, running, we saw Mrs. Csiszar painfully getting up from the floor; she was beaten and bleeding. Her clothes were torn, most of her body exposed. Her husband lay dazed on the floor. We dashed out barefoot into the cold March air, and in the first light of dawn we saw my mother and Juliska backing up toward the dung heap, the soldiers advancing toward them. My mother was screaming at them in every language she knew: Hungarian, French, German, and what Yiddish she had heard as a child at home.

"Yid! Yid! We're Jews! Why do you want to hurt us? Can't you understand, we're Jews!"

We ran to the women and they clutched us tight. Suddenly an army vehicle pulled up, and an officer got out. He was wearing a cleaner and better uniform than the other soldiers. He shouted orders as he made his way through the crowd of peasants and soldiers, and stopped in front of my mother. He looked down at us shivering and cowering, and asked sternly, "Yid?"

My mother nodded. He thought for a minute, then barked something. The meaning was obvious: Prove it!

My mother and Juliska looked at each other, and one thought passed between them: Peter was not circumcised! Then my mother took a chance. She started reciting: "Shema Yisroel, Adanoy elohenu, Adanoy echod" ("Hear O Israel: the Lord our God, the Lord is one").

The Russian officer joined her for the next line, "Boruch shem kevad malkusah lealom voed" ("Blessed be His name, whose glorious kingdom is forever and ever").

As she was about to continue, he held up his hand. It was enough. The dung heap in the farmyard was not an appropriate place to recite the Shema, the most important Hebrew prayer for Jews.

The mood in the farmyard changed immediately. The officer gave his orders. We were to be protected. The farm was off-limits. It turned out that he spoke some French and so was able to communicate with the women. If we had any trouble, all we had to do was call the Patrouille, the Russian equivalent to MPs (military police), and it would be taken care of.

The soldiers drifted off, and we were left standing by the dung heap, surrounded by the peasants looking at us with mistrust. We had deceived them. We were Jews!

There was a moment of stillness and uncertainty, until Mrs. Csiszar limped over to my mother, put her arm around her shoulder, and led her back into the farmhouse.

"I've known for a while," she said.

"Yes, I know you have," said my mother. "I wish I could have helped you before, you know . . . against the soldiers."

Mrs. Csiszar sighed. "There was nothing you could have done. At least now, because of you, we have some protection." And she smiled, wanly.

During the next two or three days we learned to fear the Russians more than we had ever feared the Germans. We did not know that the troops who occupied the village were not typical of the entire Soviet army. Those who liberated us were for the most part from Mongolia. They were totally uneducated, hardly knowing where they were, and they had been through hell. All they knew was that they were in enemy territory and that they were the victors. They raped, they looted, and shot anything in their way.

There was a tannery in the village, in front of which stood several metal barrels of vitriol, used in the tanning of the hides. The Russians assumed that anything in a barrel was alcohol and consumable. They had gone through all the bottles, be it long-treasured prewar Cologne water or homemade wine. As they were about to open the barrels, the peasants tried to stop them and warn them of the danger. The soldiers, convinced they were being denied something that they wanted, immediately shot two of them. The others peasants stood back and watched in horror as the unfortunate ignorants drank the vitriol and then writhed in agony until they finally died.

One night, the shooting began all over again. In the morning we learned that the Germans had taken back their position and were again in control of the village. Now the entire farmhouse fell into a panic. Everyone knew by now that we were Jews and under the protection of the Russians. The Csiszars had now become "harborers of Jews," unless of course they gave us up. We lived a tortured few days until the Russians fought their way back again. We were on the front, and for a couple of weeks that front constantly shifted between the two armies. But no one gave us away. By then the outcome of the war was a foregone conclusion, and the peasants were not about to jeopardize their position with the eventual victors. They kept quiet, and on the morning of March 27, 1945, our village was declared "liberated." We had managed to survive a time when millions had perished.

1945

The war was over. The Allies had won. We were free to be Jews again. These were the sentences that I kept hearing. But the war being over didn't mean very much to me; I didn't remember what peace was. The Allies were the good guys. That I knew. As far as being free to be Jews, that was puzzling. I didn't know what a Jew was. I had heard the word *Jew* ever since I could remember. In my family, it was always said in a quiet, furtive way with meaningful expressions, generally unease. When I had heard it said aloud by others, it seemed to be an insult. And I had never realized that "it" was "us." My family was not religious. There had never been a mezuzah on the door frame. I had never seen a menorah in the house, nor had I been inside a synagogue. The one time that Kati had worn the yellow star, I had ripped it off her coat. But I didn't remember why. One day, surreptitiously, we had left our home, gone into hiding, changed our names. All because it was "dangerous" and "all of our lives depended on our not giving ourselves away." But nobody had explained to me that it was because we were Jews. And now I was free to be something that I didn't know I was and wasn't sure I wanted to be.

My mother, Juliska, Peter, and I undertook the journey back to Budapest by cattle car. We sat on the floor in piles of straw. A man sitting close by asked, "What is your name, little girl?"

I didn't know what to answer and looked at my mother questioningly. She smiled. "It's all right. You can use your real name again," she said.

"Evi," I answered.

It sounded so strange. I hadn't heard or used my name for a year. I kept repeating it to myself. Ili had ceased to exist. Peace had killed her off. And Evi had been resurrected!

The train lurched to a stop. As we waited we heard shouting. My mother went to investigate, and Peter and I clambered down after her. Five bodies lay on the track. They looked dead even though they were moving. They were so thin I thought I could see through them. Their heads were shaved, and I wasn't sure whether they were men or women. They seemed to be moving in slow-motion.

Over their skeletal bodies they wore some kind of striped uniform. They were begging for someone to help them. My mother approached, spoke to them, then turned to the curious gathering crowd that had alighted from the train.

"Come on, let's help them onto the train. They walked out of a concentration camp, and they are trying to get home."

Nobody moved. My mother walked over to a group of men.

"Well, what are you waiting for? Help!"

"Not me," said one of them. "I don't want these lice-infested Jews next to me!"

Everybody nodded in agreement. She hesitated for a moment but did not reply. She then turned to Juliska, Peter, and me.

"Children, Juliska, come help lift these women onto the train."

My mother and Juliska each carried one of the women, while Peter and I tried to help a third to her feet. They couldn't have weighed more than sixty or seventy pounds. Suddenly my mother's path was barred by the other passengers.

"Lady," began the man who had spoken before. "Didn't you hear us? They are not getting on this train!"

My mother gently shifted her burden and faced the group. "Yes, they are getting on this train. And you will not stop me, because I will kill anyone who tries. You scum of the earth, you cursed people, you lowest of all animals. You will burn in hell for all eternity! Now let me pass!"

Her voice had a tone to it that we had not heard before. The pent-up pain and rage of the past few years spewed out. It was plain that, at that point, she was capable of killing. She was terrifying. Everyone was quiet. There was a strange stillness. This tiny woman, carrying a dying wisp of humanity sounded for all the world like a biblical prophet empowered by the wrath of God. Everyone stood silently for a moment. Sidestepping the man, she lifted her burden onto the train. Nobody stopped us. They just stood and watched us in hostile silence as we quietly and laboriously loaded our human cargo. We made them as comfortable as possible in the straw and lifted their heads to help them drink a few drops of water. Everyone climbed back on board, and the train lurched forward in fits and starts, jostling and shaking us like beads in a baby's rattle.

We had the whole corner of the car to ourselves. Nobody would come near us, and all averted their eyes. A few hours later when we reached Budapest, three of the women were dead. We helped one of them find her family, and one came home with us. With macabre humor, we nicknamed her Depus, shortened from *Deportalt* (deported one).

We arrived to a devastated city. The Western Railway Station was in ruins. There was no longer any covered area. The original structure was now acres of rubble and charred, twisted metal. The streets were still littered with debris. Most shops were closed. Everything was gray. People walked fast with their heads down, unsmiling, dressed in tatters. I felt uneasy. This was not how I remembered home.

We looked for our building amid the ruins. We had no idea whether or not it was still standing or who and what we would find there. We found the street. We found the building, still standing, though most of the façade fallen away from it— pockmarked with hundreds of bullet holes. We entered the apartment with Depus in tow. Kati and Klari were there alone. It was a reunion of relief, joy, and tears. My aunts were both astonished and delighted at how well we looked. Compared to the rest of the starved populace of the city, we were the picture of health. Nobody mentioned Uncle Sanyi, Uncle Miklos, Zsuzsika, or Nagyi.

There was hardly any food in the house or, indeed, in the whole of the capital. People were fighting over the flesh of dead horses in the street, and we had brought home an extra mouth to feed. Within days my mother undertook the long and dangerous journey back to the countryside to get us some food. In the meantime, we managed on dried peas, beans, and whatever Kati managed to get on the black market. Klari was still a superb cook who could make even dried peas taste good. She had not changed. She was still the hysterical, good-natured "featherbrain" who petted and cuddled me and with whom I could again be a carefree little girl.

Even with the food shortage we were in an enviable position. Our apartment was intact. The building had not been bombed, and aside from some bullet holes and erratic heating and electrical services, it seemed like paradise compared to the farm. Kati had lived in the apartment throughout most of the persecution and the Soviet siege, and this had deterred looters from stealing the furniture. Certain items that she had felt were too valuable to be kept in the apartment, in case looters did come, she had hidden in the basement of a Christian employee's home. These valuables included a suitcase full of family pictures and letters, silver, antique porcelain, and paintings. After liberation she went to retrieve her property and found most of the house gone along with everything else, except the old battered suitcase.

Kati was good at wheeling and dealing. She bartered with the Russians, who were eager for any luxury goods. One day a high-ranking Russian officer came to the door and demanded to see what she had. Dealing on the black market was illegal and carried its own perils, but everyone took chances when it came to food. She didn't dare not to show him what she had and pulled out the drawer under the convertible sofa, revealing her stash of silk stockings and other intimate apparel that she had saved from Uncle Sanyi's store. She could have been robbed, killed, or arrested, but she wasn't. The officer grinned, took an armful of goods, then dug into his pockets and handed over a fistful of U.S. hundred-dollar bills. He then ordered an armed guard to our front door. "Everything you get is for me!" he declared. Kati had found the Golden Goose!

My mother, joined by many from the capital, would go to the villages and buy or barter for food. Jewelry, silk underwear, cigarettes, gold, and dollars took the place of legal tender. Money was worthless. Inflation was spiraling at an ever increasing rate. Million-pengö notes became play money. Diamond engagement rings were exchanged for sausages and chickens, gold for eggs and lard.

With my mother's regular forays to the country for food, we were much better off than most of our neighbors. But these trips were quite dangerous. Marauding groups of Russian soldiers showed no compunction about looting; raping women was an accepted sport. After all, they were the conquerors! Many of the soldiers were from the poorest parts of the Soviet Union. Some had never seen running water. Watches were a wonder to them, and they set about collecting them at gunpoint from any unwary citizen who had forgotten to leave hers or his at home. They delighted in turning back their shirtsleeves and revealing as many as ten watches strapped on each arm. Our recourse if attacked by drunken, looting, or raping soldiers was to call the Patrouille. Sometimes they came, sometimes not. And when they did come, it was not certain that they would protect the victims. As often as not they joined the miscreants in their activities.

My mother had two chicken crates that she filled with the provisions and then strapped to her body. One in front, one in the back, leaving her hands free to carry in each a bottle of slivovitz. She then stood in the middle of a main road and waited for a convoy of Soviet military trucks. When she waved the bottles in the air, the trucks invariably stopped. The soldiers drank the liquor, and my mother was offered a ride. Then she took her chances. She came home with hair-raising stories, shrugging her shoulders at the danger. She could take care of any situation, she said, while her sisters begged her not to take such risks. After all there were trains, even if they were packed to the limit, had nonexistent schedules, and often broke down; at least there was safety in numbers. But that was not for my mother. With the convoys she could get back to Budapest in a matter of hours, instead of days. She was not afraid of anything. She flaunted her daring in her sisters' faces. Kati was constantly irritated with her.

"Why do you have to be so foolhardy? Haven't you faced enough already? You don't have to prove anything anymore."

My mother's bravado had become a dangerous habit. Death and danger had to be defied again and again!

"Why don't you try it your way then?" she taunted and challenged her sister. But Kati didn't know how to talk to peasants any more than my mother knew how to deal on the black market. They each knew their roles, and each secretly gave thanks that they didn't have to fulfill the other's. Klari's role never changed. She was the pretty one who was always happy to be taken care of by her siblings.

The day after we arrived back to Budapest, Kati, Klari, Peter, and I went down to look around the neighborhood. The Allied bombing and the two-month Russian siege had devastated the city. Rubble was everywhere. Those buildings that had not been bombed were, like ours, scarred with bullet holes. We children were fascinated by the ruined buildings. Many had been left partially standing with one or two walls totally fallen away, the interior left exposed to view. The apartments, stacked one on top of the other, with their parquet floors hanging, sofas and tables teetering on the edges, looked strangely like stage sets. Some still had pictures hanging on the walls. Not too long ago, we had played with our friends in these same buildings.

In front of the next apartment house, the child of the concierge, whom I remembered, was playing on the sidewalk. She was around eight years old. She looked up as we passed and said to me, in a matter-of-fact tone, "Hello, you stinking Jew. So you came back, after all. We thought you had all croaked."

I stopped in my tracks, not really grasping what she had said. Peter went white. Then a sound like the crack of a whip startled me. Kati's hand had shot out and slapped the child's face with such force that I thought her head was going to snap off. She fell to the ground and started to howl. Shaking with rage, Kati grabbed her arm, jerked her to her feet, and hissed at her, "You go home, right now, and tell your parents that if within twenty-four hours they have not disappeared, I am reporting them to the Russians as collaborators!" With that she gave her an extra shake and pushed her toward her front door.

Nobody said a word. We all went back upstairs. Kati locked herself in the bathroom, and we heard her retching.

While my mother was away buying food, Kati and Klari were trying to build a semblance of normalcy in our lives. Peter and I were enrolled in school. Kati had not lost her appetite for the finer things in life and decided that only the very best private schools were good enough. I was enrolled at the newly reopened Young English Ladies' School. There seemed to be plenty of money for the schools, the new clothes, the imported silk stockings that Kati could not live without, all the luxuries that were suddenly becoming available. Yet we were kept awake many a night while the sisters argued loudly about something called "dollars." Dollars were supposed to arrive, or had arrived, or were never enough, or somebody was cheating you with them. They were always mentioned in the same breath as Denes, their brother who had emigrated to Paris and married my aunt Eszter, who had brought me to Hungary.

Denes had done well before the war. He had emigrated in 1928, opened his own business a few years later, married, and changed his name to Denis. Though born in the little provincial town of Rakospalota, he was a natural cosmopolitan. He recognized early on that the backwaters of Eastern Europe were too constrictive for him. He had an innate sense for world politics, and he always saw the big picture. He understood long before anyone else in the family the dark destiny that Europe was hurtling toward. When war was declared, Denis was called up for active duty. The photograph that I have of my uncle in his French army uniform always makes me smile. Discipline in any form was an anathema to him. He was stationed somewhere in the Pyrenees, and it did not take him long to bribe a Basque shepherd to take him across the mountains to Spain. From there he boarded a ship to Cuba, where he eventually established himself as a successful garment manufacturer. He also established another family. By the time the war ended he had accumulated a small fortune and a baby daughter. The "dollars" were coming from him. He was preparing to come back to Europe, but in the meantime was making sure that whatever family was left was not going to starve. Between my uncle's money and Kati's dealings, we were living well.

Meanwhile, we tried to find out what had happened to various members of the family. People were slowly drifting back from the concentration camps and the forced labor factories, bringing with them stories of the unimaginable horrors they had witnessed and lived through. We saw and heard these tortured ghosts . . . we couldn't call them "people." They didn't look like any human beings that we had seen before, and we were awestruck. They were all looking for somebody, somewhere to live, something to eat. They brought with them valuable information, but it all had to be pieced together. Someone may have shared a cattle car with a Rozsa Pollak, possibly my grandmother, on the way to Auschwitz, but they had been separated in Krakow. So we would ask everybody if they knew anyone who was on a transport out of Krakow and so on. The detective work was exhausting, the reports devastating. It was the first time that people were seeing and hearing what had really been going on. Up until then it had all been rumors. Hopes were raised, dashed, and raised again. Official information was either inaccurate or nonexistent. Europe was still in turmoil. Spouses looking for each other, parents seeking children, children trying to remember who their real parents were. People were waiting for days at railway stations, waving photographs at those arriving home from the camps; cries of "Have you seen my husband?" "My child?" "My mother?" "My father?" echoed throughout Europe's bombed-out rail yards. We were no exception. Some information trickled through that gave us very little hope of ever seeing Uncle Sanyi, Uncle

Miklos, his wife Zsuzsika, or Nagyi again. No one ever mentioned them to us, and no explanation of their absence was ever given. Our questions were not answered. They were gone. That was all. We were going to go on without them. I don't remember sadness, just grim determination and a quiet, seething anger.

But still, people waited and hoped. There came rumors of hundreds of thousands still alive somewhere in the Soviet Union. It took time to absorb the incredible, horrible truth. In the last months of the war, while Germany was already losing, it was still putting its effort into killing as many Jews as possible. In the end, the Germans managed to massacre 60 percent of the Hungarian Jewry, or about five hundred thousand men, women, and children.

I had this awful feeling that my Nagyi and Uncle Sanyi had disappeared into the depths of those mysterious and dreadful words that I was hearing every day: *Auschwitz, Bergen-Belsen, Dachau, Theresienstadt, Mauthausen.* Words that spoke of unspeakable terrors, words that conjured up my own personal, childlike visions of hell. Of hairy black spiders and bitter cold, of exploding bombs and violent soldiers. I couldn't imagine anything worse than that.

Peter and I watched and listened to the daily parade of those lifeless shells with barely human forms who came to our door to be fed a decent meal and to ask for help in locating family. They expected to be recognized, and there was always an embarrassed silence while we were trying to guess who they were. Most of them had been friends and acquaintances. But the "Deportees" all looked the same to me. They were all gray: hair, skin, eyes, clothing. Walking skeletons, amazed themselves that they had come back from the dead. Some spewed out endless stories of their unimaginable sufferings, others sat silently eating their soup, gently stroking my hair and my face, gazing at me with wonder. Kati fed them all and doled out Uncle Sanyi's clothes. She knew that he wasn't coming back.

When they left, she sighed and said to us, "You don't know how fortunate you are. Thank God you don't understand. Soon you'll forget even this whole episode. Children are so lucky!"

We believed her.

Many of the deportees recovered physically, and I was amazed that within a few weeks I was able to recognize who they had been. But I was warned: "Don't ask about their families." Not about wives or husbands, children or parents. If they found them alive and well, they would tell us anyway.

This seemingly amazing resilience was astonishing. But the healed bodies of the camp survivors covered the bleeding wounds of inerasable memories, forever crippled emotions, and often serious mental instability. Many who came back with their bodies relatively intact from that living hell also carried home dead souls. This unholy experience could never be forgotten, forgiven, or left behind. It was like a thousand tentacles of fear, hatred, indifference, and despair gripping their hearts for the rest of their days. But those who saw them come back saw only the bodies, and they rejoiced and called it a victory, a triumph over the enemy, not ever understanding the withered life within.

Along with the deportees who straggled into the house, there also came the hairdresser, the dressmaker, and Depus, who had become the manicurist for my aunts' circle of remaining friends. She was waiting for passage to England, where her family had managed to emigrate. She had become quite plump, and Kati's clothes looked very becoming on her. Her hair had grown out and she wore it in a sleek bun at the nape of her neck. She was constantly thanking us for saving her life, for feeding her, for finding her work. She would be forever grateful, she constantly repeated.

Kati and Klari began preening again. A deportee we called Uncle Laci was courting Klari. I caught them kissing behind the kitchen door. There was a flurry of frantic activity in the air. Husbands and wives had been lost; "didn't come back" was the euphemism. New ones had to be found. There was a desperate attempt to forget, to renew, to go on.

Everyone admired the three sisters. They were young and very attractive. My mother, the youngest, was only thirty-two. She was slim and petite with a heart-shaped face and heavy blue-black hair. Her sisters teased her about her beautiful sloe eyes with their long lashes, which, they said, as a child she had always batted to get anything she wanted.

Klari, five years older, was the most sought after. Her auburn hair, curvaceous figure, and teasing eyes attracted a slew of admirers. She had the best legs, she claimed, and never hesitated in taking Kati's most expensive shoes to show them off. Kati was always regal. Platinum blond, slightly plump, always perfectly groomed, she immediately dismissed any man whose shoes or nails were not polished properly. My mother and Klari would grimace behind her back and call her "the Jewish Queen Victoria."

But everybody called them "the beautiful Pollak sisters."

My mother had to be coaxed to dress and go out while she waited for papers to be able to take me back to France. We had not yet heard anything regarding my father. We had no idea whether he was dead or alive. Since I was born in France, I retained my French citizenship and could go back. My mother, on the other hand, could only get a visa as my guardian and would, on leaving Hungary, immediately become "stateless." Kati wanted us to stay, especially me. My father, if he were still alive, would find us. If my mother returned to Paris, who knew what she would find? Where would we live? What if my father had also disappeared? Why not wait until Denis came back from Cuba? He would know what to do. At least I should be left behind in safety until things became more settled. My mother resented all advice.

"Why do I need Denis to tell me what to do?" she demanded.

The arguments went on endlessly. The tug-of-war over me between my mother and Kati continued.

Nine months after liberation, I spent my seventh birthday in a Red Cross truck rolling toward France, the land of my birth, of which I remembered nothing, not even the language, and where I would now become a refugee.

1946

Vienna was the first stop on our journey. It was as gray, sad, and bombed-out as Budapest. Kati had asked us to try and find some friends that she had known before the war. We did find them in a huge, cavernous apartment devoid of almost all its furniture. The three people who lived there, an elderly couple and their daughter, Kati's friend, looked as war torn as their city. It was so cold in the apartment that they wore threadbare coats and wrapped scarves around their necks. They invited us to spend the night. When the five of us sat down to supper, there was a loaf of dark bread and a can of sardines in the middle of the dark oak dining table, one of the few pieces of furniture left. Everybody got a slice of bread on which we spread a sardine. When I said that I was still hungry, there was an embarrassed silence.

"I'm so sorry, dear. I just don't have anything else in the house," said the old lady sadly. I looked at my mother. She gave me a warning look that meant Be quiet!

We went to bed cold and hungry. I whispered to my mother, "Why didn't you give them some of the food that Kati packed into our suitcase?"

My mother shook her head. "They would have refused it."

We had only the one suitcase with us, and my aunts had filled it with food. Anything else that we needed we would be able to get. The next morning, we left early and in a hurry in order to get a seat on the Red Cross truck, destination Paris. My mother left the suitcase behind.

The Red Cross truck arrived in Paris and deposited my mother and me in front of its headquarters. Everything we owned in the world we wore on our backs. I had on two sets of underwear, three dresses, and my coat. My mother was dressed in similar fashion. Fortunately it was January. I held her hand tightly. Everything was very confusing. The fact that I did not understand the language was frightening. The only time that had ever happened before was when the Russians had come, and that had been a terrifying experience. I kept trying to figure out what I thought was a code. I imagined that if I could figure out the code, I would be able speak the language. I yanked on my mother's arm.

"Teach me how to speak French!" I demanded.

"I can't do that immediately," she said. "It's going to take you a little while to learn. But don't worry. I'm sure it won't take too long."

"But I want to speak now!" I protested.

She smiled. "All right. Let me teach you a few words. *Bonjour,* that means 'hello.' *Au revoir,* that means 'good-bye.' Can you say that?"

Of course I could! Let's keep going!

We went on to *merci, s'il vous plaît, Je m'apelle Evi,* and onward. With every new word I racked my brain to see how it compared to its Hungarian counterpart. I was trying to break the code. Why was my mother teasing me by not revealing it to me? I kept saying, "But teach me the whole thing!"

And she kept laughing, along with the people in line closest to us. It was a conspiracy!

During this conversation our line edged forward. We were finally inside a huge hall where it was very warm and crowded, and I became hot and itchy. Especially my head. We had not undressed or washed in several days. The trip from Budapest had taken three weeks. Roads had been blown up, and many were impassable. Most railroad tracks were a mangled mess, and there were still troops moving about, so certain areas were restricted and we often had to detour for many miles. After two weeks we finally reached the French border. In Strasbourg, several truckloads of us were housed in old barracks that had been used by the Germans to assemble all "undesirables"—Jews, Socialists, Communists, homosexuals, and so on—for eventual shipment to various camps. We slept in triple-decker bunks with horse blankets distributed by the Red Cross. Our first square meal in France was *chou croûte.* It tasted wonderful. We were less pleased with the lice.

We came to the end of the line and reached a long wooden table staffed by harried Red Cross workers. My mother answered all their questions and asked some of her own. People were pressing in on all sides. This was no time for long conversations. We were given identity cards, instructions on when and where to report for food coupons, shelter, and available information on the location of any family. We were given a small amount of money, but my mother refused the temporary shelter offer. We were going to look for family immediately.

My first impression of Paris was its soft gray color. Budapest was also gray, but Paris was different. The buildings were much larger, and the gray patina seemed uniform. Then I realized the key difference: the buildings were intact!

"Don't they have bombs in Paris?" I asked.

My mother looked at me incredulously. "Paris was not bombed. And anyway, the war is over, Evi. There will be no more bombs!"

No more bombs? Bombs only came during war? I filed away the information.

With my head turning from left to right, up and down, we kept walking until we came to a dark and narrow street. The entrance to the building that we wanted to enter was barred by three women who were sheltering against the cold. They were dressed flimsily, in very bright colors, had very blond hair, and wore lots of colorful make up. I thought French women were beautiful, and I gaped at them.

"Don't stare," instructed my mother quietly in Hungarian. "Pardon," she said to the women, who very slowly slouched out of our way while looking on us with disdain.

We climbed up six flights of circular stairs and rang the bell. When the huge oak door opened, a new era opened up with it. Major changes were happening in my life. What I didn't know was that change was going to become a permanent condition. I met a new family, in a new country, speaking a new language. It was strange, and it was scary. I couldn't predict even the next minute of my life.

An odd-looking, almost gnomelike creature opened the door. She wasn't much taller than I, but she was squat and wide with a large ruddy face and wild reddish hair streaked with white. As she saw us, her expression of astonishment was immediately replaced by one of uncertainty and distaste. After three weeks of living in a truck with little opportunity to wash and wearing several layers of clothes, we must have looked like a clichéd portrait of refugees, and smelled even worse.

"My God!" she exclaimed. "Where have you come from? Is this really you? Is this Hermann's child? We were sure you were dead!"

She kept asking one question after another without waiting for an answer. She spoke in a coarse Hungarian accent, like the country people who had hidden us on the farm. I was astonished. Finally my mother interrupted her and, with not too well-masked sarcasm, said, "Hello, Regine, nice to see you, too! Is Marci here?"

Aunt Regine caught herself. "Come in, come in. You haven't changed. Still have a big mouth!" she grumbled.

From the dark recess of the back of the apartment a man emerged. He had heard the doorbell and had come to investigate. "Oh my God, Magda! You're back! You're alive! Thank God. Are you all right? Is this Evelyne? Where were you? Have you heard from Hermann?"

He grasped my mother, kissed her, and cried on her shoulder, totally overcome with emotion. I was still hanging onto my mother's hand but aware that a child had also quietly entered the foyer and was watching the scene with curiosity.

Uncle Marcel (Marci to the family), my father's eldest brother, finally collected himself. We were ushered into the "day room." Tea and biscuits were brought in and introductions made. I heard myself referred to as Evelyne for the first time. Until then I had been Evi, except for the period we had spent in hiding when my forged papers referred to me as Iluska Toth. Now seven years into my life, I found out that at birth I had been named Evelyne Juliette. I didn't even know how to pronounce it correctly!

My uncle Marci had a rough appearance. Tousled hair, a boxer's broken nose, and large upper body, all belying a sweet and gentle nature. He was completely overwhelmed by his loud and bossy wife, who obviously ruled the roost. She was abrupt but not unkind. Aunt Regine looked like a cartoon character: constantly on the go, giving orders and opinions in a gruff and rough manner, but whose intentions and instincts were good and generous. Her family allowed her to terrorize them—it was her privilege as the eldest of twelve siblings. My mother tended to brush her off as one would an annoying pest, and this left Aunt Regine angry and confused. She just never knew how to deal with this independent, younger, and prettier sister-in-law who insisted on not taking her and her constant advice seriously. We could always feel the tension when the two of them were in the same room.

Uncle Marci was greatly relieved to see us, and he and my mother spent the next hour exchanging information on what had happened the previous four-and-a-half years. We learned that my father had been picked up by the Gestapo on July 14, 1944, in Paris. Just weeks before the city was liberated by the Allies. He had been taken on a transport to Drancy, in eastern France, where deportees were collected for eventual shipment to Auschwitz. No one had heard from him since.

While my mother and Uncle Marci were catching up, my cousin Yvonne and I were getting acquainted. She was three years my senior. A vivacious, funny, and rambunctious little girl, she spoke only a little Hungarian, in a funny French-accented manner that I found hilarious, and we laughed about it together. She immediately took me under her wing.

I remember the apartment as very dark and depressing. There were large pieces of mahogany furniture, heavy old-fashioned draperies, and a long, dark hallway. It was nothing like the bright modern apartment in Budapest, especially when it came to sanitary facilities. There was no bathroom, only a *cabinet de toilette,* which was nothing more than a cubicle with a sink in it. The toilet was outside the apartment, half a flight down, and shared with other tenants. It consisted of a hole in the middle of the floor with two raised platforms on either side, the size of bricks, where one placed one's feet and then squatted. This was the usual arrangement in most of the old buildings in Paris. Many had been built after the First World War, when soldiers returning from the front were thought to be transmitting diseases via toilet seats. My mother called these toi-

lets *talpra Magyar* (literally, "Stand up, Magyar!"), referring to the title of a rousing nationalistic poem by the popular poet Petofi, which called on the Hungarian people (the Magyars) to throw off the shackles of slavery imposed on them by the Hapsburgs. Aunt Regine was not amused.

After we had eaten, Uncle Marci hauled a large zinc tub out into the middle of the old-fashioned kitchen, and water was heated on top of the stove so that my mother and I could take a much needed bath. Layer after layer of clothing came off and were dumped into another washtub. We rediscovered the luxury of feeling clean. After the bath, however, as my mother was combing my hair, she found that I had lice. It wasn't surprising, considering our journey of the previous three weeks. Yvonne and I were told not to put our heads close together until the problem had been taken care of. As soon as she was dressed again, my mother went "shopping." She came back with half a liter of gasoline, difficult to get without coupons, with which she doused both our heads. A divan in the day room was transformed into a bed for the two of us, and for the first time in three weeks we slept between clean sheets.

I awoke with a strange, tight feeling in the back of my neck. I tried to lift my head. I couldn't. It appeared that I was stuck to the pillow.

"Anyu," I cried. "I can't get up. I'm stuck."

My mother started to laugh, but her laughter ended abruptly with a sharp intake of breath. "Don't move," she said. "I'll be right back."

She came back with a basin of warm water and a washcloth. She bathed the back of my neck and slowly pulled the pillow away from me while I screamed in pain and woke up the whole household. The gasoline had certainly killed the lice, but it had also eaten away the tender skin on the back of my neck, which was now raw and very painful. Uncle Marci was appalled and set about finding a doctor. Aunt Regine, though equally distressed, felt justified in telling my mother that "as usual" she had gone about doing something "arse over teakettle" without thinking of the consequences.

After shaving the back of my head and dousing me with a stinging disinfectant, the doctor pronounced me out of danger. The "miracle drug," penicillin, was not yet available to the general public. It was in short supply and available only in hospitals to the seriously wounded, of whom there were still plenty.

For the next couple of weeks I wore a white cotton veil covering the back of my shaved head. This drew hoots of laughter from Yvonne, who called me "the bald bride." One evening while horsing around, she hit me on the head with a baguette, the long thin bread that the French eat. My mother, with mock seriousness said, "You'd better not do that. The baguette might start walking away on its own!"

Everyone laughed except Aunt Regine.

•

We needed a home. What had happened to ours? My parents had owned the modest apartment where they had lived on rue d'Enghien, and we went to find it. An insurance company had moved in. It was now an office. We were politely shown around the premises by the office manager, and an extraordinary thing happened. I was looking idly at a couple of desks placed under a window and facing each other when something jogged my memory. I saw in my mind a man, my father, of whom I had no other recollection, sitting atop a large cutting table, legs crossed, basting the horsehair-interfacing into the collar of a man's suit jacket. It was so clear in my mind.

"Yes," said my mother, totally taken aback, when I told her. "This is exactly where the cutting table was. How can you remember? You were barely two years old."

I shrugged my shoulders. "I don't know. But wasn't my crib in this corner?" I asked, walking into what I remembered as the bedroom.

"Yes, it was," said my mother quietly. "What else do you remember?"

But that was it. The flash of memory had passed. Five years is a very long time in the life of a seven year old.

The law stated that residences had to be returned to the refugees who had been the original tenants, or comparable accommodations offered. This did, in fact, take place, and we were offered a small two-bedroom apartment on rue des Ecoles on the Left Bank. My mother was happy to accept the exchange. The apartment was in a much more desirable location than rue d'Enghien. All of this, however, took time, and living with Uncle Marci and Aunt Regine was not the answer. We had to find temporary accommodations. Uncle Marci would gladly have put us up, but Aunt Regine was not too keen on the idea. My mother was too "uppity" for her taste. She read—"a waste of time." She used lipstick— "just like the girls outside." But what she most objected to was my mother's dismissal of the idea that Aunt Regine knew better. My mother did what she wanted, the way she wanted. Her mistakes were her own, and though she made plenty of them, she always accepted the consequences.

Yvonne and I, however, got along well. We spent many hours together in her big, darkened room under a large old-fashioned oak double bed or inside a heavy, mirrored armoire, hiding from Aunt Regine and trying to keep a straight face when she found and scolded us. Uncle Marci always defended us and ended up with a tongue lashing for his trouble. How different from what I had been used to! Kati and Klari doted on children. Even though Klari's hands were a little too fast and often collided with Peter's cheeks and occasionally my buttocks, our every whim was indulged and we never feared family members. Actually I knew that Aunt Regine liked me, though I'm sure that she would rather have been flayed alive than admit fondness for any living creature, especially one related to her sister-in-law Magda.

My mother decided that I would be better off in the country breathing fresh air and playing with other children, where I would learn to speak French quickly. Without further ado I was shipped off to a small children's home about an hour's train ride from Paris. I don't remember the name of the place, just the building with the walled garden in the back, where I watched the gardener pruning pear trees and training them to grow up against the wall. I spent a lot of time in the garden by myself, wandering around among the vegetables and flower beds. I didn't seem to be able to get the hang of where I was supposed to be at any given time, and a staff member was always running to find and take me to the right classroom or wherever I was supposed to be. I was disoriented, lost in a sea of strangers speaking a language that I hadn't yet mastered. I was terribly lonely and spent time writing childish notes to Peter demanding that he come and take me back to Budapest. I gave the notes to one of the teachers, telling her, in broken French, but probably more Hungarian, to mail them to my cousin. She smiled at me, and I assumed that she understood my request.

The big problem at the children's home was food. I had always been a poor eater, and getting used to French food was difficult. The woman in charge of the dining room was not sympathetic to my needs and made it her business to make my life even more unhappy. Breakfast always consisted of a big bowl of weak chicory coffee with milk, postwar French fashion, into which we dunked chunks of buttered rolls that were delivered fresh every morning. It was the best meal of the day for me. Except on Thursdays. On that day the baker did not deliver, and instead of fresh rolls we were given bowls filled to the brim with warm milk and tapioca. Just looking at the tapioca made me sick to my stomach. Under the watchful eye of the Dining-Room Woman I pretended to eat, maneuvering my spoon around the tapioca and managing to slurp just some of the milk, then escaped from the place while she was occupied with something else.

One Thursday morning, however, she positioned herself behind my chair and directed me to finish the contents of my bowl. I told her that I couldn't. She said that I could and I would—or else! I tried a few spoonfuls but I gagged, so I just sat there unhappily, waiting for a reprieve. None came. I was going to stay there until I finished, she said. Suddenly with a shock I realized that there was no one to protect me against this woman. Not my mother, not Kati or Klari or Peter. I was on my own. My unhappiness and lethargy vanished, and a rebellious anger took its place. No! I was not going to eat this horrible stuff. I didn't care if I had to sit there all day! If she wanted to be there and watch me all day, well, I would outlast her! I folded my arms and sat there scowling while all the other children filed out and went to their lessons. When the place was empty except for the two of us, she took a chair and sat down next to me, picked up my spoon, filled it with the vile stuff, and attempted to spoon-feed me. I turned my head away. She took my jaw firmly in one hand and tried to pry the spoon into my mouth, jabbing it against my teeth. I struggled. She hit me and hissed, "You will eat every spoonful of this!"

At that point I resolved that I would die before I let her get the better of me. It was a struggle to the death. Soon we were wrestling on the floor. She, half sitting on me, was still trying to jab the spoon into my mouth when I managed to get a hold of the bowl and spill the contents all over her. She sat there gasping, unable to believe my effrontery and her defeat, fuming like a bleeding bull in the corrida. I was sitting on the floor opposite her, daring her to kill me. She got up slowly and menacingly, grabbed me by the hair and, almost lifting me off the floor, carried me to the door of the garden, threw me out, and in a threatening voice told me that I would never see my mother again.

I stayed in the garden for what seemed like hours, disheveled, with my cheek burning and swelling up from the slap that I had received. The war was over, but new enemies had emerged and they had no uniforms to identify them. Any stranger could be an enemy. I had learned my first lesson in surviving on my own. I realized in terror that this was no temporary separation from Kati, Klari, and Peter. This was to be the place that I would have to live forever! Eventually, someone came and took me to the principal's office, where he informed me that since I had behaved badly I would not be allowed to see my mother on visiting day, the following Sunday.

Sunday came. So did my mother. She obviously got some concession because we were given fifteen minutes to see each other in the principal's office, where my bad behavior was discussed. When I told my mother what had happened, she told me to go and pack my valise. By the time I was back downstairs, the finances had been settled and we were ready to leave over the sputtered objections of the principal, who had obviously received an earful. As we were walking down a corridor toward the front door, I saw the Dining-Room Woman walking in front of us.

"That's her," I whispered to my mother.

"Excusez-moi, madame!" my mother called out to her. She stopped, and my mother walked up to her with a bright, wide, disarming smile. Suddenly, without warning, swift as lightning, she drew back her arm and hit the woman on the side of the head with such momentum that the big woman fell like a nine pin. She lay on the floor, looking totally disoriented. My mother stood over her.

"Touch a child again and next time you won't be able to get up!" With that, she took my hand and we walked out the front door.

I did have a protector after all! My aunts, Peter, my adored uncle Sanyi could no longer be there for me. Only my mother was there. She had become my sole savior, my sole protector. She had defended me. But, I realized, *I* had defended myself *first!*

During my absence, my mother had found another family member, my aunt Eszter, who had taken me to Budapest in 1941. While her husband, my uncle Denis, had escaped to Cuba, she had stayed behind with my cousin Claude and distinguished herself in the French underground.

Aunt Eszter, though born in Poland was the epitome of the sophisticated Parisienne. She was lovely, with beautiful blue eyes, short and tightly curled blond hair, a pleasing full figure, and great legs that she showed off in stylish high-heeled shoes. She was self-assured, elegant, loving, generous, and she had an impish sense of humor. But most of all, she had style. She commanded respect. Everyone called her "Madame Denise."

She owned an elegant little dress shop on the main street of Asnières, a suburb of Paris, and that is where I always remember her. The name of the shop was Denise. It was the French form of Denes, with whom she had started the business before the war. She had inherited the name, and when speaking French we always called her Tante Denise. In Hungarian she remained Eszter. The three Pollak sisters, my mother, Kati, and Klari, had adopted her as soon as their brother had married her. They always got along well, and long after she and my uncle ended their tempestuous marriage, the women remained close. Her one fault she shared with her sisters-in-law: she doted excessively on her child and indulged him outrageously.

Our apartment was not yet ready, so it was decided that I was going to stay with Aunt Eszter temporarily and attend school with my cousin Claude, three years my senior. My mother was going to stay in Paris, where she had found work sewing bathing suits, and hoped to start putting our lives back together. It was not the most ideal arrangement as far as I was concerned. I was getting anxious. Where was I *really* going to live? I was being thrown from pillar to post and feeling very unsettled. The excitement of the new country was fast wearing off. Well, at least I was not going to be mistreated. I had high hopes for cousin Claude. I missed my "big brother" Peter. Maybe Claude would take his place.

Things did not go quite as well as I expected. Claude was not ready to give up his privileged position as an only child and resented my presence; and I certainly was a presence! I demanded a lot of attention and used every trick to get it. Acting cute whenever anyone came to visit, curtsying sweetly, as I had been taught to do in Budapest, I charmed all the grown-ups. Claude retaliated with sneaky pinches on my arm, tripping me "accidentally" as I walked by, and just general mischief. Once, he "forgot" to wait for me after school, and I got lost on the way home. Fortunately Aunt Eszter had taught me our address, and someone walked me home while Aunt Eszter and the maid were already frantically combing the neighborhood.

Claude and I fought and squabbled and drove Aunt Eszter crazy. I was bewildered. Big brothers were not supposed to behave this way. I just had to tell Peter! I had no writing paper so I took toilet tissue and wrote a letter on it, pouring my heart out: *Claude was ugly and nasty! He didn't play with me and made me walk behind him on the way home from school. Please come and defend me!* Claude saw me writing diligently, and curiosity got the better of him. Whom was I writing to?

"Peter," I responded. "I miss him."

"So why don't you write to him on decent paper instead of toilet tissue?" he wanted to know. When I told him that I didn't have any, his better nature came through. "Here," he said, handing some nice clean sheets. "I'll even write it out for you. My handwriting is better. But you have to help me with the spelling. I don't understand any Hungarian!"

It was the perfect revenge. He was going to write out his own indictment without even knowing it. It was probably the quietest time we had together as children. We sat close together as I spelled out the Hungarian words, which he wrote down in his best hand. He even drew some pretty pictures at the bottom of the page. What I had not counted on was Claude showing the letter to his mother. Aunt Eszter blew up.

"That ungrateful little ——, a snake at my bosom!" she shouted at my mother. "I feed her. I dress her. I treat and love her as my own, and she makes my son write a nasty letter about himself. What kind of a scheming little minx did you bring into this world, Magda?"

My mother hid a smile. "Come on, Eszter, don't take it so seriously. It's just a childish prank."

"Childish prank? Why, even I couldn't think of anything sneakier!"

Claude was even madder. He had been had—by a younger girl cousin yet! It didn't improve our relationship, and the atmosphere in the household became more tense. Even though Aunt Eszter quickly forgot and forgave the whole episode, my mother decided that it was time for me to move out. Our apartment was ready. We had a bed, a table with two chairs, a bureau, and a lamp. My mother had started a new life.

Château des Groux, 1947-1948

"No one is going to hurt you here," my mother promised. "But should anyone even try they'll have me to deal with. I would kill anyone who hurt you." She said it with such fierceness that it almost frightened me.

"Paris is not a good place for a child," she continued defensively. "I have to work all day. How can I look after you, too? Especially now that the school year is coming to an end?"

I was eight years old when my mother took me to the Château. It was late May; I remember that the lilac bushes were heavy with blooms, filling the air with that particular fragrance that has ever since reminded me of the place. It was small as châteaux go, but full of tall windows, turrets, balustrades, and balconies. A wide driveway led up to the porte cochere, across from which was a low, curved limestone wall where colorful little lizards basked in the sun all summer and played tag with the children. Inside were very tall ceilings, lots of dark polished wood, carved doorways, and a grand staircase.

My mother told me that I was going to love it there. There would be lots of nice children, good food, plenty of fresh air, and everything else that I couldn't have cared less about. I wanted to be with her. I pleaded to no avail. She said it was only going to be for a short time. Just enough time to get her life together. This would really be much better, she tried to convince me. I had been back in France for over a year and was speaking French quite well. There would be no trouble about going back to school. I resigned myself to the fact that I had to stay. I was getting used to being left in various places. She promised that she would visit every Sunday. I was left in the care of Mr. Guttman, the director, who assured my mother that all the children at the Château were very happy indeed.

The Joint Distribution Committee had acquired the Château as a home for Jewish children affected by the war. Some, like me, had lost a parent, and the remaining ones were trying to pick up the pieces of her or his life. Others had become orphans and had nowhere to go. Most of the children there had been brought over temporarily from Hungary. Their parents, if they were still alive, were only too glad to know that they were in a safe place.

•

Upon my arrival I was introduced to a half dozen other little girls. A beautiful blond child named Marika was assigned to be my *kis mama* (little mother) since she was already ten years old.

"I don't need a kis mama," I protested. I'd had enough of temporary caretakers. Besides, if the grown-ups wouldn't take care of me, I wouldn't let them palm me off on a child barely two years older than I!

"Of course you do! She'll help you get dressed, tie your laces, wash, make your bed."

"I can do all that by myself." I was not going to make things easy!

A couple of days later, Marika announced that I didn't need her as I was quite capable of being a kis mama myself. I could do everything for myself, and better still, I was the only child there who spoke both French and Hungarian and could therefore help out as interpreter. Some of the children spoke only French, and the Hungarian ones were still learning the language.

There were already two Evas, and a third one would only complicate matters. Eva Ferenci, who had arrived there first, became Eva 1. Eva Berkovics became Eva 2, and I, Eva 3. We became so accustomed to these numerical appendages that if someone called "Eva 1!" I didn't even turn my head. What was one more name, at this point?

The "little mother" organizational model typified the way the orphanage was run at the beginning—namely by the children themselves. The little ones were taken care of by the older girls, the ten to twelve year olds. There were very few staff members: the cook, the laundress, and a half-witted employee of the Château's who did the gardening and some heavy cleaning. We did the rest. We cleaned our dormitories and our bathrooms. We helped in the kitchen. We set and cleared the tables. We swept the stairs and raked the leaves. A teacher came every day to tutor the Hungarian children in French. Mr. Guttman was the administrator. We rarely saw him, except at mealtimes, though he played soccer with the boys some afternoons. We were pretty much left to our own devices, and we were amazingly responsible. The war had made us grow up fast. We acted like little old people. We created a society for ourselves based on what we remembered or imagined to be ideal family life. The little mothers ran the place, while the older boys were the "helpers."

The oldest among us was only thirteen, Claudio. He was a serious, smart, and wise boy. Even now I think of him as a man. He had survived the concentration camps. His left leg had been shot away by a Nazi bullet while trying to escape, but he was not a cripple. He hopped around on his one good leg as fast as the rest of us did on two. He swam and played soccer as well as the other boys, and he was a whiz on the harmonica. He was our undisputed leader.

The grounds of the Château were beautiful. Ancient horse chestnuts shaded gently curving walks. There was a knoll with three stately pine trees that was our designated meeting place. The word would go around, *"Aux trois sapins!"* ("At the three pines!"), and within minutes all the older girls and boys were gathered there to discuss the issues of the day. Behind the Château was a large free-form basin lined in concrete that had once been filled with water, fish, frogs, and water lilies. There was even a pretty iron bridge connecting the basin to a little island in the middle. The basin was now empty, and we used it as a playground. It was the right surface for jumping rope and ball bouncing. Around the perimeter of the park were thick bushes that made wonderful hiding places.

That first summer should have been like an ideal summer camp, but we missed our parents and worried about seeing them again. So many family members had disappeared mysteriously, and we still didn't know what had really happened. Nobody wanted to tell us. We had all heard over and over the words *Auschwitz, Bergen-Belsen, Mauthausen, Theresienstadt, forced labor camp,* but we had not understood the full meaning of what these places had really been. We had all seen people who had come back. They had been more dead than alive. And we had all known many who had never come back, but how could we, as children, imagine the atrocities? How could we understand that our fathers, mothers, grandparents, aunts, and uncles had been tortured and murdered in these places simply because they were Jews? We just knew that these words meant danger and tragedy. The truth is that we were forbidden to talk about the war years. At that time the thinking was: it is over. There is nothing anyone can do about it. Talking about it does no good. It was supposed to be forgotten, to be put behind us. Even Claudio, who had been there did not speak about it, and we did not ask. Yet our own memories of the war were still very much with us. Those were our *only* memories. We were all too young to remember the prewar years. When we said "When I was little . . . ," we could only speak of wartime. And since this was not allowed, we were denied our first memories.

Waking up from nightmares was a frequent occurrence in the dormitories. Sometimes at night, we would get into one another's beds and whisper, "Do you remember the bombs? Were you frightened?"

"What was your name during the war?"

"Do you remember your daddy?"

Some of us had physical reminders, Claudio's the most obvious. In winter my hands were bandaged because of the frostbite that I had suffered. They still swelled and itched, and the skin split as soon as the weather turned cold. Two children, brother and sister, had nervous tics. Their bomb shelter had received direct hits, and they were the only ones who had survived. One boy had a hideous scar where his ear should have been. He had undergone emergency surgery on a kitchen table. Jews had not been permitted entrance to hospitals, and something had gone horribly wrong.

My mother came to visit every Sunday. She always came loaded down with packages full of goodies for all the children to share. She often brought a friend or two, and in the spring and summer the visits turned into group picnics with all the children whose parents were not able to be there also included. Occasionally she brought either my cousin Yvonne or Claude along. Everyone loved my mother and envied me. I, on the other hand, wanted my mother to myself, not to share her with everybody else. But Sunday was not only my visiting day; it was also her one day off from work that she could spend in the country with a friend or two, relaxing, and at the same time giving comfort to children who certainly needed it. The day usually ended with my crying at the gate, watching my mother walking down the road toward the railroad station, her words ringing in my ears: "Evi, don't spoil the day by crying." But I couldn't help it. I missed her, I missed my aunts. I missed Peter. I missed a home, a family. Why could my cousins go home, but not I? Every Sunday, watching my mother walk down the road, my feelings of abandonment were renewed. Eventually I hardened myself, and the day came when instead of crying I said coldly, "It's time for you to go if you want to catch your train."

She looked at me, surprised. "Are you in a hurry to see me leave?"

"No, but it's time for you to go. We have to get ready for supper. Good-bye." And I walked away toward the dining room.

I was not the one who cried that day.

Over the summer other children came, and by the time school started that October there were as many as thirty or forty of us. Those of us who were old enough to go to school were taken down to the village and enrolled. It was a typical French village setup, with the boys' and girls' schools connected to and flanking either side of the town hall. In the front building, on the girls' side and facing the street, were the older children, nine to twelve. Their teacher, Madame Salle, was also the headmistress. This allowed her to lord it over the only other teacher, Madame Coureneau, who taught the younger girls in a tiny building across the minuscule, gravel-covered playground with plane trees around the perimeter.

Though I was almost nine years old, I had had less than a year of formal schooling. I read and wrote quite well in Hungarian and French, but history, geography, and arithmetic were still a complete mystery. (The latter has remained so ever since.) It was a great shock to me when, after the Christmas holidays, I was moved up into the main building. I wasn't ready, but I was nine years old and those were the rules.

Mme Salle was a widow and one of the village's leading citizens. She was a woman of a "certain age" with what she considered to be a sophisticated Parisian look. She wore makeup and red nail polish, smoked, and her red hair had a professional permanent wave. Her clothes were tight and stylish, and above her ankle-strapped high heels she wore a gold chain. She flirted outrageously with any man who so much as came near the school. But most importantly, she considered herself *une vraie française* (a real Frenchwoman)—as opposed to us, we presumed. She seemed to derive a perverse pleasure out of having us *juives* in her classroom, just to torment us. She ridiculed the Hungarian girls when they made a mistake and gave us homework based on what she had taught the previous year, so that the village girls knew what the material was, but we didn't. She made snide remarks about us, deliberately mispronouncing our Jewish names. The village girls were encouraged to laugh at us, and her manner challenged us to defy her, if we dared, which we didn't.

For some reason I was her favorite target. Perhaps she resented that though born French, my mother tongue was Hungarian, perhaps it was because I was the youngest in the class, perhaps because I was an ugly duckling, or most likely because I would not lower my eyes or cry when she berated me as did most of the other girls. "Baissez les yeux, tout de suite, mademoiselle!" ("Lower your eyes at once, mademoiselle!"), she would scream at me. But I just stood there like a stone, focusing my eyes straight into hers, daring her to touch me. We loathed each other.

Every day started with the study of verbs. Mme Salle would pick a verb and write it on the blackboard. She would then select a pupil to come forward and conjugate the verb in the present tense. Then another pupil came and did it in the imperfect, then *passé composé, impératif, futur, passé anterieur, futur anterieur, plus-que-parfait,* until all sixteen possibilities plus the four *infinitifs and participes* were written out on several blackboards lining the walls of the schoolroom. The little French girls had a great deal of trouble learning some of these conjugations, especially of irregular verbs. For the rest of us it was almost impossible. Klari Heisler and I were up late into the night before tests learning these arcane tenses, some of which I have not to this day ever come across even in classical French literature. But we had to learn it. It was an honor and a privilege to have the opportunity to learn French. French was the most beautiful, poetic, versatile, and expressive language; indeed, the only language worth knowing. France was the only country whose geography was worth a damn. Its history was the most noble. Its art the most uplifting. All other countries were lumped together as *l'étranger,* except the United States. That was *le pays des Indiens et des sauvages* ("the country of Indians and savages"). But for France, the war against the "Bôches" would have been lost. Who was there to challenge her?

Miserable though we all were, biased as the material was, we did learn, and Mme Salle had to stifle her outrage when *les juives* carried off all the prizes for the end-of-the-year examinations. Among the orphanage students, I was the worst. That made Mme Salle happy, though she would have been happier, no doubt, had I been at the bottom of the entire class. Actually I really didn't deserve even that lowly place. I cheated whenever I could. I remember being triumphantly smug and satisfied when I received a passing mark on a particularly unfair and difficult geography test. We had to draw a map of the Saône and Rhône river valleys, with all their tributaries and major cities, from memory. I always had to sit in the center of the front row, right in front of her. It was my permanent punishment. That time, however, it worked in my favor. I opened the atlas at the right page and kept in on my lap, copying the entire assignment line for line. I figured that Mme Salle would never imagine that anyone would have the temerity to cheat so openly under her very nose. I was right, but though my map was perfect, I didn't get full credit. "It wasn't neat enough." Still, I was more than satisfied. I had put one over on Mme Salle! The look of incredulity on her face upon seeing my map was worth far more to me than a good grade.

But life was not going too well. I was very unhappy despite the fact that I had my little circle of friends to whom I was devoted. There was remarkably little friction among the children, and we were very supportive of one another. Like little old people we would gather together and discuss our problems and fears, put our arms around one another for comfort, draw little hearts and flowers on bits of scrap paper and slip them under dinner plates. But still we were children, children who had been brought up in fear and hiding, and we were wilting for lack of nurturing. I had never been a good eater. Now I ate less. I became lethargic, slow in movement. I was late for everything. The only thing that interested me was reading. I lost myself in the fantasy world of that reactionary writer of French children's books, la Comtesse de Ségur. I didn't notice that she promoted class distinction; that she was really writing for children of the nineteenth-century upper class, giving them lessons in noblesse oblige. All I understood was that all the children had homes and were loved by their parents, that wrongs were righted, the bad punished, the good rewarded. Life was just and fair. God watched over you.

My listlessness came to the attention of Mr. Guttman. He would put his hand on my head and ask me what the matter was. I would make a moue and say, "Nothing." At first he just smiled and continued to joke and play with the boys, who considered him their pal. Gradually I started getting more attention. He listened to the problems that I was having with Mme Salle. He allowed me to tele-phone my mother from his office occasionally. I was even allowed to play on his private piano. He would sit next to me on the bench, encircle me with his left arm so that his hand would guide my hand, and teach me the various notes and their names. On Sundays, my mother and he would have long conferences about me.

One morning when the idea of Mme Salle seemed just too much to bear, I dawdled instead of going down to breakfast. Mr. Guttman appeared in the girls' dormitory and wanted to know why I was still there. I said I wasn't feeling well and dragged my feet.

"Come on, come on. You're always the last one. Go have breakfast and we'll talk about how you feel later," he said. Then to make me get a move on, he nudged my backside toward the door with his foot.

I didn't like it and, giving him a dirty look, I said, "Don't kick me. I'm not a dog."

"What a mouth! Just like your mother," he said but laughed. After breakfast he said, "If you don't feel well, stay home and I'll look at you later." He acted as doctor for all minor ailments that came up.

I went up to bed and the Château emptied out as all the children left for school. A little while later he came up, took me by the hand, and said, "Come on upstairs. Let's have a look at you."

We went up to the third floor, where the "hospital" was: a room with three beds and a medicine cabinet. But instead of going in there, he took me into a room that I had not been in before. It was his room. It was small but well fur-nished with an enormous upholstered easy chair. There he sat down and lifted me onto his lap.

"All right now, little one, tell me everything."

I didn't understand. He had always been friendly, but not affectionate, never really fatherly. It seemed to us girls that he favored the boys, so his sudden fatherly concern and his ever tightening hug suddenly made me uncomfortable. "Don't be afraid, I'll look after you," he cooed.

He was stroking my hair, my back, my buttocks and holding me tight. His breath was coming in short bursts, and I felt something hard between my legs pressing into me. I tried to wriggle out of his grasp, but he was holding me too tightly. I couldn't move. I felt a sharp pain. I cried out.

"Don't cry. It's all right. I won't hurt you," he gasped.

But he was. And I was crying and struggling. Then it was over. I felt all wet and sticky and sore. I had no idea what had happened, but I knew that something was very wrong. Mr. Guttman was still sitting in his chair, fumbling with his clothing, while I slunk out of the room. I went downstairs, washed, dressed, and went to school.

My mother called to say that she wouldn't be able to come out on Sunday, but that she had made arrangements for someone to take me to the train station on Saturday evening, and she would wait for me in Paris. But it was my mother's best friend, "Aunt" Nusi, who was waiting for me.

"Don't worry, " she said. "Your mother has a rendezvous. I'll take you home, and we'll wait for her together. You'll like who she went out with." She smiled in a conspiratorial way. All this time I was wondering what and how to tell my mother.

The key turned in the lock, and my mother came in with her date. It was Mr. Guttman. I was so shocked I became totally speechless. I turned on my heels and ran into the bedroom. Later when my mother came in she asked me why I had been so rude.

"I don't like him," I said.

"Since when? Why?"

"Because he . . . ," I began. But suddenly I realized that I couldn't tell her. She had told me that if anyone hurt me she would kill them. I knew my mother. She meant it. If she killed him she would go to jail, and if she went to jail I would lose her again. I wouldn't have anybody! Thus went my childish logic. I was going to have to carry this burden alone. In the meantime my mother was waiting for me to finish my sentence.

"Because he what?" she asked.

"Because he kicked me," I blurted out.

"He what? When? Why?"

"I was late for breakfast, so he kicked me on my behind out of the dormitory, and he said I had a big mouth just like you."

"Oh, really," she said very quietly. "Don't worry. I promise you he will never touch you again."

The following week a man from the Joint Committee came and talked to all the children privately. Apparently all the little girls said that they had also been "kicked." Not the boys. There was a big fuss, and Mr. Guttman was dismissed. The boys were furious at me. He was their friend and playmate. They knew that I was the one who had told. How could I have taken that little kick so seriously? The girls said nothing. They just looked at me wonderingly. We never discussed the "kicks." And I just found it easier to bury it somewhere in the deep recesses of my memory for many years to come.

Summer of 1948

It was the end of the school year and a wonderful surprise was in store for me. I was going to spend the summer in Hungary. I was going to be with Aunt Kati and Klari and Peter. Nagyi and Uncle Sanyi were gone. It was going to be sad without them. I still hadn't quite accepted their loss. Still it was wonderful news. My mother took me to the Gare de l'Est. A woman she knew was traveling as far as Vienna. She would make sure that I was all right, help me change trains. Then I'd be on my own. Someone would wait for me at the station in Budapest. Everything went as planned, except that the lady was so happy to see her family waiting on the platform in Vienna that she forgot about me. While I was waiting, the Budapest train left and so did the lady. I was alone. Suddenly I felt very grown up. I was in charge. I had money. I had my passport and my ticket. I boldly went up to a policeman and asked him to help me find the right train. He didn't speak either French or Hungarian. My German was all but forgotten. There was a quick consultation with another policeman and they took me to the Bahnhof Mission (the railway mission) where nuns waited to look after lost travelers. There was general consternation. What to do with this lost child?

"Nothing," I said with authority. "I'm not lost. Just put me on the right train. You have no right to keep me here. My papers are in order." And I showed them my passport.

I knew the lingo. And I was right. At least they believed so. I got onto the right train and arrived several hours later than expected. Two frantic women were waiting on the platform. Kati was breathing fire. Klari was in hysterics.

"What happened?" Kati wanted to know, while Klari was squeezing the last breath out of me, covering me with kisses. I explained. A knowing, irritated glance passed between them.

"Letting a nine-year-old child go on a thirty-six hour train ride across several countries alone. Only Magda would do that!" Kati mumbled fiercely.

"Nine and a half," I inserted.

"Be quiet. You still have a big mouth. Let's go home." And we did. And it was home.

Peter and I had not seen each other in two and a half years. We looked at each other in wonder. He had become a young man. I was no longer a *kis poloska* (little bed bug). I could read and write in two languages. I had traveled on my own. I had seen the world. He was proud of me and I adored him for it. As soon as the weather got hot, we were sent to Eger, in the north, to stay with Aunt Klari's new sister-in-law, Aunt Piri, who had two sons of her own. Klari had married Uncle Laci, the deportee.

Eger is a beautiful little town shrouded in history. In the sixteenth century, the conquest of Europe by the advancing Turks was halted there. The enormous battlements surrounding the castle, which had seen so many bloody battles, still dominate the town. There are still reminders of the eventual victory and the one-hundred-fifty-year occupation of the Turks. We set about exploring everything. We climbed the minaret; we explored the catacombs. We went swimming. We had picnics. We saw old movies. We lay in the grass and daydreamed about the future. Peter was planning on becoming a famous surgeon and I was going to be his nurse. Later I decided that I, too, wanted to be a surgeon. Peter grinned and said, "A-ok."

It was a wonderful summer, the summer of 1948. But the memories would have to last me a long time. I went back to France, and the Iron Curtain slammed down, dividing us once again. By the end of that summer, I realized that my ties with Hungary were broken. I could have stayed with my aunts, but I knew that life had changed. I had become French. I had to go back to France. I belonged there.

I was very torn. I did long for the emotional security of the home that I had known as a very small child, but I understood that this world no longer existed. I had started losing respect for adults and resenting their interference in my life. I hated being a child, powerless to make my own decisions. Resigned to going back to the orphanage, I nevertheless felt a certain pride in living a different kind of life. A harder life than I would have had in Hungary. But I saw myself as a tragic victim of adult ineptitude. They had all failed me: my father, Uncle Sanyi, Uncle Miklos, even Nagyi had all abandoned me. I held them responsible for dying. And those who had remained alive were not protecting me. I refused to see their heroism, recognizing only their faults. I could no longer be Kati and Klari's spoiled little girl.

Living at the orphanage, I had become much more self-sufficient than most children of my age and felt that for the most part I could do with as few adults as possible. Kati and Klari were horrified at this streak of independence and immediately blamed my mother. She had not provided me with the proper environment. I was not sent to the proper schools, and I had been allowed to become "wild." They never acknowledged that I was living in an orphanage; it was always referred to as a "boarding school." Though I loved them both, I had no more illusions about them. I became a harsh critic, contemptuous of Kati's love of luxury and of Klari's silly, hysterical fits.

My aunts wanted to keep me in Hungary. First they begged my mother, then they threatened, then they begged again. Letters were flying back and forth across the continent. I secretly hoped that, with this pressure from her sisters, my mother would let me live in Paris with her. If I had to be dependent on an adult, let it be her. She was not the smothering kind. She encouraged my independence.

"In case something happens to me, you have to learn to stand on your own two feet," she often said.

I realized that by saying this she was defending her own actions. She wanted help and advice from no one, especially her family.

As the youngest of five siblings, she had been the closest to my grandmother. She had lost the two most important people in her life, her mother and her husband, and in some twisted way she lay the blame for my grandmother's deportation and eventual extermination in Auschwitz on the shoulders of her older sister Kati and her brother Denis. Kati had been there. She had managed to save herself by passing as a Christian. She had saved Klari, Peter, and me—and actually, even my mother—by providing us with plans for hiding and forged papers. My grandfather had also survived. Why then had Kati allowed her Anyuka to be taken away? No amount of explanation on Kati's part about the situation at the time nor her own distress over my grandmother's fate and the loss of her own husband had ever been able to satisfy my mother, or, I suspect, to assuage her guilt for surviving. Kati's desire to take charge of my life only proved to her that my aunt wanted to deprive her of the only thing left in this world that she cared about.

With Denis it was another matter. He had left his family to the mercy of the Holocaust. He had managed to get to a golden land, where he not only escaped suffering but flourished. While my mother was being beaten senseless for sabotage in a Nazi forced-labor ammunition factory, Denis was enjoying the good life under the Cuban sun, making money, and seducing women. My mother would never forgive either of them. They in turn would have to live with her bitterness and defiance for the rest of her short life.

Château Anna Szenes, 1948–1949

Great changes at the Château were well underway by the time I returned. The arrival of the new director caused general consternation among the children. Monsieur Haddad was a young Moroccan. He had dark skin, and he had a wife—a very pregnant wife who was kind and motherly. He also looked like a sober, take-charge, no-nonsense type. He called us into his office one by one and asked about life at the Château. We saw him wince at some of our stories, and we knew that our loosey-goosey ways of running things were over.

The children's population had changed as well. Several of the Hungarian children had gone home and would not be coming back. French orphans had taken their place. And one day six girls from the Ukraine arrived. They were a little older than us, probably in their early teens. Their leader was Basha, a dark-eyed, plump, serious girl of about fourteen. I can't remember how we communicated, but we did, and their influence, along with Monsieur Haddad, changed our lives.

The Ukrainian girls spoke Yiddish. They were very religious and totally appalled at our "pagan" ways. No one had paid particular attention to our religious education: our Jewish lifestyle had consisted of lighting candles on Friday nights and not going to school on the Jewish holidays. Most of us had not come from observant homes and certainly had not grown up with observances during the war. We really didn't know very much about Judaism. Basha, her friends, and Monsieur Haddad set about correcting the situation immediately. The first thing was the name of the Château. We all knew that upon acquiring the property, the Joint Distribution Committee had renamed it Anna Szenes, but it had never taken. The locals had always known it as the Château des Groux, and we just went along calling it by its old name. Monsieur Haddad was shocked: here our home was named after a young martyr of the Holocaust, whose memory should have been an inspiration to us, and we had been allowed to ignore it. A large, beautiful sign made by us children was erected at the entrance of the driveway, and it proclaimed the CHÂTEAU ANNA SZENES. When we saw it we laughed and celebrated, and we felt oddly proud, as though we had gained a victory over an unseen enemy.

The Russian girls took serious charge of our religious education. Readers were acquired, and every evening we sat in small groups in the various nooks and crannies of the Château and learned to read and write Hebrew. We learned that the Sabbath did not only consist of Friday night candle lightings but extended to sundown on Saturday and did not include bicycle riding. Monsieur Haddad conducted services, and we learned all the songs and prayers. We learned the rules of kashruth, the meaning of the various holidays, and all the rites and rituals pertaining to our religion that could be stuffed into our young heads. We loved it! We became so proud of being Jewish! Our identities became crystallized, and we followed all the rules punctiliously. Religious practice became the most important activity in our lives. We learned the blessings for everything we could think of, and on Friday nights we waited for the precise moment that the sun set so we could welcome the Sabbath properly and reverently. We became little fanatics, so devout that we tried to out do each other in piety. Whenever we managed to discover certain arcane facts or practices, we would tell the others of it with a disdainful nonchalance, as though we had known this fact all along. We just had not bothered to let anyone know until now. Being so irreligious, they had not deserved to know!

The Ukrainian girls asked us all what our Jewish names were. I had no idea whether I had one or not. I asked my mother. Her answer was a look of exasperated amusement. I didn't pursue it.

At the orphanage I told them that I didn't have one. During services on the following Saturday, I was named Chava. I chalked up one more name.

My mother's reaction to all this wavered between mild interest and concern. She had become a rabid atheist. I had become a little zealot. I tried to convert her. She tried toning me down. But she listened to me and asked questions. Questions that required me to think.

"How do you visualize God?"

"Do you think that if there were a God, he would have let the Holocaust happen?"

"Why do you think that the Jews are the Chosen People?"

I answered to the best of my ability. She took my answers seriously. She seemed to treat me as her intellectual equal. She tested my faith, and when she saw that she couldn't shake it, she shook her head, sighed, and said, "I'm happy that you can believe. I hope you'll be able to keep your faith."

Two or three months later our young indoctrinators, all orphaned, left for Israel. We continued our religious studies, and though our zeal waned with time they had left us a legacy. They had taught us who and what we were, and we began to lift our heads and walk a little taller.

•

Our religious education well underway, Monsieur Haddad turned his attention to secular matters. On October 1, the first day of school, he marched us down to school. I, as one of the "senior" members of the Château, had related to him the horrors that Mme Salle had heaped upon our heads the previous year. He had not said anything at the time, but now he walked into the girls' school ahead of us and politely confronted our nemesis.

Monsieur Haddad was an *Agrégé*. This title is reserved for those who have completed a postgraduate degree that allows one to teach at the highest academic level. Such a title commands great respect in the teaching profession and among the general French population. Madame Salle must have swallowed a lot of bile as we stood there biting our lips to stifle little smiles. In his professional manner, speaking a beautiful and perfect French, Monsieur Haddad discussed the coming year's curriculum, the homework schedule, the reading lists. Mme Salle was outclassed and by a Jew—a Moroccan Jew no less. She knew it, and she knew that we knew. It was a small victory considering the misery that she had put us through, but we settled for it gladly. We thought we saw Monsieur Haddad wink at us on the way home, but we weren't sure.

Life became more orderly under Monsieur Haddad's tutelage. Every day after school, we sat at the long refectory tables chewing on our pencils until he checked everyone's homework and then allowed us to go and play. He was always there to correct our French or to help us with long division, and he never hesitated to come to school with us if there was a problem or if he felt that any of the material was inappropriate. Someone was finally on our side! Mme Salle had to stay on her toes.

At school we never received a kind word, a smile of appreciation for good work done, but we never really expected it. We knew that the best revenge was to excel. And we did. All of us seemed to have our areas of excellence. Mine was an odd combination: geometry and sewing, the latter a required subject. While in hiding, Juliska had taught me to sew, knit, embroider, and crochet, and I had become quite adept at it. Mme Salle never praised my work, but it was always I who was told to help the younger girls with their handwork, and whenever she unraveled a buttonhole, she brought it to class for me to fix. She stuffed our heads with facts and figures, dates, and names of kings and battles, jeered at our spelling errors, harangued us about our handwriting. She was a hard taskmaster and, to her credit, also introduced us to good French literature by providing us with a creative reading list.

On the home front, Mme Haddad had given birth to little Daniel, who immediately had dozens of eager baby-sitters. "Dani" became an important part of our lives. The girls were encouraged to help with bathing and diapering, just like big sisters. We were concerned about his every activity: his diet, his development, even his bowel movements. His parents alternated between amusement and exasperation at our constant presence, interference, and comments. We somehow got a hold of some old home moviemaking equipment, and some of the older boys became very adept at using it. One Sunday afternoon they announced that instead of going to the village cinema we were going to be shown a home movie. They had concocted a story with Dani as the star. Some of it was made up of still photographs, the rest from hand-drawn cartoons. I remember one particular frame: a still photograph of Dani sitting up on a chamber pot that one of the boys had added to the picture. A white dialogue cloud was coming out of a smiling baby Dani's mouth. It read, "Kaka, pipi, Tra-la-la." Everybody loved the film, including Monsieur Haddad, who entered it in the local high school competition for creative endeavors. To our delight and surprise, it won a prize.

As the second year progressed at Anna Szenes, we were gaining confidence and we were also starting to feel our oats. Some of the more vivid memories of our experiences during the war had begun to dull, and we were becoming more accustomed to our surroundings. However, we were also growing to understand why we were there and what had really happened to us. We knew that our lives had veered off course, that something had been done to us that was not normal. Slowly we came to realize that what we had experienced, other generations of children had not, and that our future was not mapped out for us as that of previous generations had been. We were going to have to start from scratch in a new, uncharted world.

Talking about our past was still taboo, but in some obscure way. There was no actual punishment if we broke the rule. Rather, it was as though we were caught talking about a subject that was not appropriate for children, like obscenity. Yet we listened to the adults talk about their trials, which they often did, and if we joined in the conversation, we were ignored or told, "You don't understand. You're a child. Just forget about it." We were becoming angry and had no outlet for our feelings. We got into fights with the village children when they called us names. We were not going to take any more abuse! We were starting to rebel, and no one thought our feelings and behavior could have anything to do with the past, which we were expected to erase from our memory.

One evening, Eva Ferenci's little brother, Peter, eight years old, did not show up for supper. After a thorough search and hysterics from Eva, Monsieur Haddad called the local gendarmerie. Yes, Peter was there. He had been "arrested" for stealing a local boy's bicycle. Monsieur Haddad, furious, started running toward the village, several of us following behind him. Eva was crying hysterically, convinced that her little brother was being tortured. A big shouting match ensued at the gendarmerie, the gendarmes getting the worst of it. Guilty or not, Monsieur Haddad was not going to let "his" children be treated differently than any other kid in the village! The gendarme should have brought him home and let his "father" deal with him! The entire police force (three) got a dressing down, but Peter walked all the way home with his ear firmly held by Monsieur Haddad, while Eva lamented like a little old lady.

"Peter, how could you? After all we've gone through. How will I be able to face our mother? Hasn't she had enough pain? I'll never be able to lift my head again!"

She was a barely eleven years old.

I dealt with my emotional burden in a traditionally feminine way. I had a doll whose place was always on my pillow. I never played with her. She was my secret friend and confidante. Lying in bed at night, I whispered my fears, hopes, and secrets into the deaf ears of my celluloid companion. Her name was Ildiko. Large and stiff with big vacant blue eyes, she was made from molded celluloid and dressed in a snappy sailor suit. Uncle Sanyi had given her to me for my third or fourth birthday. I had admired her every day in Oswald's toyshop window, around the corner from us in Budapest. She was the biggest doll that I had ever seen, and I begged to have her only to be told that she was too expensive. On my birthday she was waiting for me at the breakfast table. Our bond was immediate. We had cowered together in the cellars during the bombing raids. We had hidden together at the farm and the haylofts during the Nazi occupation, and she had been with me in the Red Cross truck as it had lurched back to France. She was the only constant in my life, and she was my link to Uncle Sanyi, the only father that I remembered. During the day I pretended that she was just a keepsake. I was too old to play with dolls. At night, I hugged her hard body and poured my heart out. I just knew that she came to life and heard me.

At school, I discovered a new survival method. I always sat in the front row, right under Mme Salle's nose, and to add to my misery, the class bully sat behind me and tortured me to her heart's content, since Mme Salle never bothered to notice. One day in the middle of a test, I heard the sound of a small snap, followed by a moan, behind me. I knew that my classmate's pencil tip had broken, and she probably didn't have a spare. We were never allowed to speak up during a test. We were supposed to be prepared for any emergency. If we weren't, too bad! We would fail the test. I still don't understand why I did what I did, but it changed the way I perceived relationships. I had an extra pencil, and without a moment's thought I turned around and, with a smile, handed it to my tormentor. I saw the startled look on her face, the suspicion, the relief, and finally the acceptance. The exchange

of looks took but a moment, but in that moment I knew that she would never torment me again. I also realized that my "niceness" had the effect of providing me
with protection. If I were "nice," I would not be harmed. If people liked me, they
would be less likely to hurt me. It was a revelation. It became my insurance policy. So I became "nice." I lent my things. I cheerfully mended seams and hems that
had come undone. I smiled at everybody, listened to their problems, and pretended to like them. I watched how people responded with detached wonder and
cynical amusement. They were nice back. They couldn't be anything else, after all
I was so-o-o-o-o nice! Meanwhile I was contemptuous of the people that I manip-
ulated into liking me and also elated that I had found a secret way to protect
myself without the help of adults. Mme Salle was never a beneficiary of my newfound benevolence. I was no longer fearful of her, and it gave me more pleasure to
hate her and to watch her perplexed by my newfound popularity. I used this ploy
for years, to the point that saying no to any request became impossible, and I
defeated my own purpose by often being used. But I was "safe." And being "safe"
was worth being used.

Monsieur Haddad worked hard at integrating us into the community and trying
to mold us into a family. Moreover, he encouraged us to be *children*. We took
some tentative steps, self-consciously, in that direction. The boys had always had
their soccer games, but the girls spent most of their free time reading and
sewing. We did play house, but it was for real. We fretted over the younger children, we dressed them against the cold, we kissed and bandaged their "boo-
boos," we made sure that they were clean and that they ate all their dinner. We
argued with Monsieur Haddad when he wanted to take these chores from us.
But eventually we did discover the joys of sliding down a well-polished banister.
We picked poppies, cornflowers, and buttercups in the nearby fields and decorated the dining room. We learned to build campfires, around which we danced
the hora and sang Hebrew songs. The day Israel became a state, the campfire was
so big that it threatened the Château. We laughed and we cried, sang "Ha-Tikva"
("The Hope," the Jewish national anthem), and vowed to go to Israel and fight.
My mother was horrified at the thought. "One war was enough. We don't need
another one!" She held out no hope for the new nation's survival.

On Sunday afternoons we were usually escorted down to the village cinema,
where we enjoyed those wonderful 1940s films along with the rest of the French
population. I still cherish the memory of those delightful Fernandel classics,
which gave the boys enough clowning material for the rest of the week. We
became familiar with the villagers and they with us. On July 14, Bastille Day, we

were invited to join in the celebrations. We dressed in our best clothes and trotted down to the village, which was decorated with flags and banners and ribbons
and flowers, all in red, white, and blue. We hardly recognized the place. Everyone
was milling around. The excitement was infectious. A procession was getting
underway. People were lining the street to watch, and we joined them. In the hubbub, Monsieur Haddad managed to get the mayor's ear. Suddenly, we little girls
were swooped up and seated in a freshly scrubbed and painted horse-drawn carriage decorated with flowers and hundreds of tricolors. Little flags were handed
to us, and before we knew what was happening we were in the midst of the
parade, laughing and waving flags, being applauded by the crowds on the side-
walks. I can pinpoint this event as the one that inspired my becoming "French."
I called myself "Evelyne Juliette." I spoke French like all the other French children, and after all, I had been born in France. I had taken a little side trip during
the war. So what? Many people had. But I had come home. That was the important thing. Soon my life would be normal. I had not yet experienced what "normal" was, but it sounded wonderful. It was being just like everyone else. It was
being where I belonged. It was being French! I was proud of being French.

The villagers got used to our presence. They also took personal pride in
Monsieur Haddad's impressive academic credentials. He became the village
intellectual. The children at the orphanage began to rack up academic prizes,
and this reflected on the whole community. All the older children who were eli-
gible successfully applied to the better high school that was in the next big town,
Saint-Germain-en-Laye. I was expected to follow suit—if I stayed there. But, of
course, I wouldn't. I was going to live with my mother. Or so I told everyone. I
was finally going to have a home again.

My mother, on the other hand, was not feeling at home at all. She was now stateless and a widow, she thought. She didn't know for sure. Nobody knew what had
happened to hundreds of thousands of deportees. People were still hoping that
their husbands, wives, mothers, fathers, or children were still alive somewhere in
the Soviet Union and that eventually they would return. Uncle Denis, back from
Cuba, was brutally frank.

"Hermann is dead. Get used to it. Find another husband. This is a rotten
world, and the only way to survive is not to have any hopes or illusions."

They fought constantly. My mother needed time to mourn, to gather her
physical and emotional resources. He wanted her to marry right away so as not
to become a burden to him. Besides, single women had no status as far as he was
concerned. She resented his attitude and fought every attempt at help or advice,
whether it was constructive or not. Aunt Eszter tried to intervene on my

mother's behalf, only to have her rocky marriage rocked some more. Eventually my mother and her brother stopped talking to each other. This created complications within the family. Aunt Eszter would secretly see and help my mother. Denis was not to know. Denis would buy me things and give me money, but I was not to tell my mother that it came from him. Kati and Klari took sides, by mail. Kati on Denis's, Klari on my mother's. (If Denis sent her a present, Klari happily changed sides.) Both Denis and my mother wrote to Kati and Klari complaining about each other. They, in turn, were exasperated with their two younger siblings. "Haven't we had enough already? Please try and get along!" they begged and pleaded, but to no avail. Denis and my mother were both mulishly stubborn.

Denis was a man of his time. As far as he was concerned, women were dispensable—except mothers and sisters, and all they had to do was to listen to him and do as he told them to do and then everything would be fine! If they didn't, he washed his hands of them. The clever ones in the family knew how to get around him; I became the best at it. I could manipulate him at will, get almost anything I wanted from him. All I had to do was laugh at his jokes (he *was* funny!), listen to his political philosophy—and agree with him—and promise to read all the books that he recommended.

My mother disdained such tactics. She was going to make it on her own even if it killed her. And eventually it did.

Cheltenham, England, 1949-1950

My mother and I left France in the late spring of 1949 under rather mysterious circumstances. She wanted to leave France and decided to raise some money in the only way she could—illegally. She sold our apartment for cash, planning to take the money out of the country to start our new life. To this day I'm not sure which part of this transaction was against the law. I think all of it. All I know is that directly after the transaction took place, my mother's pocketbook, full of the cash, was ripped off her arm (probably by the people that she had made the deal with), and our future went down the drain. She had no legal recourse, and we didn't have a home anymore. We were, again, destitute.

For a short while we rented a furnished room on the avenue du Maine. There I remember learning to cook potatoes on a small electric ring plugged into the wall next to the sink, which we used to wash the potatoes and ourselves as well. Some time later, my mother announced that we were leaving for England. She had found work there, and I was going to be boarded with an acquaintance from her glove-making apprenticeship in Budapest who now lived in a place called Cheltenham.

Immigration to England was possible only if one signed a contract to go into domestic or hospital service. Immigrants were not allowed to rent or buy personal accommodations. England had been so badly bombed that there was not enough housing for its own citizens, let alone immigrants. My mother had somehow discovered that her old friend Rose had emigrated from Hungary before the war and married an Englishman. After much correspondence it was decided that for the sum of a pound a week and, just as important, the extra ration card, I was to live with Rose and her family while my mother worked as housekeeper for a couple who owned a small café in the seaside resort of Weston-super-Mare, about seventy miles from where I would be. Since she couldn't have her own home, there was no possibility of my living with her, "for the time being," she assured me again.

We were seen off at the railroad station in Paris by my mother's best friend, Nusi Neni (Aunt Nusi), and her daughter Yvonne, who had been with me at the Château. Nusi Neni handed me a book: since I was going to England and would have to learn English, she thought it was only right that I get a head start on some "English" literature. The book was *Tom Sawyer*. I pronounced it "Tom Savier," as did most French people.

In 1949, Cheltenham was the quintessential provincial English town. Northwest of London, it is situated about halfway between Birmingham and Bristol, in the heart of the Cotswolds. A pretty, hilly, green, and brambly countryside, with hedgerows along country lanes and sweetbrier growing along the sides of fields. Before the war, it had been a favorite retirement spot for army officers and other government officials on modest incomes. Now, after the war, it had an air of genteel poverty and a stiff upper lip.

I was lowered into these unfamiliar surroundings at the age of ten and a half. It felt as though I had been dropped off on another planet. Though England is considered to be part of Europe geographically, the English have never reconciled themselves to this fact. There is England, and the rest of Europe is "the Continent." The *English* Channel (as opposed to la Manche) was, until very recently, the "great divider." In 1949, England was indeed still very different and isolated from the Continent. The term *foreigner* could be substituted for *suspect* or *interloper* and carried an implied caution, as in "Careful, these foreigners are clever, you know!" It was also used as a derogatory term, as in "What do you expect? She's a foreigner!" Cheltenham, in the west of England with its provincial, conservative, middle- and working-class population, had seen very few immigrants, and it was obvious from the start that none were welcome. It was plain. We were not as good as they were.

I lived my first few months there in a state of complete bewilderment. It was as though I had moved to a wasteland without signposts. I had no idea what was expected of me, what role I was to play in Rose's family, or how long I should expect to stay there. This life bore no relationship to anything I had known before, not even the time I had spent at the Château. I had no connection to anyone from my previous life for months, except to my mother. And I saw her only rarely. I was isolated in the midst of a family who made no secret of the fact that I was there because my mother paid for me to live there. Then there was the language: so very odd! Those strange words that started with *w*, which sounded like little dogs barking. And the *th*'s, where I was told to put my tongue against the back of my teeth and lisp. I despaired of ever learning English.

Rose was a strange and eccentric woman. Looking back, I realize that she really was quite mad. She was bony with bright red hair. She wore severely cut bangs on exactly half of her forehead, "to hide a scar," she said mysteriously. Her husband, Harold, was a dour and unattractive Englishman whom Rose had trapped into marriage in order to avoid internment; this she admitted without shame. Their life together was a bitter disappointment to them both. Harold still held a grudging respect for Rose, but she thoroughly despised him. She had, however, made peace with the fact that he was her lot. She loved her child and her home, and if Harold came with the package, so be it. Then I dropped in, and at that tender age became Rose's confidante—the keeper of her most intimate thoughts and secrets.

My place in that family was as confusing to me as it must have been to them. Rose and Harold had a five-year-old redheaded daughter, Veronica: a precocious little thing who, according to her mother, was destined to become the world's greatest ballerina. As far as I was concerned, Veronica was not about to give up her No. 1 position in the family. For a while she was able to maintain her superior position by virtue of the fact that she spoke English and I, not a word. She treated me, in turn, as a personal protector and a lady-in-waiting. She had me follow her to all the neighbor's houses where she showed me off as though I were a new possession.

"Look, everybody. See what I got! She doesn't look like much, but she can sew doll's clothes and she'll protect me from the bigger kids!"

Harold treated me well enough. That extra pound every week was very welcome. He earned five pounds a week as a factory worker. On occasion, he would fly into a rage when he'd had enough of Rose's and my Hungarian prattle, which, he rightly suspected, was mostly about him. He did, however, take seriously the task of providing for his family. He rarely got drunk—as opposed to most of our neighbors. Many of the wives cried when they found themselves out of money at the end of the month, owing to their husbands' frequent stops at the local pub. Harold always handed over his pay envelope to Rose, untouched. She then doled out to him whatever amount of pocket money she deemed affordable. Though they often quarreled, it was never about money. Rose was a wonderful manager, and Harold, to his credit, recognized it.

We lived in a community of prefabricated houses, those postwar aluminum dwellings that the government couldn't put up fast enough to shelter its bombed-out citizens. The waiting list had thousands of names. Everybody, it seemed, wanted to live in one of those white metal boxes that were cold in winter and hot in summer. The army engineers erected them, several at a time, in the span of twenty-four hours, and the open field behind us soon added substantially to the size of our community. We called the houses "prefabs." They were rectangular boxes divided into a kitchen, living room, two bedrooms, and a bathroom. Spare and clean, the houses were more modern than any those poor

English folk had ever seen before. Around each house was a tiny plot of land where vegetable gardens and rosebushes sprouted in true English fashion. The rent was a pound a week, and if a tenant paid on time for fifty-one weeks of the year, the government waived the rent for the year's last week. I remember Rose clutching her unexpected windfall and planning to have the cat spayed with it. A pound was a big deal for a working-class family in 1949. It was the first time that I became aware of class distinction—and I was on the bottom rung.

It seemed to me that things were getting worse since the end of the war, not better, as the grown-ups thought. At night I sometimes thought about my doll, Ildiko, which I had been forced to leave behind in France with my Aunt Eszter. She was too large and bulky to take with us, and my mother had said, "You're too old for a doll, anyhow." I had been too ashamed to say that I wanted to take her. Aunt Eszter promised to keep her for me.

It soon became clear that I was not the only one who felt isolated. Rose, too, was lonely. She had no friends among the working-class women who were our neighbors. So the two of us, a friendless, frustrated, unhappy woman and a lonely, homeless child, formed a peculiar union. I helped Rose in the kitchen and while we cooked and cleaned, we talked. That is, she talked. For years Rose had had no one with whom to speak Hungarian, and stories just flowed out of her like a river that had burst its banks. She talked to me as an equal, and it made me feel very grown-up. I heard stories about her childhood, the death of her great love, her immigration—and too many details of her loveless marriage. Even then I knew that there was something not quite proper about our relationship, which was probably the reason that I never told my mother about these confidences. I was titillated by Rose's stories, feeling that I was privy to secrets that other children my age were not. Rose desperately needed companionship, and for want of an adult friend, she chose me.

True to her background, Rose was a good Hungarian cook. She made very little go very far. She taught me how to coagulate milk to get curd, which we made into cheese or used in baking. The small amount of meat that we were able to get was ground, mixed with spices, bread crumbs, garlic, and one precious egg, then fried into patties. It was delicious even the next day, cold and sliced in sandwiches. While the children in the neighborhood thought that a jam tart was the ultimate treat, we feasted on delicious little cheese pastries baked in crescent shapes and filled with nuts and apricot jelly.

Rose was also very nimble-fingered. She tatted, sewed, and embroidered. She and my mother had met in Hungary when, as young girls, they were both learning the art of sewing suede and soft leather gloves by hand. Since I was also adept at needlework, she cooked up a scheme to earn some extra money. She contacted a glove factory and talked them into letting her do piecework at home. Under her tutelage I learned this art and spent many of my evenings adding to the family's meager budget.

I exchanged weekly letters with my mother. She came to see me maybe half a dozen times in the beginning, but these were difficult visits. If it rained, which it often did, we stayed in the house with no privacy. I had to share her with Rose, who never left our side. If we went out, it was to take a walk around the perimeter of the prefab community. There was nowhere else to go. She always asked, "Are you being treated well?" But there was no point in asking whether or not I was happy there. I had the vague, uncomfortable feeling that Rose disapproved of my mother. In retrospect, I can see that she was probably jealous: I had become *her* friend. She also might have felt some envy. My mother was pretty and—from Rose's point of view—she was free. She had taken the opportunity to start a new life and could afford to pay her child's board while she did it. Rose was stuck.

My mother's visits became less frequent after she began to waitress in the café in addition to her regular work as housekeeper. Since her employers allowed her to eat in the café, she saved her own food coupons and was able (in "lieu" of her actual presence) to send sugar, chocolate, and other rationed items as special treats for Rose, Veronica, and me. There was never anything special for Harold, and he usually sulked like a child.

Postwar England provided very few luxuries. An occasional movie was a great treat. In summer, weather permitting, we took walks in the countryside and looked for various herbs that Rose would dry and use for homemade remedies. Generally we led a very modest existence. Veronica and I went to school, Harold worked at the factory, and Rose looked after all our needs. This included scrubbing the house from top to bottom every single day. Her mania for cleanliness and order caused terrible friction between her and Harold. A crumb on the floor produced a screaming fit. Shoes, naturally, could never be worn indoors. Sheets were washed every day, by hand, since a washing machine was an unknown luxury. Rose was on the move from morning till night.

The school was not memorable. I learned to speak, read, and write English, and though my classmates were friendly, their parents were wary of "foreigners." Hence my only real friend was Rose, a thirty-eight-year-old crazy woman. Once I learned the language, visits to the public library were my weekly outings, and I retreated into my books whenever I could. I left Madame de Ségur behind and made the acquaintance of Enid Blyton.

I shared Veronica's room and I should remember something about that, but I don't. I don't remember what our relationship was like at all. Was I a big sister? Did she resent that I took part of her room or her mother's attention away from her? We lived together for about a year, but I don't remember how I felt toward her—only how she looked twirling round and round in her little pink tutu or when she occasionally ran to her mother to complain that I was reading instead of playing with her.

People kept to themselves in the community. Only the children would meet at the curbside and play on sunny days. We said "good morning" and "good evening" to our neighbors, but we had little to do with them. Rose did attempt to make friends, but she was looked upon not only as a foreigner, but as an eccentric. She did, however, win over our immediate neighbors with her Hungarian cooking. Though they never crossed our threshold, they gratefully accepted samples of *fashiert* (meat patty), *pörkölt* (beef stew), and *rakott krumpli* (a dish of baked sliced potatoes layered with sausages and eggs), which no doubt supplemented their meager food budget.

The only social occasion that I remember was Veronica's birthday party. Rose invited several little girls from the neighboring prefabs. She set the dining-room table and served blancmange, a horrible, tasteless molded dessert—"The English love it," asserted Rose—and a cake with candles. Next to each plate was a "cracker." This ubiquitous English party prop consists of a cardboard tube, about four-inches long, wrapped like candy with pretty silver wrapping paper twirled at the ends into tassels. When both tassels are pulled at each end, the cracker pops open with a bang and a surprise falls out, usually a miniature whistle or a plastic animal. The children quietly ate their sweets, sang "Happy Birthday," banged their crackers, and played one round of musical chairs. After that they had to sit quietly while Veronica danced for them. They went through these motions like little automatons, with a little fidgeting during Veronica's performance. Even at that young age, the children knew that parties were a social obligation, not an event to be enjoyed. The parents came to the front door at the appointed time and waited for the children to come out. Everybody said "thank you," and the whole affair was over in about an hour, after which Rose scrubbed the house until there was not a sign that anyone had been there. I had watched from the sidelines, being too old to join the children. I had never been to a birthday party, and I took it to be strange, English ritual.

The prefab community was built on the edge of town, one stop before the cemetery on the local bus line. The conductor was already announcing the next stop as we were getting off. "Pearly gates to the boneyard!" he bellowed and then had a chuckle. The location of the community and the fact that most of the tenants were factory workers made them less accepted socially than the townspeople. We knew our place. We rarely intruded on the pretty little Georgian town. But I remember vividly when we did. Woolworth's was usually our first and favorite destination. On occasion we were allowed a small treat: a piece of candy, a little plastic ballerina, a new pencil sharpener. Next best on the agenda was the well-manicured town park, where under a gazebo the local oompah-pah band struck up favorite tunes and the local gentry sat in gleaming white chairs on the green, green lawn. Some scowled when they saw us. They knew that we were from the prefabs because we sat on the grass and brought sandwiches. This was where, at the age of two, Veronica had climbed out of her stroller and started to dance with "such incredible grace," I had been told, that her mother had the revelation that Veronica would be a great ballerina. Since that day Rose made sure that there was always enough money for ballet lessons. We could always do with a little less food, but never would her daughter miss a ballet lesson.

The other excursion into town, the memory of which still makes me wince and tightens my throat, was to the local department store, Cavendish House. It was like walking into a forbidden shrine. I remember the polished mahogany, the thick carpets, the ladies wearing hats and gloves. It was there that I saw a television set for the first time. Of course I was fascinated and stopped in front of it, but only for a moment. The vigilant eyes and stern faces of the saleswomen warned me away. They knew that we were not there to buy anything. And we knew that they knew. We stood out among the well-dressed clientele. Nonetheless, Rose put on her snooty, nonchalant face and walked slowly past the expensive merchandise as though considering a purchase. Veronica, a miniature Rose, followed suit. I always slunk behind, feeling ashamed and uncomfortable and very left out. I wanted to say, "I don't belong to them. Don't look at me like you look at them," and I attempted a half-hearted smile at the saleswomen, but it was never returned. I was so ashamed. I felt that we didn't belong there. The elegant place painfully underscored everything about my new life: the working-class poverty, my motherlessness, the strangeness of that foreign place. Cavendish House made me feel abandoned, intimidated, and very lonely. It also evoked for me a vague memory of Budapest when I was very little. It reminded me of Kati and Klari, breezing through the elegant shops in the Vaci utca, with Peter and me in tow; of being fawned over by the help, who assisted us in loading our pretty packages into a taxi. I couldn't understand why Rose wanted to be there. Obviously nobody else wanted us there. Cavendish House always made me cry.

Harold strongly disapproved of Cavendish House. It was for the "toffs": those people who had money, who thought that they were better than we were! Those who were going to be taught a lesson by the Labour Party and Clement Attlee! They'd show those Tories and Mr. Churchill where to get off!

The dreaded bimonthly outing was to Mrs. Davis's house, Harold's mother. She lived in an old working-class neighborhood where all the little brick houses are attached and look the same, their only distinguishing mark being the different colors of the front doors. In postwar England fresh paint was a luxury, so most front doors wore either peeling brown or peeling green coats. There were tiny garden patches both in front and in back of the houses, and most owners attempted to beautify their sad environment by planting flowers in their miniature plots.

Mrs. Davis was a "true Englishwoman," she proudly asserted. She was considered of lower middle class, with pretensions of gentility. She'd had two sons. One of them, her favorite, had been killed in the war. The other, Harold, had married "that crazy foreigner." To me she seemed a very bitter old woman, with a permanent scowl on her face. The "crazy foreigner," meanwhile, was an exemplary daughter-in-law. Whenever we visited the old woman, Rose cleaned the house, did the laundry by hand, and to my thorough disgust, washed the old woman's hair and clipped her toenails. Since our visits were about two weeks apart, these seemed to me most unappetizing chores.

I hated going to that house. It was old and musty and smelled like a dirty old woman. Mrs. Davis herself was sloppy and wore stained, torn dresses. Her dirty slip always showed, and she wore tattered old slippers with the backs folded down under her unwashed heels, her huge bunions poking through holes on the sides. She shuffled along mumbling nasty things under her breath about the "foreigner" who, meanwhile, was working to make the place livable. She seemed fond of Veronica and would question her affectionately and delight in the demonstrations of her most recently learned dance steps. She ignored me. Whenever possible I escaped to the tiny patch of green at the back of the house, away from the stifling smells of the interior. There was, however, something in that house that I coveted. It was a picture that hung on the wall above the dining room table. It illustrated five stages in a woman's life: each stage on a different step, as though on an open ladder, twenty years apart from birth to eighty years. The baby in the cradle was on the lowest rung on the left. On the next rung was the young bride. One rung up, in the center, was the matron aged forty with her children. Then, going down one rung on the right was the sixty-year-old grandmother, and finally, on the last rung at the same level as the baby but on the right, an old woman in black, surrounded by her large family of children, grandchildren, and great-grandchildren. Everybody in the picture was dressed in Victorian clothing and pretty colors, and the whole thing was framed in gold. I loved that picture. I wanted it so badly that I figured out all kinds of outlandish schemes for getting it. The only reason that I tolerated the visits was because of the picture. I stared at it for what seemed like hours. Perhaps I saw an untroubled continuation of life, running its course from birth to death, unencumbered by wars, untimely death, or migration. Or, who knows, maybe it was just the pretty colors.

After Rose married Harold, they had lived with his mother since no housing was available. Rose's manic cleanliness and her mother-in-law's hatred of foreigners had assured a near state of war in the household. When Rose was told by the local county council how far down the list she was for getting public housing, she burst into hysterics and screamed that she was immediately going to kill herself and her baby daughter. She couldn't spend another day at her mother-in-law's house. She must have made an incredible scene, as the very proper British bureaucrats on the council put her at the head of the list, and she and Harold were given one of the first prefabs available. She kept her little house in perfect order. It was the only one that I visited that was not permeated with the smell of boiled cabbage, aged mutton, and drying laundry. Any visit by dignitaries or various members of Parliament checking on the progress of the housing authorities always merited a stop at the Davis residence. Rose was very proud of this. She never ceased comparing her orderly house, clothing, child, and lifestyle to those of her neighbors, who always came up short.

While I was living with the Davises, they took their first vacation—ever. I went with them. Rose had scrimped and saved for heaven knows how long to be able to afford a week away from the aluminum prefab. She paid for a one-week stay in a trailer. (She evidently had a penchant for metal habitats). It was in Brixham, a lovely little fishing village on the southern coast of England. It rained every day. The trailer park, however, was booked full, and there was good cheer. In the rain, we explored the town, the next town, and the one after that, taking buses everywhere. The town council organized competitions and games for its visitors and commiserated with everyone regarding the weather. I won a prize, a basket of goodies, by finding a foreign object in an overcrowded grocery store window display. It was a shirt button. We celebrated with our neighbors at the trailer park, all squeezing into one trailer, surrounded by mud puddles on all sides. The day we left, the weather was glorious. Rose promised that the following year we would be away for two weeks. But the following year I would be back in France—in a Catholic convent.

Rose was a Spiritualist. She followed a sect started in Canada by two sisters who believed in getting in touch with the dead, who in turn revealed themselves as spiritual guides to the living. Rose truly believed. I sanctimoniously informed her that since I was Jewish I wasn't sure that all this was kosher. Rose was delighted. Didn't she remember that I'm Jewish? I wondered. She asked me all kinds of questions regarding Judaism. I answered every question whether I knew the answer or not. Heaven only knows what my ten- or eleven-year-old mind came up with regarding Jewish practices and beliefs. Rose thought it was all marvelous. Jews were the Chosen People. "But," she said sternly, as though I were responsible, "you must now share that choseness." She felt that her church was best, being that it was nonsectarian. "This way," she said, "we would all learn from one another."

I missed the inspirational Sabbath services at Anna Szenes, but France and the Château were a long way off, and eventually I grew accustomed to Rose's Spiritualist church, which she dragged Veronica and me to regularly. Harold snorted at the whole thing, but quietly, just in case. The women and men conducting the services were called mediums. They were the psychic transmitters charged with sending and receiving messages from the beyond. Indeed, I do remember some extraordinary things taking place there; occurrences that to this day I cannot explain and leave me still wondering, What if?

Rose took me to the Spiritualist healers. My fingers and toes, frostbitten during the war, were still painful and swollen in winter. As I sat in a chair very quietly, the medium would gently caress the afflicted areas, then shake his hands as though he were getting rid of the ailment. I really don't remember whether it helped the pain or the itch, but I liked the peaceful atmosphere and enjoyed the attention. I enjoyed it all. Besides all the hocus-pocus, Rose and I would discuss and dissect all the ladies of the congregation—in Hungarian, of course.

"Look at that one. Only an Englishwoman would think of wearing a red hat with that coat!"

"Huh! Widowed six months and she's already hanging on the arm of any single man who will let her."

I learned at an early age the type of clichéd gossip that frustrated, ignorant women often engage in.

Soon Rose discovered that her "guides" had given her a spiritual gift. She, who could never draw a straight line, began creating pastel portraits of people that she "saw in her mind." They were Native Americans, Indians, Arabs, and all other sorts. Actually all the portraits she drew seemed to have very similar features, only their skin color, hair, and headdresses differed. They all came equipped with names and occasionally titles. None, it seemed, had been unknown in this world. They were "guides": they looked after our spiritual welfare. She hung them around, attached to ribbons, festooning the living room, making it look like a spiritual wash day. All the neighbors admired Rose's portraits, and she gave them away freely, explaining that she was not allowed to sell them for money; this much to Harold's chagrin. We got more and more involved in occult activities, experimenting with Ouija boards, tapping table legs, going into trances, and discussing endlessly the meaning of such movies as *Pandora and the Flying Dutchman,* starring James Mason and Ava Gardner.

One day, I did something awful. Rose burnt her hand quite badly on the stove and immediately smothered it in egg whites and butter. The next day I told her that during the night, my guide had come to me and said that to cure the burn, Rose had to put salt on it. She believed me and immediately removed the bandage, dredging her burned hand in salt. It hurt like hell, and I got scared. Rose, however, said that hurt was good: it meant healing. But tears were running down her face. I didn't dare fess up. It had gone too far, and Rose really believed that I'd had a revelation. Fortunately her hand healed in spite of me, but I never played seeress again.

All this was pretty heady stuff for an eleven year old. What was even better— though very confusing—was being privy to Rose's sex life. I was thrown headlong into the complexities of marital sexual conflict, without knowing anything about the basics. I was not about to acknowledge to Rose that I didn't understand everything that she confided to me, so I just kept listening. One morning I woke up to some angry words and Harold slamming the door. Rose was steaming.

"He didn't pull out in time, the brute."

I didn't ask "Pull out what?" I just waited, and sure enough I learned about coitus interruptus and assumed that this was customary. What I didn't know was that Rose and Harold's sexual practices were anything but "the norm." Rose explained that she only had to worry about "the Brute" every three months or so. Anything more frequent and he was on "some crazy rampage."

I got a lot of advice on how to avoid sexual contact with my husband-to-be. Headaches, periods, stomach pains, and similar clichés were advanced as sound practice. Obviously, Rose had some problems regarding sex. She thought it unworthy of civilized people. It was typical. Men were brutes who didn't know any better, and women who enjoyed sex were sluts. And this is where the trouble began.

Rose, Veronica, and I had gone to spend a couple of days at the seaside where my mother worked. We shared her little room and enjoyed one of the few sandy beaches in England. My mother had shown Rose a drawer full of money that she had earned in tips while helping in the café on busy evenings after her housekeeping shift. Rose was stunned at seeing all that money. One evening after our return home, appearing as if she had just solved a difficult mathematical problem, Rose turned away from the dishes in the sink and, looking at me, said thoughtfully, "I don't believe that your mother earned all that money making tips. Besides, I saw something else in that drawer." Rose explained about condoms. Yes, come to think of it, I had seen something that looked like a rubber sleeve in the drawer. She explained about some women having to have men, about my mother placing me in Cheltenham in order to be able to live her own life, about her being an atheist (this was true). It all happened over a period of time so that—gradually—I became more and more integrated into Rose's family and eventually accepted the fact that my mother didn't want me—and that I was going to stay with the Davises forever. Rose even said that we could manage without the extra pound a week. Cheltenham had no particular appeal, but I had come to accept it as "home." I wouldn't have to move again. If my mother didn't want me, well there was a family that did. It was better than nothing.

My mother's weekly letters were read, analyzed, and reinterpreted by Rose. She always found something in them that bore out her theory that my mother considered me a burden. Then one day a letter came. My mother and I were moving to London. Rose and I panicked. Rose said she wouldn't let me go. I said I wouldn't go, so off went a letter to my mother: *I want to stay in Cheltenham. I found a family that wants me. . . .* Two days later the doorbell rang and there stood my mother. She came right to the point.

"Hello Rose, hello Harold. Evi, go pack your clothes. We are leaving."

Harold tried to be a man and stepped forward to defy her. My mother drew on her limited English, and every word was fired at him like bullets from a machine gun.

"You stupid man. You wife crazy! You crazy too? I kill you. No more pound every week. You understand?"

Understand he did. One crazy Hungarian was more than enough for him. He fled: let the women battle it out!

It wasn't much of a battle. My mother looked Rose straight in the eyes.

"Rose, you're not getting my daughter. If you try to stop her from leaving, I'm calling the police."

Rose started raving. "We know the kind of life you lead. We know about the men. My guides told me all about it. You should not be allowed to have a child. The guides are cursing you! You can't take her away from me. She belongs here. She's clean!"

My mother, totally ignoring her, located the drawer where my clothes were kept, threw them into a suitcase, and grabbing my wrist firmly, propelled me out the front door.

Not a word was spoken until we were on the train. I was apprehensive. I felt that I had done something very wrong, though at the time I was defiantly trying to escape back to the prefab, out of loyalty to what I felt was my commitment. Not a chance. My mother's vigilance never let up for a second. Looking back, she, too, must have been apprehensive, trying to figure out how to deal with her wayward child.

Finally settled in the train, sitting opposite one another, my mother held my chin up, looked at me, and said, "I want you to tell me why you want to live with Rose."

I averted my eyes, fidgeted, squirmed in my seat, but she was persistent. I mumbled and grumbled unintelligible reasons when something concrete came to mind. I blurted out accusingly, "And anyway, Rose and I saw the condoms in your drawer!"

"Condoms? What do you know about condoms?"

She was totally taken aback. She seemed not quite sure whether to be angry or not. I explained about condoms.

"Do you mean this?" she asked.

She held out her left thumb. On it was a large bandage and covering the bandage was a transparent rubber sleeve.

"Yes," I said. "That's it."

"This is not a condom," she explained. "This is a cover for a bandage to stop it from getting wet. Condoms are much larger."

What? How much larger? My eyes must have opened wide because my mother looked almost amused. I put on my I'm-not-sure-I-want-to-talk-to-you-yet face and retreated further back into my seat, looking out the window at the passing landscape.

After a few minutes my mother said, matter-of-factly, "Evi, I saw this wonderful film the other day. A French film made by a famous French artist called Jean Cocteau. It's called *La Belle et la bête*. Would you like to hear about it?"

I shrugged my shoulders. My mother started telling the story of "Beauty and the Beast." She was a good storyteller, and though at first I pretended to be absorbed by the sights outside, I soon found myself listening. By the time we arrived at Paddington Station in London, we had established a tenuous relationship. I felt as though I had awakened from a strange dream. Like Dorothy in *The Wizard of Oz*, I had been transported to a strange and warped world from which I suddenly awoke, thrust back into reality. I was again the French Hungarian refugee in England trying to make sense out of this world that I had been born into.

I never went back to Cheltenham; nor did I ever see or hear from the Davises again. My mother and I never spoke about this episode. I suspect that she felt as uneasy about it as I did. But the memory of this episode still brings huge pangs of guilt. I still feel that I betrayed my mother.

Paris and the Convent of Notre Dame, 1950–1951

The Cheltenham experience weighed heavily on both my mother and me. She was at a loss as to what to do with me. She had a job as housekeeper for a family in the north of London, and for a while I stayed with her there, sharing her room. But it was only a temporary arrangement.

I was enrolled in the local school, where I was immediately labeled "Frenchie." There my only memorable experience was when I broke up a vicious fight between two tough older girls in the playground. The smaller combatant was getting the worst of it. I could see blood and I decided to step in. I threw myself in between them, and in my agitated state mixed up my languages, shouting, "Stop! Stop! Voyons, êtes-vous folles? Arrêtez! No more fighting!" They were so astonished at this skinny little runt daring to come between them, shouting excitedly in a foreign tongue, that the bigger one actually started laughing. She had already proven her superiority and could afford to stop. She put her arm around me in a proprietary fashion.

"Hey, you're a piece of all right, Frenchie," she offered, sauntering off.

I became the heroine of the day. Frenchie had stopped a fight between the two toughest girls in the school. (Had I only known!) Teachers smiled at me and I got admiring looks. The headmistress called me in and asked me why I had done it.

"Because they were hurting each other," I answered, surprised to be asked such a question.

She smiled. "That was very brave of you. But don't do it again," she admonished. "You might have been hurt. Those are very tough girls!"

What kind of school was this, where teachers were afraid of their pupils? I thought of Mme Salle: she would have made short shrift of them! That was probably the only positive thought I ever had about Mme Salle. I told my mother what had happened. She sighed. "Do you like it here?" she asked.

"No," I said. "It's a strange country. Can't we go back to France? I finally got used to it there."

"I can't go back," she said quietly.

It was around this time that my aunt Kati escaped from Hungary. She had been tipped off that she was about to be arrested and "relocated." This was a Communist maneuver aimed at wreaking vengeance against the "capitalists." The targeted people would be gathered, put on trucks, and bundled off to the countryside where they would be dumped and abandoned. They were not allowed to take anything with them in the way of money or clothing and were left totally at the mercy of the peasantry, who were not encouraged to offer them work or help. Kati found a smuggler who, for the promise of a large sum of money to be paid once she was out of the country, took her across the border to Austria.

A few weeks as a refugee marked Kati for life. She never forgot the indignity of having to ask for refuge and then being offered a school bench to sleep on. Of having to ask for money for food and then being sent to WÖK, the government-sponsored nonprofit restaurants where blue-collar workers and students ate. Uncle Denis, in Paris, put an end to her misery and got her a visa to France. The timing was perfect for me, since I wanted to go back to France. And Kati wanted to take me, offering a temporary solution to my mother's dilemma. Though again frightened that Kati would try to keep me, she gave in and allowed me to go back to France, "for a little while. Until I make a home here," she said, again.

I joyfully recrossed the Channel and felt as though I were going home. Kati was waiting for me at the train station. She saw me and let out a shriek.

"My God! What have they done to you? Has your mother lost her mind? You look like a *proli!*" (a pejorative word for the working class). A neglected permanent wave crowned my head and my clothes were from Cheltenham, not known for its fashionable attire.

Kati was staying with Uncle Denis and Aunt Eszter (aka Tante Denise) temporarily, and I went there too. It was a little cramped, but only my cousin Claude complained. But it was painfully clear that there was no room for me.

Aunt Eszter was immediately recruited to help rehabilitate me from a *"proli"* to a *"urilany,"* loosely translated as "young lady." For this transformation, however, we needed Uncle Denis. He had always had a soft spot for me.

"Well, how is perfide Albion?" he wanted to know.

"Huh?"

"England! England! Don't they teach you anything?"

"Well, I speak English and you don't," I answered saucily.

"My God, you sound just like your mother. How is the idiot?"

"Stop it, Denis. She's only a child!" snapped Aunt Eszter.

"My mother is fine. And she's not an idiot, so don't call her that!"

"Then why did she chose to be a servant in that meshugene country rather than have a decent life here?" he demanded.

"Because she couldn't stand your bossing her around. That's why! She's the only one with any guts in your family," countered Aunt Eszter.

Nobody answered. The rivalry between Uncle Denis and my mother was a sore subject. Uncle Denis was a bully, albeit a benevolent one most of the time. Kati and Klari knew how to get around him, how to butter him up, but my mother refused. She could never compromise, and her sisters never understood what they took to be plain stubbornness. He was the only male left in the immediate family, ergo the top authority. Everyone accepted this, except my mother.

Uncle Denis reached into his pockets, took out a fistful of bills. "Here. Make her look presentable, then we'll see what to do with her."

My hair was cut short, my nails clipped, cleaned, and polished. I got new clothes, hemmed above the knee. White gloves were added to my new wardrobe. Kati eyed me critically.

"All right. Not too bad. As soon as you're old enough we'll take care of the nose. The eyes are good. The skin is good. Your legs are long. You'll probably be tall. You won't look Jewish at all."

"What's wrong with looking Jewish? And anyway my mother says my nose is distinguished looking."

"Your mother knows nothing," she snorted. "Come on, I have a job for you. You will be my interpreter."

Kati's French was still very poor, so my services came in handy. We went to a very fashionable address on avenue de la Grande Armée.

Madame Pimbel was an older aristocratic lady who had fallen on hard times. She owned a magnificent apartment overlooking the Arc de Triomphe, but since her income consisted mainly of her late husband's military pension, she rented out a couple of rooms. The renters, however, had to be *"comme il faut."* Kati's beautifully coiffed blond hair and fashionable linen suit, and my impeccable manners (encouraged by sharp pinches on my thigh), convinced Mme Pimbel that we were indeed "comme il faut." Later, Uncle Denis would come and charm her with his accented French and his knowledge and admiration of French history. Of politics she said, referring to Mendès-France, "O, vous savez, il n'est pas du notre" ("Oh, you know, he's not one of us").

Meantime Kati rented, with Uncle Denis' money, a beautiful room with a balcony, tastefully furnished in Empire style, with a beautiful single-size daybed. So where was I going to live? So far nobody had said anything. When business was settled the conversation turned toward me.

"Where does this lovely child go to school?" inquired Mme Pimbel. I translated for Kati, putting the emphasis on *lovely.*

"We were just looking for a suitable place," cooed Kati. "She has just returned from a year in England . . . to . . . to improve her language skills. You know children learn so much faster."

"Oh, the best place is the Convent of Notre Dame in Bourg-la-Reine," offered Mme Pimbel. "All my nieces went there and received a wonderful Catholic education."

"Really? What a superb idea!" said Kati, while I stared at her, eyes wide, hoping she wasn't thinking what I thought she was thinking.

I was taken for an interview at Notre Dame by Kati and a friend of hers. Tante Denise thought the whole thing crazy. Uncle Denis wasn't paying much attention.

It was a fortresslike building in the middle of Bourg-la-Reine, a sleepy little town. Inside was cool and quiet. Little girls in navy blue uniforms sat primly inside glass-doored classrooms, and the singsong of childish voices reciting their lessons by rote, in true French fashion, came wafting out into the hallways as we were escorted to the mother superior's office. I sat and listened to Kati (translated by her friend) lie blatantly about our background, trying to explain why I hadn't made my First Communion. Then mother superior turned to me.

"What is your mother doing in England now?" she asked.

"She is a cook-housekeeper," I answered. Kati almost collapsed. She jumped in, looking daggers at me.

"No, no, no. She is just helping a friend. She will be coming back soon."

Mother superior was no fool. She probably thought that even if she couldn't save my soul she would try to save me from my family. I was accepted. On the way home, Kati exploded.

"How could you do that? How could you tell someone that your mother is a cook?"

"Why? It's honest work!"

"Don't give me that communist propaganda. I knew it by heart before you were born. There's no virtue in being a servant. People judge you by things like that. You have to move in the right circles, make the right friends. You never know who you're going to need. Don't be a fool like your mother."

"Stop talking about my mother that way!"

"She's my baby sister. I can talk about her any way I like. I've known her longer and better than you. Her problem is she's too good, too honest, and she has too much pride. And you're getting to be just like her."

"That's funny. She says I'm just like you, except that you don't have a sense of humor and everybody else in the family does."

"Evi, shut up!"

A week later I was ready to move into the convent. I made a last ditch effort to avoid this fate by appealing to Uncle Denis. He took me out to a grand lunch on the Champs-Élysées.

"Listen, Evi. Go to the convent. They have a good system. Learn all you can. Not just what's in the books but about *them.* Learn their ways. Learn their lingo. Learn about what makes them tick. It's the only way to beat them. This time we escaped. Who knows what's next. We have to arm ourselves. The only thing that can't be taken away from you is what's in your head. You and I are the only true survivors in this family. We're the ones who will always have to help the others. And by the way, send this to your mother. Tell her it's pocket money that I gave you and you saved it up." He handed me an envelope full of cash.

During the war, we had passed for Protestants. At the Château, we practiced Orthodox Judaism. In Cheltenham, I was indoctrinated into Spiritualism. My mother was an avowed atheist. Now I had to take on the Catholics.

A big blue trunk and I were deposited at the Convent of Notre Dame, ready for the beginning of the school year. Once again I entered an alien environment. The sight of the nuns filled me with apprehension and curiosity. Who and what were these saintly women, covered from head to toe, whose lives were supposedly devoted to God, who could never marry and have children? I expected a kind of holiness or serenity to emanate from them, and I was terribly disappointed that it never happened. Many of them were gentle, quite devoted to children and to teaching, but they seemed to me to be so unworldly, so childlike. They talked endlessly about Heaven, Purgatory, and Hell, the mortifying of the flesh, mortal sins, that one could not go to Heaven unless baptized and free of sin. They were so earnest I wondered whether they really thought that all this was true. And if so, where did that leave the other three-quarters of the world's population who were not Catholic? One did not ask these questions, neither did we argue about matters of faith. It all had to be accepted as a package. I reminded myself that I was Jewish and all this didn't apply to me, especially when a few of the nuns who were mean-spirited and sometimes even vicious took special pleasure in describing the horrors of Purgatory and Hell to us terrified children. I would on these occasions paint a sneer on my face, rebelling against their attempts to frighten me and half hoping that they would notice the contempt that I did my best to display. I did, however, think that getting baptized might be the prudent thing to do.

A nun took me up to the dormitory. It was a huge room with several rows of iron beds all painted white and made up with white sheets and rough dark gray blankets. It looked curiously like a mammoth checkerboard. There was a row of narrow closets along one wall, and along the longer wall thirty or so washbasins with built-in cabinets, fitted with little doors, beneath. My belongings were thoroughly examined before I was allowed to put them in their assigned places, and I was warned that my nighttable would be searched periodically. I couldn't begin to guess what it was that they would be looking for, and they didn't tell me. I met my class at lunch in the refectory. They were, on the whole, nice little girls, and I made friends immediately. Bedtime, on the other hand, was a shocker. A nun stood at the door and watched us get undressed to our undershirts and panties. When we were all ready, she announced "Aux lavabos!" and we all rushed to our assigned washbasin, where we were expected to brush our teeth and use a sponge to wash our faces and upper bodies without taking our shirts off. Next, she blew a whistle, the lights went off, and there was a clatter as everyone opened the little cabinet under the sink. When every cabinet was opened, all at right angles and parallel to each other, they formed little cubicles under each sink. Now, in the dark, protected on each side by a little door, we were expected to crouch down and wash "the lower parts of the body." I giggled. Wait till I tell my mother about this. She'll be so tickled! Uncle Denis, too. Kati? No. I wouldn't tell Kati. I remembered the Château where, just as one of the little girls would be preparing to take a bath we would all jump in with her and tweak one another's bottoms while laughing and splashing hysterically. We never thought of modesty or shame.

I eased into the life of the convent. The daily classes were, I imagine, not much different from other schools in the early fifties. Great emphasis was put on orthography, penmanship, precise historical dates, grammar. Not much room was left for imaginative thinking. We learned a great deal by rote, and whether we understood or not didn't seem to matter. The big difference between other schools and this one was the religious instruction. I was introduced to catechism. Because of my age I was put in the class where all the girls were preparing for their confirmation. I had seen in previous years, always in the month of June, myriads of little girls dressed, like little brides, in ruffled white dresses invade the streets with proud parents in attendance. I had always wondered what it was that they had to do for this privilege. When I asked anybody in my family, they shrugged their shoulders. It was something the goyim did. Three times a week a jolly, rotund little priest would come and give us instruction in catechism and prepare us for "our" confirmation. I kept very quiet in class, learned the questions and answers by rote, and asked no questions in order not to draw attention to myself. When my classmates asked me where I was getting my dress and what kind it would be, I said that it was being made in England, and if my mother were not able to come to France for the ceremony, I was going to wait and be confirmed later in England.

Actually, I really would have liked to be confirmed. I thought it wouldn't hurt to have a piece of paper to prove that I was a Catholic. Having the safety valve of papers to prove different identities, religions, or whatever was still very important to me. It was also the year that Maria Goretti was canonized, and this was a really big event at the convent. It made it a big honor to be confirmed that year. This fascinated me, and one weekend home with the family at the dinner table, I was telling them about it.

"Made into a saint?" asked Uncle Denis absentmindedly, looking up from his paper. "What for?"

"Well," I explained dutifully, "she was a young girl who was raped by a neighbor and then stabbed. But she forgave him before she died."

Uncle Denis gave a long, low whistle. "Boy, he must have been terrific!"

"Denis!" both aunts screamed at him. I blushed. Claude snickered.

"Oh, for heaven's sake. That's a saint? She probably got knocked up and was riding him about getting married, and being a stupid goy, he killed her."

Both aunts considered this explanation, cocked their heads to one side, then admitted that it was probably correct. Denis went on.

"They want saints? I'll give them saints! How about the little priest in Belgium who risked his neck every day for three years by hiding, feeding, and keeping alive twenty-six Jewish children? How about Admiral Canaris? How about six million Jews? Or aren't we good enough for them? How about your mother?"

"My mother?"

"Yes, your mother! Have you any idea what she went through those accursed years? I wonder how many of their saints could do what she did?"

"Well, they do have their martyrs," I protested. "But I think the idea is to forgive the tormentors."

Denis said something totally unprintable, then turning to Kati, said, "You'd better get her out of that place before they siphon off her brain to divide it among the two hundred shiksas there. I think they've already started!"

I felt guilty and a little angry. After all, it was Denis himself who had encouraged me to go there and learn. As for Catholicism, I found it fascinating. I liked learning about this religion, this other way of thinking. Even if I didn't agree, couldn't I just learn about it? Their religion was as important to them as ours to us. Actually more, it seemed. They practiced theirs constantly, while we seemed to be defending ours constantly but without practicing it too much. After that I left anything about religion out of the conversation. If asked about school, I kept strictly to the academic subjects.

Since I spoke English, I was put into one of the upper classes for language study. My classmates were sixteen years old. They were not interested in grammar. They wanted to know colloquialisms, flirtatious phrases, and swearwords. Pretty soon Rose Davis's "sex education" became handy as a subject of secret conversations, and from there it was only a hop, skip, and a jump to Spiritual-ism. Before long Ouija boards were snuck in and table legs were tapping all over the place. Not for long, of course. The nuns' espionage system must have rivaled the KGB. We were caught and the older girls punished. Denis and Kati were called in. My influence on the other students was called into question.

"But," argued Denis, "why is a twelve year old responsible for the behavior of a bunch of sixteen year olds? Shouldn't they have exerted their good influence on her?"

Mother superior was stumped, and I was given another chance. Kati was livid; Denis, amused; and I, confused. What had I done that was such a big deal? Could I go home? No! Where would I live? There was no "home." So the drab, disciplined life of the convent continued, with a respite from Saturday afternoon to Sunday afternoon when Kati would come for me and take me to Paris.

Everything would probably have continued normally had it not been for Friday mornings. On that day we had to go to Mass first thing in the morning, without breakfast. The service was quite long, and the little chapel, filled to capacity, was hot and stifling. Every Friday at about the same place in the service I started feeling faint, and before I had a chance to pass out, a nun would quietly shove me out into the fresh air of the playground, where I had to wait for the rest of them. One time ambling around the playground, I picked up some gravel and began idly tossing the small stones into a garden that was separated from the playground by an iron fence. The garden was hardly visible as there were thick bushes lining the fence on the other side. One of the stones, however, hit something hard, and I realized that there was a stone statue of some kind, half hidden in the overgrown bushes. I started aiming for it just to hear the "plonk!" of the stone hitting the concrete. Two little girls who were also in the playground, probably for the same reason as I, came over and asked if they could join me. We became happily engaged in tossing the little stones and seeing who could hit the statue—until the head of an incensed nun popped out and stopped us in our tracks. This was too much! It turned out that the statue was that of the Virgin Mary. This time there was no question that it was my bad influence, this time exerted over younger girls, and that what I had done was sacrilegious!

Kati was called and politely but firmly asked to remove me from the premises posthaste.

I could have explained and apologized. But I didn't. I wanted out. I wanted someone in the family to take me in and give me a proper home. Surely now they had to do it! Except nobody did. I was shipped back to London, with lots of presents, lots of kisses, promises of visits, and instructions on how to behave like a "young lady" (as opposed to my mother, no doubt). My mother and I had a wonderful reunion, and within a month I was living at the Jewish Orphanage of West Norwood, under the aegis of the Jewish Board of Guardians.

Norwood Jewish Orphanage, 1951–1954

West Norwood, SW 27, is part of London's sprawling metropolis. A working-class neighborhood, it is connected to the West End by several bus lines and a train from Victoria Station. It's pretty much the same now as it was in 1951, except that the shopkeepers are mostly either East or West Indians, traffic is much heavier and now flows along one-way streets that once carried motorists in both direcions, and the old cinema is boarded up. But Saint Luke's Church, with its faded yellow façade and ancient cemetery, still stands at the bottom of Knight's Hill; I remember its dank basement where we gathered once a week for Girl Guide meetings. The same Woolworth's is still there, offering temptation to young would-be shoplifters, as it did to us. It's so easy to remember it the way it was.

The orphanage was diagonally across from the railroad station. Its long, sloping driveway led up from the street so that the building was not immediately visible to passersby. When it did come into view, it was as a surprise. In that neighborhood of tiny, brick, attached houses with little shops, it looked enormous in its Victorian pomposity. It had several acres of grounds, including a soccer field and a large grassy area in the back. Built in the heavy, fussy style of the late nineteenth century, it had a large, elaborate entrance hall with a grand staircase, flanked by a wing on each side that conveniently allowed for a girls' and a boys' wing. Behind the entrance hall was the huge, baronial-style dining hall and, just beyond, the cavernous, old-fashioned kitchens. Wide corridors led off to the left and the right. Each wing had a covered quadrangle that served as our meeting place, with basketball and netball courts and the occasional free-for-all arena. On the far end of the "quads" were the "family rooms." Children were divided up into age groups of up to fifteen members. These groups were called "families." Each family had its own family room, which was its social center, its own dormitory and bathrooms on the second floor, and its own table in the dining hall. Each family also had its own housemother or housefather, the adult responsible for the welfare of the children—the surrogate parent.

On the third floor was the synagogue, where we spent our Saturday mornings. There was also a well-equipped sick bay with matron in attendance, a "linen room" with a full-time employee, and a library. It was all organized in true British fashion, real shipshape. Occasionally, it even worked that way.

The atmosphere was very different from the Château's, where everybody knew everybody else and everything about them; where, no matter what their current circumstances, the children had all come from well-to-do, educated backgrounds. At this orphanage the children were a ragtag lot. Some were budding juvenile delinquents, some pathetic, abandoned orphans from extreme poverty, and others left orphaned because of the war. A few like me, though for various reasons, could not live at home with surviving parents. Many hadn't even the vaguest notion of the manners or other niceties one picks up automatically when living in a socialized environment. They spoke back, hit, did or didn't do whatever they wanted, and feared no one. I hadn't known that there was such a thing as a Jewish "lower class," and I wasn't thinking economics, only education. I had always taken it for granted that Jews were educated.

Each family was a microcosm of the society around us. We had our leaders, our bullies, our victims, our quiet little bookworms. Little cliques formed, mainly to exclude others. We had the "goody-goodies" (informants). We had the rebels. The smart ones and the stupid ones. "The babies" and "the toughies." And we had Mr. Conway, the headmaster who enforced discipline with a cane and whose two boys, though living on the premises, were housed in private quarters and not allowed to fraternize with us.

I arrived there already hardened to communal life. I had experienced an orphanage, a foster home, a convent, living with various families and family members in various countries. What could be so different?

My first encounter with Mr. Conway went as follows.

"What's your name?"

"Evelyne." (I pronounced it the French way, "Ev'lyn.")

"Oh, heavens, no! Not another one. Do you have a middle name?"

"Yes, Juliette."

"Good. We have enough Evelyns (pronounced the English way), so from now on you'll be called Juliette. Don't forget it!"

I didn't. It didn't seem to matter to me what name I was called. At Norwood and at school, I became Juliette. On my passport and to my French family, I was Evelyne. To my mother and Hungarian family, I was Evi.

School started and everyone over eleven was enrolled in the local secondary modern on Gypsy Hill. In the British educational system, children were sorted at the age of eleven according to their eleven-plus test scores. Top grades went to high school to prepare for college. The next level were sent to trade schools, and the rest to secondary modern, where they graduated at fifteen and then entered the workforce. I had not taken the test, nor had anyone asked me to.

Gypsy Hill was overenrolled, so five children had to be sent a bus ride away to Brixton. Mr. Conway took great pains to pick out five, those he thought were the best behaved. We had to know how to behave on the bus, in a different neighborhood where nobody knew us. The honor of the orphanage was at stake!

It was the standard school in the standard working-class neighborhood. Dull and depressing, with too few (and overworked) teachers for too many under-privileged children. In the gray concrete school yard at recess, the local children were anxious to know where we were from, especially me, as I spoke with a strange accent.

"The Jewish orphanage? No! You can't be Jewish. Jews have 'orns. My father told me."

"You were born in Paris? Co'r! Are all people there beautiful? And do they all 'ave long silk dresses?"

"Can you invite me to tea? I want to see what orphans are like."

We rolled our eyes heavenward. We felt superior to our classmates and told them all kinds of outlandish tales about our lives, which they believed and relished.

I did well in class. The nuns and Mme Salle had done their job. I was far ahead of the little Brits. So much so that I came to the attention of my teacher, Miss Peacock, and she changed the course of my life. She was an elderly spinster devoted to improving the lives of the children under her care. She questioned me at length about my background and tutored me in English during recess. A few weeks later, she took me to Saint Martin-in-the-Fields High School for Girls and introduced me to her friend, Miss Gordon-Ewen, the headmistress, with whom she had attended university.

Saint Martin's is the oldest girls' school in England, established in 1699 by the Church of Saint Martin-in-the-Fields in Trafalgar Square. Its first home was a room above a baker's shop, with eight girls from "good" families. In the 1920s, having outgrown its cramped quarters near the church, the school acquired a beautiful piece of property in Tulse Hill, halfway between Norwood and Brixton, where a modern school had been built, complete with playing fields and tennis courts. The school has a long and distinguished history. The president of the board of governors was Her Grace the Duchess of Marlborough; the chairman, the Reverend Austin Williams, the vicar of the great church. Under the 1944 Education Act, the school started receiving aid and no longer collected private tuition, but retained a certain independence in return for undertaking obligations regarding maintenance of scholastic standards and improvements to the building.

There was a long discussion between the two women, after which I was administered a battery of tests: Miss Denton tested me in math; Miss Free asked me to write an essay in English; Miss Foster, in French (No problems there!); Miss Pierce asked me about my knowledge of history; and Miss Wheeler about Latin. I passed.

Back at the orphanage, Mr. Conway almost had a coronary attack when Miss Peacock told him what she had done without his knowledge. It was impossible, he said. There was no way that I could be singled out to go to a different school. There was no money for the special uniform. How dare she interfere in the lives of the children, and so on. Miss Peacock stood her ground. Her business was education; her aim to secure for children the best education that was available according to their ability. "What about their circumstances?" Mr. Conway wanted to know. "How would I feel being the only Jewish girl in the school?" Considering that I had spent the time during the German occupation denying my Jewishness and the better part of the previous year in a Catholic convent, it seemed like a silly question. Battle lines were drawn: Miss Peacock demanding that I be allowed to fulfill my potential, Mr. Conway equally determined not to have any exceptions made. Miss Peacock won. She went above his head and petitioned the board of guardians of the orphanage, who, to everyone's surprise, not only agreed to let me go to Saint Martin's but asked whether the following year other children might be allowed to take the entrance exam.

Mr. Conway treated me differently after that day. On the one hand, he was proud that one of his children had been accepted to a prestigious high school and introduced me to any visitor who came to the orphanage. On the other hand, he knew that his authority had been thwarted, and he made me pay for it in subtle ways. To practice the piano, I had to get up before anyone else, because the only piano was in his office and only available to me before breakfast. He made no effort to spare me the embarrassment of having to wear a secondhand uniform straight out of the school's charity box, and whenever my behavior did not measure up, the comment was, "Well, for someone attending Saint Martin's one would expect better!"

We were resentful of Norwood's management of our lives. But we were so needy that no matter what had been offered, nothing would have been enough. Nevertheless, the orphanage provided us with as decent a life as could be expected during the postwar years. We were well fed, well clothed, and sheltered. Our education was designed to make us useful members of society, not to reach a higher level thereof.

There were regular visits by the trustees. One of them, Mr. Shapiro, sought me out. "So, you're the smart one who got into Saint Martin's. We expect big things from you!" On each visit he made a point of spending a few minutes with me and inquiring about my schoolwork.

Discipline was strict at Norwood, but not unreasonable, and I can't think of a single instance of abuse. Neither can I remember any special show of affection toward any child by any of our caretakers. Life was tolerable, organized, but hardly joyful. Fortunately there was a very liberal policy regarding visiting privileges. With permission from our housemother, we could invite school friends over to tea and we could also accept invitations. Those who had family could visit them on weekends and invite friends to go along. This policy prevented isolation from, and exposed us to, the world outside—a double-edged sword. We saw what family life could really be like. Much depended on whom one had for a housemother or housefather. Some of them liked children and could cope, others were woefully lacking and made themselves miserable and us rebellious. (Many of the housemothers were German Jews who had emigrated before the war.)

Mrs. Jacobs, though probably the oldest, was the most popular. She was grandmotherly and good-humored. Hers were the eleven to twelve year olds. She walked with difficulty, the outside edges of her shoe soles trodden down to almost an inch less than the inside. She shuffled along slowly and preferred to sit in her well-worn easy chair, from whence came instructions in her guttural German accent to do our various chores and her best help with our homework. Miss Salzmann, on the other hand, either feared or disliked children. In her German, humorless fashion, she marched us to and from the dining hall, to and from the dormitory, demanded quiet in the family room, forbade certain kinds of music on the radio, and showed more concern with the state of our underwear than that of our minds.

A humiliating moment in my life was when she discovered a drawer full of dirty socks in the bureau next to my bed. For some reason that I can't remember, instead of washing my socks I kept putting them away dirty, intending to get to them eventually. But I kept procrastinating, and finally on one of her inspection tours into our private bureaus, she discovered my stash of smelly socks. She claimed that when she opened the drawer the stench made her sick to her stomach, and she took great pains in imparting this information to anyone within earshot. I wanted to kill her. My saving grace was that I was more popular than she, both among the housemothers and the girls. Mrs. Jacobs, passing me in the hallway, gave me a half smile.

"You're too old to do things like that. Especially if you're in Salzmann's family!"

We took great pride in the fact that many housemothers resigned within a very short period of time. We actually made bets on how long some would last. Those of German Jewish background proved the most tenacious.

The ultimate authority regarding discipline in the girls' quarters was Matron. A formidable figure at the orphanage, Matron was the only person that we were in awe of. She was of "true" British stock, not Jewish. She treated people with a certain noblesse oblige whenever it was obvious to her that they didn't know how to behave because they had not had the good fortune to have been born British and/or Church of England. She seemed cold and remote, and she spoke very little. Fights often broke out among the kids. Girls as well as boys resorted to fisticuffs. The girls would add scratching and hair pulling to the punching and kicking. When the housemothers or housefathers were unable or too frightened to stop the melee, Matron invariably appeared. The circle around the combatants opened up and she would manage to grab one or both culprits by the scruff of the neck, pull them up straight, and in a truly British, Oxford-accented, no-nonsense, peremptory tone say something quite banal like "Now, stop this silly nonsense!"—but with such authority that, amazingly, they did just that. She looked them over and if one of them were bleeding or had a black eye, she sent them up to sick bay to be tended. She then turned to the rest of us looking as though she were distastefully studying a lower form of life. Without having to hear another word, we all slunk away.

We didn't see much of Matron. Every two or three days there would be "inspection" after breakfast. Each table in turn got up at the end of the meal and filed past her on the way out. We stopped in front of her and held out our hands, which she inspected. First palms up, then palms down. Next, we stuck out our tongues for scrutiny. Her eyes flicked over us, checking for cleanliness and neatness. If we passed muster, we were dismissed. If not, we were directed to sick bay. This last option usually created great inner conflict. It could mean staying home from school. It could also mean staying in sick bay with Matron in attendance.

One day during inspection, as I was standing in front of her, she looked at me and said, "You have beautiful hair. Keep it that way!" I blushed. Compliments were not her strong suit, and I hadn't received enough to know how to respond graciously. Actually it didn't really sound like a compliment; more like a statement of fact with a direct order attached. All the girls in my "family" had heard her and responded in the way that we always responded to Matron. What she said was gospel. From that day on, Juliette had beautiful hair! Matron had said so.

I received another compliment from Matron during the three or so years that I spent at Norwood. One evening a horrendous argument broke out between Evelyn Liebman, a generally well-behaved, athletic, blond teenager and Miss Pappenheim, our current housemother, prim and mousy. Miss Pappenheim was a fussy middle-aged spinster without any understanding or sympathy toward teenagers, orphaned or otherwise. Her heavy German accent, pinched, prunelike face, and high-pitched voice made her an object of ridicule among us. Her attempts at discipline were a dismal failure, which, very obviously to us, put her beneath contempt in Matron's eyes. That day, Evelyn spoke back. One word followed another, escalated into screams, and finally Evelyn raised her fist. Miss Pappenheim fled, pulling the door behind her to close it. The top half of the door was glass, and the momentum of Evelyn's blow carried her arm right through it. Blood gushed from a severed artery; I remember the look of utter astonishment on Evelyn's face. For a moment everything stopped. Then, as the shock wave passed: pandemonium! Miss Pappenheim, in a panic, ran off shouting, "Help, Help!" and was not heard from again for hours. Of the other girls who were there, one was gagging at the sight of the blood, others fled screaming, and another one was staring at Evelyn, eyes wide, rooted to the spot. I had just come in from a Girl Guide meeting and had only witnessed the last minute or so of the argument and accident. I was wearing my uniform of crisp blue shirt, red tie, and navy blue wool skirt. I remember a feeling of resignation. I knew that I was going to get blood all over my uniform. I took off my tie, sat Evelyn onto a chair, and started making a tourniquet on her arm the way I had learned to do at meetings. I turned to Miriam Fishman, the girl who was standing there looking at us as though in shock, and said, "Go get Matron. Tell her to come quickly. There's been an accident."

I was left alone with Evelyn, who by now was sobbing in great big gulps. "I'm going to die. I'm going to die. All because of that bitch Pappenheim!"

Matron rushed in with Nurse Fowler, took in the scene with one glance, checked the tourniquet; Evelyn was whisked away, not to be seen for six weeks. She then returned from the hospital, a real heroine in our eyes.

Meanwhile, I was left alone in my stained uniform, standing in a pool of Evelyn's blood. I started cleaning up. Slowly, methodically, I mopped, wiped off the chairs, picked up the broken glass. When I was finished I sat down. There was no one around. It was getting dark. Matron suddenly appeared.

"Come with me," she ordered.

I followed her, and we made our way to sick bay. She handed me a robe and told me to take off my stained uniform. She left me while I changed my clothes. When she came back, she handed me a big mug of cocoa.

"You did a good job, Juliette," she said. It was all she said.

This woman has remained an enigma to me. I wonder still what made her work in that place, rather than in any of the hospitals that were always understaffed. She didn't show us any love or even sympathy, but we grudgingly admitted that she always treated us fairly. She demanded respect and gave it when it was due. Ramrod straight, severe-looking, and sexless, she brought something into our lives that we had not experienced before: order. Indeed, Matron seemed to embody British Order and Discipline. The chaos of the previous years still raged within me, and her unwavering British sense of duty and order and her unemotional manner gave me a sense of security. I was not afraid of her as most of the other kids were. I admired how she commanded respect and authority.

I quickly forgot about her, along with as much else as I could, when I left Norwood. Now many years later, her image keeps tugging at my memory. By treating me with respect, she planted the seeds of self-respect. I acknowledge a debt of thanks to Matron, whose real name, I found out later, was Matron Darling.

The orphanage had a rhythm of its own. We did things according to the quirky schedule that an institution demands to make it work. To deviate even the slightest bit from the usual routine required tremendous organizational changes since a few hundred peoples' schedules would have had to be reprogrammed.

On school days, we came home and got ready for "tea," the main meal of the day. We then assembled in our family rooms for homework. After homework there was free time, depending on the day of the week. At eight o'clock we had to polish our shoes. At eight thirty, supper trays (peanut butter and jelly sandwiches or bread with beef drippings) were brought to the family room, and then we went to bed. On Tuesday and Thursday evenings, and Sunday mornings, there were two hours of Hebrew instruction. It became a sport to see who could get out of it with the most creative excuse. On Wednesdays those who wished could go to Boy Scout or Girl Guide meetings. This, however, always created a scheduling problem that was never resolved. Wednesday was the day that the laundry came back and had to be sorted. All socks were dropped into a big basket to be paired and returned to the rightful owner (our names were written into our socks); one then had to check for holes and start darning. It was not a skill that everyone had, and I racked up quite a few favors for darning my friends' socks. I was fast and good at it. The problem was that it all had to be finished on Wednesday night, the night of my Girl Guide meetings.

Once a week we were given pocket money, six pence each. Everybody had a bankbook, and we were expected to save part of our allowance. I couldn't. Every penny was accounted for. One went into the Girl Guide box, two pence was for my weekly Roundtree chocolate bar, and three pence was allotted to the thrill of the week, *School Friend*. This was the most exciting weekly comic book geared to schoolgirls. We could hardly wait for Thursday afternoons, when on our way home from school we stopped at the local candy shop to pick up our copy. I read it from cover to cover, relishing every adventure of the blond, blue-eyed, upper-class English heroines, with names like Imogen and Millicent, who had been denied their birthright by a greedy relative and discovered proof of this by exploring dangerous, hidden underground passages in their ancestral homes. They were always saved, in the nick of time, by the gentle, seemingly bumbling (but handsome) hero, whom they had originally despised. They then lived happily ever after in a splendid platonic relationship.

Mrs. Jacobs shook her head. "Three pennies for this? Better you should put it in the bank!"

The adults were there to look after our physical needs and to keep us in line. It never occurred to us to confide in them. Problems, feelings, sadness, loneliness, or even the occasional treat from home were all reserved for our "best friend"—for those of us lucky enough to have one. Mine was Elsa: a quiet, studious girl with an infectious laugh, shiny black curls, and very large dark eyes. We were a natural duo. We were different from the others. We generally kept to ourselves and read anything we could lay our hands on. Though hardly "goody-goodies," the adults considered us responsible and generally well behaved. We rarely got into trouble, especially Elsa. Though when she did, she did it in style. Once, she was caught red-handed in the branches of an irate farmer's apple tree, nonchalantly helping herself and throwing down a bountiful harvest to the other miscreants on the ground, who departed posthaste when the farmer showed up with a shotgun, leaving Elsa to face the music alone.

With teenage boys and girls under one roof, there were always plenty of ways to break the rules. Nothing serious ever happened, but often our aim was to make life harder for the adults around us. The big "dare" was the midnight raid. This meant getting up in the middle of the night and sneaking over to the boys' side of the building, or vice versa, without getting caught. Once we arrived, there was the problem of what to do. Sex was not yet an option. We didn't think boys were *that* great! There were occasional smoochy kisses and clumsy groping among the most daring, of which I was not one. No one was ever going to touch me! The very thought of it brought on chills of disgust. Having a "boyfriend," though, was very important, especially if the boy was good-looking or smart or popular. When one had such a prize, it was expected that he was one's official smooching partner. We were certainly not mature enough to admit that we were not interested in such activities. The catch-22 for me was to get a boyfriend for appearance's sake and not engage in any activity that I found distasteful. Fortunately there was David Myers. He was a smart and good-looking boy who, to my great delight, felt very much as I did. We talked and read together and generally enjoyed each other's company. We even tried kissing once but decided that we didn't particularly like it. When anyone asked about our "activities," we both smiled slyly and giggled. Let everybody think what they liked. We let our sleeping hormones lie.

Both Elsa and I were generally liked. We were not particularly sought out, but we were "safe." Neither adults nor children feared us. We shunned cliques, didn't start arguments, didn't tattle or tease. We were a negative-plus. And I had an extra edge with the boys and the housefathers. I could draw pinups! Since early childhood I've had a facility with a pencil and could draw, with a few quick lines, caricatures that made people laugh. What the boys liked were the busty, sexy, curvy pinups (this was before the days of *Playboy* magazine) that I knocked out in a few seconds, which they in turn could swap for candy or whatever. Some of the housefathers liked them, too, and I exchanged them for certain privileges or treats. One housefather provided me with fresh drawing pads whenever I needed any!

Some of the kids considered Elsa and me "eggheads" because we liked to read. But our two resident bullies, Shirley Bligh and Sheila Goldman, natural best friends, gave up on us. We were not good victims. Without conscious awareness, we countered their taunts by not acknowledging that they were attempting to bully us. Shirley was a dark, chubby, prematurely well-developed girl with sneaky eyes and a defiant manner. Her sidekick, Sheila, was heavy and awkward-looking, with kinky blond hair and vacant blue eyes. Neither was too bright. They would come up to us in the communal bathroom, and Shirley, thrusting her size 38D-cup breasts forward, would taunt, "Hey you two, you think you'll ever grow any tits?"

Elsa and I looked at each other, an immediate understanding passing between us. We shrugged our shoulders, smiled sweetly, and one of us took up the challenge. "I suppose we will eventually. It takes a little longer when one is small and slim and not overweight!"

The other girls around us, usual victims of Shirley's and Sheila's nastiness, giggled, delighted that their tormentors had been brought down a peg. Shirley glared. "Oh, you two think you're so smart. Just you wait!" she threatened. Then she swiped one of the smaller girls on the shoulder and for good measure added, "What do you think is so funny, you little runt?"

Most of the housemothers were afraid of those two girls, so they ignored them, giving them tacit leave to make the other girls' lives miserable.

There was another reason why the bullies usually gave me a wide berth. Very soon after my arrival to Norwood, one of the oldest girls, she must have been fifteen (as we all had to leave at that age), was disciplining a younger child in a very harsh way. The little girl was howling, and the older one was holding her by the ear and tugging at it.

"Leave her alone," I said. "Can't you see you're hurting her?"

"Mind your own business, Frenchie!" she retorted and kept at it.

I got between her and the child. "I said leave her alone."

She let go of the child, who ran off as fast as her skinny little legs could carry her, and put her face close to mine. She was three years older and a full head taller than I.

"I told you to mind your own business, you bloody little French pip-squeak. So BUZZ OFF!" She punctuated the last two words with such sharp punches to my left shoulder that I reeled back. I lost it. I had an absolute horror of being touched, and being attacked has always evoked in me a feeling of uncontrollable rage that has taken me many years to restrain. I drew back my arm and with all my strength hit her in the face with my open palm. For a moment she was so astonished that she couldn't react. Then I saw the look on her face, her eyes narrowed, her teeth clenched. I knew that I was in for the fight of my life. I didn't care. The only way I could lose was by dying, and that was a better option than allowing myself to be hit! By the time she collected herself and lunged at me, I was ready. I fell on her kicking and punching, scratching and biting. I don't know what she did to me because I couldn't feel anything, except her hair in my grasp and the taste of her blood in my mouth. Like a whirlwind in a fury, I couldn't stop. I just kept lashing with everything I could. Legs, arms, fingers, teeth, knees, everything was moving furiously. I was vaguely aware of shouting in the background, but nothing was deterring me from my wish to maim. Finally, two very strong arms pried me loose, and a housefather carried me away still shaking and crying from rage. We were both taken to sick bay. The girl was crying.

"She's crazy, she's crazy! Look what she did. I probably have rabies!"

Fortunately for me, it was Matron's day off. Nurse Fowler cleaned me up, shook her head, and said, "Very nice, very nice indeed!" Then she made me drink a cup of tea to calm me down, but I vomited for hours afterward. Curiously, I was never punished. Nothing more was ever said. The other girl left the orphanage very soon after. This performance earned me a dubious reputation: Don't mess with her. She's crazy!

Elsa never had to resort to such drastic actions. She had a quiet strength about her. She could take teasing up to a point, then she got a look in her eyes. It was clear warning: Enough! Or else! As far as I know, nobody ever dared to test her.

Elsa had a much older brother, who used to come and visit her and sometimes take her out. She never talked about having any other family. A long time elapsed before she confided in me. She used to come with me occasionally when I visited my mother. We explored the West End of London, went to the cinema, and my mother would prepare a feast for us. We always had a good time. Then, she asked me if I'd like to go with her and visit her mother. I didn't let on how surprised I was. I had assumed that she was an orphan. All I remember was a dark and gloomy apartment, with a dark and gloomy lady. She seemed too old to be Elsa's mother until I remembered that she had a much older brother. The visit was nothing like the ones to my mother. Elsa's mother never laughed or joked with us like mine did. She sat alone observing us, like old grandmothers do when they have lost the strength and will to deal with the young. Elsa's mother was sick. She suffered from paranoia. Her father had left long ago, before Elsa was born. He was from South Africa, so Elsa had no other relatives that she knew of. Her brother and her mother were her only family. I, on the other hand, had a whole slew of relatives, all slightly crazy, all strewn around the continent, and all still struggling to salvage the life that the war had taken away.

Just about the time that I arrived at Norwood, the terrible consequences of Kati's defection from Hungary bore fruit.

In 1951, when Kati fled Hungary, she had left part of the money for the smuggler in Klari's hands, with instructions to hand it over on demand once she was safely out of the country. Klari, in her typical scatterbrained fashion, decided to take matters into her own incapable hands. No one in the family, to this day, really knows what happened to the money. Kati claimed that Klari spent it. Klari claimed that Kati's boyfriend showed up and asked for it, saying that he would pass it on. The upshot was that the smuggler did not get his money. Later, when he was caught by the authorities, he named Klari as an accessory, probably in revenge for not having received his fee. She was arrested, tortured, and imprisoned in the notorious Kistarcsa jail, where she spent four years. Meanwhile, Peter was left on his own. Uncle Laci, Klari's new husband, largely ignored him, busy with his many lady friends. Our grandfather was similarly employed. The three males shared the old apartment, but Peter had to fend largely for himself. Kati, my mother, and Denis sent packages full of things to be sold for food and necessities. What was not stolen by the customs officials, Uncle Laci generously distributed among his own numerous brothers and sisters. Grandfather grabbed what he could, and Peter was left with very meager pickings. His clothing became increasingly threadbare, and food became a luxury. Every Sunday he got on his ancient and rusty bicycle and pedaled twenty miles so his mother could catch a glimpse of him from the prison windows. He kept going to school, his dream of becoming a doctor untarnished. Most of this we found out much later, since communication with any country behind the Iron Curtain was very limited. Mail was censored, travel practically nonexistent. We just knew that they were in need, and whenever I visited my mother, one of my chores was to haul the heavy packages to the post office.

Meanwhile, I lived at the orphanage. My life continued on an evermore divergent path from that of the rest of the family.

Religion was an aspect of my life that was always in conflict. We hated Hebrew classes. Our teachers were the very religious members of the local synagogue, who were very rigid and humorless. The younger children were taught Bible stories and Hebrew songs, but after the age of ten we were expected to study and translate from the Old Testament. Six hours a week plus Saturday morning services was too much, and most of us rebelled against it one way or another.

The synagogue was on the third floor, and to make sure that we all attended services we had to assemble, family by family, at the bottom of the stairs and be counted as we went up. Nobody, however, counted us as we arrived. A favorite ploy to "cut services" was to go up the stairs, as expected, and not stop at the synagogue entrance, but keep going up another half a flight to the roof. There, those who were daring enough snuck across the roof, entered another stairwell, waited till services started, and then snuck down those stairs and out a side door. One of the local cinemas, which usually played vintage films, was only half a block away, and that was the destination of the escapees. The movies always ended before services, so there was enough time to retrace our steps and be back in line to join those coming out of the synagogue. I did this once. Only once!

That Saturday I allowed myself to be persuaded by Lillian to play hooky. Braving the roof and the possible wrath of Mr. Conway, I, along with a sprinkling of boys, snuck off to the movies.

Lillian Jacobs was one of the "tough girls." Afraid of nothing and no one, she was our Robin Hood. She defended the weaker ones against the staff or the bullies and always did whatever she wanted regardless of the consequences. I envied her and she tolerated me. The cinema was playing *The Phantom of the Opera,* with Claude Rains. It scared me out of my wits. My terror was probably heightened by my fear of getting caught. I wanted to leave, but where was I going to go? I couldn't sneak back by myself, and if I wandered the streets, someone I knew could spot me and ask embarrassing questions. I was stuck in the dark with the disfigured phantom.

We got back without getting caught and, it seemed, without any consequences. Till that night. I lay awake afraid to close my eyes, the vision of the phantom in front of me. I bolted upright in my bed, seeking him and fearing to see him in the darkness of the dormitory. Terrified, I listened to the even breathing of the fourteen other girls, fast asleep in their narrow beds around the perimeter of the enormous room, while I tried to stay awake to stave off any possible attack, finally falling asleep from sheer exhaustion. My vigils lasted about a week, after which God forgave me my lapse and let me sleep in peace!

Our rebellion against the formal display of our religion did not show the way we really felt. In another way we were quite devout. We were proud of being Jews. We loved hearing about Jews who had made good, who were famous. When we heard of someone achieving a great feat, we asked "Is he Jewish?" and we were disappointed if he were not. In front of strangers, we practiced our religion fiercely, conspicuously eating only kosher foods and being careful to say the correct *Brochas* (blessings). Being Jewish was the only thing that identified us. We were "We" and they were "Them," the goyim! We knew and felt that we were outsiders, and were defiantly proud of it. We had survived in spite of the rest of the world so F.U. all! We had what is called an "attitude." But not the swaggering adolescent attitude of the 1990s. Ours was grim and relentless. We were angry and hostile.

When the summer holidays came, most of the children stayed at the orphanage the whole summer. I was one of the luckier ones. I was able to spend some time with my family; sometimes with my mother, depending on where she was working at the time. Or I went to France and stayed with Aunt Eszter and my cousin Claude. Hungary was no longer accessible. It was behind the Iron Curtain.

Quite often the orphanage was able to send us to either a summer camp or to families who lived in resort locales and offered, sometimes for a fee, sometimes gratis, to give poor Jewish children a couple of weeks away from the city. I remember two such vacations. During my first summer at Norwood, three older boys and I were sent to a family in Southend-on-Sea, a seaside resort on the southeast coast of England. The family consisted of Emma, a tarty-looking woman with a cigarette hanging out of her mouth most of the time, her burly husband who was never home, and their slightly mentally handicapped son of about ten.

Emma seemed very disappointed when she saw me arrive with the boys; she ignored me completely and concentrated on them. She gave them seductive looks, brushed up against them, fondled their behinds, and walked around the house in a clingy silk robe, with nothing underneath and one sleeve falling off and baring her shoulder. The boys loved it. I, on the other hand, blushed to the roots of my hair while she made off-color remarks to the boys, who thought that she was the greatest thing that had ever came down the pike!

We went to see the annual summer parade down by the pier. As we stood on the crowded sidewalk waiting for the parade to start, we began chatting with two old women who were standing in front of us. They told us that they lived in Southend all year long. I remarked on how lucky they were, but wondered what it was like during the winter.

"It's much better than in the summer," one of them replied. "There aren't any Jews here then!"

Nobody said anything. The boys looked embarrassed. Emma pretended that she had not heard. I felt myself grow red in the face and then heard myself say, very loudly, "It might interest you to know that we are Jewish!"

Again, silence. Someone tapped me on the shoulder. I looked back. A tall young blond couple was standing behind me. The woman smiled at me. "Good for you!" she said. I smiled back, so relieved.

On the way home, Emma grumbled, "You didn't have to make a scene. Everybody knows me here!"

At dinner that night she served us Spam. And I snitched. I called the orphanage on the telephone and sanctimoniously told Mr. Conway that we had been sent to a home that was not kosher. We were immediately fetched and taken back to London. The boys never forgave me.

The other summer holiday was quite wonderful. It was the summer of 1952. I was picked to go to a summer camp on the border of Wales, near Oswestry, where a lot of French children had been sent. I spoke French for two whole weeks, acted as interpreter for the staff, and fell in love with Jean-Pierre, the incredibly handsome and gentle junior counselor for the French kids. He never knew it, of course. But he became my friend, and we wandered the Welsh hills, attended sheepdog trials (contests), lolled on the beaches of Rhyl and Llundudno; he even gave me the lead in the play that we put on for our farewell performance. We corresponded till at least the end of that year.

Through my mother's various jobs, I met some very interesting people and my friends envied me. One of my mother's employers was Mr. Baron Nahum, court photographer, friend of Prince Philip, Duke of Edinburgh, and of Ninette de Valois, director of the Sadler's Wells Ballet, now the Royal Ballet. He offered to get me a scholarship to the ballet school. Unfortunately I showed not even an ounce of talent for dance, and that career never got a chance.

Mr. Baron often allowed me to stay weekends with my mother at his mews house in Mayfair. When he gave dinner parties, I helped my mother in the kitchen and got peeks at many of the rich and famous that he entertained and that my mother cooked for. I regaled my friends with stories about the people that I had seen, what my mother had cooked for them, and occasionally what the conversation had been around the dining table; the latter only when it was loud enough for me to hear from the darkened hallway outside the dining room, where I crouched and shamelessly eavesdropped.

My mother always picked her jobs well and prided herself on working for interesting and mostly very rich people. Another family that she worked for was the Westons. Mr. Weston was a Canadian magnate, "the Ryvita king." He manufactured the cracker of that name and other brands of bread and cookies. They were immensely wealthy, and I got a good look at the lifestyle of the very rich. The Westons had several children, six or seven. The two younger ones were around my age, and one summer I was allowed to stay at their magnificent estate in

Buckinghamshire. It was a beautiful and grand house, with woods, flower and vegetable gardens, greenhouses, and extensive lawns leading down to the banks of the Thames. The house was furnished with things that I had before only seen in museums. The whole of my Aunt Eszter's lovely Parisian apartment could have fit into their vast living room. When there was no one around I would explore the house, inspecting paintings, rugs, furniture, and sculptures at leisure. It amazed me that people could own such things. I had no envy, since it never occurred to me that I could also own pretty or valuable things. That right belonged to the privileged, and I was not one of them. The home where I had lived in Budapest bore no relationship to my present circumstances. It was another world. My mother owned nothing of value. All her belongings fit into a couple of suitcases, and her home was a room in someone else's house.

Saint Martin-in-the-Fields High School for Girls, 1951–1957

"Learn their ways. Learn their lingo. Learn about what makes them tick. It's the only way to beat them!" my uncle Denis had advised me. I learned it all, probably as well as any "foreigner" ever did.

This was my second time in England, and the milieu that I was to enter differed radically from the one I had known in Cheltenham, where it was that of postwar England's provincial working class.

The obvious signs of the war were lessening with each year, but the memory and other after-effects continued to rule everyone's life. Many foods and clothing were still rationed, and though the rubble left behind by the heavy bombing had been cleared away, there were still many empty lots covered with weeds, inescapable reminders of the death and destruction that had been visited on that land.

The British were proud of having beaten the "Krauts" and hated to be reminded that they'd had a little help from their American ally across the ocean. The people were poor, but in true British fashion they "carried on." Understated British humor thrived, as it always does under adversity. They had buried their dead, and now it was time to give their attention back to their gardens, their church choirs, and their devotion to their beloved king and his family. They wanted to forget, to return to the old days of isolation on their island at the edge of Europe.

But it was not to be. England had been changed forever. The British Empire was in its death throes. Immigrants were knocking at her door. Labor unions were gaining strength. Politically and geographically, England was joining the rest of the world, especially Continental Europe. Most Britons, however, in their heart of hearts, knew that they were different, better, prouder. They would tolerate foreigners but they would never be like them.

I entered Saint Martin's in the middle of the fall term of 1951, and my education began: not only in geography, history, literature, or languages, but the stuff that the British were made of.

I was an immediate curiosity. A Jewish refugee from Continental Europe, living in an orphanage, speaking with a French accent, and wearing a secondhand uniform. Actually, the fact that I wore a used uniform only made a difference in my mind, not in anyone else's. Nobody but I really paid any attention to it. There were others girls whose families were poor and could not afford a new uniform, but to me it was an excruciating humiliation. I hated my brown blazer with the school badge on the breast pocket and the tiny tear (near the hem on the right side) that someone had repaired with black thread. I hated the brown-and-white check gingham dress because the shoulders were too big and hung down over my arms, and most of all I hated the brown beret that was too big for my head and which we were obliged to wear at all times when in uniform off school grounds.

My classmates gathered around me and showered me with questions. As my complicated background emerged, some budding wit nicknamed me "Heinz 57 Varieties." Eventually Varieties was dropped, and I became plain Heinz 57. There was no malice. Everyone had a nickname. Mine seemed quite appropriate.

I was placed into the "lower third," a year behind where I should have been according to my age. It was the highest level in the lower school, which was being eliminated year by year, one class at a time, so that the following year the "upper third" would be the entrance class. Miss Gordon-Ewen, the elegant, white-haired, and dignified headmistress, felt that I needed the extra year to prepare for high school and to adjust to Saint Martin's. It was a small price to pay for being allowed to attend such a prestigious school.

My new teacher, Mrs. Davies, was a tall, horsey Englishwoman. Her home-dyed, unkempt, ginger-red hair and very thick glasses gave her a most peculiar and comical air. The little girls giggled behind her back, while the other teachers, not one of whom had a "Mrs." in front of her name, passed her in the corridor with a slight frown and a quizzical look that said "Oh dear, oh dear, what are we to think of her?" quickly wiping all expression off their faces if a student chanced by. We were not supposed to know *their* opinion of our teacher.

Mrs. Davies was a good and dedicated teacher. She immediately set about introducing us to essay writing, demanding absolutely perfect grammar and spelling, promising to give any student six pence if we could find a word beginning with the letter *q* without a *u* following it.

"*Not* a proper noun, thank you very much, ladies," she said tartly as we all dove for our atlases.

She seemed totally oblivious to the fact that I had joined the class in the middle of the semester or that I was in any way different from the other students.

The only time that she singled out an error that I made in English was when, in an essay, I wrote the word "moonshine" instead of "moonlight."

"Moonshine? What do you mean, *moonshine?"* she scolded. "You mean *moonlight!"*

I didn't know the difference. She was aghast, till one of my classmates spoke up. "Juliette isn't English. She's French. Maybe it's the same in French."

"No, it is not," she said shortly and continued in perfect French. *"Moonlight* c'est 'clair de lune.' *Moonshine* c'est 'balivernes.' Vous comprenez, Mademoiselle?"

"Oui, Madame. Merci."

Mrs. Davies spoke French better than I did.

She was determined to get us ready for the upper school the following year. We had to be ready to start Latin and Algebra and SHAKESPEARE. Shakespeare? I had heard that he was the greatest playwright the world had ever known, and I was going to be studying his works. This indeed was a serious school, I thought. I was thrilled and not a little intimidated! From then on, every trimester, in every class, every year, we studied a different Shakespearean play, starting with the easier ones, such as *The Merchant of Venice,* and *A Midsummer Night's Dream,* and working our way up to *Hamlet* and *Othello* before graduating. It was fortunate that England's bard had been so prolific!

The upper-school teachers seemed, indeed, to be like teachers that I had read about in schoolgirl literature: middle-aged, energetic, gray-haired bluestockings. They walked the corridors of Saint Martin's with dignity, carrying heavy books and stacks of papers waiting to be marked, talking of things intellectual and dotting their conversation with Latin quotations. Their black robes flapped about them as they strode the hallways between classes, acknowledging students with curt nods of the head. The students were equally impressive. Rosy-cheeked and self-assured, they acted and talked like young ladies, seemingly free of the hostility or, at best, the wariness that I had always encountered as a newcomer.

I met Jill and Maureen the first day of class, and we became friends immediately. They introduced me to the British psyche. They and their families were the very essence of that ancient island on the western edge of Europe, on whose empire the sun was setting.

Jill's parents were people of moderate means, very warm and welcoming. Mr. Howell worked in an office; Mrs. Howell was a housewife. Jill also had a younger brother, Peter. I watched them with longing and some envy. I always missed *my* Peter. They were a true family, so secure in the knowledge of who they were, where they came from, where they belonged. I envied their orderly life, their quiet understanding of one another, their lack of unrealistic ambitions, their faith in their church and their traditions. Their lives were so tied to the land of their birth, their language, their history. I watched Mr. Howell tend his rosebushes in his tiny front yard and Mrs. Howell baking pies for the church supper. I loved being around them, as though some part of the predictability of their lives would rub off on me. Yet I knew that I could never be like them. I felt that I knew more of life than they did. I marveled at their trust in people and, at first, even wondered whether they had some ulterior motive for inviting me.

With permission from our housemother at Norwood, we could accept invitations "to tea" at friends' houses; since I was always eager to go, I made myself as agreeable as possible to ensure future invitations.

I spent many an afternoon at the Howells' house. Jill and I would hurry home after school to be able to play a game of tennis in the park before her mother served tea. When Mr. Howell came home from work, we would all sit around the big oak dining-room table and be served typical English fare. I was, at first, embarrassed that I just couldn't bear to eat certain foods and would insist that I wasn't a bit hungry, so please, PLEASE, don't serve me any "bubble and squeak"! I'd plead silently.

The Howells were quite aware of my dilemma, and as I became more and more accepted in their midst, Mr. Howell would turn to his wife and say, deadpan, "Please, dear, make sure Juliette gets an extra helping of kippers. She loves to choke on fish bones. She didn't have that privilege in France . . . or Hungermany . . . or wherever."

Soon I became comfortable enough that I could answer in like fashion. "Oh, yes, please give me more. If I don't have a mouthful of fish bones, how will I ever be able to master a British accent?" I felt comfortable and welcome in their house, even while knowing that I was different.

Maureen came from a more upscale family. Her father, Mr. Clare, was a well-to-do businessman, and they had a beautiful Tudor-style home with lovely grounds on Beulah Hill. When we had tea at her house it was in the parlor, overlooking the landscaped gardens at the back of the house. Mrs. Clare, dressed in a cashmere twin set, tweed skirt, and a string of pearls, graciously poured tea from a silver teapot.

It didn't seem to matter that we all came from such different backgrounds. Jill, Maureen, and I made a threesome that lasted throughout our time together at Saint Martin's. We accepted everything about one another. We started out as eleven- and twelve-year-old gigglers and proceeded to serious homework and tennis partnerships; by the time we were eighteen or so, we were formidable debaters, having practiced among ourselves by constantly arguing about politics, religion, and social issues.

My first lesson in British Tradition, which I learned from my new friends, was tolerance. It didn't matter that we had different points of view. Everybody listened to everybody else. Weight and respect was given to all opinions. Not quite the way that we operated at the orphanage or even in my family. Our way of persuasion was to insult our opponent into submission and giving up her or his point of view through humiliation.

"What are you, a meshugene?"

"Are you too stupid to understand that you are wrong?"

"No intelligent person can talk to you!"

Occasionally it could stoop as low as, "For heaven's sake, get your brains out of your arse!"

Jill, Maureen, and I spent seven years together in high school. We visited one another's homes, we played tennis, we went to movies, plays, and concerts together. Yet our parents never met. There was no occasion on which a refugee cook-housekeeper, the family of a government functionary, and that of a wealthy businessman would meet.

We talked about everything except our personal feelings. I'm not sure whether my silence was because I had absorbed the idea of British reticence or because I felt that no one, not even my friends, could possibly understand what I felt was missing in my life. I would have been much too ashamed to admit that I missed being part of a real family, like theirs. I didn't want them to feel sorry for me, and, besides, I had started to acquire a patina of outer toughness that said, with a little too much bravado, I can deal with anything. Don't worry about me!

Saint Martin's became my secret refuge. Secret, because I never admitted this to anyone and behaved in a manner that no one should ever suspect it. No self-respecting teenager could admit to liking school better than any other place. I admired the British "no-nonsense" attitude, their nonemotional, "sensible" behavior, the proud tradition that I deluded myself into thinking I could become a part of. There was no yelling and screaming, fistfights, or bullying like at the orphanage. There were no emotional scenes as there were when I visited my mother, during which I always felt an overwhelming sense of guilt and anger. I still resented that she was not providing me with a home, knowing full well that she really couldn't. I watched her doing physical labor, knowing that she was killing herself yet refusing to acknowledge it. I couldn't wait for weekends to be over so I could return to the rarefied atmosphere of Saint Martin's, where life was so orderly, where there were neat cloakrooms, gymnastics hall, art studio, chemistry, biology, and physics labs, a well-equipped kitchen for cooking classes, a well-stocked library, five tennis courts, and a large athletic field where we played field hockey. Inwardly I reveled in this luxury; outwardly I joined the other girls in mocking the teachers and complaining about the school. I felt sorry for the other kids at the orphanage who did not have the privilege of going to such a school, the bright ones who never got the opportunity for a better education.

I walked in every Monday with a sigh of relief.

I graduated into the upper school without any fanfare. Nobody noticed me much the first couple of years. I kept a low profile. I did my work well enough not to be admonished but not so well as to be noticed. The fact that I did better than anyone in French was normal. I did not distinguish myself in any other way.

I enjoyed going to classes. I was eager to learn everything about my host country. My best subject became history. It was the first time in a school situation that I was not singled out for one particular reason or another: not for being Jewish nor for having joined midterm and not knowing anything about the previous year's curriculum. As far as being a foreigner, it hardly ever came up anymore. I finished one class and graduated into the next, just as one was supposed to do. I felt at home. Saint Martin's was my school. I knew that I was coming back after each vacation, that I had my place in class, that I was meeting with the same friends that I'd had before. I had my favorite subjects and my favorite teachers, though I never succumbed to the English schoolgirl's habit of having crushes on them. Still, on the surface, I fit in.

As long as I lived at Norwood, I was assured of attending Saint Martin's. However, everyone left Norwood at the age of fifteen and went to work. Somewhere in the back of my mind there was an uneasy feeling about this knowledge. Something different was going to have to be done about me. As usual, there was a hurdle ahead, but I was going to ignore it for as long as possible.

We were, I supposed, a pretty typical bunch of schoolgirls. In my own little circle of friends, we were quick and smart, funny and witty. We enjoyed satire, and we made up rhymes and ditties to show that we didn't "follow the crowd." When we read that American schoolgirls were swooning over a new singer called Elvis Presley, we listened to his music and made faces, and Pauline Masters, our designated "poet laureate" came up with lyrics that made us feel very superior:

> Elvis Presley has a yell
> Like a foghorn down a well.
> Pardon an indiscreet question:
> Are they words, or indigestion?

Between classes, my irreverent chalk cartoons depicting various teachers were always a big hit. The picture of a delicate little piano stool groaning under the bulk of our music teacher Miss Copeland's enormous derriere sent my classmates into delicious peels of laughter. The daring deed was to leave the cartoon on the blackboard till the last possible moment before a teacher entered the class. I delighted everyone by waiting till the doorknob turned then nonchalantly picking up the board eraser, slowly and calmly erasing the offensive picture while politely greeting the next teacher, who usually thanked me for preparing the board for her.

Twice a week we had music lessons with the dreadfully obese Miss Copeland. She had us do breathing exercises before any singing was allowed. "Breathe in deeply, girls. Expand that diaphragm. Ho-o-o-o-ld it. Good! Breathe out."

We sang mostly psalms and hymns, which were repeated every morning at "assembly," when the entire school body congregated before classes, with Miss Gordon-Ewen presiding. The study of classical music was not a part of the curriculum. I learned to sing fervently William Blake's "Jerusalem" and Sir Cecil Spring-Rice's "I Vow to Thee, My Country." I never saw any conflict between the songs I sang in school and those that I sang in the synagogue, but the Christian hymns provoked little pangs of guilt, especially when Jesus was mentioned. I was glad that no one knew that I was singing those songs. But I liked them anyway. There was a similarity between rock-ribbed British tradition and the Judaism that had become so important to me. Both had a long and distinguished history, great traditions, and, most of all, deep roots.

After the prayers and singing at assembly, daily notices were imparted. Anyone not familiar with Saint Martin's would have been totally baffled at some of our "notices." The school did not operate on a five-day schedule, rather a seven-day one. We called them Day 1, Day 2, Day 3, and so on. Day 1 would be a Monday, Day 2, Tuesday, with the following Monday being Day 6, and Tuesday, Day 7. The cycle then began again, making Wednesday, Day 1. This allowed, for example, for more English studies during a seven-day period and only one art class, which was deemed less important. We were perfectly used to the system, with occasional lapses, and then we would reassure ourselves by asking a classmate: "Is today Day 1 or 2?" the same way that one would inquire, "Is today Monday or Tuesday?" The notices, however, became hilarious and totally perplexing to any visitor to the school:

"Miss Free is taking her class on a trip to Stoke Poges. She will therefore not be able to give English classes today. Consequently, today will be Day 1 instead of Day 2. Except the afternoon, when the sixth form will have Day 4, the fourth form, Day 3. The rest of the school will revert to Day 2 after second period in the afternoon."

"And," we added quietly, grinning, "the third floor will become the second floor. The indoors will become the outdoors. Miss Copeland will lose weight and Miss Gordon-Ewen will sprout wings."

After my second year at Saint Martin's, another girl from Norwood, Sheila Kaye, was admitted. Then another Jewish girl, Edna Bliss, whose family had moved to Streatham, joined the school. One day someone remarked that we should not be attending the morning religious services with the rest of the school, but should have a parallel meeting with Hebrew morning prayers. Mr. Conway and the local rabbi petitioned Miss Gordon-Ewen, and to my great annoyance, we were granted our own morning prayer meeting. We had to time our prayers, so as to finish at the same time as the rest of the student body, in order to file in and join them in time for notices. Naturally, every head turned in our direction when we opened the large door and walked in. I was incensed at what I considered a ridiculous and totally superfluous change. For heaven's sake, this was a Church of England school; what were we doing? Demanding equal time? I had worked so hard at not standing out, and now some religious maniac was interfering with my agenda. I thought about objecting, but I didn't know how. Truth was I liked being in a non-Jewish environment. I liked singing the Christian hymns. And I liked being part of the crowd. I also knew that these were not excuses that I could articulate to anyone. I grumbled to myself and avenged the injustice by singing twice as loudly in choir practice, joining the Saint Martin's choir to sing carols on Christmas Eve in Trafalgar Square. I did not let anyone at the orphanage know about this transgression.

Saint Martin's philosophy was based on common sense, self-control, team work, and honor, a moral code that had probably never occurred to anyone in my immediate family. Our code of ethics, if spelled out, would have been far more basic: Survive! Whatever you have to do, survive!

If we asked how to solve a problem, we were told, "Use your common sense! None were more despised than those who did not use their common sense. If something made us angry, teary, or in any way emotional, we had to "use self-control." One did not go about allowing one's emotions to get in the way of good judgment. Neither were we supposed to allow anyone to observe any personal emotions. These were private feelings, not open to public scrutiny. If we didn't have them in private either, so much the better. One did not get hysterical on seeing a spider on the windowsill. Neither did one panic over a little blood gushing out of a gaping wound. Fainting in biology class while dissecting a frog drew exasperated tut-tuts from Miss Jenkins. Why couldn't everyone just control themselves?!

There certainly was no place for passion about anything, not while we were "controlling ourselves." Passion was the realm of the great poets, Shelley and Keats and Lord Byron, not for mere mortals—unless they were foreigners, who just played at being passionate and meant something quite different, since they couldn't "control themselves."

Saint Martin's was a sexless and passionless environment. Or so it seemed to my naive eyes during the first couple of years. I later discovered that under Saint Martin's veneer of proper British behavior there existed relationships that could have scandalized society—as it was at the time. All this, however, did not rule out compassion and empathy, always doled out in a quiet, subdued, and "sensible" manner. Miss Buzzard, our athletics and gym teacher, looked at my hands at the onset of winter. My fingers were red and swollen. The frostbite that I contracted while in hiding seemed to be recurring every winter. I not only suffered from the itching and burning of my swollen fingers but also hid my ugly hands shamefully behind my back whenever in company.

"Juliette," said Miss Buzzard, "your hands are swollen and red. Is there heat at the orphanage?"

"Oh, yes, plenty. This is the frostbite that I got during the war. It comes back every winter."

"We call it chilblains. You have a very bad case. It must hurt."

"Yes, a little." I was learning how to communicate with British understatedness and stoicism.

"I will speak to your matron at the orphanage. Come to school twenty minutes early every day and we'll get your circulation going. You're very pale, too!"

Yes, I was pale and skinny. But so were many kids at that time. British food did not do anything to entice me to eat. Many children were anemic. We were given extra doses of a concentrated liquid called "orange juice" that the government doled out for all children. It bore no resemblance whatsoever, in taste or content, to real oranges. The name must have referred to the color, I suppose. We also got a paste called Marmite, still a favorite among Britons, a strong-tasting yeast extract that we were supposed to spread on bread. These additives, along with our daily servings of sticky porridge, were meant to keep us healthy. Matron checked our hair and nails. If these were all right, the rest of the body couldn't be far behind.

Every morning I got to school early, and Miss Buzzard and I jumped rope. Miss Buzzard, who was not a young woman, was in excellent physical shape. She was such an archetypal English Gym Mistress that she seemed a parody of herself. She sported very short gray hair in a masculine cut, a strong, stocky, and muscled body, and a rah-rah attitude toward everything. She always wore an oxford-type shirt with a short navy blue jumper that came just above the knee, lisle hose, and plimsolls. Her jumper distinguished her from the rest of the student body, since we all wore brown. She looked like a middle-aged woman who had forgotten to take off her high school uniform.

Miss Buzzard not only gave up twenty minutes of her time every morning for my benefit, she also took me under her wing. Me, the least athletic, skinny, pale orphanage kid with the secondhand uniform. Miss Buzzard was actually Lady Sylvia Buzzard, a titled lady who chose to be a gym teacher and part-time social worker.

Every June Miss Buzzard arrived to school and handed out several passes to the Tennis Championships at Wimbledon that she had wangled from her brother, the president of the club. We were great tennis enthusiasts. The crushes that I denied my teachers I lavished on the tennis stars of the time. I dreamed of Lew Hoad, played imaginary games with Vic Seixas, and envied Little Mo Connolly in her frilly panties. I loved it when my mother told me that my father had been a very good tennis player, and when she found a picture of him in his tennis whites, I took it to school and showed it to anyone who would look.

As far as Miss Buzzard was concerned, the secret of life was "teamwork." Anything could be achieved if only we all worked together. The game of field hockey exemplified teamwork. Whenever we missed the ball, due to the clumsy wielding of our hockey sticks, Miss Buzzard was running right beside us, blowing her whistle and admonishing us. "Teamwork, girls, teamwork. Remember the R.A.F.!" We never did figure out how remembering the Royal Air Force would make us better hockey players, but it must have had something to do with Upper-Class Teamwork! We had a tennis team, a hockey team, a netball team, a debating team. Saint Martin's was a TEAM.

I tried hard to fit in, yet I still had ambivalent feelings about my considered "difference." To be different at the orphanage was fine. To be different at Saint Martin's was not! I wanted to be selective in my differentness. I pretended to myself that I was really a British schoolgirl and thought up bizarre stories of my "real past," blithely ignoring reality.

I looked and I listened and I imitated the British Way. I became as enthusiastic as any during the yearly Oxford versus Cambridge boat races, deciding to wear the royal blue rosette in support of Oxford, rather than the pale blue of Cambridge. (Not that I knew anything about either university; I just liked the color better.) On these occasions there was always friendly banter between the teachers and students regarding the merits of the two institutions, and I tried to become part of it.

•

I had been at Saint Martin's for a few months when an event shook me out of my complacent illusions. It was February 6, 1952. We were all sitting in our classrooms when a monitor came in and spoke quietly to Mrs. Davies. When she left, Mrs. Davies interrupted the lesson.

"Girls, when the bell rings, you will get up and file into the assembly hall. Miss Gordon-Ewen has something very important to tell us."

We looked at one another in amazement. It was unheard of to be summoned to the assembly hall in the middle of the day. What possibly could have happened in the world to have occasioned such a radical departure from the normal routine? Suddenly I knew. I knew that I knew. WAR. That was the only thing that could have happened that was important enough to interrupt our lessons.

In 1952 we were living in the Cold War. Everybody was frightened, paranoid, expecting hostilities to erupt at any moment. I was thirteen at this time. I didn't understand much about politics but I was as afraid as anyone who had already gone through a war. I had been through one. I would not go through another.

As we lined up outside the assembly hall and waited to go in, I started to plan. I was going to kill myself. But how? I couldn't get a gun. I didn't know what kind of drugs or medication to ask for, and I didn't think I had the courage to jump out of a window. Then I knew. Gas. That was it. Close the windows, close the doors, stuff some rags into the cracks, and open the taps. I wasn't at all afraid of the thought of death, only of living through another war. Then I thought, Oh, my God, I forgot about my mother. I can't kill myself without her. Right! We'll have to do it together. She'll want to do it as much as I do.

Slowly we filed into the hall, six hundred girls and about thirty teachers. When we were all quietly standing in our places, Miss Gordon-Ewen walked up unto the dais. She was wearing her mortarboard, which she only wore on special occasions. She looked very grave. Taking a deep breath she said, "Ladies, girls, I have very sad news to tell you. Our beloved King George VI died this morning."

Five hundred and ninety-nine girls caught their breath, and a communal "Oh" mixed with shock and horror filled the hall. One girl let out an "Ahh": a long sigh of relief, and I thought, I'm going to live a little while longer.

The entire nation was in mourning. Everyone pitied and admired the "plucky" young Queen Elizabeth, who had flown home from her tour of South Africa with her handsome husband. The true grief, the adoration, the awe shown by the population toward their sovereign totally baffled my mother and her friends, who joked about it; but I, somehow, without being able to articulate it, felt that the reverence of the British toward the royal family was not hero-worship but a respect paid to the embodiment of everything British—the history, the culture, the traditions of which they were so proud, to which they clung so desperately and which had very nearly been destroyed. I knew that I could never feel what they felt, but I understood them, and with secret envy, joined my mother in mocking them behind their backs.

Another lesson to learn was honor, the British version thereof. During any test, the teacher could leave the classroom and be assured that not a word would be spoken, not a sign made. All she had to say was "Girls, you are on your honor!" Cheating was unheard of. Penny McIntyre, the curly-headed, freckled class cut-up, would make a funny noise only to have several stern glances thrown in her direction. If she wanted to act up, she could do it when the teacher was present, when she had to take her chances on getting caught and punished. Otherwise it wasn't cricket! I lived up to what was expected. Not because I believed in it but because I knew that if I were the one who broke the rule, it would be because I was "different." Foreigners were always different. They didn't understand British Honor. That's why they were not as good. So, yes, I would be accepted, as long as I acted just like them *and* accepted the absolute correctness of their rules and behavior. But to me, lying was a way of survival. My life had been spared because I had been taught to lie. To lie well required skill, and I took pride in being a good liar. I didn't blush. I could look someone straight in the eyes and lie, and I never, ever, owned up to a lie. Once told, the lie became my truth and could not be changed.

At the orphanage I had plenty of competition and therefore abstained from lying, perversely deciding that I did not want to be like the other kids there. But at school it gave me an edge.

I remember one particular instance when a history paper had to be turned in on time or receive a failing grade. Miss Mayer, with whom I was not always on the best of terms, met me in the hall.

"Juliette, I did not get your essay on Henry VIII's foreign policy. It was due yesterday."

"But I put it on your desk, with everybody else's," I lied, totally barefaced.

She searched my face. I knew that she didn't trust me, but I didn't even blink. "I'll look for it immediately," she said in a matter-of-fact tone that nevertheless carried a clear warning.

I went home, finished the essay, got to school early, and slipped it in her drawer, in the attendance book. The pages fell out the minute she took the book out. She looked at me across the classroom and I flashed my friendliest smile at her, as though oblivious. There was nothing she could do. No one could accuse a student of such an unspeakable crime without proof. It would not be cricket.

The following week, Miss Mayer's special friend, Miss Free, our English teacher, gave us an essay to write: "Can Lying Ever Be Justified?" The girls looked at one another. What an odd subject! And why we didn't get a choice of essays? We always did.

"See what you can do with this girls!" was Miss Free's answer.

I did marvelously well with it. Yes, there were instances when lying could be justified. My own history proved it. I maintained that if no one was hurt, including the liar, then lying was acceptable. Aye, but there's the rub! Could there be lies that didn't hurt? I wrote an entire argument, and as I remember, wrote it well. As I finished the piece, I came upon a truth with which I ended the essay: Not having to lie is a privilege.

Miss Free was dumbfounded and scandalized. Ethically speaking, she was mortally wounded. The argument that lying had saved my life hardly impressed her. Was my life worth the compromising of one's ethics? She obviously didn't think so. My essay provoked a debate in class. Penny McIn-tyre was on my side. So were Jill and Maureen, but only out of loyalty, not conviction. Someone pointed out that I had lied to Nazis. *That* made all the difference. Nazis were foreigners. They didn't count. One just didn't lie at home (i.e., the confines of the British Isles and the Commonwealth, excluding various and sundry natives). That saved the day. My essay received a decent grade and we got a lecture on what it meant to play devil's advocate.

"Which you did quite well, Juliette," commented Miss Free generously, saving face.

The last line of my essay remained with me. I had come upon the thought inadvertently, and it made a difference in my life. Yes, not having to lie was indeed a privilege.

As year followed year, I became more and more absorbed into British culture. I steeped myself in English history. Miss Pierce, our history teacher, remarked that she was embarrassed that the only student who knew the dates of all the reigns of the English kings and queens was a foreigner. I knew the geography of the British Isles as well as any well-traveled native. I learned all the camp songs, the silly poems, the serious ones, and even the nursery rhymes. I understood and loved British humor. While my mother sat by the radio, totally mystified by "'Ancock's 'alf 'our" on the BBC's light program, I was roaring with laughter. I read everything, willy-nilly, good and awful, that fell into my hands, from Sir Walter Scott to Jane Austen to Thomas Hardy to the trashy comic books and Penguin paperbacks left strewn about the family room in Norwood. I made Saint Martin's my real world. The orphanage and my mother's environment were places that I was passing through on my way to my real life. During holidays when I went back to

France, I compared everything French to everything English. Besides the food and the weather, everything made more sense in England. I felt more comfortable there. England had become my home. I had decided to become an English schoolgirl. I no longer wanted to leave Norwood; I knew that as long as I was there, I could attend Saint Martin's. When I left, who knew where I'd have to go?

In June of 1953, the young Queen Elizabeth was to be crowned in Westminster Abbey. The entire country was celebrating. We were all caught up in the excitement of the great pageant about to be played out. At the orphanage, Mr. Conway was figuring out how to rig up the two available television sets so that everyone would be able to witness this historical event.

The Victoria Embankment, along the Thames and part of the procession route, was reserved for emissaries of London's high schools, and Saint Martin's had a spot reserved just large enough to hold a couple of dozen students. Miss Gordon-Ewen decided that all class captains would go plus another student from each class to be chosen by the students themselves. We held a secret ballot (Never did we miss an opportunity to demonstrate democracy in action!), and my class chose me. I knew that I had not been chosen because I was the most popular or the smartest or that I in any other way deserved it, but because I lived in an orphanage and my classmates wanted me to have something special. They were being charitable. I was humiliated. The vote had been unanimous, less one— mine, which made me suspect that it had been discussed in my absence. I thanked everyone graciously and promised to report everything to the last detail.

Jill, Maureen, and I walked down the hill from school that day without a word, until Maureen broke the silence. "Everybody *really* wanted you to be the one, Juliette," she said as convincingly as she possibly could.

I went to the coronation, getting up at four o'clock in the morning in order to get to school in time to assemble and be at the Embankment by seven. Rain drizzled all day. By the time I got home I had missed the televised coronation ceremony at Westminster Abbey. But I had seen, in the flesh, a real British coronation procession. It was a historic event that would most likely not be repeated in my lifetime.

I redeemed my self-esteem by giving an account of all that I had seen to my class. Not the kind of account that they had heard repeated a thousand times by the media, but the Saint Martin's kind, the kind that made me part of their crowd and that they had come to expect of me. Standing in front of the class by the teacher's desk, I acted out, very theatrically and with tongue in cheek, the role of a newsreporter. Pretend microphone in hand, a fedora pulled down over one eye, my raincoat tightly belted, I held forth dramatically, my voice forced down several octaves.

"The Queen of Tonga is coming into view. At least I think it's the Queen of Tonga. It looks like an enormous black female Neptune rising from the frothy, misty seas. She is six feet and three inches tall, dressed in layers of flowing silk, the colors of a stormy sea. On her head she is wearing a four-masted galleon. The wind and rain are swaying the craft unmercifully. The Queen is sloshing about in huge puddles. If the rain does not let up, I fear for the ship. Next to her, striving vainly to keep up is a tiny little man. I'm told that it's her prime minister. Actually, it looks like her lunch. . . . And here, driving up in an open golden carriage drawn by four white horses, is . . . is . . . a very large cigar . . . attached at one end to Sir Winston Churchill. A footman is standing behind him, holding an enormous umbrella. The umbrella covers Sir Winston, but, unfortunately, it is not large enough to cover the cigar, which is getting soggier and limper with each drop of rain that lands on it. Sir Winston is not happy. . . ."

The class cheered at my account of the procession. Parody was a favorite pastime at school. I knew that everyone was fair game—except the royal family. They were sacrosanct. That part of my account was reserved for my mother and her friends.

As the years passed my scholastic abilities improved, my accent became less obvious, and I grew to understand my milieu. I was one of the crowd, and yet the differences were always there, though I chose to ignore them. Sometimes, I was the one who seemed to be the privileged one among my friends. I was the one who went abroad for vacations, the one who had a mysterious uncle who sent gifts from around the world, the one who had access to famous people's houses. My extracurricular education was far broader than that of my friends'. But no matter how hard I tried I could never be a "real" Saint Martin's girl.

What Color the Chameleon?

RESIDENCE: Norwood Jewish Orphanage
Language: English, untutored, regional
Religion: Orthodox Jewish
Socioeconomic environment: Lower-class orphans/refugees/Blitz victims
Cultural environment: Strictly Jewish
Name used: Juliette

SCHOOL: Saint Martin-in-the-Fields
Language: The Queen's English
Religion: Church of England
Socioeconomic environment: Postwar British middle class
Cultural environment: Strictly English
Name used: Juliette

VACATIONS: France (if not with my mother)
Language: French
Religion: Jewish (nonpracticing)
Socioeconomic environment: Well-to-do Jewish immigrants
Cultural environment: Urbane, tentatively reaching toward appreciation of
    the arts
Name used: Evelyne (pronounced "Ev'lyn" in French)

VACATIONS: With my mother, wherever
Language: Hungarian
Religion: Atheist
Socioeconomic environment: Poor immigrants living and working in wealthy,
    cosmopolitan, upper-class homes
Cultural environment: Undefinable mishmash of poor immigrants and/or sur-
    vivors, originally from wealthy and educated backgrounds
Name used: Evi

These were my worlds. I moved between them like an actor, changing roles, costumes, and languages for the different parts, as though I were performing in several plays at once.

It never occurred to me to question who I really was. The roles I played were all parts of me. Besides, I didn't know then about the concept of identity. All four parts of my life were further subdivided along their divergent routes.

The orphanage would send me for a week's vacation by the sea, where I was expected to behave and was treated as a charity case. Thence, I'd take the ferry to France, where my aunts Kati and Eszter would immediately outfit me in expensive clothes and take me to the opera, the ballet, expensive restaurants, and occasionally a trip to Biarritz, Monte Carlo, or a tour of the châteaux of the Loire before shipping me back to the "British boarding school." I loved their lifestyle and envied my cousin Claude, despite the fact that the family around him was becoming increasingly dysfunctional. Aunt Eszter and Uncle Denis's marriage was a series of raging explosions and battles that we were all privy to. Both were intelligent and attractive and totally unsuited for each other. Denis imperiously demanded total loyalty and obedience from the women around him. Aunt Eszter thought he was mad. "Il est fou, totalement fou!" ("He's crazy. Totally crazy!"), she kept repeating to anyone who would listen. He cruelly taunted her with his Cuban family. She countered by throwing a lead crystal vase at his head. He told her that her brothers had forced him into marrying her. She shouted that he could only be a man to submissive, simpering twenty year olds. Claude and I would listen to the fights with our ears pressed against the door, and occasionally heard slaps, screams, and dull thuds against the wall as a variety of missiles, thrown by Aunt Eszter, landed there.

Claude had no respect for either of them and used them against each other, as they did him. If Claude asked Denis for money and Denis refused him, Aunt Eszter immediately gave it to him. If Denis gave Claude money, then Aunt Eszter gave him more. If Aunt Eszter planned a skiing trip for Claude, Denis decided he couldn't go because his grades were not good enough, then sent him to Spain under the pretext that he had to practice his Spanish. Still I envied him. He lived in a beautiful environment, had his own piano, a motorcycle, and met his friends in coffeehouses in the Latin Quarter. Whenever he let me tag along, I felt very shy and mousy, totally inadequate among his "sophisticated," espresso-sipping, black-clad friends. Yet, I detected something not-quite-right among these youngsters. They mocked everything and everybody. They saw themselves as disciples of Jean-Paul Sartre. They were "existentialists." They hid behind a mask of jaded sophistication, a world-weariness that made them old beyond their years, and I was uneasy around them. I was thoroughly intimidated and I envied them still.

The subject of conversation at home with my aunts and Denis was, first, money. How to get it, how to spend it, and who had how much. But most important, how to keep it liquid. That was always the theme and the scheme. All assets had to be available in case we had to flee—and it was always assumed that we would have to at some point. Loose diamonds and gold napoleons were always on hand, though Kati preferred jewelry. That way she could make better use of her property.

"Always live and talk and look as though you have a lot of money. People respect that!" Kati and Denis insisted, while Aunt Eszter looked on aghast. I was living in an orphanage, my mother was a cook. Whom was I going to show off to, I wondered.

Politics came next. Denis read many newspapers, from the extreme left wing to the extreme right. Then he lectured us. But he did not invite discussion. We were there to listen to him. If we asked questions, they had to be "intelligent" questions. Denis was the judge. If he deemed the question "stupid," he would stop talking for a moment, shake his head sadly, then keep going, ignoring the questioner. I think I was the only one who really paid attention. I was fascinated by how he deduced the hidden agendas of the various politicians, how he detected new movements, how he sensed who was dangerous and who was an up-and-coming leader. He knew his history, and he knew the background of every world leader. I stored away all the information, and when I went back to England I explained it all to my mother and my friends. My friends gave me strange looks. They believed the newspapers. My mother listened. She respected Denis's political acumen, but would never admit it. She wondered why I enjoyed being around her brother, even when I always had to watch my step. He was volatile. We never quite knew what was going to set him off. But I knew how to play to his ego. I asked lots of questions about things I knew he liked to talk about. He also enjoyed the understated, subtle humor that I had acquired in England. We sparred with words, and he laughed delightedly when I got one over on him. When he was in a good mood and flush with money, he was a charmer and a wit. Women adored him. His jokes, perfectly on target and well told, were the delight of company. There was always a group around his table at the family's favorite coffeehouse, La Belle Ferronniere, just off the Champs-Élysées, where he sat contentedly, sealing business deals while stirring his espresso and winking at the pretty waitresses. To all our friends, he was the clever and charming rogue; to Aunt Eszter, he was "Le Fou" (the Crazy One); to me, he was my savior.

Cultural discussions, though not first priority, were important on the agenda. Uncle Denis quizzed me on my knowledge of literature and thought that the syllabus at Saint Martin's was too narrow in its scope, since it concentrated mostly on English literature. The family made sure that I took back stacks of French books to

England. Claude and I were shipped off on many an afternoon to the Louvre, then quizzed on what we had seen. We had to get our stories straight. We often ended up in le Bois de Vincennes or le Jardin du Luxembourg.

The subject of religion was never mentioned, as though there were something vaguely embarrassing about it. Any new acquaintance, however, personal or business, was always evaluated according to his faith.

"He's Jewish?" (Subtext: "Is he one of us?")

"Well he was before the war!" (Subtext: "Yes, but he is trying to hide his past and infiltrate Christian society.")

"Aha!" (Subtext: "So, we can let him know that we know who he is, but we won't reveal it to anyone . . . unless we have reason to want to embarrass him.")

Denis delighted in taking digs at my mother and watching my reaction. I was always fiercely loyal in my defense of her and often raised my voice to him. The family was always astonished that he tolerated that from me. I was the only one who could get away with such open defiance. I took a perverse pride in being allied with the family outcast. I stared at Denis with narrowed eyes and thought, If you hit me or even shout at me, I'm going straight back to England. I'm not afraid of you.

It seemed as though he read my mind. He always had an amused look on his face when I challenged or confronted him. He never touched me in anger. I think I was the only one in the family he respected; Klari, the only one he loved. He pitied my mother and tolerated everyone else. He felt a sense of duty toward the family, but resented them as a weight around his neck. He spent more and more time abroad on business and finally divided his time between Venezuela and the United States, with only occasional visits to Paris and London.

I loved visiting France, but it no longer felt like home. Neither did the orphanage, which I hoped to get away from as soon as my mother established the home she had been promising and that we often spoke about . . . but was not yet able to achieve.

Back in London, my mother was outspoken about her atheism, her disdain for the easy life that the family led in Paris, the blame that she thrust on Kati and Denis for the death of my grandmother and her own situation. I then changed roles and defended Kati and Denis. Often her anger exploded, and I became her target. She regarded religion the same way that the Communists did. It was the opium of the people.

"How could there be a God?" she would challenge. "Would a God allow the misery, the hatred, the unfairness of this world? A Devil? Yes, there is a Devil, but no God. There is no God! It's just convenient for the powers that be to scare the people into believing. That way they can keep them in check with threats of everlasting suffering after they die. What do they think this is, life?"

My friends from Saint Martin's invited me to their homes. With them I was an English schoolgirl, almost. We played tennis, we had high tea, we took the obligatory trips to Stratford-upon-Avon, Stoke Poges, and Runnymede, and we giggled over silly limericks. When I slept over, however, I felt a difference that I couldn't quite articulate. I was never totally comfortable. I felt I was in an alien environment. In Maureen's house, Mrs. Clare woke me up at six o'clock for the early morning cup of tea. Was I supposed to drink it and get up? Drink it and then go back to bed? Did the English bathe in the morning or in the evening? When was I supposed to be down for breakfast? What was early? What was late? If I asked, they would know that I wasn't one of them. If I made a mistake, would they think that it was because I was (1) Jewish, (2) Continental, (3) an "orphan"? Did I have to join them in saying grace before meals, and would they think it a sign of disrespect if I didn't make the sign of the cross? It seemed the answer to all these things came naturally to them. Would I ever feel that way somewhere, anywhere?

With Jill it was usually something about religion that showed up our differences. A Fundamentalist, she was aghast when I ventured to point out to her that the temptation that Adam and Eve were led into by the serpent in Genesis was sex. Jill was very devout and involved with her church. One day, she had an idea.

"Juliette, why don't you come to hear Billy Graham with us? He's coming to Wembley Stadium."

"Who's Billy Graham?"

"He's a new evangelist from America. You must have seen the ads. They're all over." We were riding on the top deck of the bus, and she pointed out the window excitedly. "Look! Over there. That's Billy Graham on the poster. Haven't you seen them?"

"Oh, that! I thought it was a shaving-cream ad. He looks like a model!"

We went, and I listened to the rousing and inspirational sermon. At the end, I watched in wonder the streams of people getting out of their seats and walking down the aisles to "register their souls with Jesus." Jill was sitting next to me, praying quietly, and I knew that she was praying for me. Were people really this naive? I wondered. I could never trust anything or anyone that much! Should I just go down there to please her? I decided not to. I would have to follow up. I resisted the urge to please. The minutes dragged by. More and more people joined the throngs already in the arena, while the choir sang and Mr. Graham prayed quietly. Finally it ended, and, I suppose, Jill resigned herself to having a Jewish friend.

I went along from role to role. Jewish orphanage resident, English schoolgirl, favored French niece, daughter of refugee cook, waiting to find out where these roles led. Waiting for my real life to begin.

From Pillar to Post

Our fifteenth birthday marked our release from the orphanage. About three months before that date, we each had to meet Mrs. Brash. We looked forward to that event with excitement and trepidation. Most of the boys and girls left school at that point, got jobs, and went out into the world. Mrs. Brash was responsible for our transition to the outside world. She decided what kind of work each child was suited for, found accommodations, and took each of us to Marks & Spencer, who donated the clothes for our trousseau. For the next two to three years she kept tabs on the "Old Girls" (graduates) until they were considered "on their own" or just disappeared and melted into the amorphous masses of humanity in various large cities around England.

Our introduction to Mrs. Brash marked the beginning of the end of our "stretch"; it was the start of a new life. It meant the adventure of our real lives was beginning. We were no longer to be considered children. We were finally gaining control over our own lives. My life, I knew, was not going to change as radically as that of my friends. I was in high school, with another three or four years before graduation.

My first interview with Mrs. Brash took place on a fall afternoon. She came to the orphanage, and I was summoned to Mr. Conway's office, which was given over to us for an hour. She greeted me with a firm handshake. She was quite tall with short dark hair, very dark eyes, and olive skin. She wore unfashionably loose clothing, rather 1920s in style, I thought, and sensible, low-heeled walking shoes. She was imposing, and I was immediately intimidated. The rumor was that she came from a very wealthy Sephardic family. She gave me a cold smile and invited me to sit down and tell her about myself. As I spoke she took notes, then fired off a lot of questions.

"You were born in Paris? You lived in Hungary? Why? Your mother speaks Hungarian! Why? Doesn't she want to learn English? Oh, you speak French and Hungarian? . . . interesting. How can you remember a language that you only spoke as a small child? You read French books? Why?"

I tried to explain my background, but she kept interrupting with new questions, looking at me in disbelief as though she were thinking that I was making up outlandish stories. Finally she said, impatiently, "Oh well, never mind. It's not important. Let's see how your English is. After all, that's what's important, isn't it?"

She handed me a book and asked me to read a passage and explain it to her. It was kid's stuff, and I felt insulted that anyone would even think of testing me on that level. She then dictated a couple of sentences and checked my spelling and handwriting. Finally she asked me to add a column of pounds, shillings, and pence.

"Well," she said in a business-like tone, "that's quite good. Maybe we can even justify the fact that you are allowed to go to high school. Maybe you could attend Miss Grimble's academy for a year and then, with your skills, become a creditable secretary. What do you think of that?"

"Well, actually, I would really like to go to university and become a surgeon," I answered tentatively.

"A surgeon?" she repeated in an incredulous, high-pitched voice.

After what seemed like an eternity, a condescending smile touched her lips. She cocked her head to one side and kept looking at me, a slight frown on her face. Was I making fun of her? she seemed to ask.

"Well," she continued finally, with a long sigh. "I really don't know how you could ever manage that. Let's just be realistic, shall we? It takes a great deal of money to put someone through medical school, with no guarantee of success. If the board of guardians spent all that on you, what would be left for the others? We must all be satisfied with what we are allotted in life. Especially if it is charity!"

I was properly humiliated and put in my place. I mumbled something about being sorry. Surgery had always fascinated me. I wasn't squeamish like girls were supposed to be. I enjoyed helping in the infirmary, lancing boils, stitching up various cuts. I spent hours looking through old medical books that were gathering dust on a forgotten shelf in our library. Someone brought in tea on a tray, and Mrs. Brash asked me to pour. I knew that she was checking my manners. She asked me about my mother; what she did, where she lived—and did she keep a kosher house?

My mother had just moved to a bed-sitter. There were always boarding houses around, and eventually immigrants starting renting rooms. She had finally taken her first step toward having a place of her own. I mentioned that there was a possibility that she would get two rooms, and that way I would be able to live with her. Mrs. Brash immediately dismissed that. An atheistic environment with no kosher food was not a fit place for one of her charges! She would find me something near school, "with a nice family."

She said good-bye and told me that she would be in touch. I left the office and tears immediately welled up, and I ran into the bathroom. I felt angry and humiliated. There was a leaden feeling in my stomach. There was no chance now of going to the university. No chance of getting out from under the burden of poverty, refugeeism, the "lower-class" milieu. No chance at that "other" kind of life. All I wanted was to return to that secure middle-class existence that I had once known, which part of the family was enjoying again. I clung to that hope, fearing that if I ever let it go I would never reach it again. But I couldn't do it alone. I wasn't strong enough. My mother couldn't help me here. And she thought I could do anything I wanted. I spoke the language. I attended a prestigious school. I wasn't a refugee like she was! She didn't understand the system. She didn't understand England or that I needed someone's encouragement, someone to inspire me. And she certainly would never understand that some philanthropic Jews had embraced the British class system.

The fact was that a cultural and generational chasm had opened up between us. Though she had crossed the English Channel, she would always be Continental European. Though she eventually learned English, she would never understand the nuances of the language, the humor of the people, their eccentricities. Her roots were in prewar Europe. I had no roots, but I began to understand that I could never put them down in this country. No matter how long I lived in England, how well I spoke the language, how deeply I absorbed the culture, I would always be a foreigner. Denis now became my only hope. I was going to work hard and ask him to help me through medical school. My mother sat me down and looked at me very seriously.

"You know that my brother and I don't get along, but this has nothing to do with what I'm telling you. Never, ever, rely on Denis for anything. You cannot count on him. He will resent any demands that you make on him. He will give you what he wants to when he wants to, never what you need. Take care that you don't allow him to disappoint you."

I didn't believe her.

Mrs. Brash found a "suitable" home for me in Brixton, close to the school.

Mr. and Miss Goldschmidt were elderly brother and sister. Neither had ever married and they lived together in a "council flat," apartments rented and maintained by the Greater London County Council to provide decent housing for low-income families. I was given a room, modestly furnished like the rest of the apartment, and I was expected to become part of the family.

"But I have my own family," I explained. "I am not an orphan!"

A knowing, gentle smile passed between them. We know better, it seemed to say.

Mrs. Brash had done her homework. The Goldschmidt household was extremely religious, far more so than the orphanage had been. Mr. Goldschmidt, a retired merchant with a long beard, wore a yarmulke and spent most of his time on Talmudic studies. His sister worked a few hours at the local library but dedicated her time to the synagogue.

They expected me to continue with Hebrew school, go to services every Saturday, and during leisure hours to join the youth group at the temple. My friends from Saint Martin's were not welcome. It was one thing to attend a Christian school since it was the best one around, but socializing with the goyim was frowned upon.

Visiting my mother became a logistical problem. I couldn't leave for the weekend on Friday, because I couldn't get to her before sundown, the onset of the Sabbath, when travel was no longer permitted. I couldn't leave Saturday night because I had to go to Hebrew classes Sunday morning. That left only Sunday afternoon to do my visiting and my homework for school, which had become a heavy load. I was allowed to read on Saturday, but could not pick up a pen, a telephone, or even flush the toilet. The Goldschmidts were simple, decent, devout people, and I was terribly miserable living with them. I spent most of my time in my room, doing homework and reading to ward off the loneliness. The Goldschmidts and I had nothing to talk about.

It was about that time that I received news that broke my heart.

Peter and I corresponded, but infrequently. Neither one had happy news to report. His life behind the Iron Curtain was certainly not easier than mine in the Free World; and since mail was heavily censored, we couldn't write about anything that really mattered. We knew that Klari had been released from prison the previous year with six other women, but only because they were all dying. Apparently the authorities did not like to bother with funerals on prison premises. Five of the women did indeed die. Klari was nursed back to life. We knew that they were in great need, and whenever I visited my mother, we hauled packages to the post office. We became quite ingenious at getting things past customs. Klari had asked for fancy buttons, needles, and thread. It seemed there were still people in Communist Hungary who could afford dressmakers, but supplies were not available. We got old used clothing, sometimes with holes in them, that no one would want and sewed fancy buttons on them and hid precious sewing-machine parts in the pockets. Shoulder pads were stuffed with anything that couldn't be detected, and rolls of cotton, in themselves useful, were also filled with minute necessities.

In my mind, Peter had always remained my big brother: someone that I would always be able to count on as he would me. Though we lived thousands of miles apart and had not seen each other for several years, I felt that the bond we had forged as children was as strong as ever. I was too young to understand and accept that though Peter loved me, he could also love another. A letter and a picture came from Klari. Peter was married. I was in shock. I felt totally abandoned, my heart broken. How could Peter do this to me? I cried myself to sleep every night for weeks. The picture that Klari had sent showed a beautiful girl with enormous dark eyes and black wavy hair. She was twenty-one, a woman. I was an awkward and homely sixteen year old. I had no illusions about my looks and had the usual teenage insecurities. I hated Erika on sight. Why did she have to be beautiful when I was such an ugly duckling? She could probably have anyone she wanted. Why did she have to take my Peter? I pictured her a hussy. There was no one that I could talk to. I knew that there was no one who would understand. Not even my mother. Since I couldn't articulate or understand what I felt, how could I have explained it to anyone else? I carried my pain alone for a long time.

I had to leave the Goldschmidts. I couldn't bear it anymore.

To Mrs. Brash's great disapproval, I announced that I was going to live with my mother. She had stopped working as a live-in housekeeper and had taken a job as chef in a restaurant. The money was much better, but the work was brutal and totally unsuitable for her weak heart condition. She was, however, determined to become independent and to have her own home. She rented the bed-sitter from Mrs. Rosenberg.

Mrs. Rosenberg was a legend among the Jewish Hungarian refugees in London. She was a big, handsome woman with a huge, roaring laugh. She had come to England in the late 1930s, been interned during the war, then married a well-to-do and much older man, who conveniently died shortly afterward. She legally defeated his family's claim to his money, and with that she set herself up in business by buying two large, adjoining Victorian homes in Warrington Crescent, a few blocks from Maida Vale. She converted the buildings into a boardinghouse over which she ruled like a ruthless mother hen. Her rules were rigid, and any boarder who broke them found himself or herself thrown out into the street bodily, with Mrs. Rosenberg herself doing the throwing. Rent had to be paid promptly on Sunday before 10:00 A.M. for the following week. All the tenants lined up in front of her office door, meekly clutching their money, while she took out a heavy ledger and ceremoniously entered everyone's allotment. By eleven o'clock her loud knocks could be heard on the doors of the would-be deadbeats. There was never any credit given. The rooms had to be kept clean, and she spot-checked regularly. No noise was tolerated. No children. No pets. Mrs. Rosenberg lived on the premises in a comfortable, nicely furnished apartment.

She lived well, dressed well, never fraternized with her tenants, my mother being the exception. Every Saturday she attended the synagogue.

My mother's bed-sitter was reached by the basement entrance at the front of the house, but it had French doors opening onto the communal garden of the houses surrounding it. This gave the room a feeling larger than it actually was. Still, it was a little dank and dark, the large oak tree in front of the window keeping out most of the light and the English weather keeping out any warmth. In one corner was a sink, a stove, and a food cupboard. That was our kitchen. The rest of the room was fairly comfortable with its mismatched jumble of furniture: a couple of overstuffed fauteuils, a table with four chairs, a carpet of indistinguishable color, a chest of drawers, and a "put-u-up," otherwise known as a sofa that opened into a double bed. We were now going to live together for the first time since I could remember.

It was about that time that my mother got word through the International Red Cross that documents had been found proving my father's extermination in Auschwitz. Her mourning period started all over again. She had never reconciled herself to my father's death, hoping against hope that he was still alive somewhere in the Soviet Union. I dismissed the news with, "I never knew my father, so how can I miss him?"

But this attitude was bravado on my part. I would have liked to mourn, but didn't know how. Truth was, I didn't remember my father, but I felt the void in my life and I would have liked to speak about him, to find out who he had been and what had happened to him. But my mother guarded the information jealously, as though I were not yet worthy of this knowledge. Consequently, I was an adult and my mother long dead before I found out the details of my father's deportation and eventual murder.

Our reunion was dreadful. Within a short period of time, all the pent-up pain and resentment that we both unknowingly harbored toward one another came spewing out. The short periods of time that we had spent with each other was nothing like living together. Neither of us had any understanding for the other. The work that my mother did was physically demanding, and her health was weak. She came home exhausted, complaining about her shortness of breath and the pain in her back.

"How can a back hurt?" I asked with the impatience and thoughtlessness of a teenager.

I resented the chores and the running of errands that she was asking me to do, especially when it was for her friends.

"But you're young and healthy. They have no one. What's an hour out of your day to help someone out?" But I needed all my time for schoolwork, I insisted. Besides, I had an hour-and-a-half commute to and from school.

The "home" that she now offered me was not what I had imagined a home would be. It was not a cozy place where I could invite my friends for an overnight. I was alone a great deal. I left for school long before she got up and was often asleep when she got home from work. She assumed that I could take care of myself, and I could, but I resented her expectation. Now that I was home, I wanted to be taken care of. I wanted what I didn't get as a child.

"But, why do you need me here? You're sixteen years old. At your age I was already earning a living," she said. But I knew that she was feeling guilty, because she also said, "You know that I would do anything for you. If you're ever in any trouble, you must always come to me."

"Why?" I asked.

"Because I'm your mother."

She never said, "Because I love you." And I angrily resented it when she said that she stayed alive only as a duty to me. I think she was afraid to admit that she loved me, fearing that anyone she ever loved would only be lost, like she had lost her husband and mother. She had also lost her faith, her interest in life, and her ability to even admit to loving. With her failing health, her erstwhile boldness also waned and the bravado that I had so admired as a child now embarrassed me. She still had a charming cockiness that made her endearing to others, but it irritated me, as did her heavy accent and her wisecracks, the more so because I was very shy with strangers, and hated being so. But I saw that she was vulnerable, and I went in for the kill.

"You've never let me live with you. You've always farmed me out. Now you want me to live with you your way. Well, it's too late!"

For her everything ended in 1945, and for me it should have been a new beginning. She knew that and blamed herself not only for failing to provide me with a better life but also for not permitting the other members of the family to try. I never allowed her to unburden herself; nor was I able to articulate my own anger. I did not acknowledge that she was sick. I insisted to myself that she was just looking for sympathy. I kept a loud silence, nursing my anger, knowing that I was reinforcing her feelings of guilt yet unable to help myself. My teenage rebelliousness was laced with more rage and desperation than either of us understood, while her own bitterness over the direction of her life was often misdirected toward me.

I even thought that my life would be easier without her. It was a terrible time for both of us, even more so because we had expected so much. We both had a fantasy about what our life together should be. But they were different fantasies.

I wanted a mother who was powerful, who inspired respect, someone well educated in the subjects that I thought were important, someone to come to school with me and discuss my future confidently with my teachers—in perfect English. Instead I had an immigrant mother with faltering health, whose English was halting, whose jokes were greeted with either blank stares or polite smiles; whose knowledge of English literature was a vague memory of the stories of Hamlet, Romeo and Juliet, and Oliver Twist.

My mother, on the other hand, fantasized of a relationship that she once had with her mother. The two of us against the world. Me, the younger and stronger, looking out for her, loving her unconditionally, recognizing the many sacrifices that she had made.

I once unburdened myself to our doctor and to Mrs. Rosenberg, who seemed to be sympathetic to me. Concerned, they both immediately repeated everything that I had confided to them to my mother. She was angry, hurt, and humiliated that I had talked about her with anyone.

"How could you say such things about me? It's for you that I do what I do, that I stay alive. How could I have brought such an ungrateful child into the world? Me, to whom my mother was a sacred being. You don't understand how good you have it. I hope you're ashamed of yourself! You've never really been hungry. You're like Kati and Denes and the rest of them. You want to go to Paris? Go!"

"Ashamed of myself? What have *I* to be ashamed of?" I demanded angrily.

We never talked about the past. She lived with her memories and I with mine. I felt betrayed by Mrs. Rosenberg and the doctor, and avoided them for months.

Yet, there was also a spark in our relationship that eventually saved it. It was our own brand of humor. In the middle of a senseless screaming match, some absurdity would strike us. Then, unable to stop ourselves, we would guffaw. Sometimes only one of us would laugh and the other would wind up even angrier, but eventually this common ground offered a mutual safe haven where we both found refuge.

I once spent too much money on a very green outfit, complete with matching shoes, bag, gloves, and beret. Our fight started over something totally different but deteriorated to be about the outfit.

My mother sputtered, "You . . . you . . . look like a . . . a . . . vegetable in that outfit!"

"A vegetable?" I taunted back. "What vegetable? A carrot? A beet? An aubergine?"

"No, a skinny bean, you dope!" This ridiculous exchange ended with both of us sprawled on the bed, doubled over in helpless laughter.

Sometimes we could look at each other across the room and know that we were sharing one thought, and smile. Meanwhile we were undeclared enemies, moving through a complex dance of love and hate, loyalty and betrayal, protection and abandonment.

•

I called Mrs. Brash and told her that my mother's place was too far from school. The trip was too long, I said, and asked her to find me another place to live. My mother stood and watched me pack my things.

"By next year, I'll have a real home where you'll have your own room," she promised.

"All right," I answered, not daring to believe her anymore.

The Cohens owned a retail business in the East End of London. They had hoped to pass it on to their only daughter. She, however, had taken a trip to Canada and had become so enamored of the country that she had decided not to come back to England. They had a large, comfortable apartment in West Kensington, along a modern block of flats, the kind that I had not yet seen in England. There was a lobby, elevators, central heating, and modern bathrooms. Mr. and Mrs. Cohen were uncomplicated people who had spent their lives running their business. They were not well educated and were actually quite contemptuous of any higher learning for females. According to them, teaching school was the highest pinnacle of achievement that women should strive for. Marriage and helping their husbands in business was what women were meant for, and they were pleased that their daughter's chances of finding a "nice Jewish boy" were much enhanced in Toronto.

Mrs. Cohen was a brusk little woman with very curly red hair, a mustache, and an enormous belly. She reminded me of my aunt Regine in France. She was bossy, good-hearted, and shrewd. Mr. Cohen was a dapper little man, quiet and good-natured. He missed his daughter, and I suspect that this was the reason that they filled the apartment with young people. They rented out another room to a young school teacher, Rina, who hated her job and her pupils and whose apparent sole aim was to get married to a rich man and be taken care of. Terry, a nephew of the Cohens, was another boarder. He was attending technical school, learning how to build and fix television sets. He also had no use for academics, but he was quite bright and funny, and somehow the two of us became allies against poor Rina, whom we teased unmercifully. She had a terrible disposition, and though the Cohens tried to fix her up with every young man that they could find, Rina never managed to get a second date.

"Hey, Rina," Terry would suddenly say, very cheerfully. "No date tonight? I heard Prince Philip was abandoning Queen Elizabeth for you. Or did you refuse him because he's not Jewish?

"Oh, leave her alone," Mr. Cohen would admonish good-naturedly. "She'll find someone in good time."

"What's 'good time,' fifty years?" I'd pipe in, earning Rina's eternal wrath.

Every night right after supper, Rina was always slouched in an armchair in front of the television, a scowl on her face, picking at her bad skin. It was the first time that I had access to a television, and I would have enjoyed it had it not been for Rina's unappetizing grooming habits being practiced in the next chair.

The time that I spent with the Cohens was like a hiatus. They made few demands on me, and I was left alone to do what I liked best, read. I was now in the sixth form, and schoolwork was plentiful and serious.

I failed miserably at developing a social life. Mr. Shapiro, the trustee who had taken an interest in me while at Norwood, introduced me to a family with a daughter my age in Hendon, a wealthy Jewish suburb. Anita was a smart, perky, and privileged teenager, a popular member of her synagogue's youth group. She generously invited me to the dances, the sleepovers, the shopping trips with her friends. But I felt in a foreign land where I didn't know the language. I didn't know how to play at these common "girl" activities. I didn't know how to talk about boys and clothes and upcoming parties. I didn't dance. At Norwood, I had always been a spectator when the other girls had jumped up at the sound of a catchy tune on the radio and started gyrating and twisting to the rhythm, totally unselfconscious, as though born to the beat of the big bands. In Anita's world, dancing was the entrée to the magic of the social circle.

I felt awkward and dowdy among her friends. I saw them eyeing me silently when I showed up to a dance in my new, gun-metal colored, open-toed high heels and my circular felt skirt with the poodle appliqué. The shoes were too high, too showy, in bad taste; the skirt a year out of style. It was all such a contrast to their elegant little pumps and pretty, multilayered petticoats. Painfully I pictured Anita explaining my constant presence to her friends, and I wanted to sink into the ground and disappear. There was no chance of a genuine friendship developing in that quarter, and sparing us both further embarrassment, I made excuses whenever an invitation was extended. I retreated to my room, immersed myself in books to cover up the pangs of loneliness.

Occasionally, Mr. Cohen poked his head into my room.

"Come on, that's enough reading. There's a good program on the telly. Come and join us."

Mr. Cohen liked me because I often helped his wife in the kitchen. I always did the dishes. Not because I liked to, but because Mrs. Cohen was a terrible housekeeper and unless I did them, the dishes and pans were dirty. Every Friday, Mrs. Cohen made gefilte fish; the pan that she used was heavily encrusted with burned-on fat, which she said added to the flavor. I loved the fish, but couldn't bear to eat it, until I spent an entire afternoon scrubbing the pan till it looked like new. Mrs. Cohen was not happy. I had ruined the flavor of her gefilte fish.

We were in the kitchen one day when, without warning, she turned to me and asked, "Why aren't you living with your mother?"

"It's too far from school."

"Nonsense! Did she do something bad to you?"

"No, of course not! It's just that her bed-sitter is too small for the two of us."

"She can get her own flat now. The laws have changed."

I didn't answer. Since we weren't living together, the relationship between my mother and me had improved. We visited. I took her to see the sights of London, explaining the history. We went to Hampton Court, Blenheim Palace, the Tower. We were talking and laughing again.

"Juliette, don't be a bad daughter. Go make a home with her. Mr. Cohen and I will be joining our daughter in Canada. We're emigrating."

The law had indeed changed. My mother could now legally rent her own home. The problem was that it was very hard to find anything that she could afford. Then something came up. A little flat became available, but she had to move fast. The landlord wanted twenty-five pounds, "key money." If she came up with it immediately, she could move in. She didn't have twenty-five pounds, and she didn't have time to ask the family. Mrs. Rosenberg was out of the country. She knew only one other person that she felt confident she could go to and borrow money.

We had kept in touch with Depus's family, the woman whose life my mother had saved on the way back from hiding. Depus herself had married and moved to Canada, but her mother still lived in London, in very good circumstances, and her brother was a well-known political cartoonist who worked for the *Evening Standard*. We visited them occasionally, and they always said that if my mother ever needed anything, all she had to do was ask. They would always be "eternally grateful." She called on the old lady, explained the circumstances, and asked to borrow the twenty-five pounds.

"I'm sorry, Magda, I don't keep money around."

My mother didn't understand. "Oh, I can give it to the landlord tomorrow. I'm sure he would wait one day."

"Magda, I don't have twenty-five pounds right now."

"Well, could you ask Vicky? It's very important. I could finally have my own home."

"No, Magda. I don't think he would be interested. You see this is really not a good time to lend money. I'm sorry."

My mother was so shocked that she was unable respond. She turned on her heels and stumbled out of the apartment. It was one of the few times that I saw her cry.

She had a small coterie of friends, all refugees, most of them also working as cooks and housekeepers. They all immediately rallied around. Whatever they had, they gave, and the landlord got his twenty-five pounds in the nick of time. Ten years after the end of the war, my mother finally moved into a home of her own.

62 Chippenham Road, 1956–1958

A flat in a row of aging, three-storied Victorian houses, attached and made of brick, was my mother's new home. It was a working-class neighborhood off Elgin Avenue, the kind where the garbage cans stood outside the front door and the local women dawdled about gossiping while wiping the snot from the noses of their unruly toddlers. The children played in the street and chased one another around the solitary plane tree gracing the curb.

On the main floor lived an immigrant Irish family, the O'Sullivans, with their large brood of impish, freckle-faced children. We lived above them, and upstairs from us, in a couple of rooms, lived a middle-aged bachelor whom we rarely saw or heard. He was chauffeur to some important person in government and occasionally parked a shiny Rolls Royce in front of the house overnight. The children stood around it in a circle, eyes round, mouths slightly open, silently admiring the beautiful machine but never daring to touch it.

A half story up from the front door of the house was a tiny room, about six feet by ten feet, which was designated as mine. It had a small window looking into a bleak and empty backyard. I drew a sign and nailed it up: *CHEZ MOI*. I had just enough room for a bed, a small desk, and a narrow wardrobe. Mr. O'Sullivan helped me to put shelves on the wall to house my collection of books, which was getting quite extensive. I was content. It was mine and I had a key to it.

On the same small landing as my room was the only toilet in the house, shared by all the tenants. A few more steps up was our kitchen—large, airy, old-fashioned. Next to the kitchen was the main room, which was also where my mother slept. It had a fireplace that was blocked up with a gas heater put in its place. Two large windows faced the street, giving us a view of the old gray Catholic Church that the O'Sullivans attended faithfully every Sunday, scrubbed and dressed to the nines. There was no bathroom or hot water. The kitchen sink was the only place to wash. My mother swallowed her pride and wrote to Denis that she needed a bathtub. This was an emergency, and he immediately responded with a generous check for which my mother never bothered to thank him. The tub and a water heater were installed in the corner of the large kitchen. The former had a large wooden cover that made it look like another table when not in use. Above the tub was our *fregoli,* a device widely used in Hungary for drying clothes. It consisted of a large wooden frame, about three feet by six feet, with five dowels running lengthwise inside the frame. Wet clothes were hung on the dowels and the entire contraption was hauled up toward the ceiling by means of a pulley. The tub and the fregoli were a wonder to the neighborhood. All the neighbors agreed: my mother was an "educated and fine lady."

Mrs. O'Sullivan kept the staircase, hallways, and communal bathroom spotless in exchange for my tutoring her two oldest children in French. But the house still looked dingy. The steps were old and worn, the hallways were painted dark brown, and there was linoleum covering the floors. Still, we were very fortunate; in our house reigned a congenial, neighborly atmosphere.

We slowly acquired a mélange of odd-looking furniture. The Cohens, upon leaving for Canada, gave me a glass-fronted bookcase, an easy chair, and a pair of brass candlesticks. The previous tenants had left behind a large pine kitchen table, and our new landlord generously presented us with four matching, red plastic-covered kitchen chairs. The only new items were the beds and mattresses. It was an unspoken rule: one did not sleep in a stranger's bed. Mrs. Rosenberg cleaned out her attic, and we got a large, Victorian-type floral rug and a standing lamp. We sewed curtains, bedcovers, and tablecloths; we painted and we scrubbed; and though hardly elegant or even particularly tasteful, the little flat acquired a homey feel.

Having my own room for the very first time gave me a feeling of independence that I relished. I spent a great deal of time in my tiny quarters. No doubt it would have been far more comfortable to be able to spread out on the kitchen table to do my homework, but I preferred to be *chez moi.* I even attempted decorating—with disastrous results. I was dazzled by the cardboard top of a chocolate box that had a picture of an ersatz Renoir on it, real kitsch. The eyes were exaggerated, too large, too black, vacant. The colors were naive pastels. The border was cheap red brocade. I loved it. Holding it in my hands, I slowly spun around my tiny room, looking for the perfect spot to hang it. It was my first attempt to aesthetically improve my surroundings.

Mr. H. came for his biweekly English lesson. A recent émigré, he was a dapper little man, cultured and proper. I proudly showed him the picture. He looked at it politely, raised his eyebrows, and gave a little, closed-mouthed smile. I knew immediately that the picture was wrong. I saw it in his face. It was common and gauche. I had committed a faux pas in even showing it to him. I was mortified, ashamed of my lack of sophistication, humiliated beyond words.

I stared at the picture every night from my bed, still liking it, taking pleasure in its gaudiness, until one day I threw it in the trash as my mother looked on, biting her lip to hide a smile, which I ignored.

Our relationship, though still stormy at times, had improved a great deal. We trod very carefully. We never talked of the pain that we had inflicted on each other the previous year. We just avoided doing it again. Both of us became more settled in our own home, and we led separate, busy lives. My mother worked very long hours at the restaurant where she was now a chef, and I gave French and English lessons in my spare time for extra money. We fell into a routine. I got up very early in the morning, picked up the newspaper that had been pushed through the slot in the front door, went up to the kitchen, and started making coffee. If, while I was having my breakfast, I heard a knock on the wall, it meant that my mother was up and would like me to bring in a cup for her. We exchanged a few words, then I made the long commute to school. When I got home she was at work. I did my school assignments, tutored on certain days, ate, read and was usually asleep by the time she came home. We caught up on Saturday nights and Sundays.

That year, winter Saturday nights were our best times together, ever. At nine o'clock there was "Saturday Night Theater" on the BBC radio station. We both got into my mother's big double bed with a big tray between us. On the tray was a large pile of fried bread rubbed with lots of garlic and huge glasses of tea with plenty of sugar and lemon. We turned on the radio to listen to the play and munched on the garlic bread, getting crumbs all over the bed but feeling cozy and at ease with each other.

"You'd better enjoy this now, because once you're married, that's the end of garlic at night," she said.

"What if my husband also likes garlic?" I challenged.

"Don't be silly. What kind of Englishman likes garlic?" We assumed that I would marry and stay in England.

I had very little social life to speak of. There were no opportunities to meet young men, since Saint Martin's was an all-girls' school, and I had abandoned the synagogue's youth program. The young people there were so much better off financially than I was that I didn't feel comfortable around them. I felt that I couldn't invite them to my home, nor could I dress the way the girls did. I was too shy to learn how to dance and at four feet eleven inches tall, I was taken for twelve when I was already seventeen years old. I rarely saw the handful of friends I had from Norwood. They were working, and we had less and less in common as time passed. I saw Elsa from time to time. She was unhappy in her job, but she had met other young women at her workplace and had even started dating.

She was talking about going to Israel. Jill, Maureen, and I sometimes went to the theater, mostly the Old Vic, but their social life was tied to their church. I spent most of my free time reading alone in my room.

My mother's house became the gathering place for her friends. They were all Hungarian refugees, mostly Holocaust survivors who had come to England as domestics after losing all their families. There was Bolond Rozsi (Crazy Rose), who looked like a Cockney charwoman. Hair dyed a bright henna, topped by a hat bought at a church jumble sale, she walked around with her stockings always hanging and her coat pinned together with huge safety pins. Rose came from a wealthy family who had objected to her becoming an opera singer. Her husband, a brilliant young surgeon, had encouraged her, and she had sung the title role of Madame Butterfly at the Budapest Opera House. She was the only one of her family to survive the war. Now she cleaned houses for the rich and famous of London society. Her favorite employer was a famous art dealer because he allowed her to play his opera records while she worked and look at his art collection. Sometimes on a Sunday afternoon, sitting at our kitchen table, she broke into "Un bel dì," and her face was transformed from a charwoman's to a diva's. Her voice filled the room and the other women wept.

I never found out what had happened to Irene. She was tall and stately and looked more like the lady of the grand house than its housekeeper. She had been married and had two daughters. Now she had no one. All she ever said that referred to her life before the war was, "Thank God my mother insisted that I learn cooking and housekeeping, otherwise I would starve."

Mrs. Rosenberg was also a regular visitor, and her big laugh could be heard all the way to the street. Women drifted in and out of our kitchen. There was always a pot of soup on the stove, along with espresso and my mother's inimitable strudels. Sunday afternoon, we all sat around the kitchen table laughing, gossiping, exchanging books and recipes, discussing politics. I was always included in the conversation, and whenever I came out with what my family called my "sitzers," quick, sharp remarks, just this side of impertinent, my mother would throw me a warning look. But the women laughed and thought I was very clever.

Whenever there was any official business to be handled for anyone, I was the one who filled out forms, made telephone calls, or visited various government agencies. The history and English papers that I wrote for school were passed around the table and read as though they were precious manuscripts. If I ever received anything less than an A, the teachers were, at best, "stupid," at worst, "anti-Semitic." The women were very impressed and sometimes skeptical. "Otto von Bismarck's domestic policy? Why does a young girl have to know that? Besides, he was a German, wasn't he?"

They were very proud of me and envied my mother for having me. I became their surrogate child, along with interpreter, correspondent, and general troubleshooter. I took over the paying of our monthly bills. My mother could never learn to spell numbers, so it just became easier to write out all the checks myself rather than correct my mother's spelling. Eventually I just signed her name to the checks and sent them out. Mr. Summers, the bank manager called one day and in a very concerned voice told me that he had reason to believe that someone was forging my mother's name to her checks—would she please stop in at the bank as soon as possible? I asked whom the checks were made out to, and when he reeled off our landlord, the electric company, the telephone company, etc., I told him not to worry, I had made out the checks and had been doing so for the past year. Poor Mr. Summers was totally beside himself. He called us both in and lectured us as though we were two naughty children, then he opened a joint account and backdated it six months. We left the bank, mimicking the grave look and stern voice of Mr. Summers, and laughed over the stuffiness of English bank managers.

Soon after my mother acquired the apartment, Kati came to visit. We were sure that it would not be to her liking, and on the way home from the airport I warned Kati to keep her mouth shut, no matter what she thought. But Kati surprised us. She kept her criticism to a minimum; in fact as she walked around the apartment, looking at our various knickknacks, she said wistfully, "Well, at least it's yours!" Her two suggestions, delivered in a very serious and schoolmarmy tone, which made us raise our eyes to heaven, were (1) take half the upstairs apartment ("He's a bachelor, he doesn't need more than one room") and build a proper bathroom, and (2) move the garbage cans to the front of the neighbor's house, and put geranium pots in their places. "It will tone up the place!"

Kati came to tell us that she was moving to Munich. Denis was doing some export-import business with Germany and wanted her to be his liaison there. Laws had been passed in that country demanding that restitution be paid to Holocaust survivors. While she was there, she was going to put in her claim and wanted to do the same for us. There ensued a heated discussion. My mother wanted nothing to do with "blood money." Kati was horrified. Her raised fist punched the air as she shouted, "Are you crazy? You must try to get every penny you can. You lost everything. You lost your husband, your health, your home, your means of support. Evi's hands and feet are still painful. And who knows whether they'll ever heal properly. They owe it to you. They owe Evi the education that her father would have given her had he lived."

"You think there is a price for what they did?"

"Of course not. But let them pay. Let them bleed. Let them watch us live on their earnings! Let them see us grow strong again on their money!"

The women around the kitchen table nodded vigorously in response to Kati's impassioned battle cries. They wanted to join her in putting in their claims. Kati took everyone's story and claim back to Germany with her.

Denis also came. He sat at the big kitchen table and ate his sister's cooking with relish. "You cook just like Anyuka and even better than I remember Klari's cooking, but never tell her I said so."

"I wish I could tell her something . . . anything," answered my mother wistfully. They both sighed. None of us had seen Klari, Peter, Pista, or my grandfather since 1948.

With any two Pollak siblings in one room, peace could not reign for very long. Denis strutted around the little apartment and declared, "Well, you must admit, I got you a pretty nice place here!"

"What?"

"What do you mean 'what'? Didn't you buy it with the money I sent you?"

"They money you sent me bought the bathtub. Period. With what was left over, Evi got a winter coat."

"Chinchilla?"

"Yes, but after the first season we gave it to the poor."

"You probably did!"

I left the room. The silliness escalated into a full-fledged quarrel. Then I heard my mother's gasps. I ran to get her pills and shot Denis an annoyed look. He looked startled.

"How long has this been going on?" he asked.

"Since 1942, you idiot!" said my mother between gasps, fighting for air. She chose the moment well to insult him. He didn't dare answer her.

He stayed only a day or two when he came. His visits were like a whirlwind. I cut school and he took me shopping in the West End and to elegant restaurants where we met people whom I had never heard of but who knew and inquired after my mother and told me to tell her to call them.

"You see," Denis said, "she doesn't have to do what she does. She could meet a better class of people, get married, or at least get into a decent line of work. But your mother refuses to take any sane advice. She thinks that because your father was a Communist, she would be betraying his memory by not being 'one of the masses.' Don't grow up like her!"

We always took in a couple of new movies, and I usually took him to see some interesting historical or architectural sight where I was the one who knew more than he did, the Whispering Gallery in Saint Paul's or Poet's Corner in Westminster Abbey. He always ended his visits with the same sneer. "Napoleon was right. They are just a nation of shopkeepers!" And I knew that he felt inferior to the English.

He usually gave me money to give to my mother. She took it and sniffed, "I guess we're supposed to buy Buckingham Palace with this."

For a few years, my mother made the best of the short English summer season. She took a job at a seaside family hotel in Ilfracombe, in Sommerset, as their seasonal chef. Before the era of luxury hotels and resorts, middle-class families in England would spend their two-week summer holiday in old-fashioned, weather-beaten, family-owned hotels, stacked with peeling wicker furniture, close to the rocky beaches, where they could have a modest room and three meals a day for a reasonable price. The English, accustomed to their mediocre food, were delighted with tasty, well-prepared and attractively served meals. They always wanted to "meet the chef" and left generous tips at the end of their stay. My mother's reputation grew and her hotel was always booked solid during July and August. For a couple of summers I joined her for a few weeks and helped out. For breakfast large stacks of buttered bread and sectioned grapefruit halves were placed on each table, and my job was to butter the bread and section the grapefruit. I became so adept at these chores that I amused the kitchen help who stopped what they were doing and came to gape at the ever escalating speed with which I performed my tasks. Eventually they even timed me with a stop watch. My mother would tolerate this interruption of work for only a short time, then shoo everybody back to their stations, while shaking her head at me. I made a game of my tedious chores and everyday tried to beat my own record. I stood at the ready in front of the large wooden table with all my "props" in the correct spot, my left hand placed on top of a stack of sliced bread, my right holding a blunt knife above a mound of softened butter. Then, one, two, three, start! Simultaneously my hands swung toward the center. The knife had picked up a dollop of butter, swung left, spread itself on the oncoming slice of bread going toward it to the right. The buttered slice ended up on the right side, starting the "buttered stack" while my hands swung back and started the procedure all over again.

The particular "twist of the wrist" I developed for rapid grapefruit sectioning became a legend in the hotel and I was asked to demonstrate it to the rest of the staff. The sharp, curved and serrated knife sliced into the flesh of the fruit and the famous "twist" did its trick. Not a smidgeon of membrane remained attached to the pulp. The fruit came away free with each spoonful. I was the heroine of the breakfast room! My mother's tart remark was, "Well, you can always make a living as a glorified kitchen maid!"

I didn't get paid by the hotel. I was my mother's "employee," but they did give me the tiniest garret room, which I found very romantic and where I had a marvelous view of the ocean. I enjoyed these weeks at the seashore. Aside from the bread buttering and the grapefruit sectioning, I sometimes helped set the tables in the dining room and decorated the dinner plates with sprigs of parsley and rosettes of radishes. The rest of the time I was free to roam on the rocky seashore and find secluded coves where I read for hours without a soul to disturb me. On rainy days, of which there were plenty, I haunted the local used-book stores and found treasures that I hauled back to the hotel and holed up with in my little garret hideaway.

My mother joined me when she had a couple of hours off. She liked to sit high on a cliff, look out toward the ocean, and listen to my reading aloud to her. Though she worked very hard at the job, these weeks together had a vacation-like quality. Away from our usual routine, at the seashore, we never quarreled and were relaxed with each other. We often later referred to the "nice summers" in Ilfracombe. In the summer of 1956, my mother was getting ready to go to her summer job, and expected me to join her, but it was not to be.

Summer 1956

Denis appeared on our doorstep on a rainy late June day in 1956.

"Evi, ask your mother if you can come with me to Munich. Kati and I need an English interpreter for a few weeks."

My mother shrugged her shoulders. "It's up to her," she said to Denis. She was loathe to see me go, but I chose to ignore that. I was always ready for an adventure.

We arrived in Munich, where Kati was waiting for us. She had rented an elegant little apartment in Schwabbing, the trendy part of Munich, and there was a man in her life.

Kati always recognized quality, whether it was a dusty, forgotten piece of antique furniture left in the cellar or a sad older gentleman walking the streets of Munich with worn shoes and a shabby overcoat. Kati could resurrect either one, if she thought it worth her while.

Andreas Gedeon (Uncle Bandi, as he became known to me) was a gentleman of the old school and scion of one of the wealthiest Jewish families in Hungary. Their fortune came originally from wines and liquors but had expanded into real estate. His only brother had opted for the intellectual life and was a music critic and biographer, while Uncle Bandi had taken on the running of the family business. During the war most of their assets were confiscated and he had been conscripted into forced labor. His mother and brother had been saved by the latter's wife, who was not Jewish. What the Nazis did not take, the Communists did, and the family was left practically penniless. After his return from deportation, Bandi was "relocated" by the Communists, as were all former "capitalists," into the hinterlands, from whence he escaped in the early 1950s and ended up in Munich; there he made a meager living by brokering business deals. He had excellent contacts from the prewar years, and his reputation was spotless. When Denis was looking for an entrée into the German business community, someone recommended Uncle Bandi. Kati recognized the name and remembered that when she was a young girl, she had dreamed of moving in the same social circles and meeting him. Now he lived in the most modest circumstances. Every spare penny he had was sent back to his aged mother and his brother, living in a cottage on the banks of the Danube outside Budapest.

Kati took one look and knew. Here was a subject worthy of her talents. She fed him, spruced him up, made him clean his shoes, and unstuffed his pockets, in which he carried two thick Hebrew prayer books plus a fat envelope full of pictures of his mother. Under Kati's care he blossomed, and this unlikely pair stayed together till his death twenty-five years later. Aunt Kati, the attractive, ambitious, energetic, shrewd social climber and Uncle Bandi, the gentle, cultured, unassuming gentleman with the quiet sense of humor became a totally devoted couple to the end.

There was someone else in the apartment besides Uncle Bandi. Without warning to anyone, Denis had brought his Cuban daughter, by then about ten years old, to visit the family. Her name was Magda: a total surprise to everyone, since my mother was still alive. We dubbed her Little Magda. She spoke only Spanish and was totally confused by her new environment. In addition to removing her from the only home she had ever known, Havana, he had left her with Kati in Munich while he had flown to England. Little Magda was frightened and became completely wild. She bit, scratched, and broke everything in sight. Denis laughed and thought the whole thing hilarious, while Kati, at her wit's end, told him in no uncertain terms to remove his child forthwith from her apartment. She was not going to jeopardize her new relationship because of this "savage." Uncle Bandi suggested boarding her for the summer with a woman he knew who took several children into her cottage. It was in a beautiful Bavarian setting on the edge of a lake in Bad Wiessee, about an hour south of Munich. We drove there, and when all the arrangements had been made, Denis had the brilliant idea that since Little Magda was going to have such a wonderful vacation, I should stay there, too. What about their need for an interpreter? Well that was no longer necessary, since Uncle Bandi was there. I could not stay at the cottage, which was for small children, so Denis rented a room for me at a nearby inn. Before I realized what was happening I was alone in a hotel room, in a town where I knew no one, with instructions to watch over Little Magda.

The first night I went down to the common dining room, with its single long refectory table and cheery, country-style furnishings. The smell of sausages and sauerbraten wafted in from the kitchen. Everyone seemed to be in a happy mood. There was a *gemütliche,* or "homey," atmosphere. I was standing alone, hesitantly, when one of the guests asked whether I was waiting for someone.

"Nein, Ich bin allein" ("No, I am alone").

"Na den, kommen Sie schon und setzen Sie sich mit uns" ("Well then, come and sit with us"), they invited.

I sat down next to them. They were a middle-aged, florid-faced couple dressed in the traditional Bavarian dirndl and lederhosen, real Germans. We talked and they asked questions. It was odd for a seventeen-year-old girl to be staying at an inn on her own, and they were curious. I answered all their questions about where I lived, went to school, and so on, but then came the questions about my family. Where was my father? What did he do?

"Mein Vater ist gestorben. Er war in Auschwitz getötet" ("My father is dead. He was killed in Auschwitz").

The entire table stopped talking. The laughter stopped. All heads turned toward me. My first reaction was embarrassment. Why did I say that? Why didn't I just say that he was dead? Why did I have to add that he was killed in Auschwitz? A few moments passed. No one said anything, and my feeling of embarrassment turned to anger. Why doesn't anyone say anything? Can't they at least say "I'm sorry"? I thought. It never occurred to me that they were embarrassed, too.

I wanted to leave, but I didn't. People started talking again quietly, but the mood had changed. The couple didn't say anything further. We finished our dinner in silence. I said "gutte Nacht" and returned to my room. I wanted to cry, but I couldn't. I just stared at the ceiling for a long time.

I didn't go back to the dining room. I went out for my meals and sometimes ate with the children at Frau Smetana's, where Little Magda was. It was the oddest vacation ever. For the most part I spent my time alone reading, leaning against a headstone in the local cemetery, looking out over the lake.

Frau Smetana's youngest son, a tall, blond, intelligent young man and a student at the university in Munich, was home for the summer working in one of the local restaurants. He took pity on me and spent some of his free time with me. We became friendly, and I told him about the incident at the inn. He sighed. "Yes, we have a terrible problem. We are a nation divided. There are plenty of ex-Nazis, and there are also plenty like my mother. They were not Nazis, they did nothing bad, but they closed their eyes to what was going on. Now they can't live with themselves. And then there is our generation. We are disgusted with our parents, deeply ashamed of them, yet they are our parents and we love them. What are we going to tell our children about their grandparents? And nobody admits to what their role was during the war, because they don't know what their neighbor did. We are afraid of ourselves and of each other."

"Perhaps," I said, not caring in the least.

A couple of weeks later, Denis roared into town in his brand-new American car that he'd had shipped over from the States. It was a Chevy Bel Air, two-tone blue, chrome-laden, and gorgeous. The innkeepers were stone-faced when he paid the bill.

"What's the problem? What did you do?" he asked.

"Nothing. Perhaps they don't like Jews with fancy cars."

"Let them get used to it," he answered grimly as he handed the porter a huge tip.

Little Magda, Denis, and I headed back to Munich. After a couple of days with her littlest niece, Kati was verging on a nervous breakdown.

"All right, all right. Everybody is leaving," announced Denis. "Magda's going home, and Evi and I are going to Vienna."

"Vienna? What for?"

"I have business there. Evi, are you ready?"

Of course I was ready. We got into the Chevy, dropped Little Magda at the airport into the care of an obliging stewardess, got on the Autobahn, and roared toward Vienna, Denis never giving his child another thought.

Denis was flush and in a good mood. We stopped at wonderful restaurants, he told jokes and stories, listened to mine and told me that we no longer had to worry about the future. He was expecting his first shipment of slot machines to arrive in Germany any day, and he had sold them at a good price. Now he was ready to do some negotiating in Austria.

In Vienna, Denis went to his business meetings, letting me roam and explore the city. We had been in Vienna for a few days when he rushed into the hotel one evening.

"How would you like to go to Budapest?" he asked.

"Budapest? How? Did you buy the American army, or just a Soviet tank?"

We were very aware how near, and yet how far, we were from *Haza*. But we never thought that there was a possibility of crossing the Iron Curtain.

"Listen," said Denis excitedly, "I just found out that there is an international football match this Saturday in Budapest and that they are issuing weekend visas. We have to apply three days in advance. Today is Tuesday, we may just make it."

At eight o'clock the next morning we were at Ibusz, the Hungarian state-travel bureau, with our passports. Mine was French, Denis's Cuban. We had to give a reason for wanting to enter the Hungarian People's Republic, and for the next five minutes we became avid soccer fans. We would not find out till Friday afternoon whether we would be granted the visas that would allow us to enter the country.

We were both in a feverish state of excitement, though Denis pretended to be very philosophical about it. "Look, either we go or we don't. There's no use worrying about it." But by Friday afternoon he was pacing the pavement outside Ibusz.

If we got the visas, we would have to shop for a lot of things that we wanted to bring the family, but we couldn't start shopping until we knew whether we were going or not. A friend of Denis's joined us in our wait, and at four thirty the visas were issued. We were on the list! At five o'clock the stores closed.

Denis dug into his pockets and handed me an enormous wad of bills. "Evi, you go to Julius Meinl and get everything you can before they close. Jancsi, you go get those watches you said you could get wholesale. I'll meet you both back at the hotel. Hurry!"

We ran. I still don't know how I managed to drag back to the hotel several pounds of coffee, tea, cocoa, oranges, lemons, chocolate, and any other delicacy that I could grab.

Jancsi showed up with his watches and even a couple of cameras. Denis made a triumphant entry with dozens of nylon stockings, silk blouses, lace night-gowns, perfume, and other feminine accoutrements. Everything was thrown into the trunk of the car and we took off, destination Budapest.

Neither one of us said very much on the drive to Budapest. We were too excited and too apprehensive about getting across the border. Until we were in front of the house, we didn't dare believe in what was happening.

"You just never know what the Communists might pull," muttered Denis.

At the border the young soldiers were friendly as they examined our pass-ports, though the machine guns, nonchalantly slung over their shoulders, made us very uneasy. They opened the trunk and looked in amazement at the array of luxury so carelessly thrown in. Denis immediately offered them chocolates, oranges, and nylon stockings, which they eagerly accepted before waving us on, wishing us the pleasure of seeing our favorite team win.

We arrived in front of the building around eleven o'clock that night and just sat there for a few moments, at a loss for what to do next. We drove around the block where we found a coffeehouse that was open and had a telephone. Denis asked the proprietor to call Klari's number; if a woman answered, ask for Peter. Peter answered, and Denis took the receiver.

"Peter. It's Denis."

"Denis! How are you? How great to hear from you. Where are you calling from? Paris?"

"No, I'm downstairs."

"What? What did you say?"

"Peter, Evi and I are downstairs. We didn't dare come up in case Klari became hysterical or had a heart attack."

"But . . . but . . . how? Denis, you're joking, right?"

"No. We'll explain when we come up. Prepare your mother!"

"Give me five minutes. And I hope I'm not dreaming."

Getting into the building was not that easy. The front door was locked. We rang the bell and a sleepy concierge shuffled out and asked us what we wanted. We told him whom we had come to see. He looked us over, saw the fancy car behind us, and said, "I need to see your papers!"

We exchanged glances and handed over our passports, which he examined upside down.

"Well, I don't know about this," he said uncertainly.

"Oh yes, you do," said Denis, handing him a large bill, picking up the bags, and walking toward the elevator.

"It's broken," said the man.

We heard someone running down the stairs, taking them three at a time, and in a second I was picked up and hugged and kissed and kissed again. Peter half carried me up five flights of stairs. Klari was standing in the doorway of the old apartment, half crying, half laughing. "Oh my God, Oh my God, I don't believe it. Denes, Evi, how did you do it? How is it possible?"

Oh, the excitement, the tears, the laughter, the hugs, the kisses, the questions that didn't wait for answers. It seemed to go on and on. Finally things quieted down, and they were ready to hear how we had managed this miracle.

"All right," said Denis, "I'll tell you. But first make me a nice cup of English tea with lots of lemon and sugar."

"The sugar we can give you, the rest you have to imagine. You are in Hungary!" said Peter with a wry grin.

"Nonsense," said Denis as he reached into his bag and pulled out a whole bag of lemons and a box of English tea.

"Oh, my God," wailed Klari. "Do you know how long it's been since I've held a real lemon in my hands?"

"Well, don't just hold it! Squeeze!"

My grandfather sat in his chair, speechless, looking at his son as though seeing the Messiah. Klari's husband, Uncle Laci, patted Denis on the back, looked wise, twirled his mustache, and shook his head as if to say, "We men of the world are different from them. We understand things they don't."

Peter had one arm around me and the other one around Erika, who stood shyly, feeling left out. Damn, she's pretty! I thought. And obviously pregnant!

We talked, we laughed, we told stories, we cried and laughed again.

Around four in the morning we finally petered out, loathe to miss even one minute of this miraculous reunion.

I woke up before anyone. Denis was sleeping on the brown cut velvet sofa bed that I had shared with Uncle Sanyi the night Klari had threatened to take me down to the cellar. I walked out onto the balcony where Peter had been stranded during a bombing raid; the sash that pulled up the wooden shades still showed where it had been mended after it broke and the shades had come crashing down on me, leaving Peter outside. The furniture was the same, just older and shabbier. I recognized every single one of the knickknacks in the showcase with the sliding-glass doors. As a small child, I used to stand in front of it on tiptoe to look at the little Dresden china ballerinas that Kati prized so much she never allowed me to touch them. There was a framed scene of a Greek legend hanging above the sofa that had been embroidered in petit point by Peter's father and had always held such fascination for me. I felt as if I were in a time warp. I was back in the only place where I had ever felt secure. The surroundings were still there, so were some of the people; but the world had changed and so had I. Those of us who were still around, whether in the Free World or behind the Iron Curtain, had been battered and bloodied, but we had survived and, incredibly, were still hopeful for the future.

I sat down in the deep armchair where Nagyi used to sit when she came to visit. I tried to feel her presence. I closed my eyes and remembered the sound of Uncle Sanyi's voice. These walls were the repository of so many of my childhood memories. I was lost in thought when Denis's voice broke the silence.

"So, what do you think they'll say when we get back?"

"They won't believe us."

"That's why we have a camera!" he said triumphantly.

Everybody woke up to the smell of real coffee. We were all gathering in the dining room when the doorbell rang and to Klari's great annoyance an invasion began. Word had gotten out, "the Westerners were here!"

Auntie Erna from next door, whom I knew since babyhood, charged in with her own pot of coffee as a tribute to us.

"Erna, for heaven's sake, what are you bringing in that old pot?" asked Klari crossly.

"Coffee for everybody! Where's Evike?"

"Coffee? Your coffee? It's so weak it can't get out of the pot!"

"Oh, don't say that. I put my heart and soul into it!" said a hurt Auntie Erna.

"You should leave your heart and soul out of it and use coffee instead," muttered Klari, annoyed that she had to share us with friends and neighbors.

Peter had run out to fetch our cousin Pista, who held a special spot in Denis's heart, as had his father, Denis's older brother Miklos, who had died in Auschwitz. At age twenty-four, Pista had the eyes of an old man. When he was eighteen, he had tried to escape from Hungary and had been caught at the border with his pockets stuffed with revolutionary literature. He had been tried as an "enemy of the state" and sentenced to four years in a Communist prison. Never too strong emotionally, he was showing signs of instability since his release. He and Klari shared memories that the rest of us did not dare to intrude upon.

So many people wanted to see us. The doorbell and the telephone didn't stop ringing. Denis took charge. "Ok, everybody out! We are going to a big outdoor place. Klari, where? The restaurant on Margaret Island? Ok. Anybody who wants to see us can come there. We will sit in comfort and have lunch. Let's go!"

Eight of us piled into the Chevy, which already had a curious crowd around it, and we took off for Margaret Island, to the hotel restaurant usually frequented by Iron Curtain dignitaries.

Tables were pushed together, Denis ordered the best and most expensive things on the menu, and anybody who came to see us shared in the feast. Suddenly we realized that my grandfather was missing. It didn't take long to find him. A crowd of about two hundred people had gathered around our car, and Nagypapa was holding forth.

"This car belongs to my son. He is a very rich and famous man in America. You've all heard of the island of Manhattan? Well, he owns it. And this car has a 500-horsepower engine and a gas tank so capacious that he can drive clear across Europe without stopping. Only very respected people are allowed to paint their cars in two colors, and blue is the most honorable color. . . ." He kept on talking in this outrageous fashion for as long as we were there, never stopping for lunch or to join us.

We drove around the city, looking at the sights, recognizing the old ones, disliking the new ones, till exhausted we went home, horrified that half the time we were allowed to spend there had already passed.

Pista, Peter, and I managed to take a walk together while the adults were getting ready for dinner and planning the following day. We strolled to the park where we had played as children. We sat there looking at one another and smiling.

"We'd better talk," said Pista. "We don't have much time. Who knows when we'll see each other again."

"Yeah, probably not for years," sighed Peter.

"I don't think so," I said. "I feel that there are changes happening. We may be together again sooner than you think."

"Evi, you're a Westerner. You don't understand how we live here. Nothing is going to change unless there is a major war. And why should the West sacrifice their peaceful existence for us? No, unfortunately nothing is going to change. Let's just hope that there will be lots more international football games in the future and that you'll get visas to come."

"No, you're wrong!" I said loudly and emphatically. "You're too close to it.

You can't see it. You can't feel it. It's in the air here. I can't explain it. There's a revolutionary smell."

Both young men clamped their hands over my mouth simultaneously.

"Ssh, Evi. Are you crazy? You can't talk like that here! Someone might hear!"

The old fear was back. Watch what you say! Don't give yourself away! I had forgotten what it was like not to be able to say what I felt like saying. It was a shock to realize that they had never stopped being afraid!

We huddled together on a bench and talked about our lives, about my mother and Kati who would both be so disappointed for not having had the chance to come with us. They whispered the latest anti-regime jokes making the rounds and asked about the political situation in the West, especially the Suez Crisis, which had just exploded.

"We don't believe anything we read in the newspapers here. As a matter of fact, we don't even believe the opposite of what we read!"

Our two days together passed all too quickly. As I kissed Erika good-bye, I slipped a package into her hands—the prettiest lace nightgown that we had brought with us. Klari would have to sell something else!

We left with tears and promises to write more often and a list from Klari, reminding us what to send in future packages.

Denis went back to Munich, then New York. I went back to London and school, where I made a big splash because I had visited behind the Iron Curtain. Our lives reverted to the usual routine.

October 24, 1956

It was a school day, and as usual, I got up and ran down the half flight of stairs to the front door to pick up the newspaper. A cold wind was blowing through the mail slot in the door, and I hurried back up the stairs toward the warmth of the kitchen and a fresh cup of coffee. I glanced at the headline and stopped dead in my tracks: UPRISING IN HUNGARY. I scanned the article. The previous day some university students had held a political protest meeting, which got out of hand. Word spread to other universities, and by the next day there was a full-fledged popular revolt. Communist leaders were dragged out of their beds, beaten, and hanged. Prisons were opened and prisoners freed. Some people were fleeing toward the Austrian border.

I flung open my mother's door, rushed in, turned on the radio, shouting at her to wake up. "Look, look what's going on! What's going to happen to them? Can we call them?"

International telephone calls were still very expensive luxuries reserved for very special occasions. But as soon as she had grasped the situation, my mother reached for the telephone. Impatiently we waited for the operator to make the connection.

"I'm sorry, madam, all the lines are busy and we have been told to take names and put them on waiting lists. Do you wish to be put on?"

"Yes, yes, of course! How long will we have to wait?"

"It's impossible to tell. But someone must be by the telephone at all times. If we call you back and you're not there, you'll lose your turn."

"All right, just put us on. Meanwhile, can you get us through to Munich?" Maybe Kati had heard something; it was an hour later there. But Kati had not. She had also been trying to call, but couldn't. Nobody knew where Denis was. We were at a loss as to what to do. How could we help? What was there to do? We sat by the radio, school and work forgotten, waiting for news bulletins. My mother's friends all came by and sat with us. We jumped every time the telephone rang and told everyone to stay off the line in case the call from Budapest came through.

For the next few days we camped in my mother's room, where the telephone was. One of us was there at all times. The radio was on day and night. The Suez Crisis was again uppermost in the news. Israel was involved. Would the Russians intervene in Hungary or in Egypt or both? Would there be another war? We argued endlessly and senselessly and agonized over what was happening to the family in Budapest.

A week went by before we got our one minute on the telephone. We learned very little. They were all fine. They were being careful. We had nothing to worry about. Obviously they did not trust their newfound freedom and assumed that the phones were still wiretapped, which they had always been led to believe. We immediately put our names on the waiting list for another call.

Within a few days the headlines announced that Soviet tanks had entered the country "at the request of the Hungarian people," and true fighting had begun.

Every news bulletin brought terror into our living room. The tanks thundered through Budapest, shooting indiscriminately and mercilessly. Young revolutionaries risked and often lost their lives by throwing Molotov cocktails under the tanks. Russian and Hungarian bodies littered the streets of the Hungarian capital. There was looting and burning. Eleven years after the siege of Budapest, the Soviet army was back, again under the guise of liberators. We hoped against hope that no one in the family aspired to heroism this time around.

The next one-minute telephone call that came through brought with it dread and hope. Klari came on the line. "The children have left," she said to my mother, then burst into tears.

We sat there silently, afraid to look at each other—both of us picturing Peter and Erika in the minefields separating Hungary from Austria. Erika, nine months pregnant. How were they going to make it across?

Reunion

In early December, a little band of disoriented refugees arrived at our doorstep. Peter with Erika, who was nine months pregnant, and another young couple, Panni and George, with their six-month-old baby girl. Panni's family and Klari had been friends since the births of Peter and Panni, which were on the same day and in the same hospital. The two young mothers were fast friends. When the decision to leave was made, the parents consolidated plans. Panni's father had possible "connections" at the border, and Peter had family abroad. They would help one another.

Upon hearing the news of the revolt, Denis had flown to Vienna and miraculously found the group among tens of thousands of refugees. He put them on a train bound for London and stayed behind to find Pista, who had disappeared from Budapest. No one knew where he was.

It was logical that Peter and Erika should come to England. Where else could they go? Kati still had no home of her own. Denis was wandering the world. Ironically, we had become the most settled, in our little flat on Chippenham Road.

Our lives, which had finally achieved some measure of stability, now exploded again into frantic chaos and confusion. Amid the relief and joy of seeing Peter and Erika safe in England were real and immediate needs. Beds and linen, crib and diapers, clothes and food—lots of food—and money. My mother worked her shift at the restaurant, then ran home to tend to the needs of the expanded family. I answered a plea from the Red Cross requesting the help of interpreters. Refugees were pouring in, and there was a desperate need for people who spoke Hungarian and English to process them on arrival. Miss Gordon-Ewen announced my involvement to the whole school and granted me a leave of absence.

We cooked, we shopped, we rocked the baby to sleep. Our place became a refugee camp/soup kitchen. I ran to railroad stations and airports at all hours of the day or night, wherever the Red Cross directed me. In between we registered our refugees with the agencies that offered help, temporary living quarters, clothes, funds, English lessons, jobs.

Kati called, offering advice but little else, alluding to some financial disaster and warning us not to expect any help from Denis when he surfaced again, which he did when Pista showed up at Kati's doorstep in Munich.

As far as Denis was concerned the revolution could not have happened at a worse time. His big financial deals that were supposed to ensure security for the entire family had fallen through. He had sunk everything he owned into that ill-fated deal, and now he was broke and devastated. He put Pista on a refugee transport to the United States and immediately advised Peter and Erika to stay where they were. He didn't have the means to help them. He made it very simple. "You can't count on me now. I have my own problems. You're young. You're in a good place. There is help available. You'll make it. I'll see what can be done about Pista in America. I can't take on any more."

That was it. He left and we didn't hear from him for months. My mother was the only one who was not disappointed in him. She had never harbored any illusions about help from that quarter.

Day by day, some things became settled while other problems arose. But the wonder of it remained. We would look at one another and marvel, "Did this really happen? Are we really together again? In England?"

Ten days after their arrival, Erika gave birth to baby Andre, the first British-born citizen of the family.

The British people were wonderful. They mobilized and rallied around the newcomers, though until then many were totally unaware of such a place as Hungary, except as a small blob of color in the center of a European map. Offers of clothes, shelter, and jobs came pouring in. George got a job within days. He was a brilliant young engineer and spoke English. Panni was a qualified draftsman. Peter and Erika had been in their last year of medical school and were specializing in dental surgery. As soon as they could pass the necessary English-language requirements, they would be able to resume their studies, courtesy of the British government. Soon our little families found living quarters and hesitantly settled into their new reality.

But as everyone else's life settled down, an upheaval began in mine. The arrival of the two young couples gave me a whole new perspective on my life, and it was not a comforting one. I saw the look of confusion on their faces as they assessed our surroundings. Our home in a working-class neighborhood with no bathroom. Our lack of social or cultural life. My mother's menial type of work. How long, if ever, would it take for them to achieve the degree of comfort that they had known in Hungary? England was very strange to them, the language, the people, the customs, and our lifestyle was not what they had been prepared for: Is this what life was like in the "Western world," in England? They lamented that they would be forever strangers. They were articulating what I had always felt, but I had nothing to compare it to. They, on the other hand, had grown up with roots, with a culture and a history that they were familiar with and that they called their own. Their parents were known in the community, and though their means had certainly been curtailed by the war and then under the Communist regime, they had grown up in a culturally sophisticated environment. They were well educated, polished, and accomplished. They had a common frame of reference. They had known the same people all their lives. They had the same circle of friends since their early childhood. I recognized something that I could not name. Something that I had been missing. A sense of belonging to somewhere, of knowing who you are. And it made me feel even more a stranger. I wasn't like them, even though we spoke the same language. I understood the words but not the meaning of the poetry that they quoted to one another wistfully. I couldn't grasp their innate sense of what was in "good taste" and what was not. Panni sat with her eyes closed, rocking her baby, listening to classical music on the radio, telling me about her life in Budapest and what she had left behind. Her father was a leader in the old Jewish community, her husband a respected professional. She had enjoyed a comfortable home and lots of friends. Now she was frightened and wondered whether she had given up too much for that ephemeral ideal of "democratic freedom."

I had grown up in a "free society" but was isolated from the inherited traditions and comradeship that they had taken for granted, even under their restricted lifestyle. While we could travel, talk, think, and argue freely, we also had to fend for ourselves and fight hard for our little corner of a foreign world, without ever being granted the feeling of belonging. While having to watch their every word and every thought, their lives were organized, their education secure. In some ways they even kept their status as an educated middle class. They understood how and when to circumvent the system because it was *their* system. They had grown up with it. But we'd had to learn a new system every time we moved, without anyone being there to give us a helping hand.

A mirror was held up, and I saw my life as shabby and dismal. The one place that I had always counted on, Saint Martin's, now became the target of my anger. Why wasn't I like Peter, Erika, Panni, and George? Why didn't I have a better education? How come I had not been introduced to classical music, to philosophy, to the theater? I completely disregarded the fact that I was still in high school and that our guests were all university graduates. I felt betrayed and ashamed of my lack of knowledge and sophistication. I, who had grown up in the "Free West," should feel inferior to refugees of an oppressive system that I had grown up believing was secondary to "ours"?

I wanted so much to be important in their lives. I fantasized about getting

them wonderful jobs, easing their paths, being their guide. But these young people were not my mother's war-damaged friends. They were a different kind of
refugee. They were not intimidated by their hosts. They knew that they had
something to offer in return for the refuge that they were being given. They had
left their country voluntarily because they had been betrayed. They knew that
they deserved better. They were skilled, proud of themselves, confident of their
own abilities. We had been a beaten lot, unsure, tired, and battle scarred. We had
been beggars, and the feeling had never left us.

To everyone's surprise and great delight, Klari and her husband Laci, being over
fifty, were granted visas that enabled them to leave Hungary legally, and within
a few months they joined the rest of us in England. The two sisters, my mother
and Klari, had always gotten along well, and it was a truly joyful reunion for
both of them.

Now that we were a "family," my position in it shifted from a twosome in
which I had a quasi-equal standing with my mother to being the youngest and
therefore the least prominent. Decisions were no longer mine to make. There
was a man in the family now, Laci, and I didn't particularly care for him. I found
his fastidious ways irritating and the fact that he expected to be waited on hand
and foot by the women, demeaning. I was not used to having a man around and
had become adept at doing traditional "men's work," like electrical wiring and
minor carpentry. The fact that Laci couldn't do these things, and felt that it was
beneath him to try, made me contemptuous of him. He also had a roving eye
and often made off-color jokes that embarrassed me and which I pretended
either not to have heard or understood.

"What's the matter, Evi? Doesn't your English educational system include the
teaching of male and female anatomy?" he would ask with an accompanying
leer, which I found particularly nauseating and which generally provoked a
quick and cutting answer. "Yes, it does. It also teaches us what is acceptable conversation and what is gutter talk!"

He complained bitterly about my lack of respect.

I became very unsettled, completely unsure of my position in our newly
reunited ménage. My mother and Klari became inseparable. They and Laci were
the elders; Peter, Erika, and the baby were the young family; and I was hanging
somewhere in limbo, the odd one out. One of the things that accentuated my
difference was language. By then, English was my language of choice, the one
that I expressed myself best in. My mother and I spoke a mixture of Hungarian,
French, and English, with a generous dose of Yiddish and German expressions
thrown in for good measure. In common, everyday communication I could hold

my own in Hungarian; in fact, I had no noticeable foreign accent. But when it came to serious conversation, I often halted in midsentence searching for the right word, and often I just automatically substituted the English or French equivalent as I was used to doing, which either amused or irritated the listener. My vocabulary was not much above that of a seven year old, which was how old I was when I left Hungary. Fact was, *they* were Hungarian. I was not. They remembered songs, books, stories, mythical and historical characters and laughed, sang, or reminisced while I just sat there, unable to join in. Yes, English had become the language that I expressed myself in, but it was not *my* language. I didn't have a "mother tongue." Even my language was adopted, and I would always speak it with an accent—the accent of a language that I shall never speak as well as my adopted one.

Conversation among the older generation often revolved around the war. Laci had been in a concentration camp and had evidently suffered terrible hardships. We often heard him cry out in his sleep, but I was hard put to feel any sympathy for him, disliking him immensely. Klari told stories of the torture that she had undergone during her incarceration by the Communists, and even my mother occasionally spoke of her experiences in the slave labor camp. It was as though no other time of their lives was important enough to talk about, except that time of suffering. It was the high point of their lives. It was something that they all had in common.

My memories or perceptions of that time were of no consequence during these discussions. I had been a small child and couldn't possibly have understood what was at stake. And after liberation I had been plain "lucky." I had been looked after, fed, clothed, and couldn't have had any worries about the future. Astonishingly, it was the first time that I heard the details of my mother's incarceration in the forced labor camp. She had never spoken of it to me, and I had never dared to ask. There had always been a feeling of buried secrets in our family. About all kinds of things. Things were alluded to but never spelled out. How often my mother had spoken the unfinished sentence "If you only knew . . ." whenever certain subjects had come up. Occasionally I'd get up the nerve to ask, "Knew what?" But she would only shake her head and mutter, "Never mind. Maybe one day. . . ."

The same thing happened with Kati, Klari, and Denis. Denis would add a little teaser, such as, "One day ask Kati why she came to Paris in February 1938. See what she tells you" or "Ask Klari why her first husband was divorced." It was as though there were a common conspiracy among the siblings to weave a tapestry of intrigue and innuendo around themselves. They had lived through a time of fear and secrets, never knowing what kind of knowledge carried what kind of danger, and even though it should have been over, it still carried right through into every part of their lives. Knowing someone else's secret was for them a cloak of safety. It was their bargaining power with one another. We, the younger generation, were not privy to these mysteries, but, as I learned much later, there was nothing quite as dreadful in any of their pasts as the horrors that my imagination had conjured up after years of listening to their weighty silences. We learned that we were not supposed to know, so we gave up asking, and we remained ignorant of very basic facts about our family's history.

The newcomers were vaguely amused and thought it quaint that I had been brought up Jewish. Peter and Erika had had no exposure to Jewish learning and tradition. Customs and holidays were foreign to them. No young person in the Communist bloc pursued any religious practices if they wanted to remain in mainstream society. Besides, our family had been assimilated long ago. Laci was the only one who approved. He was from an Orthodox family, and every morning he put on his tefillin and prayed. But his alliance was abhorrent to me, and I made a point of telling him that I was not particularly religious. Judaism, however, had become an anchor for me, and it was just one more thing that separated me from the rest of the family.

I found that I was constantly explaining myself and my adopted surroundings. On one hand, I was proud of my family's sophistication; on the other, I was embarrassed and annoyed by them when they made fun of or derided the British for their "strange" customs and behavior, which they didn't bother or even try to understand. And they made fun of me when I defended the British. It was all in good humor on their part. But not on mine! I wanted them to blend in as soon as possible, not be so different, so foreign!

While preparing for his university exams, Peter was given a job in a dental supply warehouse filling orders that had to be shipped. It was a boring and mechanical job where he was not likely to improve his language skills. His coworkers were mostly uneducated, blue-collar Cockney youths, who told him to slow down, not work so hard in order not to show them up. We decided to go back to the Jewish agency that had found him the job and ask whether there was something more appropriate available.

We walked into the offices of the agency where a half dozen well-dressed and obviously well-heeled volunteer ladies were chatting and sipping tea while sitting behind their desks, looking important and officious. I told them why we had come, and we were told coldly to wait. We sat forlornly on a bench, I in my brown school-uniform winter coat, Peter in his unfashionable jacket, a scarf around his neck, looking much younger than his twenty-three years, the picture of a refugee. The ladies went about their business, ignoring us for along time. Finally I approached one of them and asked how long we would have to wait.

"What is it that you actually want?" she asked in an irritated tone.

I took a deep breath and answered. "As I said before. This is my cousin. He is one of the newly arrived Hungarian refugees. He was in his last year of medical school in Hungary and it is very important that he learn English as soon as possible so that he can finish his studies. Since he does have a limited knowledge of English, we were wondering whether there might be a job available that would be better suited to his circumstances."

She frowned, looked Peter up and down, shook her head, then turned to her colleagues. "These people are unbelievable. Nothing you do is good enough for them. We take them in, we give them accommodations, clothes, jobs, and they're still not satisfied. If things aren't satisfactory enough for you maybe you should have stayed in Hungary," she said, turning back to Peter.

Something within me stirred. It was Mrs. Brash all over again. The humiliation that she had inflicted on me three years previously in Norwood was now being visited on Peter, and I couldn't bear it. The unfairness, the mortification, the affront so outraged me that an overwhelming anger flooded over me and I found my voice. All the indignation that I had not been able to articulate to Mrs. Brash came spewing out of me in a torrent of rage. And I screamed at the women.

"How dare you talk to us like this, you pampered silly women! Have you any idea what being a refugee is? Could you ever imagine having to leave your fancy Hendon homes, with nothing but the clothes on your backs, to go to a country where you don't know the language, the customs? And then to be at the mercy of people like you? You call yourselves Jews? You think because your husbands send money to Israel that makes *you* a good Jew? Read the Torah and see what it has to say about humiliating someone who is asking for work! How would you like to go begging for work? Having to leave your child behind with strangers? You think you suffered here because a few doodlebugs fell on London, or because you had to be evacuated? At least you had somewhere to go! Your families stayed intact. Nobody went hunting for you! You think because you speak the language and you have money, and you dress well, that you are different from us? You have no idea how fast you can lose it all if you're a Jew! Then you can wander around from country to country, away from your family, living in orphanages, having no control over your life. . . ."

I went on and on, out of control, unable to stop whilst realizing that what I was screaming was becoming incoherent and totally irrelevant to our visit. Finally, out of breath and determined not to cry, I rushed for the door, Peter, wide-eyed, right behind me.

We had almost reached the front door when one of the women caught up with us. She put her hand on my shoulder. She looked very subdued. "Don't upset yourself so. She didn't really mean what she said. We'll see what we can do. Don't worry. Things will be fine."

I was annoyed at her. I wanted to stay angry, because if I didn't, I would cry. I just nodded my head and kept going.

Out on the street, I leaned against the building, taking deep breaths, astonished at my own temerity. Peter looked at me, grinned, and tousled my hair. "I'm not sure what you carried on about in there, Nyunyus, but whatever it was, I think it worked."

This episode only served to confuse me further. Just where did I belong? I loved my family. I defended them the best way I knew how; but we were so different! We had so little in common! I knew I wasn't English, and I knew that I wasn't French. Yes, I was Jewish. But these were not the Jews that I belonged with either, nor with that sad lot in Norwood. I felt as though I existed in a vacuum.

Without my being conscious of it, the previous ten years of my young life had been a search for an identity. I was bewildered, totally at a loss. I didn't understand what was happening to me. Something was giving way. My world was crashing in on me. I kept crying in secret and repeating to myself, I can't do this anymore. It's too hard. I just can't. But I couldn't define what was so hard, what it was that I couldn't do anymore.

A few months before our final exams and graduation from Saint Martin's, I announced that I wasn't going back.

"Why?" asked my mother in surprise.

"There's nothing more that they can teach me. I'm wasting my time. I don't need a piece of paper to tell me that I attended their precious school."

"What about university? Won't you need a graduation certificate to get in?"

"There is no graduation certificate in England. There are the Advanced-Level Exams. If I decide to go to university, I'll take them later, on my own. I don't have to stay at Saint Martin's for that."

My mother shrugged her shoulders. "I suppose you know what you're doing. You're old enough."

I wanted to scream, No, I don't know what I'm doing. I'm not old enough. Help me! But I didn't. I couldn't ask for help. They would never understand! I vowed that I would show them. Show them what? I didn't know. I was lost in a maelstrom of confusing and conflicting identities, angry at a world that seemed to have no place for me, drowning in my inner turmoil and self-pity.

I walked hesitantly into the inner sanctum of Miss Gordon-Ewen's elegant office. She asked me to sit and waited for me to begin.

"I'm leaving Saint Martin's," I said in a bold tone that I didn't feel.

She raised her eyebrows. "Now? Before exams? Why?"

"I'm too busy helping the refugees. I don't have time to study. I'll take my finals later, independently."

"I see," she said. "Well, there's nothing more to be said then. Good-bye, Juliette, and good luck!"

I was stunned. She had not even attempted to change my mind. She had let me burn my bridges. I felt more alone than I ever had before.

Without telling anyone, I scanned the papers and went on job interviews; jobs that would take me out of the country. I interviewed for a nanny's position in Switzerland, a secretary's in Saudi Arabia, a training program for airline stewardesses and another for news reporters. But it seemed that I wasn't qualified for anything.

I wrote a letter to Denis. He had an address in New York City, the office of a friend, that he used for poste restante. I begged him to let me come to the States. I couldn't stand living in England anymore. I needed to get away. I would do anything he wanted me to if he let me come. Back came an telegramlike answer from somewhere in South America: *Can't help now. Traveling all over. Go stay with Kati. How's the family? Love, Denis.*

Everyone was busy. Peter, Erika, and Laci got jobs and studied. My mother worked as usual. Klari looked after baby Andre. Everyone was looking to the future but me. I had gathered a few refugees as English students and that kept me busy enough, so nobody noticed that anything was wrong.

Then I got sick. The damp English winters had always been hard on me. I was pale and anemic. My confused and depressed state probably contributed to the deterioration of my health, and I ended up in the hospital with pneumonia, seriously underweight.

The crowded hospital ward was like heaven. The nurses were kind, jolly, and efficient, and even when the matron came on her rounds and everyone trembled, I felt safe. I didn't want to leave.

My mother came. "Evi, please tell me what's wrong."

"I don't know."

"Don't you want to come home?"

"I don't know."

"What do you want to do when you get better?"

"I don't know."

I saw her confer with the doctors and nurses. She looked so crushed. But I was on a different plane, not feeling anything.

Peace, I thought. That's all I want. Just peace. Not to hurt. Not to remember. Not to feel.

Peter came to see me every day, and sometimes we talked. "Hey, Nyunyus," he asked one day, "what do you dream of being one day?"

"I want to be famous!"

"Why?"

"Because I want to be important. I want everyone to know who I am. I want to be somebody!"

"But Nyunyus, you *are* important and you're certainly somebody, and two out of three isn't bad. And being famous isn't necessarily great. Look, he was famous!" He did his Charlie Chaplin-doing-Adolf Hitler routine, which always broke me up, and I laughed for the first time in weeks.

The British Health Service provided me with a few weeks in a convalescent home by the sea. By the time I came home, Kati had been mobilized.

"Bandi and I are moving to Vienna. Would you like to come for a while? You could attend the university there."

"I haven't taken my Advanced Level Exams."

"So, take them! When can you do it?"

"June." I couldn't humiliate myself and ask go back to Saint Martin's. I enrolled in a business school for a semester and took the exams there while learning shorthand, typing, and business correspondence.

At the end of the summer I packed my bags and left England.

Vienna, 1957–1960

In 1957, Vienna was still recovering from the Allied occupation. For ten years following the war, the Americans, British, French, and Soviets had occupied the city. It had been carved up into four different sectors. Each sector under the administration of its occupying forces. Those in the American sector had considered themselves very fortunate, while people in the Soviet sector had been in constant fear that the Iron Curtain would one day cut them off from the Free World. Finally, after a decade Vienna became whole again. There was a frenzy of rebuilding and restoration. I was there for the openings of the new Vienna State Opera and the Burg Theater, as well as the final restoration of Saint Stephen's Cathedral. The old rococo façades were cleaned up, and people were lovingly rediscovering those beautiful eighteenth-century buildings, the pride of Viennese architecture, that had not been destroyed by Allied bombs. The Viennese were jubilant: they were free of the Germans, they were free of the Western Allies, they were free of the Russians. They appointed themselves as the saviors of Western culture, and there were endless classical music concerts and classical theater performances. The museums were refurbished, the churches were restored to their original baroque glory, and Herbert von Karajan ruled at the new opera house.

Kati and Uncle Bandi were living in a tiny sublet in a modern apartment building in the third district, just off Schwartzenberg Platz, certainly a more than respectable neighborhood. Kati would always opt for the fashionable address over the comfort of space. Since there was not enough space for me, a rented room had been arranged within a five-minute's walk of their apartment.

I loved the "student's digs" that Uncle Bandi had found for me. It was in one of those old, gray, massive, nineteenth-century Viennese buildings with a wide, circular marble staircase and elaborate iron handrails, mile-high ceilings, and baroque statuary flanking the front entrance. It was in some disrepair and remained war-damaged, but still, oh so grand! In my room I had a magnificent tiled stove reaching all the way to the ceiling. The furniture was all slightly shabby and worn, but highly polished and authentic Biedermeier. It had an aura of long bygone days. I felt as though I were on stage in an operetta or some period piece. Kati had begun to sniff at it from the first time she saw it until she found out who my landlady would be.

Die Prinzessin Helena von Cröy, grandniece of the emperor Franz Joseph, had become old and impoverished. All that remained of her former wealth and grandeur were her apartment, her top-flight education, and her reputation. She had never married, and like the rest the Habsburg royal family, had never allied herself with the Nazis. Later, she worked as an interpreter for the American army. She rented out all the rooms in her enormous apartment, contenting herself with living in the former maid's room next to the kitchen. She had a part-time job as an interpreter at the fledgling International Atomic Energy Agency and on weekends worked as a tour guide. She and Uncle Bandi had met at the American Reading Room and formed a pleasant acquaintanceship, which resulted in my being considered for, then accepted as one of her boarders.

The Prinzessin was eccentric in what I considered to be a very aristocratic manner. If anyone that I knew had had her eccentricities, they would have been labeled "crazy." But rank and title still had their privileges. She loved music and saved from her meager income to be able to attend as many concerts as her money allowed. She positively refused, however, to listen to music on the radio or on a record. That was "canned" music, not fit for human ears, and she was quite put out if she heard the sounds of "canned music" coming from the room of any of her boarders.

We all had cooking privileges in the big sprawling old-fashioned kitchen, but she disapproved of meat and made horrible choking sounds if someone had the temerity to cook any while she was home. She claimed that mushrooms were the perfect substitute, and we were subjected to the constant smell of cooking mushrooms, which she prepared in innumerable ways while extolling the virtues of vegetarianism. She was also prudish and would surreptitiously supervise her boarders' reading matter. Nabokov's *Lolita* was the hot new controversial book that everyone was reading. She saw it on my nighttable and demanded that either "it" or I leave her home forthwith! The book was transferred to Kati and Uncle Bandi's apartment, and my diary was immediately placed out of sight. Still, she had a certain charm, and she was a very cultured and educated lady who never bemoaned her fate. What she bemoaned was the apostasy of her fellow Austrians. She detested them, though she never thought of emigrating. The remains of the Austrian royal family were dispersed throughout the world, and occasionally a cousin would send her an airline ticket for a visit. While I was there she visited Tulsa, Oklahoma, a couple of times, courtesy of a favorite family member, but she always hurried home complaining of a lack of cultural life and the smell of oil wells.

Most nights, after dinner, Uncle Bandi walked me home and occasionally stayed and chatted with the Prinzessin. They talked about old times and music. She wryly described her former life as the aristocratic debutante, and he discussed the latest productions at the opera or the various upcoming concerts. He never talked about his former life as the scion of a wealthy Jewish family. But she well knew who he had been.

Kati was left out of these evening encounters and feigned to be glad of it. She would have had very little patience with the Prinzessin's blue-blooded manners and little to add to the conversation. However, she never failed to mention to her friends "our association" with Prinzessin Helena von Cröy.

I registered for classes in the foreign students' program. Before entering the mainstream university programs, we had to pass a rigorous language examination. Since having reluctantly given up the idea of medical school, I had decided to enter the Interpreters Institute. My mother had always said that, no matter what, I would always be able to make a living using my knowledge of languages. I was worried about entering the university, feeling that perhaps Saint Martin's had not prepared me adequately, but found to my relief that the work was easier than I thought. Probably the most useful thing that I had been taught was the discipline of study. And besides having taken German for several years in high school, I had heard it spoken around me all my life and I seemed to have a knack for languages. I took to my new lifestyle and surroundings like the proverbial duck to water.

I enjoyed being a student. Studying had never been particularly hard for me and I had a lot of freedom. I took to exploring the city and found favorite places to sit and read. I met a number of young people at the university. Dita was my first American friend, and she typified what I thought was "American." She was carefree, trusting, generous, with a marvelous sense of wonder and excitement. There was an openness and confidence about her that I envied from the start. It was easy to tell that she had always felt secure and free, that she had been coddled and loved. She disturbed my other new friend, George, a serious young Hungarian Jew who thought of her as he did anything American, "frivolous," "a piece of fluff." George was a recent refugee from Budapest. He lived with his mother and younger sister. They had gone through the war hiding just like we had, suffered under Communism, then ended up as refugees in Austria. He felt that Dita's sense of wonder and excitement was childish. And for the first time I saw clearly how those of us who had been denied our childhood felt a sense of disdain and superiority toward those who had been fortunate enough to have enjoyed theirs. We had no idea what childhood and youth were for. We thought it was a waste of time! Always we had to be adults, ready for anything that came along. Oh, but how I loved talking with, just looking at, Dita. She was not afraid of this world, she was embracing it, all of it. Europe may be culture and history and experience, but America was freedom and newness and exploration, and Dita, the first American that I met, embodied everything wonderful that I believed was American.

My second encounter with Americans was not quite as uplifting. One evening a group of us went to Grinzing, a quaint area on the outskirts of the city where the new wine from the local vineyards is served to guests, along with fried chicken and such. There's usually singing and dancing, and in the 1950s it was a great favorite of students, where a good meal, wine, and a good time could be had at a very modest cost. We sat at a long wooden table with other students and some American tourists from a place called Arkansas. They spoke with the strangest accent and seemed only to be interested in drinking their way around the world. They had never been to New York, they said. Dita screwed up her nose.

"Not all Americans are like that, you know," she said crossly.

My German improved steadily. I read like a demon. Professor Trebitz advised me to take some courses at the business school where he also taught, and he gave me extra work. This caused an amusing incident that, at the time, caused me great embarrassment.

I turned in a paper that, he informed me, contained several grammatical errors. When I told him that I had consulted a native Austrian for help, he wanted to know whom. I informed him that it was our cleaning woman. The professor just about exploded.

"Das Dienstmädchen? Sie wollen von dem Dienstmädchen Deutsch lernen?" ("The maid? You want to learn German from the maid?"), he screamed. To my horror everyone was laughing at me. "Do you ask the maids in England to teach you the Queen's English?"

No, I thought, sheepish and embarrassed, I would hardly consult a Cockney char regarding the correct use of English, but I just thought that anyone born here would certainly know more than I did. Despite such small setbacks, my studies continued steadily with daily routines hardly changing. But my studies were the least of my concerns.

A disturbing aspect of my new life was the introduction of young men into it. By the time I was nineteen I'd had a few dates. But it was high school stuff, with boys, not men. Nothing but awkward experiments in asking and accepting an evening at the movies and worrying about how to avoid having to accede to the obligatory goodnight kiss. I knew that I was not attractive in the way that young boys look for in young girls. I was painfully thin and small, looking much younger than my years. And I also knew that they were just experimenting any-way. Well, not on me they wouldn't! I became terribly sarcastic. I had a biting wit that the boys did not or could not deal with, which made me all the more con-temptuous of them. Besides, I hated to be touched by anyone. A light kiss on the cheek was the best I was able to give, and that only to close family members.

Before I got to Vienna, there had been no one of particular interest to me. My reticence had never bothered me. Now as a student at the university, where I came into close contact with bright young men, where there were daily fervent discussions at the local coffeehouses, where we all laughed and flirted together, I started to become afraid. Whenever a young man showed the slightest roman-tic interest, I visualized him laughing behind my back, teasing me for fun. I became a potential victim. I felt humiliated.

I was aware that my feelings were not the norm; still, I craved male friends. So I turned flirtations into platonic friendships. I compensated by being a "pal." I liked young men, but only so long as I didn't have to allow myself to trust them. Even then I was able to distinguish that my anxiety really had nothing so much to do with sex as trust. The idea of intimacy with anyone brought thoughts of fear and betrayal. Males especially were creatures to be feared. There was no one that I could ever allow myself to trust with my feelings . . . or my body. I imag-ined "their" sadistic satisfaction in hurting me. The humiliation of it . . . the pow-erlessness. I wondered how my girlfriends could let themselves fall in love. And when they found out that the young man was cheating, they would cry and tell me that their heart was broken. How could they bear it? I would rather die! Being a friend was easy, but romance, love, even infatuation, impossible. I talked and listened as a friend. It seemed that everyone trusted my sympathetic ear. I gave good, "sensible" advice, but I never trusted anyone enough to seek any. There was a constant vigilance about me. I couldn't bear the thought of allowing anyone to hurt me.

With women, it was easier to hide. If I held back from a woman's embrace, they would generally just knowingly smile and say, "Oh yes, the English upbringing. Very reserved." Nobody noticed my paranoia.

I had friends, young men, young women. Between study and work, we all went to the theater together, to the Heurigen (a Viennese specialty, an inn that serves its own new wine to guests, sometimes along with food), skiing, swim-ming. I wove an air of mystery around myself, by not answering certain personal questions, ignoring them and just smiling. My fellow students assumed that I had some secret romance that I didn't want to share. Maybe a married man . . . that wasn't uncommon among students. Nobody pried. It kept me safe and it kept me lonely. So I played my little charades. Everything was fine. I was a pal. I became quite popular in my circle of friends and even felt that so far this was the best time of my life.

Kati was delighted when she saw me surrounded by friends. "Evi will end up all right," she'd say to her friends, right in front of me. "She's smart, she's talented, and eventually we'll fix her nose. Let's just hope she's smarter than her mother and goes where the money is."

"Ah yes," sighed one of her friends. "It's as easy to love a rich man as it is a poet."

"Why couldn't she love both and only marry one?" inquired a more pragmatic friend, winking at me. I laughed while Kati threw a scowl at her friend.

At the university there were many Arab students. They came from all over the Middle East and were conspicuous in their number. These were the sons of the very wealthy. They were handsome young men, always immaculately dressed in suits, white shirts, and ties, carrying expensive leather briefcases. Many Austrians liked them because they spent money lavishly. Several of them were in my foreign students' class, but we never mingled. One day, however, the topic of conversation turned toward the emergence of new nations. When Israel was mentioned, one of the Arab students jumped up and, waving his arms, started screaming as though in a frenzy.

"There is no such place as Israel! Those occupying our land will be driven into the sea. All the Jews will be exterminated. In twenty years there will be no more Jews in Palestine. Muslim blood will be avenged. Jewish blood will flow in the streets and Allah will reign supreme!"

It was an electrifying moment. Everyone sat up, stunned. I had never been confronted with such raw fanaticism, and it felt like a punch in the gut. I couldn't draw a breath. I felt as though this young man could and would have liked to kill Jews right then and there! I was totally mesmerized by the energy he generated—and I sat there looking in amazement at the contorted face, the uncontrolled rage that had taken over his body. I couldn't understand what made someone act like that. I should have been frightened, but the scene had such a surreal, bizarre quality that I was totally fascinated. Only later did I grasp the fact that among the objects of his irrational hatred was me.

Professor Trebitz shot out of his chair like a bullet, pointed at the screaming student, and roared so loudly that he drowned him out.

"You will not spew your venom in my class. And you don't know what you are talking about, because in twenty years Israel will still be there, stronger than ever, while your people will be beaten and still living in poverty and ignorance! Now get out of my class!"

The professor was not a Jew, and it amazed me to see an Austrian taking

Israel's side in public.

The Arab students walked out of the class. I knew that they would not return. We sat there in silence for a minute or so till the professor collected himself, then we just continued the discussion as though nothing had occurred. After class I did not talk to anyone and rushed to a tutoring session.

That night I related the incident to Uncle Bandi. He was not surprised by the student's behavior but rather by the professor's actions, and he was concerned that Professor Trebitz might be censured by the head of the faculty. And that was when I found myself reacting to what had happened. I wavered between despair and anger. Doesn't it ever end? I thought hopelessly. What made these young people so full of hate? What did we ever do to them? Then my feelings turned to anger. Enough already! How much more were we supposed to swallow? No country wants us, but neither are we allowed to have our own. What are we supposed to do? Lie down and die? Disappear? Just to make the rest of the world feel better? Damn them all! That night I wrote in my diary:

> *This is outrageous! Censured? For what? For not allowing a fanatic to "spew his venom" as he said. Isn't that a teacher's job? What kind of a university is this? It's really ironic. Everyone is running to take their children to the doctor for the new vaccine against polio that has just become available. I'd love to take out an advert. in* Die Presse *[Austria's foremost newspaper]: "Oyez, Oyez! Come and get your Jewish vaccine! Oyez, Oyez, We're giving them out at Hubner's [elegant coffeehouse in Vienna's Stadtpark], the place where 'Jews and dogs' were not allowed to enter from 1938 to 1945. Oyez, Oyez!"*
>
> *From now on I'm wearing my Mogen Dovid, whether Kati likes it or not!*

I had never worn the little gold Star of David that my cousin Yvonne had sent me from Paris one year for my birthday. There was something that I had never liked about overtly showing symbols of one's religion. I'd always felt that it created a division between people. It was "Us" being different from "Them." I winced when I saw crucifixes, as much as I did when I saw the Star of David, hanging from anyone's neck. Now, however, it was different. I had a reason for wearing it! I wanted the Austrians and the Arabs at the university to know that I was Jewish. It had nothing to do with religion. It was my demanding, "Wanna make something of it?"

In 1958 anti-Semitism was still rampant in Vienna.

Most evenings I showed up for dinner at Kati and Uncle Bandi's apartment, and complicated new relationships were formed: an elaborate dance that all three of us participated in but that none of us would ever acknowledge or maybe even be consciously aware of. To Uncle Bandi, I was "a young soul to be saved," someone to help, someone who needed him to save me from Kati's materialism while allowing her to show me "a better side of life"; to help me with my balancing act between my mother and her oldest sister. He treated me as a young "buddy." We were allies against Kati's stuffiness. We plotted to meet in galleries when Kati had assigned us to go for haircuts or shoe shines. We snuck away to feast on *cevapcici* in the little Serbian restaurant that Kati wouldn't set foot in because it didn't live up to her standards of cleanliness. We talked about Heine's poetry, and we debated whether a Jew should or shouldn't listen to Wagner's music. Kati, on the other hand, finally had me to herself without my mother's interference, and she was ready to exert her influence over me, to teach me how one should live "like a lady" and move "in better circles," as she put it. But she trod carefully. She feared that to overtly show her superiority over my mother would force my loyalty and that I would rebel against her. Uncle Bandi kept her in check. He admired and respected my mother. He clearly saw her as the family victim, and tried to do his best for me out of respect for her. He understood the mother/child relationship as sacred, and he very subtly protected me from Kati's sense of ownership. But he also knew that, at this point in my life, Vienna was a better place for me than London. And I felt that I was finally breathing free. I was grateful to Uncle Bandi and to Kati too, though how I wished that she had been blessed with a little humor. I felt that I was being given a new life, though there were pangs of guilt attached. It was at the cost of abandoning my mother and life in England. Still, I was filling up my emotional well.

Uncle Bandi and Uncle Sanyi merged into one. On the way home in the evenings, we used to stop either at a pastry shop or at Barry's, the big coffeehouse on the corner of Schwartzenberg Platz, for a *Gemüse* sandwich, a delicious concoction of crunchy parboiled vegetables atop a square of crustless bread, covered in aspic with a curlicue of mayonnaise on top. He introduced me to the Musikverein, the elegant Viennese concert hall that had first heard Beethoven's *Eroica*. He bought me Hermann Hesse's books, and we went to the Burg Theater to see Goethe's *Faust*. Kati, meanwhile, took charge of my wardrobe, my coiffure, and my manicures, and checked out all my new friends.

It was understood that I would get tutoring jobs to help pay for my keep. Kati had already alerted her circle of friends to the fact that I was a linguistic genius who might consent to taking a few students in order to keep "my hand in," so to speak, while attending the university. Within a couple of weeks of my arrival, I had gathered a number of students. They included high schoolers who needed tutoring in either English or French and adult friends, or friends of friends, of

Kati's who wanted to practice their language skills, especially those who were refugees and were hoping to emigrate to America or Canada. Almost from the start I was busy running from class to teaching and from teaching to studying.

Vienna was a city full of refugees. And for the first time on my arrival in a new country, I was not one of them. The very word *refugee* immediately brought to my mind the homelessness, the poverty, the humiliation. Never did I want to be a refugee again. I knew how people in host countries felt about refugees. They were, at best, tolerated but usually held in contempt as though they had no one to blame but themselves for their condition. Refugees were accused of using too many resources; of taking jobs away from their hosts and, paradoxically, of an unwillingness to work; of not wanting to learn the language, laughed at for their accents. And they were admonished for "looking like peasants," for expecting too much, and for never, ever being grateful enough for the refuge that they were being granted, however grudgingly. I knew what it was like to be on the receiving end, and I consciously tried to keep away from them, as though they would contaminate me with their condition.

The refugees were mostly the Hungarians who had come out the previous year during the revolution, having decided to either settle in Austria or wait for visas to other countries. Remembering how it was after the war, I, along with other self-righteous former refugees, felt that this newest wave of refugees was luckier than they knew. The world had calmed down enough to be able to give a helping hand, and besides, the West was happy to give all kinds of aid while gloating about a "people's revolution" in one of the USSR's satellite countries. Though I tried to keep my distance, by virtue of being related to Kati, I was swallowed up into the Viennese–Jewish Hungarian refugee world. But I refused to consider myself Hungarian. Some odd left-brain activity had caused me to speak German with a French accent, so nobody who didn't know my family connections mistook me for Hungarian, and at the university I was just another foreign student.

Among the Hungarian Jewish refugees were various categories that formed a kind of hierarchy. The elite were those who had left Hungary soon after the Iron Curtain had come down, around 1949–1950, usually by having paid a smuggler who slipped them into Austria by rowing across the Neusiedler See (a lake separating Hungary and Austria) at night, avoiding the border patrols. These people had time to settle, to establish businesses or get jobs. They had permanent homes, and their children were going to Austrian schools and spoke the language like natives. Many of them avoided the newest wave of refugees, fearing that their association with them could jeopardize their standing with their newly acquired Austrian friends. Among the newest, 1956 wave were the "older generation," those over fifty. They were all Holocaust survivors, most had been in the camps, most had remarried, having lost their first mates, and often their children, to Hitler's ovens. This group was split in two. Some had been able to smuggle out money and jewels, and they lived lavishly and conspicuously, and often by their wits. The established Jews avoided them carefully, fearful that they would cause a new outbreak of anti-Semitism. The other half of this older group was the most pathetic. They had nothing. They had dared to come out because they had family somewhere in the West, who they were convinced would help them start a new life. They had for years received loving letters, parcels, and words of sympathy regarding their lives under the yoke of Communism. But encouraging words from afar were not the same as taking responsibility, and many Western relatives were in no hurry to help their refugee brothers, sisters, uncles, and cousins. There were many whose disappointment with their families was heart wrenching. All they wanted was a leg up. They were willing to do anything. In Austria there was nothing for them, especially if their knowledge of German was poor. Most had meager means and lived on donations from various charitable organizations while waiting for visas to the United States, Canada, or South America. Meanwhile they were languishing in a hostile environment, unable to go forward and unable to return to Hungary, only two hundred miles to the east.

Then there were the young people. Most had come on their own, a few with parents. These young people were different. Like Peter, Erika, Panni, and George, they refused to act like refugees. They felt that they had left of their own free will and were looking to build a life. They were not asking for charity. They wanted to contribute, to get an education, to assimilate into Western society. They did not have the "ghetto mentality," nor did they differentiate between themselves and non-Jews. They knew that they were Jews, but it wasn't important to them and they didn't understand why it should be important to anyone else.

There were mutterings among the Austrians about "too many Jews around. More came back than were ever taken." The older people shuddered and lay low. The younger people shrugged their shoulders or got into fights.

Although being Jewish was not always what I wanted to be, it never occurred to me that there was an alternative. Yes, I knew that there were people who converted, but they were simply Jews-who-had-converted. They may have worshiped another way, but they were still Jews. So it came as a shock to me to discover that fifteen years after the war, some people simply denied that they were Jews, even though everybody else knew that they were.

Kati and Uncle Bandi were friends with a Hungarian family who had also survived the war in hiding, then had been "relocated" by the Communists; they finally escaped Hungary by means similar to Kati and Uncle Bandi's. Their only child, Juliana, who was born in the last year of the war, had been spirited out of Hungary by her father's childless sister, Frederica, who had kept her in Vienna until her parents rejoined her in the early 1950s. The family had established itself in business and was doing very well. Juliana, now in her teens, was a model student at the convent school Sacré Coeur, well known for its very thorough classical education. Sweet-tempered, submissive, and shy, she was reminiscent of a nineteenth-century Jane Austen heroine, which was, indeed, how her family seemed to be rearing her. Her family cosseted and sheltered her, watching her every move; her parents were determined to see Juliana become an educated, cultured, and rich member of Viennese society.

Kati and Frederica were the best of friends, and soon I was spending two hours a week giving "Aunt Fritzi" conversational lessons in French and English. She was a lovely, cultured lady with a quiet sense of fun who usually insisted on taking her lessons in one of Vienna's comfortable and atmospheric coffeehouses, where we shared the traditional whipped cream–topped *Einspanner* with delicate pastries while she practiced her already perfect French. Soon I was asked to tutor Juliana, and there began a lifelong friendship. I marveled at her charmed life, and she found mine exotic and interesting. Despite the five-year difference in our ages, which at that time seemed enormous, we became friends, and largely because her family knew mine, she was allowed to spend unchaperoned leisure time with me. We went ice-skating and to the theater, and sometimes we took walks in the Vienna woods. On one occasion we were discussing the traditions of various cultural groups. Quite innocently, I started to rebut a point she had made, stating, "We Jews have a different point of view on the subject . . . "

"Maybe you do, but I'm not Jewish!" she replied.

"Juli, of course you're Jewish. When your parents are Jewish, so are you. Even if you don't practice the religion."

"Yes, I understand that. But my parents aren't Jewish either."

I was quite astounded and, being nineteen years old, didn't have the sense to let the subject drop. I pursued it and told her that of course her parents were Jewish; how come she didn't know that?

That night Kati received an incensed telephone call from Juliana's father. He was outraged that I had dared to open up such a subject with his daughter. While Kati was vainly trying to sputter apologies into the receiver, Uncle Bandi grabbed it from her and quietly but very firmly said, "Tibor, you are not doing your daughter a favor by lying about her background. Harbor no illusions, everyone in Vienna knows that you are a Jew. Consider it fortunate that it was Evi who broke the news to Juliana, sparing her the humiliation of eventually being ostracized by the very society you want her to infiltrate and being told the reason why by some spiteful anti-Semite."

It was rare for Uncle Bandi to take a firm stand on anything. He generally just smiled and allowed everyone their own opinions and rarely disagreed with anybody. This was such a radical departure from his usual behavior that it left everyone quite speechless, even Kati, though not before she made a tart aside to me, "Next time, keep your mouth shut!"

This little drama made quite an impression on a lot of people. Juliana, of course, found out about her roots. Kati saw a side of her husband that called for more respect. It made a hole in the feeling of smug security in Juliana's family, and it gave me a whole new perspective on Jewish refugees. This family was well established, in fact quite wealthy, yet they had still felt the need to hide their origins, to assimilate. They were still afraid, and in spite of all their efforts, Uncle Bandi had revealed to them that their worst fears were true. And we all knew him to be right. What did it take for a Jew to feel safe? Not to be beholden to anyone? Where did one go? Israel? Was that the only safe place for us in the world? But Israel was *not* safe. It was being attacked daily. Where could one go and be free to just be?

My mother had said, "I don't know how Kati can even think of living in Vienna, let alone Munich. I know I couldn't. And knowing you, always having to say your piece, you won't be too happy there either!"

I thought that she had just wanted to talk me out of leaving her, but now I understood her. Vienna would be a constant reminder of the past. It would be too much. She was tired, too tired to hate anymore. She just wanted to be left in peace. She didn't want to look at people and wonder what they had been doing fifteen years earlier. She didn't want to search their faces and wonder if one of them had been the one who had beaten her, or the one who had pulled the lever that released the Zyklon-B to pour through the showerhead, causing her husband or her mother to choke to death. She didn't want to have to avoid eye contact or stop herself from smiling at a stranger on the street lest it might be one who had been *there.*

Kati, on the other hand, thrived on her loathing. She strutted down the Kartnerstrasse, daring them all. There was such passion in her hate that it seemed to energize her, and she channeled it all into "her" restitution cases. She worked tirelessly on them, typing letters late into the night, feverishly pecking away at her typewriter with her two index fingers pounding like two miniature pneumatic drills, constantly poring through the legal documents that came in an endless stream from Germany, and sending back her daily missives to the German Restitution Committee's lawyers. Uncle Bandi sat with her at her desk, patiently correcting her shaky German while at the same time trying to tone down the arrogant tone of the letters. Kati would often hit the roof.

"Don't tell me to pussyfoot around with those bastards. I know what language those German animals understand!"

"Katika!"

"Don't 'Katika' me. Just leave it the way it is. Do you really think they understand human language?"

He just shook his head and smiled sadly. They were such an incongruous couple. She, so bossy, so peremptory, while he was so gentle and obliging. But I wondered if, sometimes, he wasn't grateful to his wife for the anger that she was able to spew, which he could only feel somewhere deep inside himself but never express. She was determined to get back whatever she could for herself and the family, and she badgered everyone constantly: "You must remember names . . . you must recall places . . . the names of other inmates. Some must still be alive and we must get documentation, affidavits. Get that doctor in Paris to give you a letter attesting to your condition when you returned in 1946. . . . Fortunately we have plenty of proof regarding the condition of Evi's hands and feet. We must do this. They can't get away with everything!"

My mother often sighed, "Oh, I just wish she'd leave me alone already and find something else to do. We'll never get anything, anyway." But we grudgingly got the affidavits and the letters and the doctors' certificates, and Kati sent them all to the right places. An entry in my diary from March 1958 reads:

> I've been helping Kati with her "Wiedergutmachung" correspondence. She works at it day and night. She has become such an expert in the restitution law that the lawyers in Germany have hired her to do the preliminary work on some cases. She eats and breathes restitution. She is constantly working on Mamcsi's dossier and swears that she'll get her a pension or "die in the attempt." Kati is never going to die! She'll just kill everyone else. It's her hate that keeps her going. How much can one hate? . . . with such passion? Mamcsi doesn't and she has much more reason to. Mamcsi just seems indifferent . . . like she doesn't feel anything . . . maybe that's worse. I can't hate either . . . I don't know how. That sounds so strange. "I don't know how to hate." But it's true. Does that mean that I don't know how to love either? Probably. It's really so much easier not to feel these emotions, because then they can't hurt.

I was busy. I tried to be as financially independent as I could. I took any job that was offered to me. The Prinzessin got me some part-time work at the Internationsal Atomic Energy Agency and also at the tourist bureau where she worked as a guide. I loved that best. I had become very familiar with Vienna. I loved the architecture, the history, the museums, the gardens, the special places that one becomes familiar with only by living there. Like the exquisite Auersperg Palais, that architectural gem, which opened its winter garden to the public and had a little coffeehouse inside that served the best hot chocolate in the world! Its walls were adorned with original Renaissance art. I could sit and sip my *kleine Braune* while admiring a jewel of Fra Angelico, right there, next to the table, as though I were in my own living room. And across from the university, the romantic Drei Mädel House, where Schubert was a constant visitor and where he fell in love with one of the daughters, who then married another and for whose wedding mass he composed his haunting *Ave Maria.*

There were a lot of tourists in Vienna, and the office sometimes needed extra guides. The Americans were the easiest to please and the nicest. I liked the English, too. I always felt so much more at ease with them than with any other nationality. But the English rarely hired guides. They usually traveled on a shoestring budget.

I remember one particular quartet of Californians that I went to meet at the fanciest hotel in Vienna. The office had not given me the paperwork that indicated the type of tour that the customer had requested, so in my friendly-but-businesslike voice, I asked, "What type of tour did you have in mind, architecture, history, art, shopping?"

One of the women giggled and said breezily, "Oh, we'll leave it up to you. Just give us enough time for a good lunch and make it fun."

I took them all over and led them to Demel's for lunch, telling that I'd pick them up again in an hour.

"No, no," they protested. "Please join us. We'd love to have you. Besides, we can't order without you!"

They wondered where I had learned to speak English so well and asked me where I was from, and as usual I didn't quite know how to answer. One of the women interrupted, "Oh, you'd make a perfect American. Everybody there is from somewhere else!"

She said that she herself was Swedish, her husband, Irish. The other couple described themselves as Italian and Polish. I looked at them, wide-eyed. It seemed that nobody in America was "American." They all referred to their ancestry, and none of them spoke the language of their heritage. I recounted this exchange with relish to Uncle Bandi and Kati that night. Especially the part about "every American being from somewhere else!" We laughed, but I really liked that little ditty. America was a place anyone could go to and be at home.

•

I exchanged weekly letters with my mother and kept up with the news from home. Erika and Peter had both been accepted to dental school. They only had to repeat the last year of their studies. All their previous work had been accepted. Within a year they would have their degrees and they would be on their way. I felt left behind.

Little Andre was thriving under Klari's care, though she had not changed her habit of spoiling rotten every child she could lay her hands on. My mother wrote me that Uncle Laci adored Andre and behaved as though he were the natural grandfather. A comment in my diary dated March 1958:

> *Got a letter from Mamcsi today, with picture of baby Andris. He is soooooo cute! I'm amazed that Laci is such a good grandfather. I would never have believed it of him . . . Andris is like a new limb on a tree come to life again . . . a transplanted tree. I wonder where my children will be born? What will they call themselves, English? French? Hungarian? Peruvian? Maybe even Chinese? Who knows . . . with our history!*

Time passed. I studied and got into the Interpreters' Institute. Everyone in the family approved; after all, it was one less thing for them to worry about. Even Denis wrote: *I'm glad that you gave up thoughts of medical school. This is much more fitting for you. Besides I have ideas and big plans for you.* That was the first time that I really got angry with my uncle Denis—and felt totally helpless in expressing my anger. *Who does he think he is ordering us about like that?* I wrote, fuming, in my diary: *I wish he'd just give up the 'idea' that he can just walk in and out of our lives and control us at will.*

We had not heard from Denis in months, but Kati kept writing to him at his poste restante, and once in a while he'd send a telegram from some remote South American backwater: *Everything all right. Don't worry. Things look well. Denis.*

Soon it was time for me to get my diploma as an interpreter, but what was I going to do with it? If I wanted a job at the International Atomic Energy Agency, I would have to stay in Vienna, at least for the foreseeable future. I didn't want to do that. It was a fine place to be a student, but to live and work? It was too confining. It really was a small town with a small town mentality in spite of its pretentiousness. Vienna was a "cliquey" town. One had to conform to certain standards in order to belong to a so-called decent social circle. Vienna clung to its past and its old-fashioned ways. As a Jew, I just didn't feel comfortable in Vienna. I had come there as a shy student, grateful to have been allowed to leave England. But I was growing up. I wanted to see more of the world. The thought of going back to England was painful. It was a place that I wasn't ready to face yet. I knew that it would hurt my mother terribly that I wasn't coming home. But I felt that I just couldn't. I would be stuck there forever, in the same environment, in the same dismal life as before.

All my friends had plans. Dita was going back to the States. George was in architecture school. Lite was going to graduate school in Sweden. I started interviewing with private companies that required interpreters for jobs abroad. These companies were mostly Middle Eastern, and it would have meant relocating to a variety of Arab countries. Kati was horrified, actually so was Uncle Bandi. As far as they were concerned, all the Arabs were looking for were "white slaves."

And suddenly there was a reprieve! As we were sitting down to dinner one night, Kati, grinning from ear to ear, held out a letter.

"Look what I have. A letter from Denis."

"Oh? A whole letter? What's gotten into him? He remembered he has a family?" I asked sarcastically.

"Oh, he remembered all right. It's not just a letter. Look!" She held out a check and I took it from her nonchalantly. Ten thousand dollars! Was this a joke?

"Is it real?"

"Yes, it's real. What do you think of it?"

"What is one supposed to think of ten thousand dollars? What's it for?"

"He says he wants to pay us back for all the loans these past couple of years, plus a lot of interest."

"Anything for Mamcsi?"

"I don't know. I just got this. I hope he sends your mother something, too, if he has so much to throw around." Ten thousand dollars in 1960 was a lot of money!

"Wait! That's not all," said Kati. "There's another check here." That check was made out to me, Evelyne Juliette Weisz, for $2,000. A note was attached: *Get yourself a bathing suit and a ticket to Caracas. I need an interpreter for the new business. Denis.*

I was totally bewildered. Caracas, Venezuela! It sounded so exotic. I was in shock. He really wanted me. And it was *he* who needed *me* this time. It wasn't just a "let's do something for the kid" type of thing.

Caracas! Away from Europe and its oppressive history. I felt the thrill of advancing toward a new and exciting adventure. And this time I would be working, earning money, because I was worth something now. Denis had finally come through.

"Does he mean it?" I asked quietly, terrified that perhaps my imagination was running away with me.

"Denis doesn't kid where money and work are concerned," Kati said tartly.

Everything had changed again. No more worry about what to do next, where to go, how to get a job; only to tell my mother that I was going even farther away from her. I quieted my conscience by telling myself that now that Kati had succeeded in getting my mother's restitution pension from the German government, she really didn't need me around anymore. She had just stopped working and was coming for a visit. We would be able to visit anywhere from now on. Life was really getting back on track.

The last of the exams were over, and I started to take daily Spanish lessons, Castilian—learning to lisp and substitute *b*'s for *v*'s. My mother came for a visit. She shared my room, and to my absolute astonishment and Kati's perplexity, my mother and the Prinzessin became great friends.

"Just be careful what you tell her," Kati warned my mother. "She doesn't have to know about the kind of work you did."

Uncle Bandi, my mother, and I guffawed, while Kati, exasperated with our complete lack of *Weltanschauung,* shrugged her shoulders and left the room.

My mother also gave warnings. "Go to Caracas. It'll be an adventure. Learn and see as much as you can. Just don't be disappointed if Denis is not everything you expect."

With my diploma, my passport, and my ticket in my pocket, at age twenty-one I left for Venezuela.

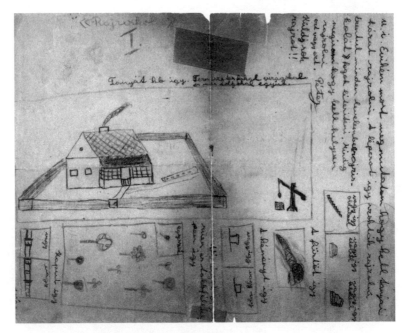

Letter from Peter. Budapest, June 18, 1946.

My Darling Evi, I got your drawings and I can't tell you how
happy I was. Now I am sending you mine and you can judge
whether it's good or not. I hope you are well. I feel wonderful and
I think a lot about you. I hear that Claudi (I'm not sure that I'm
spelling it correctly) is bothering you a lot. Just tell him that if he
doesn't leave you alone, I shall break his bones when I come. You
got my previous drawings, let me know if you like them and what
you want me to draw next. These drawings that I'm sending are
not just for you but also for Magda, so be careful with them, don't
crumple them. Now, Young Lady . . . a special request. Please write
otherwise. . . . I will write more often too. Since you weren't here
for your birthday I'm sending you congratulations and wish you
lots of chocolates (you can send me some of it). Wishing you
everything good. Write a lot. Till we see each other again, lots of
kisses. Peter and Pista

Château des Groux (back).

Elementary school in Verneuille-sur-Seine, 1947. Evi, top row, far right.

At the Château des Groux orphanage, 1947. Claudio, standing, far left; Peter Ferenczi; Eva Berkovics (Eva 2), third from left; Klara Heisler, fourth from left; Eva Ferenczi (Eva 1), fifth from left; Evi (Eva 3), front center.

At Saint Martin's, 1951.

"To Evi, a keepsake for Evi's eleventh birthday. Peter." 1950.

Saint Martin's class in *A Midsummer Night's Dream*. Evi, top row, third from left; Pauline Masters, standing, far left; Maureen Clare, with lantern, top row, far right; Jill Howell, directly under Maureen.

Rose, Veronica, and Evi (eleven years).
Cheltenham, England, 1950.

Peter. Budapest, 1947–8?

Evi, Magda, "Bolond" Rozsi. London, 1955.

With cousin Yvonne. Paris, 1957.

With Peter during visit to Budapest, 1956.

Peter, Erika, and Andre. London, 1960.

Andreas Gedeon (Uncle Bandi). Vienna, 1958–9?

Caracas, 1960

We came in from the ocean, directly onto a landing strip, and the plane skidded to a stop right across from the bare, terra-cotta-colored mountains. Through the small window, I could see palm trees and a small crowd of people on the edge of a tarmac in front of a couple of low buildings with metal roofs—with the words *La Guaira* on them—shimmering from the heat. As I stepped out of the plane, sultry, hot, humid air with that distinctly tropical odor of decay hit me in the face, and immediately I started to perspire. The palm trees were not those stately trees that always grace pictures of the tropics, but thick and dumpy with heavy fronds, some of them dead and brown, hanging from the trunk. Airport personnel, with open shirts, their caps perched carelessly on the back of their heads were moving about casually chatting with one another. The air was heavy with the heat and it slowed everything down to a different pace. I took a breath and felt how different the air smelled and tasted. The light was so much brighter than I had ever experienced and seemed to be pulsating. I squinted at the sun, huge and blazing, and in that moment realized how far away I was from everything that was familiar. How alien this world was.

By the time I reached the bottom of the stairs, Denis was there waiting with an amused smile on his face.

"Well, well well, look at the little Pollak. She's made the break! Did you at least bring me a good strudl?"

"As a matter of fact," I laughed, "I did."

"Good. I hope you don't travel like the rest of the family, with everything you own packed into a few dozen suitcases?"

"No. You told me to just bring a bathing suit. So that's what I brought. Oh, yes, and a toothbrush. Is that OK?"

His eyebrows shot up, and he laughed. "Well, looks like there's hope for you yet."

He walked me through passport control and customs, talking to the officials as though they were old friends. He spoke Spanish rapidly and seemingly well. I didn't catch most of what he said, but I understood that he was introducing me as *mi hija*.

When the formalities were dispensed with, he said, "Come on, there's some-one I want you to meet," and he steered me toward a young light-haired and fair-skinned woman, very thin, dressed in a crisp cotton shirtwaist and very white shoes.

"This is Jean. You two had better get along, since we are all living together. Evi I'm counting on you to teach her how to cook a good chicken paprikás with *nokedli*."

"How do you do?" said Jean, formally. "Did you have a pleasant flight?"

The British accent threw me. "Er, . . . yes, thank you. How do *you* do?"

My heart sank. What did he mean by "we are all living together"? I had thought that he was alone and needed me. Had this young woman, probably less than ten years my senior, usurped my place? While I was wondering who this young Englishwoman could be, Denis hailed a taxi, bundled Jean and me in the backseat, got in next to the driver, gave directions then immediately turned back toward me and began talking in Hungarian. Jean looked out the window.

"Shouldn't we be speaking English?" I asked tentatively.

"No, my English is terrible. Let her learn Hungarian if she wants to. Besides, I want to know about the family. It's none of her business."

"Can we talk when we get home? This place is so different. I'd like to look out the window," I continued in English, embarrassed for Jean.

"Oh, all right," he grumbled, as Jean began pointing out the sights to me.

The road curved and climbed. Half-naked children with distended bellies and dirty faces were lining our route; behind them, covering the entire hillside, were hovels on top of hovels. Pieces of wood, corrugated metal, cardboard, and hang-ing rags all in a jumble, at odd angles and on top of one another, formed the most primitive living quarters.

"What is this place?" I asked, horrified.

"They call them barrios. The poor people live in them. They're all over."

"This is terrible. I've never seen anything like this."

"Don't worry, you'll get used to it. Everyone does. Americans and Europeans are shocked at first. They think that nothing is worse than their slums. Then they see this. But as I said, you'll get used to it."

"I hope not," I muttered.

We kept climbing. The air became clearer and less humid. Soon we reached the outskirts of Caracas. We rode through narrow streets lined with small pastel-colored houses with iron gates. Vividly colored flowers and enormous dark green leaves were struggling to grow through the bars. I marveled at the brilliant hues. It looked like miniature jungles were sprouting behind those gates, a world away from the delicate daffodils and subtly colored English roses. A vaguely remembered poem crept into my mind, something about a "a gaudy melon-flower." Ah yes, Robert Browning's "Home-Thoughts, from Abroad." Poor Robert, I thought. He was so homesick. And he was only in Italy. He should have seen the colors in Venezuela!

Soon we were driving on broad avenues, lined with apartment houses, all looking very square and modern. The streets were quite empty of people.

"Where are the people?" I asked. "There's hardly anyone around."

"It's siesta time. Nobody works in the middle of the day. We start very early, take three to four hours off in the middle of the day, then back to work till evening," said Denis. "Sleep well tonight because I'm waking you up at 5:30 tomorrow. The two of us are going to work. No time for sight-seeing now. This is my busy season. You'll do your tourist stuff later."

Ah, so Jean wasn't working for him? So what was she doing? I resented her presence, but this was mitigated by the fact that she was English. In the midst of these foreign surroundings, she was a stabilizing factor. She gave me a feeling of security. I knew how to talk and behave with English people.

We stopped in front of an apartment building, la Residencia los Caobos, on la Avenida el Libertador. It sounded so romantic!

The apartment was a nondescript one-bedroom: kitchen, one bath, balcony. Nothing fancy. It looked like a bachelor pad, complete with a bar and matching stools in one corner. It could have been anywhere, in any modern, unimaginative building in any postwar country. I was disappointed.

"Well, how do you like it?" asked Denis. "You'll have to sleep on the couch. We only have one bedroom."

"Oh, well, that's OK," I said. "I don't suppose we'll spend much time at home."

"That's what I keep telling her!" cried Denis triumphantly. "She always wants to get a big fancy apartment like all her friends have!"

"No," protested Jean, "I just want something comfortable, where we can invite our friends and maybe an extra room where guests can stay."

"She's not a guest," growled Denis. "She'll be fine."

"Well, yes. It's certainly more modern than her mother's flat in London," said Jean.

"You've been to my mother's flat?"

"Yes. I visited her last time I went home to England."

I was totally bewildered, very tired, and suddenly, very alone. Who was this woman that I had never heard of, who knew my mother and with whom I obviously had to share Denis? I didn't know what her role was, nor what mine would be in regard to the two of them. I had come halfway around the world to sleep on a living-room couch, to be the extra wheel, an afterthought.

I settled in and was allowed a short rest. Soon after Denis announced that we were going out to dinner and that I would be meeting "their crowd."

By the time we set out for the restaurant, it was already dark. Darkness comes very suddenly in the tropics. I remembered a geography lesson from my school days: The equator is the closest point to the sun, therefore as the earth rotates, it takes the least amount of time for the sun to "disappear" at this part of the globe. Now I finally understood what they had meant.

Tables on the sidewalk were pushed and pulled together, and Denis took center place. As people drifted in, they greeted us and sat down. I was introduced to everyone. Many were Hungarian, some American, none were Venezuelan. Some said they remembered me as a little girl in Paris or Budapest and inquired after various members of the family. The atmosphere was reminiscent of the café La Belle Ferronniere, off the Champs-Élysées, where Denis had held court years before in Paris. Several of these people evidently followed one another around the world, constantly in search of better business pastures.

On one side of the table Denis was speaking Hungarian with his friends, while Jean was chatting in English with the Americans on the other. I caught some bemused looks thrown in my direction and wondered what Jean was saying about me. My head was going like a Ping-Pong ball, answering questions and trying to keep up with several conversations at once. Meanwhile, the food came and Denis was pressing me to try all kinds of new foods that I had never heard of before. That evening, for the first time, I ate avocado, mango, and papaya, had lime juice in my tea, and tasted several different cuts of beef, sizzling on a hibachi set right in the center of our table. Yes, this place was very different, very exciting. Maybe it would work out after all!

I was enjoying my dinner and the attention when something large and flying, the size of a small bird, knocked against me and startled me. Everyone laughed.

"Get used to strange creatures," said Denis. "These are just large moths. Totally harmless."

Not so harmless and frightening was the snake that I found in the shower at 5:30 the following morning, when Denis woke me up. My startled scream woke Jean up.

"Well," she said, quite put out. "We've never had *that* before. Now you see why we should move to a better neighborhood and a place that is better maintained."

Denis pooh-poohed her, and by six o'clock he and I were on our way to the docks.

The harbor was a chaotic jumble of cargo ships, tugboats, various fishing vessels, and what seemed like rusty WWI battleships. It was still very early in the morning, but the air was heavy and humid, and the heat was already closing in on us. Barefoot dockworkers were running hither and dither, dressed in ragged clothing. I noticed that the local people ranged in skin color from very fair to deep dark chocolate brown. And their language sounded quite different from the Spanish that I had been studying. I could barely make out anything. Denis laughed at my confusion.

"Of course it's different. Is English the same the world over? Jean keeps laughing at the way the Americans speak, and they, in turn, laugh at the Australians, who probably wonder what language the New Zealanders speak. Everybody in every language thinks that they are the only ones who speak without an accent."

"And most of them don't even speak their own language correctly," I concurred, thinking back to that episode in Vienna when I had asked our cleaning woman to help me with my homework and she had it all wrong. It was the same all over the world.

Denis made his way purposefully to a large cargo ship. "I have a large shipment coming in and have to see the customs official. I want you to see what I do, because a lot of the correspondence that I need from you will relate to it."

"Relate to what? Shipment of what? What's your business?"

"Fabrics. I import from the U.S. and sell it here. I've never made so much money in my life!"

We boarded a cargo ship and located the captain and the customs official, who were waiting for Denis. Huge bales were ready to be unloaded onto the dock. They were assigned to "Denis Palmer, c/o Latin American Trading Co., Maiquetía, Venezuela."

Denis again introduced me as mi hija, the men greeted me, and then the four of us stepped to the side of the ship, where an intense negotiation took place between Denis and the men. I understood the gist of it. They were negotiating the weight of the shipment. Denis was handing over large bills and the men were countering with numbers of kilos. The more money Denis handed over, the less kilos the men quoted. Finally, they all agreed and shook hands. The customs official gave orders for the bales to be unloaded and handed Denis some papers on which he had hastily filled out the blank spaces, and we made our way to the customs office. The man behind the desk also received some money. Denis filled out more papers and paid the duty on his shipment, based on the "weight" that the customs official had just written.

"OK, this was a good morning's work," he observed. "Let's get out of here, it's getting hot. I'll show you the office now."

We took a taxi back to Caracas. The taxis, all numbered, drive along a particular route and take up to five passengers, who then can ask the driver to drop them off anywhere along their particular route; the driver will also pick up anyone who hails him along the way, as long as there is room in the cab.

We were let off a couple of blocks away from Denis's office, so I got the feel of downtown Caracas. It was old, crowded, and dirty with some dilapidated, colonial-style buildings mixed in with unattractive, modern office buildings.

The shops seemed garish to me, and I was curious to see what kinds of wares were being sold. But Denis was hurrying along, so I scurried behind him.

A horribly misshapen beggar was lying across the entrance to the building that Denis entered. He was missing one leg completely, and the other one was bloated to twice normal size, covered in oozing sores. Flies were buzzing around him and feeding on his pus. His eyes were rolled back in his head, and he looked more dead than alive. Denis stepped over him into the entrance hall, while I stood there horrified, tasting the bile coming up from my stomach.

"Come on," said Denis, "Just step over him."

"I can't."

Denis stood on the other side of the beggar, trying not to look at him and uncertain as to what to do. At that moment, a man carrying a large, wide broom emerged from the building and started shouting at the beggar, who seemed incapable of moving on his own. The man pushed him to the side with his broom, and Denis held out his hand to help me across the threshold. I was on the point of vomiting and was feeling faint.

"Look," said Denis, "this is South America. You can't let these sights get to you. I know how you feel. I was the same way when I first came. You have to learn not to look. If you had become a doctor, like you wanted to, you would have to look at things like this all the time."

"That's not what's making me sick. It's seeing him dying there, with the flies feeding off him, and people stepping over him as though he weren't even there."

"We had it much worse and nobody gave a damn about us. On the contrary, they were happy we were dying. Why should we care?"

"Because . . . because we're not like them."

Denis sighed. "Evi, this is a tough world and you'd better get used to it. Otherwise, you'll end up like your mother and Don Quixote: fighting windmills. Come on, we don't have time to talk about this now. Let's get to work."

I tried to put the sight of the beggar out of my mind and looked around the office. It was small, somewhat messy, but functional. Denis directed me to a desk with a typewriter and started dictating letters immediately. I wrote orders to fabric houses in New York, a letter to a lawyer in Germany, and while waiting for Denis to give me other work, a letter to my mother. Among the details of my journey and safe arrival, I casually asked what she knew of a woman called Jean, who was living here with Denis.

A visitor came. Denis introduced me to a tall, haughty-looking, very handsome, and well-dressed Venezuelan.

"This is Armando. We do business together. We're going out for half an hour. You don't have to let anyone in. If you think your Spanish is good enough to answer the phone go ahead. When I come back we'll go to lunch."

I looked around the office. There were pictures of all of us, the family, strewn around, propped up on his desk, against a telephone book, or in the drawers. Hanging on the wall, not high up, but next to the desk, was a photograph of Uncle Miklos in an old-fashioned oval frame. A faded snapshot of my grandmother and another one of my grandfather were pushed between the glass and the frame. Uncle Miklos was the second oldest of my mother's siblings, just a year younger than Kati. He was a bit of a mystery to me. I remembered very little of him. By the time I got to Hungary, he was divorced and living with his second wife in Miskolc, in northern Hungary. That was the reason that he had been deported very soon after the Germans had entered Hungary. The northern towns were the first to be emptied of Jews. I remember him visiting occasionally and making a fuss over me, while I looked surreptitiously at his limp arm, not daring to ask what was wrong with it. While looking at his picture, I remembered his silky mustache and his beautiful eyes and I remembered something else. He had a different family name, as had Pista, his son, my cousin. The name was Lengyel, not Pollak. Lengyel means "Polish" in Hungarian, as I suppose Pollak does in either Polish or Yiddish. I wondered vaguely why he had changed it if he intended to stay in Hungary. Denis had anglicized his name to Palmer.

I straightened up the office, trying to organize the various piles of letters, orders, and files. In the drawer of the desk where I was working, I found an envelope with a great deal of cash in it.

When Denis came back, he explained about Armando. "He is my banker. Very useful. He understands the way to do business. Anything new here?"

"No. But should you leave all this cash around?" I asked, handing him the envelope that I had found.

"Did you take any of it?"

"Of course not."

"Then you can't be a member of our family!" he said tartly. "How much do you need?" I shrugged my shoulders. "Here," he said, handing me a large wad. "This should last you a while. If you need anything ask Jean to help you. She's a very good shopper, only please don't buy all that paint that she puts on her face. I call her Mrs. Sherwin Williams."

"Denis, why was Miklos called Lengyel?" Denis sat down at his desk and stared at his brother's picture.

"He got himself adopted by one of our uncles, who had had his named Hungarianized when he got baptized."

"Why did he want to be adopted?"

"Because he wanted to go the university, and Anyuka couldn't afford to send him. By promising to become a Christian, Uncle Armin adopted him and paid for his schooling."

"What about you? Didn't you want to go to the university?"

"Anyuka said one goy among her children was already one too many, and anyway I wanted to go into business. Besides, he was much smarter than I."

"Smarter than you? Come on!" I said, teasing him.

"Don't be a smart-ass. Have you read his poetry, his plays, his articles?"

"No, I didn't even know that they still existed."

"They are fantastic. Very deep. Even I don't understand them all."

"It didn't help him much, did it, becoming Christian?"

"No. Those bastards took everybody. And they would still take them given half a chance. And so would three-quarters of the world. I'm telling you, Evi, don't feel sorry for the others. Think of your family and what was done to us. Protect yourself and yours. Let others look out for themselves."

Uncle Miklos, eight years his senior, had been Denis's hero, big brother, and father figure. He never really got over his brother's murder, and I suspect that he always felt guilty for having been far away from Europe at the time. He didn't talk much about his brother, cutting short any conversation about him; always when his voice started to crack.

I found out much later, and not from Denis, that Uncle Miklos had written a book about his conversion and had dedicated it to Pope Pius XII.

He had prostrated himself and for his trouble had been sacrificed in Auschwitz.

I dreaded leaving the office. I didn't want to see the beggar in the doorway, and I steeled myself as the elevator hit the main floor. The beggar was gone and I was left wandering what could possibly have happened to him. I wondered if Denis had anything to do with his disappearance, but I didn't ask him.

We caught another taxi that had the destination sign Tamanaco on the front and headed through much wealthier parts of the city. There were beautiful plazas with gardens, luxurious apartment houses, and streets lined with well-tended trees and flower borders. We came to a hill with lush vegetation on the sides and drove up a long, winding driveway lined with tall, stately palm trees, till the Tamanaco came into sight. It was at that time, and I think is still, the plushest hotel in the city, and the European business community headed there every day at noon. There were beautiful terraces where lunch was served by waiters in spanking white uniforms, a very large, clear blue kidney-shaped pool (the first one that I had ever seen), tennis courts, and lots of comfortable lounge chairs dotting the lawns bordered by flowering shrubs. Jean was already there, chatting with another friend, both of them in snappy bathing suits, comfortably ensconced in lounge chairs. I was introduced to those whom I had not met the night before and greeted by those I already knew.

Jean's friend was a luscious, amber-haired American named Hilda. She had a cur-vaceous, well-tanned body, and a beautiful complexion, and she wore expensive sun-glasses and chunky gold jewelry. She looked rich and healthy, and compared to her, Jean appeared like an spinsterish old schoolmarm. I immediately liked Hilda, but felt that she was off-limits. She was Jean's friend, and I felt that I was not going to be admitted to make a threesome. So after lunch on the terrace, when Denis joined the men, I took a lounge chair and placed it at a discreet distance from Jean: close enough that it would allow her to say "bring your chair closer" if she wanted, but far enough not to seem that I was encroaching on her friendship. She didn't say anything.

Jean was very reserved with me. I felt a wariness about her that told me that she didn't trust me, that I was invading her territory. And I felt the same way toward her. But she appeared surer of herself than I was. I felt off-balance, wish-ing that I had known about her before coming.

She treated me as a guest. She was always polite and did not let me do things around the house, such as cooking or cleaning, just as one wouldn't allow a guest to do that. I wasn't for one moment to think that as a member of Denis's family, I could assume privileges that she did not bestow on me. The couch in the living room remained my "place." Jean never bought anything for the apartment nor did she made any attempt to make it more attractive. She wanted to underscore the fact that Denis chose to live in such a place, and she was not going to make the best of it; she considered it a "dump." No one was ever invited there. When Denis insisted that I show her how to make nokedli with chicken paprikas, she stood in the kitchen watching me with a look of resignation on her face and finally said, "It takes too long to make and it's too heavy a food for this climate."

Occasionally, she would ask when I was planning to go home. I always said that I didn't know, that it was up to Denis. Besides, I really didn't know where "home" would be.

After three hours of lunch, napping, swimming, and general R&R, Denis and I went back to the office, while Jean and the rest of the wives either stayed behind or went shopping. At seven o'clock we went home, showered, changed, picked up Jean and went out to dinner. This became our general routine, although things varied depending on when Denis received shipments. When he did, we went to the docks early, bribed and paid the customs people, then imme-diately arranged for the direct transfer of the merchandise to the customers. Denis hardly had to check his merchandise or even warehouse anything. Whatever came from the United States could be sold on the spot for cash. Enormous profits were being made, especially when saving on the import duty.

In slow times we took time off, and I had the opportunity to see more of the city and the surrounding areas, though not to my satisfaction. I was not allowed to go alone. I was told that it wasn't safe and that it would be an insult to Jean not to want her to come along, and going with Jean was a not a bit of fun. She was doing her duty, taking Denis's niece and showing her "around." But we saw only the tourist sights, nothing of the real Venezuela. The only Venezuelans I met socially were the banker Armando and his beautiful wife, who looked like a Goya portrait of a Spanish grandee's wife. In the office I met his girlfriend, who seemed more like an extra from *Carmen*.

Caracas was a city of extremes. Before arriving in South America, I never could have imagined the misery and poverty nor the extravagant wealth that I saw displayed there. Through my mother's various jobs I had seen and met some very wealthy people, but they had been different. There had been a quiet, settled air to them, an elegance and a reserve, a quiet confidence. Everyone *knew* that they had money, but one never *talked* about it. Here it was quite the contrary. I didn't know the term at that time, but in Caracas was an explosion, a veritable fireworks display of nouveau riche-ism. The main topic of conversation was money and the things one could get with it. People were making fortunes and spending lavishly.

Hilda and her husband invited us to dinner one night at their apartment in one of the loveliest sections of the city. They lived in a very elegant and modern apartment house situated on the periphery of a grand plaza, magnificently laid out with palms, fountains, flowers, and marble statuary. The apartment matched the plaza. It was vast. The floors were marble, the ceilings very high, and the décor, very costly.

Denis walked around slowly, examining everything. Then, turning to his host with a sober look, he said, "Congratulations. It's all very beautiful. You must be making an enormous amount of money."

"Probably no more than you. Why are you living like a pauper?"

"Like a pauper? We live exactly as you do, except that I do not see the point of investing in an elegant home for a short period of time."

"A short period of time! Don't you intend to settle down here?"

"Settle down? How long do you think this boom is going to last? How long till they get wise to us and start throwing us out?"

"Us? Why would they throw us out? We're helping the economy!"

"We're helping ourselves! We're all sending our money out. Besides, they'll soon see that there are too many rich Jews and too many poor Venezuelans!"

"Denis, this isn't Europe twenty years ago!"

Denis sighed. I could feel him thinking: How could an American understand? Jean cut in. "We could certainly live better if every member of his family were not constantly demanding money."

Instantly it was quiet. Eyes turned toward me, then, just as quickly, away. I wanted to disappear into oblivion. Denis looked thoughtfully at Jean.

"I was not aware that you were eating any less or buying fewer dresses because of my family," he said very quietly.

"I just meant that if you feel that this boom is not going to continue, you should keep your money for future security," answered Jean defensively.

"How very thoughtful," came the sarcastic reply.

Uncomfortable as I was feeling and embarrassed by Jean's tactlessness, I still resented Denis more than Jean. Obviously he was the one who had told her that the family was constantly demanding money, while to me he was always making fun of Jean, calling her "the skinny English shiksa" and ridiculing her thin body, her use of makeup, her idleness, and her lack of culinary skills. I now understood why Jean didn't particularly like me. She probably thinks we are all a bunch of leeches, I thought indignantly. Nevertheless, I felt that there was some truth to what Jean implied. Everyone in the family, except for my mother, thought of Denis as the family mainstay, the savior, the ultimate authority. Nothing happened without his knowledge or approval. He was the "alpha male."

Meanwhile, I had received a letter from my mother, surprised that Jean was in Caracas: *I thought she was Claude's girlfriend. They came to visit me from Paris on the way to Venezuela. I didn't know that she stayed there. . . .*

I knew from keeping records at the office that Denis was sending huge sums of money abroad. To Claude in Paris, to Kati in Austria, to an account in the United States. I figured that he sensed that the good life in Caracas was not going to last forever and he wanted to be prepared, just as Jean had suggested. I also knew that there was a large sum of money in Jean's name, too, so it was with a sense of indignation that I confronted Denis.

"Why did you tell Jean that we were always asking you for money?"

"Why not? Otherwise she'd want everything for herself. Let her think I have commitments."

"But if you think so little of her, why do you keep her around?"

"She has advantages."

"Wasn't she Claude's girlfriend?"

"Evi, don't you know when you've asked enough questions? Teach her how to cook instead."

We lived in an uneasy threesome—uneasy, at least, for Jean and me. Denis seemed oblivious to any problems. For his part, he was busy trotting out young men for me to meet. There were very few single European Jewish girls in Caracas, and plenty of young men eager to date me. In the last two years I had filled out in the right places. A little lipstick, a good haircut, and pretty clothes did the rest. Hilda had nicknamed me Pocket Venus, and to Denis's total disgust, suggested that I only go on dates at the beach or the pool since I looked a lot better in a bikini than dressed up. But Denis made no bones about the fact that he wanted me married off.

"Take your pick," he urged. "I'll buy you whichever one you want!"

I asked him what kind of a life he visualized for me in South America. The European wives didn't work at anything, and all the husbands had mistresses.

"Is that what you want for me?"

"South America, North America, what's the difference? What else is there for a woman?"

What else indeed? Grandmother had toiled to raise her five children alone. Kati's way out of poverty had been by her own labor. My mother had worked since the age of nine. My aunt Eszter owned and operated her own dress shop. But now, it was 1960. The men made the money, the women spent it. Denis thought that was a better way. At least that kept the women in check!

One evening I came home late from a date. Denis was in the living room drinking cognac. Denis never drank liquor. It was a family joke. Every time Denis attempted to drink, for the sake of social appearances, he screwed up his face and looked as though he was going to be ill. I was just about to make a joke, when I heard muffled sobs coming from the bedroom.

"What's going on?" I asked, alarmed.

"Nothing. I'm going out. If you don't see me in the morning, get to the office early by yourself." He left, and I didn't dare knock on the bedroom door.

I got up early and just caught a glimpse of Jean scurrying out of the bathroom and back into the bedroom, sporting a black eye and a bruised face. I pretended that I had not seen her and hurried to the office. Denis was in a foul mood. The customs official had been arrested and he couldn't reach Armando. But I couldn't be sympathetic. I couldn't even look at him. I just went about my work without a word.

"All right, all right!" he finally shouted at me. "So I hit her. She deserved it. Why are you making such a big thing out of it? I have other problems. You want to be next?"

I got off my chair and went to face him, just as I had years ago, in Paris.

"I will kill anyone who ever touches me," I said.

Denis looked at me quizzically, then walked away, muttering, "Women, they just don't have a sense of humor."

By the time we got home, Jean was gone.

"She went to the States," he said. "Listen, I think our days in Caracas are coming to an end. Why don't you go visit your mother for a couple of weeks? When you come back, we'll wind things up and see what to do next." He handed me five hundred dollars and the next day bought me a ticket to England via New York.

Before the plane even landed at Idlewild (now JFK International Airport), I had decided to visit New York City. Denis had stuffed me with enough cash to last me for some time, and I needed a little of that time to think. What was I going to do now? Denis said that the political situation in Venezuela was becoming too unstable. He even predicted a bloody revolution.

I didn't know what I wanted to do from then on. I really didn't want to stay in South America. I didn't want to go back to Vienna either. Even though England was the place I felt most at home, I just knew my future wasn't there. Now that my mother had her pension I didn't feel the same obligation to go back. She could come to wherever I was going to be.

I took the bus to Manhattan. The wide highway that we were riding on was lined with huge billboards advertising all kinds of things. Suddenly the road took a turn, and for the first time I saw the famous skyline. I don't know why, but tears came to my eyes. From the movies that I had seen, I recognized the Empire State Building and the Chrysler Building. They were so much taller than I had imagined. No wonder they call them skyscrapers, I thought. The view took my breath away. Another billboard appeared that advertised, in huge six-foot letters, Hebrew National Kosher Salami, and there was an enormous Star of David right in the middle.

I was flabbergasted. Somewhere in the world, outside of Israel, Jews were feeling so free that they could advertise this way! This was the place where "everybody was from somewhere else," where buildings were tall and proud and had never been bombed, where beggars were not left to rot and die in the streets!

In that moment I knew that I was staying. Alone or not, it didn't matter. This was where I was going to start my real life. I felt that I had finally found my home.

Before I was able to go back to my new home, I had to return to Caracas for a second visit. This time I was the mistress of the house. My cousin Claude came to visit and so did Rebecca, Little Magda's mother. Denis and I lived like children who had been left alone at home while their parents had gone away on vacation. We invited people to the house and cooked all kinds of Hungarian foods. I filled the house with flowers and rearranged the furniture. But it was all over very fast. Denis had to leave in a hurry, owing to several arrests on the waterfront and a change in administration. The boom was over. I was left alone for a couple of weeks to clean things up, pack, lock up, and leave.

I took a plane straight to New York.

Part Two

Magda. Vienna, 1959.
Evi. New York City, 2003.

New York City, June 1960

America, the land of our dreams. In the summer of 1960, America was riding high and New York City was at the apex. The American Dream had come true . . . the *white* American Dream, that is. The mass immigrations of Latinos and Asians to the States had not yet taken place, and the civil rights movement had not yet taken off. General Eisenhower, a war hero who had "won the war for freedom and democracy in the Western world," was at the helm. Americans saw themselves as the richest, the best, the freest. Everyone had the opportunity to become whatever *he* wanted to. It was the last stage of the age of innocence. The turmoil that was seething beneath the glossy surface would wait for another few years to erupt. Meanwhile, the most recent wave of immigrants, the Hungarians who had fled during the 1956 revolution, had found jobs or were going to school. They had been absorbed into the mainstream and had quickly adapted to the ways of their host nation. As model citizens of their new country, they paid their taxes and sat in front of their television sets enjoying Milton Berle's antics and believing in the *Ozzie and Harriet* lifestyle. Another group of immigrants, the Cubans fleeing from Castro's revolution, had settled mostly in and around Miami. Many of them did not believe the revolution would last and wanted to be close to their homeland when it was time to return. They stayed and became the force behind the economic and cultural revival of the region.

Jews believed that New York City was God's acre in the Diaspora. They became lawyers, doctors, teachers, and even baseball players. They could own homes almost anywhere they wanted, and their children went to college, even Harvard, if they could get in under the quota system. Everyone knew which industries and big firms did not employ Catholics or Jews. But who cared anyway? There were plenty of others, and there was work for everyone. The "strange-looking" black-clothed Jews who wore beards and yarmulkes and owned shops on Manhattan's Lower East Side were regarded by many as oddities, tourist attractions in a way, like the Amish in Pennsylva-nia. They were not visible unless they were sought out. The places that were off-limits even became the target of jokes, as Groucho Marx saucily cracked, tapping on his cigar, "I don't want to belong to any club that will have me as a member."

I was unaware of the undercurrents beneath the American political landscape. I was twenty-one, and to me America was the golden land, where anything was possible, where opportunities beckoned around every corner, where everyone had an equal chance at success and all one needed was a willingness to work hard. Jobs were plentiful. I didn't know that certain jobs were only for certain people; that a name like Gallagher or Grunblatt could keep one out of certain careers. And had I known, I probably would have shrugged my shoulders and thought, So, change your name! Who cares? Circumventing the system was what I had always been taught to do because that was the only way to get ahead. Had I reflected on any of this at the time, I would have thought of myself as a realist. Equal rights for all was an ideal, a pipe dream, not for this world. Yet I devoured Upton Sinclair's World's End series and fell in love with its hero, Lanny Budd, never grasping the fact that he represented everything that I couldn't trust myself to believe in.

I sat on the steps of the public library at Fifth Avenue and Forty-second Street in a dreamlike trance. I turned my head slowly, surveying the buildings around me. They were so huge! I had never seen buildings so tall and so massive. I peered closely at the street signs. I wanted to make sure that I was really there . . . New York City! Utopia, El Dorado. Yes, here I was, twenty-one, enough money in my pocket to last for a while and speaking the language as well as any native. I can fit in here. Nobody can tell that I am not from here, I thought. I felt so free, ready to take on the world. I just knew that this was the place that would become my home. I felt that I was shedding the heavy mantle of my European past. I didn't need it anymore!

I watched the people walking fast and purposefully. Nobody was strolling. The men were wearing seersucker suits and straw hats. They all looked so clean-cut. The women wore high heels, white gloves, lots of petticoats, and some had cute little hats perched on well-shampooed, shiny hair. They all looked like movie stars.

I started walking south and was mystified by the steam emerging from the middle of the street. Hot springs? And what were those big ugly boxes affixed to windows, with water dripping from some of them? I came to a department store and walked in, marveling at the lavish displays, the perfectly groomed salesladies, the myriad of different items. In a display case I saw a little brooch in the shape of the American flag, studded with red, white, and blue stones. I asked a saleslady to show it to me.

"Sure, honey," she said, with a familiarity that shocked me. "D' you just get off the boat?"

"Excuse me?"

"It's just that you speak different. Like you just got here."

"I did. But I speak the same language that you do," I insisted.

"Yeah, kinda, but it don't sound American."

American? There was language called "American?" Obviously there was, and grammar was not the first priority. So they could tell that I wasn't from here. It was a shock. I thought that I had finally found a place where nobody needed to know that I wasn't born there. Where I could make my home because "everybody was from somewhere else." But I could never talk like that! I felt as though I had been found out.

I left the store, a little chastened, with my brooch, which the saleslady called a "pin," packaged in a pretty box, then placed in a beautiful little shopping bag with string handles, a red rose printed on it and, in red lettering, "Lord & Taylor." And I marveled that the shopping bag was free.

The streets were all numbered, so I found Denis's New York office very easily. It was right off Fifth Avenue. I had sent many a letter to that address to be forwarded to wherever Denis happened to be. It was a disappointment. In this city of magnificent skyscrapers, 12 West Thirty-first Street was a dingy, sooty little building with a dirty and shaky elevator. The office was seedy and unclean, with papers strewn around the desks, dirty coffee cups everywhere, and the stale smell of cigarette butts enveloping the entire area. I felt embarrassed that Denis should have this kind of office. He had always talked of the New York office as though if were the nucleus of an important worldwide financial organization. Two men looked up as I walked in. I introduced myself, and one of them jumped up from behind his desk.

"Little Evi! Denis told me a lot about you. Especially to look after you if you ever showed up."

Friendly and fatherly, Morris immediately took me under his wing. He assumed that I was just passing through and wanted me to have a safe sojourn. There was, of course, the question of where I was going to stay. But first he took me out to eat, and I experienced my first visit to a real American luncheonette, just like I had seen in the movies. Sitting on a tall stool at a pink Formica-covered, horseshoe-shaped counter, I watched in wonder as members of the American workforce hurriedly gulped down their overstuffed sandwiches along with a watery brown liquid that they called "coffee" and which made me screw up my face in distaste.

We picked up my luggage at the East Side Terminal, where I had left it, and Morris steered me to the Barbizon Hotel. As I was checking in, the white-haired lady behind the desk read the rules of the hotel to me, while I stood there wide-eyed. Men could escort the "ladies" into the lobby but were not allowed above the first floor. Any guest who broke this rule would be asked to vacate her room immediately. I was completely taken aback. Why would I want to take a man to my room? And if I did whose business was it? I had never heard of such a hotel.

"It's for your safety and reputation," Morris said, completely serious.

I had no idea what he was talking about. It was my first glimpse of American puritanism; but at the time all I attributed to it was that Morris must be a very old-fashioned man, which didn't fit in with my mental picture of a modern American.

I stayed at the hotel for three days, out of courtesy to Morris, while exploring and getting to know the city, then decided that more normal accommodations were in order. Morris was quite distressed and generously invited me to stay with his family on Long Island. I thanked him but declined. Denis had recently come into contact with a cousin who had left Hungary in 1956 and settled in New York City. I knew that this cousin had a daughter attending Columbia University, and I looked them up. Marianne, my second cousin, once or twice removed, and close to my own age, was indeed studying library science, and we became friendly. She and her mother lived near the university, and I decided to look for something in the same neighborhood. From the Columbia students' bulletin board I gleaned a few addresses where accommodations were being offered. This was how I met Cecile Blatt.

Miss Blatt, as I called her, owned a large apartment on Broadway a few blocks from the university and was looking to let out a couple of her rooms to students. She was a woman in her late fifties, tiny and round with very bright black eyes that darted like a bird's. Her hands and feet were the smallest that I had ever seen on an adult, and she had a shock of gray-tinged ringlets caught on the back of her head, usually covered with a turban. She had a high-pitched, childish voice that did not befit a woman her age and a cute flirtatious manner that was startling but not at all offensive; usually it elicited smiles and got her exactly what she wanted. When she scolded, she looked like a little girl wagging a chastising finger at her dolls. It seemed as though her persona had never caught up with her age. To my astonishment, she informed me that she had just retired from teaching political science at Barnard College.

I was invited in to look at the apartment, which was filled with oriental furniture, rugs, carvings, and various objets d'art. Over a cup of coffee, she asked me to tell her about myself. She frowned when she heard that I had no family in the country and tut-tutted that I was allowed to "gad about the world" on my own. We chatted, and she said that I could easily get a job at the university if I wanted one. It was clear that she liked me, and she took me to see the room that I was to occupy. It was beautiful, large, well furnished, and airy.

"I'm glad you're Jewish, since you're European," she said. "I certainly would never rent a room to an Italian or a Greek."

"Why ever not?" I asked.

"Well, you must know what they are like!" she said defensively.

"No, I don't know what you mean." I was genuinely curious. She lowered her voice.

"The Italians, they're all mafia," she whispered. "And the Greeks, oily, unreliable, sneaky." She pursed her lips and nodded knowingly.

I looked at her in disbelief. Italians? Greeks? Descendants of great artists, guardians of great cultures, respected members of the European community? What was she talking about? I smiled to myself. Looks like I'm destined to have eccentric landladies, I thought. I didn't quite know what to make of her. I took the room and told her that I would be back the following day.

As I was leaving, she said, "Oh, and of course, I don't need to tell you, this is a very respectable house."

"Naturally," I said.

"I myself have never been married. And I'm proud to say I've never been with a man. Good-bye."

With that she closed the door. I stood there, dead in my tracks, dumbfounded. What? What was that she had said?

I repeated the entire conversation to Marianne.

"I know," she said. "Americans are very strange. So contradictory. I've been here almost four years and I still don't understand them. Girls are categorized as "good girls" or "bad girls." This has nothing to do with good or bad, just whether they take lovers or not, a word, by the way, you're not supposed to use. But most "good girls" that I know have lovers, only no one is supposed to know. This is a big topic here. They have the most outrageous prejudices against anyone not American yet are generous to fault. They have a strong sense of morality and set themselves ideals that they can't possibly attain. Jews, Catholics, Protestants all mix at school and are friends, but they shun and fear Negroes. I went to a jazz concert with a Negro classmate, and you should have heard the hullabaloo . . . from the Jews, yet! And then of course, God forbid you should mention what went on during the war. They look at you as though you were crazy. My mother's Jewish landlady actually said to her 'Oh, yes, we also had a terrible time during the war. Gasoline was rationed and we couldn't get nylon stockings!' I could go on and on, but you'll see for yourself. And by the way, don't bother talking about anything cultural, they'll know immediately that you're European."

I listened to Marianne with amusement. She lowered her voice when she said *Negro* (as we did in the 1960s) because we were speaking Hungarian, in which the word is *Neger*—sounds much too close to the unacceptable English word. Strangely enough, the word for "black" is *fekete,* which nobody would have understood but which, in Hungarian, is the unacceptable word that she couldn't bring herself to use. She sounded a little exasperated.

"Don't you like it here?"

"I love it. I wouldn't want to be anywhere else. I just wish it were more like home. Or that home were more like here."

I moved into my rented room the following day. As I was unpacking my clothes, an earsplitting but oddly familiar sound filled the air. I stood there for a moment paralyzed, my mind in a strange confusion. I felt myself panicking and becoming short of breath. Something was not right, but I couldn't think what. Before I even was able to gather my thoughts, I took refuge under a large round oak table, close to the wall. I had my hands over my ears and I was trying to catch my breath, when the sound of the siren stopped. Then I realized: it was an air-raid signal. I hadn't heard one in years, not since childhood, but before my mind had been able to identify it, I had instinctively taken refuge. Like Pavlov's dogs, I was conditioned. I got up off the floor and ran to the kitchen, where Miss Blatt was making herself lunch.

"Why did they sound an air-raid alarm?" I asked shakily.

"Air-raid alarm? What are you talking about?" she said, looking at me with some suspicion.

"The siren! I heard it!"

"That's the twelve-noon signal. It sounds every day on the West Side."

"Why?"

"To tell everyone that it's twelve o'clock, of course," she said impatiently.

"Oh, oh I see."

I retreated slowly, back into my room, where I laid down on the bed and closed my eyes. Suddenly I felt very tired, very confused. There was an anxiety, a knot of fear forming in the pit of my stomach. I had felt so free, so liberated. I was in America, where life could start anew, where the past couldn't intrude. Yet I felt as though a malevolent force had reached out, like a hand, and pulled me back into the past, giving me an ominous warning and mocking me. I fell into an agitated sleep.

When I woke up, I felt embarrassed. How could I have let something so trivial upset me? Obviously sirens were used for things other than air-raid warnings. I'd have to get used to many different things in this country. Sirens signaling twelve-noon was just one of them.

I went to the personnel department at Columbia and asked whether there was any work available. I still felt part of the student community and considered the possibility of returning to school. Classes had ended, and the new semester didn't begin till the fall—but if I were interested, they said, there would soon be an opening at the university's bookstore. All I needed was a Social Security card.

With the guilelessness of the truly innocent, I presented myself at the nearest Social Security office to ask for one. The administrator recorded my vital statistics, and ten minutes later, I walked out with my new card, totally unaware of the value that hundreds of thousands of future immigrants would place on such a document (a document that I really had no business having, since I had entered the United States on a tourist visa).

I got the job at the bookstore. All who worked there, except the manager, were graduate students, overwhelmingly male and Jewish. They were all hardworking, cocky, smart, and curious about student life in Europe, and they ungrudgingly accepted me into their midst. Meanwhile, Miss Blatt had rented a room to another Jewish girl, whose family lived in Brooklyn. Susie was entering her senior year at Barnard, and her mother came to inspect us all before allowing Susie to move in. She planned to do some serious work and wasn't going to have time to commute home every day.

I developed a little circle of friends with Marianne, Susie, and various young men and women from the bookstore. I felt very comfortable among them. Students were students all over the world, the difference being that these were Americans, born and bred, and feeling at home in their own country. Their problems, if any, were mostly financial. But they knew that it was a temporary phase. They were all putting themselves through school, preparing for their future professions as doctors, lawyers, journalists, architects, and filmmakers. It was all part of the Jewish tradition.

We went to Lewisohn Stadium and to Central Park for concerts or picnics, or sat around talking, comparing European education, fashion, mores, and movies to their American counterparts. Miss Blatt watched over us like an eagle-eyed mother hen, always monitoring our discussions, which irritated Susie to no end.

"No wonder my mother agreed to let me live here. She knows a fellow member of the morality squad when she sees one," she grumbled.

Morris also kept tabs on me and frequently invited me to join family dinners at his suburban home on Long Island. It was understood that Denis, if he were in town, and I would always be at Morris's house for all Jewish holidays.

I was having a wonderful time: working, socializing, getting to know new people and new places. I celebrated my first paycheck with a shopping trip. At Macy's, "the world's largest department store," I bought two dresses and a gold-dipped pin with a pearl in the center for my mother. Total $26.45, including tax. At Rockefeller Center I had discovered the Librairie de France. Leon Uris's *Exodus* had just been translated into French, and I knew Kati would be pleased for three reasons to get it. First, she would be the first one in her circle to get it, since it was not yet available in German. Second, she could brag to all her friends, "Evi sent it to me from

America." And last (and least), she would enjoy reading it. She still had it in her possession when she died almost four decades later.

It was a wonderful feeling to be sending packages to Europe. From the time I was a small child, I remembered packages from America: the CARE packages that we received from the Red Cross; those sent by Jewish organizations to the orphanage; and then the rare treats that came from Denis. They were always filled with surprises. Sometimes we didn't even know what those surprises were supposed to be. There was that time at the orphanage when we unpacked a huge block of bright yellow American cheese and thought that it was soap, or the time that Denis announced that he was sending the latest American invention, a "Weather Topper," which turned out to be a piece of accordion-pleated plastic with a ribbon at each end, to be worn over the head in case of rain. Some invention! My mother and I laughed till our bellies hurt. But the best ones were those that came directly after the war and contained Nescafé and Carnation Condensed Milk! What a treat that was in the late 1940s! Now I was the one sending the packages with surprises.

Every day at five minutes to noon, I would get anxious, as though I feared a repeat performance of my instinctive flight to the shelter of the oak table. But as soon as the sound of the siren had died away, I uttered a sigh of relief and forgot all anxiety until the following noon.

By the time Denis arrived to New York, I was happily ensconced in my rented room, earning enough to pay for my modest needs and enjoying a busy social life. I thought he would be so pleased with me. He came to see where I lived, and Miss Blatt immediately began to scold him for leaving me on my own. Denis listened to her with amusement, told her how wonderful it was to meet such a charming, intelligent American lady, and praised her good taste and good judgment. When she was thoroughly charmed and mollified, we left. He didn't say anything till we were seated across from each other in a local diner. Then he looked at me thoughtfully. "So, you've decided to abandon your mother for good?" he asked with ice in his voice.

"I'm not abandoning her," I protested as guilt washed over me.

"Well, you're her only child. And now she's alone."

"She's not alone. Klari is with her."

"Klari is not her daughter. You are." There was no defense when Denis was on the attack. I was in tears.

"Look, if this is what you want to do, I can't stop you. But it hardly seems worthwhile for a job selling books. What good is your education?"

"It's only for a little while. Until I decide what I want to do."

"You don't have that luxury. Either get married or do something worthwhile.

I'm about to start up a new company. You'll run the office downtown. You do speak English as well as they do, don't you? It would help if you looked a little sexier, but some men like that little-girl look. Not me personally, but if you do what I tell you, we'll clean up."

My spirits were shattered. I hated that dingy office on Thirty-second street. Morris was kind and fatherly, but the other partner leered at me every time I walked in.

I wrote to Kati and my mother, telling them of Denis's plans. Their answers were predictable and came by return mail. My mother wrote: *You know what I think of my brother. Make yourself independent so you never have to rely on anybody. . . .* From Kati: *Don't say no to Denis. Use the time to perfect your skills and get a job as secretary to a senator or somebody through whom you can travel and meet people. That way you'll meet the right person to marry.*

At the bottom of Kati's letter, in pencil and unsigned, there was a note in Uncle Bandi's handwriting: *Do what you want. Don't listen to your family!*

Autumn was coming on. Denis seemed to have forgotten about wanting me in the office, and I didn't remind him. People were talking about the upcoming presidential elections. I asked Miss Blatt a lot of questions about the American political system, and she let me have the full benefit of her academic knowledge.

One evening she said, "I'm taking you down to our local political club. You'll see things firsthand. Besides, there are a lot of fine young men for you to meet. The district leader is an Irish Catholic."

The clubhouse had a sign in front: West Side Independent Democratic Club for the Election of Senator John F. Kennedy for President. I had never heard of Senator Kennedy, but then neither had most Americans, which came as a great surprise to me. How could an unknown junior senator from one of the smallest states run for the presidency against the current vice president, Richard Nixon? Everybody knew who Richard Nixon was. Even in Europe we had heard of Richard Nixon! American politics was a mystery.

There was a great hubbub in the club. Young men and a few women were engaged in loud conversations, carrying stacks of posters and long sheets full of signatures from one place to another, giving and taking orders. In their midst was a burly, middle-aged man with dark curly hair and a very loud voice. Miss Blatt took me to him.

"Hello, Bob," she chirped. "This is a young lady from France, or England or . . . somewhere. Anyway, she's interested in knowing what's going on. I thought I'd bring her down. She might be able to lend a hand."

"Hi, Cil. Hello, young lady. I hope you're a Democrat!"

"I think so. I'm for Labour in England."

"England? Who cares about England? We're Irish Americans and we're working to elect an Irish American! Yessiree, they can't tell us that there can't be a Catholic in the White House! This is America. Anybody can be president!"

"Yeah, you tell 'em, Bob!" came the reply from several quarters.

I looked at Miss Blatt. Had that little speech been directed at me? Before she could say anything, Bob continued.

"All right, little lady, if you want to work, we got plenty to do. Hey, Donald, come over here." He summoned a younger version of himself, with blond hair, blue eyes, and a military crew cut. "This here is my son. Served in the United States Marine Corps. He'll show you the ropes. We can always use more doorbell ringers."

The young man smiled at me and we shook hands. Miss Blatt disappeared.

"Hi, I'm Don. Don't mind my father. He gets a little carried away. We're going to ring some doorbells and campaign. Would you like to come with us?"

I was introduced around. Lists of tenants in the area buildings were handed out, and several of us headed for the door. The group broke into pairs and each pair took a list. Don and I went together. I stood and watched in wonder as people willingly opened their doors and listened to Don enumerating Senator Kennedy's achievements, asking them to vote for him, handing out literature with the candidate's handsome young face on the front flap. A few asked questions. Don had the answers ready. He was charming and polite, and everybody reacted to him in a friendly fashion. I had never in my life been part of anything like this. In fact, one of our unspoken rules was to stay away from any political organizations, or actually any kind of organization. Organizations had your name. Your name was kept on a list. Lists were dangerous because people could find out about you and use your affiliations against you. It took years before I was able to add my name to the even the most benign of petitions, feeling an alarm go off in my head.

Don and I ended up in Miss Blatt's kitchen, talking till late into the night. We were like alien creatures to each other. Born in New York, Manhattan, in fact—in Beth Israel Hospital, of all places—twenty-four years ago, he had gone to Catholic parochial schools with priests as teachers, then to a Catholic college, Notre Dame. Instead of graduating, he had impulsively joined the Marine Corps. With the corps he had traveled to Asia ending up in Japan, teaching ABC (Anatomical, Biological, and Chemical) warfare to officers. He was a staunch Catholic and attended church every Sunday. I had never met anyone like him. He was ever so polite and chivalrous; smart, but not well educated or cultured. His time abroad evidently had not served to broaden his horizons. He had spent most of his time with other American soldiers. He told me about his father, a first-generation American, whose passion in life was politics, whose greatest disappointment was that he had not been able to serve in WWII, who thought that American football was the only worthwhile sport for a man, and who, in the best of American tradition, had built up a successful business from nothing. All he had to say about his mother was that she was "elegant" and liked to "decorate." His grandmother, however, was described as a "doll". He asked me to tell him my life story, and when I did, in a nutshell, he looked as though his heart would break. He spoke to me and treated me as though I were a delicate flower in need of protection. This amused me, since I felt eons older and wiser.

We spent several evenings campaigning together, and I met his friends. Almost all of them were friends from his school days who had lived in the same neighborhood and whom he had known all his life. They came from well-to-do Catholic families, went to Catholic elementary and secondary schools, and for the most part were Catholic college alumni. The young men were all starting their careers in brokerage firms, insurance agencies, banks. The young women opted mostly for secretarial work. I became as much a curiosity for them as they were for me. When they talked politics, it was local politics, the affairs of New York City, or at best, national. They were unaware or uninterested in international affairs. They knew, of course, that the Soviets (always called Russians) were Communists, and Communists were "bad" because they didn't believe in God. Their knowledge of history was limited to American history. Their unquestioning loyalty belonged to God, as represented by the Catholic Church, and to Country. Their lives lay before them, planned and predictable: marriage, a house in suburbia, children, and a station wagon in the garage. The women raising the children, keeping a well-ordered house. The men rising in their chosen professions, making a good living for their families, doing good works and having fun at the Knights of Columbus. Eventually, retirement and golf. All the while living a good Catholic life.

But all this was in the future. Right now it was all the excitement of a first new car, first jobs, and their first political campaign for president, supporting a handsome, young, and charismatic candidate, an Irish Catholic to boot. Besides, there was dating, and baseball and pizza and dancing. The girls were all "good girls," the young men, neat, polite, and gallant. They were all very sweet and kind and terribly, terribly innocent.

I knew that I was a disturbing presence in their midst. As usual, I was different. I asked too many questions, and when they answered I always had another "why" ready.

"Why is the president's religion such an issue?"

"Because we've never had a Catholic before."

"What difference does it make? This country doesn't have a state religion. You have separation of church and state."

"But the WASPs are a large majority," Don explained.

"The what?"

"W-A-S-P, White Anglo-Saxon Protestant."

"But if they have no religious say-so, what difference does it make?"

"They're afraid that a Catholic president's loyalty would be first to the pope and the teachings of the Catholic Church."

"Would it?"

"Well . . . of course not. Anyway it's not an issue. Any policy of the U.S.A. is not at odds with the Vatican."

"But suppose it were?"

"Why would it be?"

"I'm just asking a hypothetical question. What if? Where do you suppose a Catholic president's loyalty would lie?"

This was exactly the kind of topic that my student friends at Columbia would have argued about endlessly. But not these young people. They were from a different world. They spoke, acted, and thought differently. And they were uncomfortable with questions that challenged their beliefs, especially if the questions were asked by an outsider. The subject was changed immediately to baseball, movies, or the latest television programs.

The major division that I had witnessed before among people of the same country had been one of class: the Haves versus the Have-nots. But the underlying culture was the same. What separated people in Europe was national culture. The French were different from the Germans, who were different from the English, et cetera. But here were two sets of young people that lived side by side, belonged more or less to the same economic class, spoke the same language—and yet grew up in parallel but different cultures. In a country that did not allow religious discrimination, people still separated themselves from one another based on their various faiths. In a paradoxical twist, the Jews and the Catholics of New York City were drawn together, forming a political alliance of relative newcomers against the entrenched and powerful WASPs.

Meeting Don became a daily habit. He came to visit the bookstore right before closing and walked me home. One evening he took me to his home, a cavernous apartment overlooking the Hudson River, to introduce me to his parents.

The atmosphere in their home was tense and stiff. There was a chilly hush in the apartment. The gray silk Austrian shades were down. The Chippendale sofas looked very formal, flanked by antique mahogany tables topped with bronze lamps. There were exquisite Meissen pieces in the polished English breakfronts and very good paintings on the walls. But the immediate impression was not "home." It was a showplace for beautiful things. The only cozy and friendly space was Nanny's room, which was full of gaudy keepsakes, old-fashioned photographs, and half-finished multicolored afghans, the crochet hooks still attached, thrown in the easy chair.

Don's grandmother, a sweet-faced old lady, welcomed me warmly. His mother, tall, elegant, and unsmiling, looked me up and down and asked whether all my clothes were from Europe, where I was from, who my parents were. She didn't seem pleased with any of my answers, and though his father had previously been friendly to me, I felt a cold blast of suspicion blowing my way. This reaction confused me. I didn't understand why they didn't like me. I was polite, had good manners, was educated, looked presentable. I knew that they had Jewish friends, so anti-Semitism didn't occur to me. What was wrong? Then the cat got out of the bag.

"I suppose all your family wants to come to the United States?" asked his father.

"No, not really. My uncle has been coming and going for years. But he's the only one."

"Yeah, that's what they all say. Then one comes, gets herself married to some poor schnook, and the next day the whole family arrives. Soon there won't be room for real Americans here," said the political leader of the West Side Independent Democratic Club, first-generation Irish American.

I sat there stunned by such tactlessness and coldly answered, "My family is not waiting to sneak into this country or any other, but if I know my history correctly, the only "real" Americans are the Indians. Everyone one else is descended from immigrants."

I did not feel the confidence that I spoke with. In truth I was intimidated. The lavish surroundings, the mother's haughtiness, the father's antagonism all made me feel very unsure of myself. Yet it seemed that they were the ones who were shocked. Evidently a person my age had no business answering them in kind, and I never was forgiven for my "rudeness." Don was mortified. As he walked me home, a rebelliousness surfaced—he railed against his parents' discourtesy. We kept on seeing each other. His openness, his little-boy charm, his clean-cut American looks, his cocky "can-do-anything" attitude appealed to me, and I knew that he was very taken with me. We were both intrigued and interested in finding out what made the other one "tick," and we marveled at each discovery.

Kati had a magic spyglass, and she didn't miss anything. Soon Denis called.

"Kati says you must be dating American young men, and that it's time for you to have your nose fixed and not look so Jewish. I asked some friends and they recommended someone. We'll go see him tomorrow."

Dr. Lewin examined me and said, "Ah yes, a deviated septum, and one nostril almost completely blocked. This has to be fixed, otherwise you'll never breathe properly. We'll check you into Montefiore Hospital next Monday."

That was it. It never occurred to me to protest, enquire about the procedure, or even wonder how I had managed to breathe for twenty-one years. Denis took care of the financial arrangements and told me that I had to go to the hospital by myself, as he had a horror of them. I told Don that I had to go away for a couple of weeks and that I would call him when I got back. The procedure was performed, and I came out looking like a generic European.

When I saw Don again, he looked at me a little puzzled and asked, "Did you change your hairstyle or something?"

But only I saw the difference. Every time I looked in the mirror, I wondered who this person with the cute upturned nose was. There was something frivolous in her looks. Her thoughtful, serious air had disappeared, and in her place was a silly, vacuous-looking creature. I wasn't sure who she was and how she should behave. Kati was delighted with the picture I sent her. *Perfect. You look like a smart Shiksa!* she wrote. My mother's reaction was *Have you gone crazy? What did you do that for?*

I resumed my life where I had left off, but always observing people's reaction to me. Now that I didn't look Jewish, did they treat me differently?

Don and I resumed our daily meetings and used Miss Blatt's kitchen for late-night talks. She felt totally free in joining in our conversations, imagining herself in the role of chaperone. We laughed and we flirted, and I felt very safe with him. It never occurred to me that he would ever want to hurt me. Eventually we became lovers, and Miss Blatt's virginal antennae immediately picked up this information, causing her to frown whenever she saw us, while we exchanged glances and giggled.

I was living a dream existence in this marvelous country. I had good friends and a lover who treated me like a china doll. I loved being at the bookstore and would have paid them to work there, had they asked me to. I had no other decisions to make but how to best enjoy my life. But Don didn't feel like I did. His Catholic conscience was bothering him, and he proposed that we be married. Confession was not helping him. One had to feel penitent in order to have the sin forgiven, and he just wasn't. Consequently, for him marriage was the answer. His simplistic views touched me. It seemed he wanted to "do right by me." But for me it was just a love affair with a charming and sweet young man. I introduced him to Denis, whose first reaction was surprise.

"I'll never understand what men see in you. You look like a child, and he's a good-looking guy. He could get anyone he wanted. What does he want with you?"

"He says he loves me and wants to marry me."

"Marry you? Have you met his family?"

"Yes, and they don't like me."

"Why not? Anti-Semites?"

"I'm not sure. More like anti-European."

"Uh oh! So why do you want to marry him?"

"I didn't say that I wanted to marry him!"

Denis's eyes narrowed, and his voice became urgent. "Of course you do! You will always be a poor little Jewish refugee no matter how you try to hide it. And he is an all-American, good-looking, decent young man. Grab him and make peace with his parents. You have found a way to protect yourself, use it!"

I felt like a stone had settled in my stomach. I genuinely liked Don, maybe I even loved him. I just didn't know. What was love? I had heard that it was the feeling that if the object of that love were not there anymore, life would not be worth living. Well, I didn't think life was so great anyway, but I had hope. Don gave me hope. I certainly felt very maternal toward him, and he was the first man in my life that I didn't fear. Maybe, I thought, this was love.

The prospect of a marriage made me realize what new avenues my life could take, and I began to think about them. Denis was right, I would be safe. So would my children. They would grow up with two parents, a mother and a father, speak their own language, live in their own country, the country where they would be born. Once I was married I would become an American and nobody could hurt me, make me leave, take away my family, and if they tried, Don would be there to protect me. I imagined a secure uncomplicated life. I could be like those friends of Don's, whose lives were planned out until the day they died. I was sure that I could be a good wife, though I had virtually no personal knowledge of what a marriage consisted of. Almost everyone I knew had lost their first mates. I had never known a family with all its original members intact. My knowledge came from books and movies, and I didn't know necessarily how to distinguish truth from sentimentality. There was no one to turn to for impartial advice. Kati was delighted that I had found an American, and enthusiastic in her encouragement for me to marry. Her concern was that he should have good manners and earn a good living. My mother was skeptical, even surprised that I might choose to marry a non-Jew, but as usual her response was "You know best what you need."

The thought of not being alone anymore, of being cherished, of finally having the possibility of achieving a "normal" life overcame my doubts, and I agreed to marry Don. The thought of being related to Don's parents was daunting. But my need for security, my desire to shed my background, to belong anywhere but where I did, overcame any uncertainty. Don, in his enthusiasm, overrode all objections, insisting that once we were married his parents would "come around."

Denis met my future in-laws. He immediately charmed Don's mother and even managed to amuse his father, who nonetheless always considered him an incorrigible rake. We started by immediately shocking Don's parents. Since Denis wanted to leave for Europe and my visa was running out, we wanted to be married within a couple of weeks. But according to Don's mother, a wedding needed at least six months to plan. There were invitations to send out, a party to organize, dresses to buy, flowers to chose, and hopefully, she probably thought, minds to change. Denis pooh-poohed everything.

"Just invite your friends by telephone. Two weeks from Sunday, we'll have a wedding." Then, to my dismay, he added, "Well, at least we don't have to worry about a *chuppah* (a ceremonial canopy at Jewish weddings)."

Don's parents were scandalized. We were just proving how gauche and un-American we were. They muttered something about people thinking "we had to get married," to which Denis's flip answer was "So, let them think."

He became a man on a mission. He went to his favorite hotel, the Sheraton Atlantic, straight into the manager's office, and ordered a wedding lunch for seventy to one hundred people two weeks hence. The manager fairly sputtered.

"Two weeks? For a wedding? Impossible. There's no way we can get a wedding menu ready."

"How about a party? A buffet party?"

"Just a party? Not a wedding? Yes, that's possible."

"Good. We'll have a buffet party. And just for a joke we'll call it 'a wedding!'"

A few days before the wedding, Don's father declared that he was not going to attend such a fiasco. I sat down and wrote him a long letter. In the most conciliatory and respectful tone, I urged him to reconsider. I promised that I would do my very best to be a good wife to his son and a good daughter-in-law to him and his wife. I consented to be married in church and that his grandchildren would be Catholic.

In the taxi with Denis on the way to the church, I realized the enormity of what I was doing and agonized over whether I was making a terrible mistake.

"Look," he said. "Nothing is carved in stone. You can always get a divorce."

"I don't want to think divorce on my wedding day!"

"Think of why you are getting married. Become an American. Raise Americans! Don is very pliant. You will be the force in this marriage. Use it well and don't look back!"

In June of 1961, I became Mrs. Donald Blaikie in the Church of the Ascension, on the Upper West Side of Manhattan, according to the rites of the Roman Catholic Church, while Morris and a few other Jewish friends waited outside, on the street, ready to join us for the reception at the hotel.

An American Marriage, 1961–1978

The Kennedy years ushered in a new era of chivalry, excitement, youth, and magic—a time dubbed Camelot. Many young people were caught up in the flush of this exciting new administration. They had only known old men as presidents: serious, imposing leaders who were a distant two generations and a world war away. But here was a charming, witty, handsome young man with his beautiful wife inspiring them to "do" something for their country. They felt part of this administration that they had helped to elect and invigorated by Kennedy's dynamism and his smile. There was a burst of energy in the air.

My new father-in-law was involved in the political machinery of the city, and my husband had also "caught the political bug." This was a side of life that I had never encountered anywhere before. Always there had been political discussions going on around me, but personal involvement was not something that the Jews I knew engaged in. When it came to politics, it was best to keep a low profile. But the enthusiasm was infectious, and I was caught up in the excitement of being part of a new political era. I began to read the local section of the newspapers and take part in political discussions—not on a philosophical level but about actual issues affecting us locally. These issues became "my" issues. For me, it was something daring and new. I was again "fitting in," as I did at Saint Martin's when I took sides in the rivalry between Oxford and Cambridge. But now I was attempting to fit in as Mrs. Donald Blaikie. Though years away from U.S. citizenship, I spoke in terms of "we, the Kennedy Democrats . . ."

We started out, like most young married people, by looking for a place to live. Denis put us in touch with a young Cuban woman who wanted to sublet a studio apartment. It was well situated, in the low thirties just off Park Avenue. As soon as we called her, Lucy said that yes, we could have the apartment—if we took it immediately and fully furnished. She had to leave for Miami right away. The keys were with the doorman. She'd let us know where to send the rent. It was so reasonable that we took it sight unseen and gasped out loud when we looked at it for the first time. A gold lamp with colored glass "flames" shooting off its main stem definitely took center stage in the décor department. The furniture, the colors, and every ornament and knickknack loudly proclaimed the profession of our landlady. We did our best to make it look somewhat more presentable, but The Lamp, our major source of light, immediately gave away the apartment's pedigree. The first time that Don's parents visited, my mother-in-law looked around shocked and, eyes wide with naïveté, finally declared, "Who on earth would ever decorate a place like this?"

My father-in-law's answer was a loud snort. "Oh, fer cryin' out loud, Tilda!"

Soon after, we received our first wedding present from them: a beautiful, handpainted, antique porcelain lamp with a handmade silk shade. We immediately hid the "flamethrower" in the closet, but our first treasure only served to bring out even more the vulgar appearance of the little apartment, in contrast to our new lamp's tasteful elegance

Within a week we received a visitor from the police department looking for our landlady, who had disappeared into Miami's large Cuban community and was never heard of again. My father-in-law did not miss the opportunity to remark on Denis's dubious acquaintanceship.

There were plenty of jobs for young people, young white people, in the early 1960s. Corporations were eager to enroll young men in their training programs. Women's careers lay in teaching, secretarial work, and for some of the more adventurous, in offshoots of New York's huge clothing industry: textiles, sales, marketing, and fashion design. My language skills evidently were not considered enough of an asset if I could not type at least fifty words a minute. I finally landed work as a sketcher in a large manufacturing company in New York's Garment Center. Sketching had always been a pleasant pastime for me, plus the pleasure of being surrounded by the traditionally feminine accoutrements of pretty fabrics, laces, belts, buttons, and bows was an unexpected and delightful surprise. I abandoned the thought of further academic pursuit without looking back. I was going to fit into my husband's world. Unknowingly I had stumbled into New York's "Jewish" industry—garment manufacturing. My immediate superior—Anne, a designer—was a Jewish Viennese woman, as was the pattern-maker. The head designer was a German Jew. In spite of the frowning and disapproving looks of the women at the sewing machines, German was the language of the designing room, and I fit right in. I was hired on the spot and became the company mascot.

S. Augstein and Co. was a wonderful place to learn the business. They had their own knitting mill right on the premises, where I learned about yarns and colors and how to paint up patterns, the sizes of buttons, and the width of ribbons. Fritzi, the pattern-maker, taught me how to fit a dress and lamented that her son had just married a shiksa instead of a "nice Jewish girl" like me. And what, pray tell, was I doing with a *schegetz*?

I loved my job and hurried home every night to cook dinner for my new husband, who ate my European goulashes and overcooked vegetables with hardly a grimace. We were happily "playing house." Soon, however, the reality of our new life caught up with us when I realized that I was pregnant. Small though my salary was, we needed it. We had started out with very little. Denis's wedding present to us had been a fancy automobile, a Lancia, that he had received as payment for a debt. For us it was nothing but an unwanted expense, especially since it was a lemon and constantly needed repair. To that Denis answered, "Good. It will make you work harder to be able to afford it!"

Don had started out as an insurance salesman, hated it, and was not doing particularly well, plus we were going to need a larger place to live. Don's parents' made their point clear: "You made your bed. Lie in it!" Nevertheless his father pointed us in the right direction by advising us to look into a downtown development called Stuyvesant Town.

Young veterans returning to the States after the war, many newly married, had been in desperate need of housing. The East Side of Manhattan between Fourteenth and Twentieth Streets, First Avenue and the East River was an neglected area of old gas tanks, mildewed cold-water walk-ups, and questionable residents. In 1947, the Metropolitan Life Insurance Company, in return for a tax abatement and the right to select their tenants, razed the old tenements and gas tanks and erected eighty-nine twelve-story buildings around a central oval with fountains and surrounded by playgrounds and gardens. The apartments were not luxurious but comfortable, very functional, and greatly appreciated. By the time we moved in, in 1962, Stuyvesant Town was a model community of the original veterans, raising their baby boom teenagers and established in their careers as young up-and-coming executives, lawyers, medical students, and, it seemed, every young FBI agent in New York City. It became a very desirable place to live for newlyweds, and the administration thoroughly interviewed every applicant before offering them tenancy. My father-in-law's political influence ensured us an interview, and we considered ourselves very fortunate when we were offered an apartment. Stuyvesant Town seemed a haven of calm and security in the "city that never sleeps," where the energy could be palpable and where one could easily feel lost in the crowd. It was the best of suburbia with all the advantages of the big city. Everybody knew their neighbors, children ran in and out of neighbors' apartments. Lifelong friendships were formed on the benches lining the playgrounds. Stuyvesant Town was also known for its political involvement, with one of the highest percentages of voter turnout at elections in the entire country. The population was mixed ethnically and politically but only to a very small degree racially. Jews, Catholics, WASPs, Southerners, people of modest means, and sons of wealthy families mingled and prospered, but there were very few people of color.

Between the end of our lease at "Lucy's place" and the beginning of our tenancy in our new apartment was a two-week gap during which we were going to live in Don's old room at his parents' home. Since Don's parents were still not overjoyed at my having become their daughter-in-law, I was determined to show them that I was worthy of becoming a member of their family. Already very pregnant but still working, we moved our few belongings and settled into our temporary quarters. Almost immediately our first culture clash occurred. One of my mother-in-law's neighbors and friends, a judge's wife who had attended our wedding, came to visit and noticed that I was sewing myself a maternity blouse by hand. She asked whether I knew how to operate a sewing machine. I told her that I did but didn't own one.

"I have a machine downstairs. Nobody uses it. You are welcome to use it anytime."

I thanked her and looked forward to being able to run up a few things for myself in the following two weeks. The next afternoon I rang her doorbell. Only her adult daughter was home, and I explained that I had been given permission to use the machine. She led me to the bedroom. I was happily engaged in my work when the lady of the house came home and seemed very put out that I was there, using her equipment. I gathered my things and left wondering what I could have done to irritate her. I didn't have to wonder long. When Don came home, he was greeted by a veritable deluge of complaints against his wife, who had the "unmitigated gall" to walk into someone's bedroom and use their sewing machine while they were not home. My mother-in-law, I was told, was mortified. And I, of course, was the cause.

"But . . . but," I stuttered, confused and upset. "You were here. You heard her say that I was welcome to use it anytime. What did I do wrong?"

"Oh, for heaven's sake. Don, explain to your wife about American good manners," she said, not looking at me and marching out of the room. I was humiliated and bewildered.

Don took me aside and said, "You know, you really should have called first and asked if it was convenient."

"But she said I could go anytime. Doesn't that mean 'anytime'?"

"Not really. Not unless you call first."

I offered to apologize, but nobody cared. I had confirmed their worst fears. I had no idea how well-mannered Americans behaved. My mother-in-law passed me in the hallway, looked at the handful of socks I was carrying, and said with disdain, "And in America, we don't darn old socks. We just throw them away!"

I got the message—loud and clear: We are not poor refugees. We don't wear old mended clothes like you do.

I left the apartment to take a walk. The confidence that I had felt a year ago when I arrived was slowly slipping away. I felt very young and vulnerable. My in-laws seemed so formidable and unforgiving. By opting for the safety of a Christian world, I had left behind the milieu that I understood and knew how to function within. I consoled myself with the thought that Don would lead and protect me, but clung to the women in my workplace to whom I tearfully related every unpleasant incident and who offered solace, along with, "So what did you expect, marrying into a goyishe family?"

As I sat forlornly on a bench in the center mall on Broadway, I noticed people were buying up a special edition of the *Post*. I looked at the headlines: MARILYN MONROE DEAD, it said, and SLEEPING PILL OVERDOSE. I bought a paper, avoiding my return to my in-laws' apartment as long as possible. Poor Marilyn, her life story in pictures and print was spread out for everyone to gawk at and relish in her tragedy. I suddenly felt a strange sense of kinship with the beautiful Hollywood star. I had a feeling that her death was not an accident. I felt that I understood her. She couldn't function in a world that was so different from the one that she grew up in no matter how hard she tried. I felt a new determination rise up within me: Well, I'm not going to conveniently die like Marilyn. I *will* make it in *their* world!

Don's parents were avid antique collectors and haunted all the auction houses and estate sales. So my next tête-à-tête with my mother-in-law was over the furniture that we would need in our new apartment.

"I found something wonderful for you," she declared, rushing in from one of her shopping sprees. "Two antique canopied beds are coming up on Saturday. I think we could get them for $600!"

"Six hundred dollars?" I gasped. "But that's all we have to spend on furniture. We can't possibly spend all that on beds. Besides, don't you think canopied beds will look overwhelming in a small bedroom?"

She sniffed. "I think I know how to decorate, thank you. And I want you to know that my son has never slept in a cheap bed."

This last remark sounded so ridiculous that I stifled a laugh, but couldn't resist asking mischievously, "Did they have canopied beds in the Marine Corps?"

Humor was not my mother-in-law's forte. I chalked up one more demerit.

We settled down in Stuyvesant Town, in a small two-bedroom apartment, in the summer of 1962, just six weeks before my first child was born. My mother came to be on hand for the birth of her first grandchild. She brought with her all the traditional gifts that are given to a European bride when she gets married, monogrammed sheets and towels, featherbeds (snuck passed customs), table-cloths, and napkins—all the things that she had enjoyed only for a very short time when she had married. She also brought with her a full set of Rosenthal china from Kati and Uncle Bandi. She then took me shopping for silver and the best quality pots and pans. My mother was making sure that my standing as a daughter of a respectable family who knew the meaning of tradition would be established in the eyes of my in-laws. Denis looked at all the stuff with disapproval.

"You can't afford all this. It's time you looked after yourself instead of spending it all on useless stuff."

"Denis, Anyuka would be so disappointed to know that of all her children, you are the only one capable of having good judgment." Denis sniffed but refrained from any more comments.

My baby girl was born a month early. She was a tiny little thing with black curly hair and intense dark eyes that looked as though she were aware of all that was going on around her. My in-laws eyed her critically. She was too small, too dark, too much like me. I watched my mother handle this tiny bundle with a gentle tenderness that I had never witnessed in her before. A tidal wave of repressed love flooded from her and enveloped this little baby. She, at last, felt free to love. She was not afraid anymore. I watched with envy and wonder. Would I ever be able to feel what she felt?

Don liked the name Jennifer, and the baby was named without my giving a thought to naming her after one of our dead relatives, as is traditional in the Jewish faith. She was baptized in a Catholic Church, with Don's favorite uncle and aunt acting as godparents. As the priest sprinkled holy water on my baby, my mother and I exchanged glances, and one thought passed between us: Is this what will keep her safe?

My mother stayed with us a few months, looking after Jennifer, while I went back to work. For the first time in her life, my mother was calm and worry free, but her heart was getting weaker. She carried nitroglycerin with her at all times. We made plans to get her a little apartment close to us, so she could stay in New York permanently. But first, she said, she needed to go home and get her things in order. I felt wretched when she left. We had finally felt comfortable with each other. We laughed together, we cooked together, we cooed over the baby together. She commanded respect from my in-laws, who for those few months refrained from making any allusions to the inferiority of Europeans and refugees. Besides, they were overwhelmed by her incredible cooking.

Denis had also behaved well. Whenever not traveling, he visited often to dine on home cooking and play with the baby. The first time he saw her, he brought her his own brand of baby gifts: a wig, a brassiere, and a set of false teeth. He said he had heard that she had been born without "some necessary feminine assets!"

A calmness had descended on the family. Nobody was fighting. There were no crises. Don had gone into his father's business and had started to take great interest in local politics. Now that my mother was going back to London, I was going to become a full-time housewife and mother. I told myself that I was finally headed toward what I had always wanted—a normal life in a home of my own.

I was losing touch with my friends from Columbia. I didn't have time to meet with them. Denis and his cousin, Marianne's mother, had rekindled an old family argument having to do with their fathers (my grandfather and his brother). Denis suddenly remembered that his uncle had slighted his father, and he no longer wanted to keep these renewed family ties. Consequently, I was not to see my cousin either. This was an old ploy of Denis's. If he ever had a fight with anyone, nobody in the family was allowed to speak to that person. His way of enforcing this order was, It's either him or me. You choose.

I got to know my neighbors and the other young mothers with whom I shared the benches in the playground and forged new friendships. I had one Hungarian Jewish friend, Ildiko. We had been introduced through a network of aunts and mothers. She was a refugee who had married the young man with whom she had escaped during the 1956 revolution. As soon as she arrived in the United States, she embarked on fulfilling a lifelong dream and had enrolled in fashion design school. She graduated and started to work her way up New York's Seventh Avenue ladder. Ildi was talented and elegant, but her marriage was unhappy. We became friends immediately. Our background was a mutual meeting point. We would unconsciously slip into Hungarian, cook a traditional meal, or start singing old Hungarian children's songs. She became a frequent visitor at our apartment, and we were her support system when she divorced her husband. Since my family was not around me, she was my only link to my earlier environment.

In 1964, I was pregnant again and this time I panicked. It suddenly seemed too much. I was fencing myself in. I was closing off all options. Denis came to visit, and I broke down and cried.

"Hey, isn't this what you wanted? A husband, a family, a home? What are you complaining about?"

"I don't know. I just wish Mamcsi were here."

"You've never consulted your mother before for anything, why do you need her now?"

I truly didn't know, but it was probably the first time that I reached out instinctively toward her. Her visit had made a marked effect, and I really wanted my mother around. Denis, in a sudden gesture of compassion, took out a wad of cash.

"Go get yourself an airline ticket and go to London. A visit will do you both good."

I didn't need to be coaxed. Leaving husband, home, and disapproving in-laws behind, Jennifer and I were on the next plane to London.

Kati got the news and flew in from Vienna. She had felt left out. As far as she was concerned, Jennifer was as much her granddaughter as my mother's. Klari came and declared that my toddler looked exactly as I had at her age. Peter and I watched in awe as our children played together, and we remembered our games with the spent shells of Soviet and German artillery, pondering the mysteries of our complicated, bewildering lives. Could we ever have imagined in 1944 that our children would play together in a place called London?

It was a wonderful visit. Had I dared I would have stayed right where I was for a long time. As it was, two weeks later I was back in New York, much becalmed, eagerly expecting the birth of my next child, and unaware that I had seen my mother for the last time.

My belly was growing at an alarming rate, and by the time I was seven months pregnant, I was moving with difficulty, with Don usually having to help me to get out of bed or off the sofa. But early on a Saturday morning in September, I leapt out of bed screaming hysterically, startling my husband and waking my little daughter. I had seen a huge black hairy spider on my blanket crawling toward me. Don tried to calm me, assuring me that it must have been a bad dream, but I wouldn't believe him. I had seen it. It was real. I sat in the living room trembling while he shook out all the bedclothes and cleaned out the bedroom from top to bottom without finding anything. When I finally pulled myself together enough to drink a cup of tea, the doorbell rang and Denis came in. He sat down on the sofa and started fidgeting. Suddenly he got to his feet and said very quickly, "There's no other way to tell you. Your mother died this morning."

I thought he had gone mad. How could he say such a thing? I had talked to my mother just ten days before on her birthday, her fifty-second. Denis continued. "You shouldn't have let her look after the baby. It was too much for her. That's probably what killed her."

Oh, how I hated him at that moment. I had also felt that it was too much for my mother to look after the baby, and I had said so. But she had been so happy doing it. She said that it was the best time she ever had in her life.

I turned on my heels and walked into the bedroom, locking the door behind me. Anger welled up in me. Why now? Just when, for the first time in her life, she could have taken it easy? Why just when I was really beginning to understand her? Why when for the first time in her life she had a chance to be happy? I railed inside. But it wasn't just anger that I felt. It was also the deepest sense of loneliness and loss imaginable. I had just found her! I felt completely alone and abandoned. As though I had lost the only person that ever cared for me, that I could count on, without having to give something in return.

I got dressed and walked through the living room toward the front door. Denis had gone. Don came toward me ready to console and hug me. I pushed him away roughly.

"Leave me alone. I'm going out."

"Let me come with you," he begged.

"No!" And I slammed the front door in his face.

I walked till I felt tired, then into the first movie house that I saw. I sat in the dark watching the images on the screen, keeping my mind blank. I didn't want to think. I didn't want to feel anything but the anger. I knew that I had hurt Don by not allowing him to be with me. But I wasn't yet ready to handle the grief, the pain, and the guilt that I knew were lying in wait around a dark corner. When I got home my mother's last letter to me was waiting in my mailbox.

My anger stayed with me till I delivered my baby boy two months later.

While delivering my second child, I felt my mother's presence. Whether I imagined it or wished it was immaterial, but I felt that she wanted me to become reconciled to her death. It seemed right. She had suffered so much, but she had stayed as long as she could, as long as she was needed. It was time to go. I had a feeling that she was in a better place, and I smiled while also crying, thinking that she had been an atheist. I hoped that she was wrong.

At eight-and-a-half pounds, my baby was the largest in the nursery, and I, the smallest mother.

"That's more like it!" commented my father-in-law, as I struggled with the seventeen stitches that closed my episiotomy.

My in-laws decided that the baby should be named after his father, but this time I said it was my turn to name the baby, and I wanted to name him after my uncle Miklos, who had been killed in Auschwitz. An argument ensued. I thought that I was compromising by having the baby christened Donald Nicholas but calling him Nicky. That did not please my in-laws, who thought that they would settle the issue by sending a gift, a multipiece, multicolored wall plaque of a choo-choo train; a little engineer peeked out of the locomotive window with the name Donald written on his hat. I dutifully hung up the little train above the crib, got out my paint set, and renamed the engineer Nicky. Don stood above the fray, waiting to see the outcome, then finally decided to call the baby Nicky as well. Denis was ecstatic. Miklos had been his favorite sibling, and his murder was one of his deepest hurts. My in-laws grudgingly accepted their defeat.

There were periods of truce with Don's parents. I helped out with the political campaigns that my father-in-law was involved in, and when he was running for office, I rigged up a sign to Jennifer's baby carriage that proclaimed If I could vote I'd vote for my grand pa Bob Blaikie for Councilman at Large. We collected many smiles and got the attention of our local newspaper.

My father-in-law, however, was not the kind of man that one could get close to. We eyed each other warily and circled each other like two boxers in the ring, never quite knowing what move the other was planning. Don was in my corner, my mother-in-law in his, but we were the major adversaries.

He was a Gordian knot of contradictions and inner conflicts. He supported black politicians because he felt they would best represent their own community and had Jewish friends, and he would usually endorse any legislation guaranteeing personal freedoms. Yet he could burst out with the most unforgivably racist and homophobic remarks, and took delight in seeing me offended.

During the summer following Nicky's birth, we spent a few days on the Jersey Shore. After a couple of hours playing on the beach with the children, I was changing Nicky's diaper when my father-in-law appeared at my side and, looking around furtively, said, "Don't do that! Only Jews do that in public!"

Yet, following the horrible massacre of the Israeli athletes at the Munich Olympics in 1972, he wrote me the most touching note, wherein he lamented, *When will we learn to live in peace with each other, forgetting our differences and realize that violence only begets violence and changes nothing for the better?*

He was very devout, never missing mass on Sunday and kneeling in prayer every night of his life before retiring. He adored and respected his mother yet felt contemptuous of other women, including his wife, who, I soon realized, was the closest and easiest victim of his need to control everything and everybody around him. She was a woman of very limited intelligence and emotional maturity who followed his lead in everything. She once confided to me, "I read a book once. Someone had left it at the beauty parlor and I picked it up. It was about a Scottish lord. He was so romantic! His name was Donald. That's how Don came to be named, you know."

I asked her why she didn't read more if she had enjoyed that book. She looked at me suspiciously, obviously feeling that she had revealed something that she shouldn't have, and said, haughtily, "I have better things to do."

She was totally disengaged from joining her husband in any of his interests, nor did she have the emotional means to develop deep friendships. Consequently, she was a terribly lonely and neglected woman. She spent her life in pursuit of what she called "gracious living," which in her mind was what every "lady" should aspire to. Her husband forbade her to hire anyone to help maintain their ten-room apartment for fear that someone might damage his precious antiques. The lion's share of housework fell to his elderly mother-in-law, who lived with them and who was terrified of him. His passion for antiques extended to fixing and refinishing his treasures in the most proficient and professional way. One of the maids' rooms in the rear of the enormous apartment was converted into an atelier, which he retired to immediately after coming home from his office, leaving it only to eat and sleep. He sweated and labored over his "finds" and was proud of being able to restore the most damaged pieces to their original beauty. Yet he never bothered to learn their surrounding history, which would have enhanced his knowledge of the pieces he loved so much.

He once brought home a magnificent bronze eagle, badly in need of cleaning and restoration. In its talons the eagle held several banners, and there were holes in its outspread wings, which my father-in-law bemoaned. I examined the eagle, and noticing that the flags each had the words *Austerlitz, Jena,* and *Tilsit* etched on them, I ventured to suggest that this was a representation of the Napoleonic eagle and that the holes in the wings were symbolic of the battles he had fought. My father-in-law was intrigued but skeptical of my deduction. Nonetheless he took the eagle to one of the major auction houses, where it was authenticated and proved to have been the work of a major French sculptor. He acknowledged that I had made a good "guess," however it was his "eye" that had found the eagle. To my astonishment, he winked and smiled at me on saying this, and such occasional glimpses of humor and humanity managed to imbue him with a certain charm that his wife totally lacked, endearing him to many people who had no occasion to know his darker side.

His wife adorned his environment with her good looks and stylish clothes, but being unable to join in the conversation, she sat through the innumerable political dinners and cocktail parties sipping drink after drink, with the terrible result of alcoholism. It took many years for me to understand the pathos that was her life. She lived in luxury, surrounded by family and with all the possibilities that life could offer available to her. Yet she withered away like a neglected plant.

During the eight years that we spent living in Stuyvesant Town, I learned to become an American. I had already learned how to adapt to different environments, and this was no different, except that this environment was of my own choosing. This is what, I was convinced, I wanted for myself and my children. I had a mental image of the person I should be, and I tried to become that image. Pieces were missing in the image, but at the time I wasn't aware of this. I ran our household, sewed the curtains and clothes, and learned to entertain as well as any American hostess. I thought that that was what it meant to be a wife. To share my inner thoughts and feelings with the man whose bed I shared was unthinkable. There had never been anyone that I could share such intimacies with, and I never even imagined that there could be.

I cuddled my children, fed and clothed them, and watched anxiously if the mercury climbed in the thermometer, indicating a fever. But I didn't know how to play with them or how to talk to them. I didn't remember being a child, neither did I know how that felt. I always thought of them as little adults. At each birthday, I would make a mental list of how much they could contribute to their own survival without me, if necessary. At two they could bang on doors for help. At three, Jennifer could talk and find food in the cupboard, and Nicky could climb over the fence in the playground. At four, Jennifer could call for help on the telephone. At six, she had a keen sense of which grown-ups to trust and which to avoid. I observed her playing with her brother, listened to her childish patter, and wondered whether or not she would be capable of forgetting her name and taking on a new one without ever making a mistake like I had done at her age. I wasn't able to enjoy their babyhood because I was rushing them to grow up. I was afraid of not being there if they needed help. It never occurred to me that their father had a role to play in their protection. They had to be able to take care of themselves as soon as possible! At the time I was not aware of why I had these expectations for my children. I very rarely thought of my childhood. It didn't seem important anymore. It was a different lifetime, very very far away. I had built a new life. I was putting down roots.

The young mothers in the playgrounds were bright, happy young women that I enjoyed being with, and we formed very close friendships. We were of different religions and backgrounds and completely tolerant of one another. It was a society of women. We were the organizers. On Jewish holidays we often joined Jewish friends for a celebratory dinner, and at Christmastime I was the one who trimmed the tree. The only Jewish tradition that I kept was the lighting of the *Yahrzeit* candles for dead members of the family at appropriate times during the year. We introduced our husbands, and we entertained one another with dinners and parties. We were all young and money was short, so we exchanged baby clothes and economical recipes. We watched one another's children, forming baby-sitting clubs and playgroups. The men brought home the money, and we made sure that the budget stretched as much as it had to. We shopped, we cleaned, we cooked, we laundered, sent out the bills, raised the children, entertained the boss and his wife. We consoled one another after domestic fights, laughed at one another's and our husbands' foibles, depended on one another in emergencies, and gave advice on everything from pediatricians to dealing with mothers-in-law.

One nugget of advice that I cherished was from my friend Helen. Nicky was born in November, and I was hoping that my in-laws would buy him a much needed snowsuit for his second birthday. He was a very active and mischievous toddler who upon seeing a puddle in the street would give me a wicked grin and run to throw himself in the dirty water, daring me to catch him first. In early fall, when the weather was turning cooler, I crocheted him a little blue coat and matching hat that I could easily wash and that would see him through till winter. On his birthday came, a huge, beautifully wrapped box from Saks Fifth Avenue department store. Inside was a beige cashmere coat with velvet collar, matching jodhpurs and hat. A telephone call from my mother-in-law followed.

"Won't he look beautiful? Now he won't have to wear that blue thing you made him."

On the bench in the playground, I wailed to my friend, "What am I going to do with such an outfit? It will be at the cleaners more than on the child's back!"

"Oh, that one's easy!" Helen laughed. "Dress the kid up. Take a beautiful picture and send it to your in-laws with a thank-you note. Then take the whole kit and caboodle back to Saks and exchange it for whatever the kid needs!"

"But what do I do if they come and want to see Nicky in the outfit?"

"It will always be at the cleaner's, of course. By spring he'll have outgrown it."

Nicky looked like Little Lord Fauntleroy in the photograph. I exchanged the expensive outfit for two smashing, washable snowsuits, one for each of the children, and had enough leftover for a couple pairs of overalls!

The children were beautiful and healthy. We looked like the average or even ideal American family. Don became more and more involved with local politics, and when he ran for a minor local office, I helped as much as I could. I wrote pamphlets, slid them under doors, talked to people in the playground, and organized the traditional coffee klatches. After all this work, it dawned on us that I would not be able to vote for Don since I wasn't a citizen.

"What are you waiting for?" asked Don impatiently.

I didn't know what I was waiting for. Somehow American citizenship seemed like something beyond my grasp, like genius or immense riches. I remembered people talking about Americans when I was a child. Americans were the "gods of the Earth." They were the All-Powerful, the Beautiful, the Rich. America was mecca. To reach America was the ultimate goal in life, as was heaven after it.

How lucky were those who had relatives there! When Denis visited, he was always surrounded by a crowd hanging on his every word about that wonderful land of opportunity and freedom. But to actually be a citizen of that land? I felt that I was about to become one of the privileged few on earth. I applied and went for my citizenship test. First I read and wrote English to the official's satisfaction, then he turned to American history and civics.

"What do we celebrate on July 4?"

"The Declaration of Independence."

"How long is a congressional term?"

"Two years."

"Who are the two senators from New York?"

"Jacob Javits and Charles Goodell."

"Jacob Javits and who?"

"Charles Goodell."

"Who the heck is. . . . Oh yeah." Charles Goodell had been appointed to finish out Robert Kennedy's term after the latter had been assassinated. Few people knew who he was. His name never became familiar to most people since he didn't run for reelection. The official grinned at me sheepishly.

"You got me," he said. "You pass."

I became a citizen of the United States of America and had strange and mixed feelings about that. How could I become a member of this elite class of people just because I had sworn loyalty and a judge had formally endorsed it? I was still the same person, still the same jumble of French, Hungarian, English, Jewish. How does that make me an American? Or maybe that is the ideal American? Don thought my reasoning very odd.

"Oh, just forget it! What's the difference? You're a citizen. You can vote. That's what matters."

Was it really that simple?

By the end of the 1960s, tremendous changes had taken place on the political and social landscape. The Vietnam War was dividing the nation, flower children were invading our neighborhoods, women's consciousness was being raised, and the civil rights movement showed the best and the worst that America had to offer. Then there were the killings, the assassinations. Medgar Evers, John Kennedy, Martin Luther King, Jr., Robert Kennedy, the civil rights workers, the Kent State students. The country was in turmoil. But not me, oh no! I squashed any rumblings of fear. I was fine, smugly content. I had created and lived the life I wanted: a home, a husband, children. I had a normal life. I looked around and complacently decided that people who had problems were responsible for them.

And I was certainly not one of those people. I was struggling to become mistress of my own destiny. I would not allow these world-shattering events to intrude on my agenda!

But there were rumblings. Working for his father, Don was unhappy and discouraged. He had received no encouragement and in fact had to learn the business on his own. It was as though his father were daring him to make it alone, seemingly rejoicing when Don made a mistake. There was an unspoken challenge: I made it alone. Let's see if you're as good as I am. Don's salary was minimal, so we struggled to make ends meet while his parents lived the lavish lifestyle that Don had been brought up in. Life under these much more modest circumstances bothered him terribly. His father was punishing him for marrying me. The situation made me angry, but at the same time I didn't understand Don's attitude. As far as I was concerned, we had a nice roof over our heads, were warm, and had plenty to eat. The rest was gravy!

"If you're so unhappy, why don't you leave and find something that you like to do?" I asked.

"I can't leave my father. Besides, I have a family to support, and this is going to be my business someday."

"But if you are losing interest, how can you be doing your best?"

Don was not doing his best. He was becoming demoralized. There were afternoons that he spent at the movies instead of the office. I hated the fact that his father had reason to criticize him, and I also hated that he was spoiling the perfect little world that I was trying to create. The only work that made Don happy was being involved with some aspect of political life. He loved campaigning, petitioning, talking and arguing politics. Politics was also the one area where he and his father could communicate in a civil manner.

Nevertheless, my father-in-law was becoming more and more rigid in his outlook and was drinking more and more as well. He kept talking about "real men." Real men only played football, not tennis as Don liked to do. Real men wore their hair short. Real men didn't kowtow to women. Real men were self-made. But it seemed there were very few real men. Most males were "sissies," "cream puffs," and "dipsy doodles." Along with this were the not-so-veiled implications that it was the women who were at fault for "sissifying" their men. Sometimes I ignored him, other times I deliberately baited him.

"I just read somewhere that homosexuals love to wallow in the mud together. Do you think that's why some many men like to play football?" I asked innocently. Don raised his eyes to the ceiling with a here-we-go-again look of resignation on his face as his father exploded with indignant denials, while I sat there grinning like the Cheshire cat.

Another aspect of "the American Way of Life" that was very difficult for me to adjust to was liquor and drinking. In Europe, as far as I knew, only peasants drank or got drunk. The only liquor I knew of was brandy, which was served on holidays. A small shot of it was served to break the fast on Yom Kippur, and wine was occasionally served with dinner. When guests came, we served espresso. The habit of just drinking for pleasure was unheard of among the people that I knew. Klari was always teased because we knew that she liked to sip sweet liqueurs. But getting drunk? Nobody I knew had ever been drunk. Yet here we were, attending political cocktail parties and dinners where after an hour or so, people started to raise their voices, slur their speech, lurch about, and generally behave in a way that made me very uncomfortable. Don kept talking to these people as though nothing were happening. But the minute I felt that someone had lost their sobriety, I retreated from the conversation and looked for the nearest exit. Drinking frightened me. Losing control frightened me. How could people deliberately do that to themselves? I couldn't begin to understand how a person could allow himself to be so stripped of any dignity. Once drinking became serious, I effaced myself in a corner and impatiently waited for a suitable moment to leave. My in-laws drank more and more, and constantly scoffed at me as I nursed my glass of ginger ale. There was no doubt that they were alcoholics, and I started avoiding them as much as possible. I tried to talk to Denis, who shrugged his shoulders, "What did you expect? They're goyim!"

Don didn't understand my fear. He had seen it all his life and wasn't above having a few himself with the boys when the spirit moved him. On those nights, I made sure that by the time he came home, the lights were out and I asleep, or pretending to be. I worried constantly that Don might follow in his father's drinking habits.

But that wasn't the trait that Don followed; instead, it was his father's love of politics. He became very involved with a gubernatorial campaign, spending a great deal of time working for one of the candidates and distinguishing himself with his political acumen. I had never seen him so happy and energized. Though the candidate whom he supported lost the race, he got an appointment in the new administration and immediately asked Don to join his staff. Don was overjoyed. It was the job that he had dreamed about for years. He knew that this was what he really wanted to do, but he also wanted his father's approval. Don broached the subject by asking his advice. Back came a chilling and terse response.

"You take that job and you're never coming back here!"

Don was devastated, but he didn't have it in him to defy his father. He went back to the office. A chasm opened up between him and his father, while I watched and realized that I was losing ground in the struggle to gain control over my life—and so was my husband.

•

Denis had settled in New York and for a time even reconnected with Jean, who had prudently invested her money by purchasing an apartment on Park Avenue. But the relationship fell apart again, and Jean disappeared from our lives for good. There followed a series of women. Denis would show up with one of them and one or two other friends whenever he felt like it, usually at dinnertime, calling my house "the best Hungarian restaurant in the city." But things were not going well for him. He was playing the stock market frantically, convinced that from the small fortune he had made in South America he could now make himself a big one. He was losing money daily, buying stocks on margin against the advice of wiser heads. He lost almost everything and raved and ranted that all the money that he had sent to Claude and Kati for safekeeping had been spent: they were the real culprits responsible for his financial troubles. There was just enough money left for him to open a retail store on Herald Square, selling dresses. He asked me to come and work for him. He paid for a nanny to take care of the children, but he couldn't afford to pay me a salary. It was the first time that I saw him truly depressed and worried. He was approaching sixty and feared that he was no longer able to do the things he had done as a younger man.

For a few months, I sold dresses, decorated the windows, did alterations, cleaned the store, then ran home and took care of my family. Don was unhappy, the children were miserable, and I was exhausted. The job had to go. Denis seemed to be philosophical about it. So what else was new? Another member of his family had let him down. Our relationship changed from that point on. I was no longer to be trusted.

In 1970, I was expecting again and we knew that it was time to find a larger apartment. Our friends were slowly drifting out of Stuyvesant Town, one by one, some to larger apartments in other parts of the city, others buying homes in the suburbs. The older children had started school. We were moving up the age ladder, and the new decade was bringing changes yet again.

My in-laws bought a home in Florida and suggested that we move into their big apartment on the West Side. This way, said my father-in-law, we would have plenty of space for the three children, while he would have a place to stay on the occasions he came up north (until he retired for good). I was skeptical. The thought of spending even a short time with him in one house was anything but pleasant. However, the promise of all that space was very seductive. Don was excited at the prospect of returning to the elegant surroundings that he had grown up in. He had missed the fancy lifestyle of his earlier days, whereas I had luxuriated in the settled middle-class environment of Stuyvesant Town. I was worried about having to deal with yet more of my in-laws' interference, but I allowed Don to quell my fears because I could see how very anxious he was to return to his old home.

The scale of the West Side apartment was far too large and grand for the hodgepodge of furniture that I had lovingly collected over the first few years of my marriage.

"Never mind," said my in-laws. "Look at all the furniture we have here. It's much nicer anyway. These are authentic Chippendale settees. These tables are Hepplewhite and these bronze lamps were a fortune. They came from the estate of the Count of . . ."

I listened stonily, realizing that we had agreed to give up yet another piece of our separate and private life. Our furniture was dispersed among friends, and we packed the rest of our belongings, ready to start the new decade in our new home.

With a new baby on the way, this was our last chance for taking a comfortable family vacation for quite some time, and we planned to go to Europe between moves. I couldn't wait to show off my American family. Don's parents objected.

"Europe? What's in Europe that we don't have here? What if you go into labor, what will happen?"

"I dare say the medical care in Europe is at least as good as here. Lots of babies have been born there already. As for what's in Europe that we don't have here, how about London, Paris, Vienna, Budapest?"

"Always a smart answer!" growled my father-in-law.

As we landed at Heathrow, Don looked around the airport and observed, "Look at all the foreign cars!" Then he grinned.

Awaiting us in Europe was my scattered family. Peter, Erika, their children, Klari and Laci in London. In Paris, my cousin Claude and his family. In Vienna, Kati and Uncle Bandi. In Budapest, Pista. It was Don who was the outsider now, and I was anxious for everyone to like and accept him. I need not have worried: he was gracious and warm and interested in whatever they had to say to him. Still, he was different. But not in the way we, the newcomers, were different in America, of course. Americans carried a cachet with them. After all, they were the leaders of the Free World, and if some resented their air of superiority, very few dared to confront them directly. But Don had a natural charm, he liked people and they liked him. I was proud of my family's gracious welcome and the generosity with which they treated us. Many of the people that he was introduced to were of the older generation— friends of my mother, Klari, and Kati, who had known me as a child and were curious about this non-Jewish American husband. Before each meeting, I gave Don a quick rundown of the family history.

"Aunt Manci, not a real aunt, of course. We just call her that because she lost her children. Lajos is her second husband." Or, "The children are Aliz's but not Imre's."

Don was puzzled. "How come everybody is remarried? Doesn't anyone stay married in Europe?"

"Don, they are remarried because their first spouses were killed, and often their children, too."

"But there must be some intact families!"

"No. Among European Jews there aren't any."

This side of the devastation had never occurred to him. He had heard the number, six million, as had everyone, but now he was seeing its face, not just reading statistics. Seeing Europe for the first time, with a refugee wife, besides, was not what he had expected. It sobered him. I saw him through my family's eyes, and suddenly he seemed a stranger . . . this privileged American, a stranger among us. Though I had never felt that I really belonged anywhere, now I felt as though I had come home. And that sobered me. I wanted America to be my home. I wanted to feel it. I hated that my history was tugging at me.

We picked up our new Volkswagen "square back" and headed east to Hungary. Don was feeling apprehensive about going behind the Iron Curtain. His father had been very antagonistic about that. "Giving American dollars to those Commie bums! I'd rather throw it out the window!"

Don was shocked that bullet holes still marked many of the buildings' façades. But he waded through the antique shops, marveling that people were willing to sell for pennies things that Americans would spend fortunes on; but the items allowed out of the country were strictly limited. And Pista was not well. He had episodes of serious paranoia and often spent time in the psychiatric wing of the hospital.

Budapest was not beautiful, not at all the way I remembered. The broad avenues were still there, but the buildings on both sides were shabby, unpainted, with rusty gates and broken windows. There were no gardens, just empty lots. Even the trees were gray. The statues were dirty with pigeon droppings, and the water in the fountains was foul. We stayed only a short time . . . not long enough to visit Lovászpatona, the place where we had hidden during the war and where I really longed to go. But we were there just long enough notice the poverty and the depression, the drabness, the petty nastiness and envy that seem to breed among the oppressed and hopeless. We said hasty good-byes and packed our bags sooner than we had planned.

On leaving Hungary, we stopped at the border for passport control. It was late evening and the two children were sleeping in the back of the car. Don handed the border guards our passports. We had decided that I would not disclose that I spoke

Hungarian. The Hungarians who came to visit with foreign passports were generally those who had fled in 1956, and they were not popular with the authorities, who often held them up at the border for hours. As far as anyone could tell from the place of my birth, noted in my passport, I was French.

"Please get out of the car!" a young soldier ordered.

"What does he want?" asked Don.

"He wants us to get out of the car."

"Well, we don't understand him!" Don smiled at the soldier, who immediately raised his rifle and gave an unmistakable sign for us to get out. He then motioned us to get the children out.

Don protested, "They're asleep!"

"Out!" came the order.

Don was seething. An ex-U.S. Marine did not take kindly to being ordered about by foreign soldiers. The car was thoroughly searched, and a long oblong mirror on wheels was pushed under the car to make sure that nothing and no one was being smuggled out. The children were whining, and I was leaning against a post trying to relieve the weight of my big belly from my feet. Our passports had disappeared into a wooden building, and there was nothing to do but wait. Don was pacing up and down, smoking, while the soldier with the rifle was eyeing him enviously. He was very young, maybe eighteen. He came over and motioned to me to go sit down in the car, then went over to the side of the road, picked a rose from a bush and handed it to me with a shy smile. At that moment, another soldier came and returned our passports. We were free to proceed. As the level crossing was lifted manually by the young soldier, Don sighed and, with a resigned smile, handed the rest of his Lucky Strike pack to him. A big grin, a quick salute, and we were on our way, out from behind the forbidding Iron Curtain headed for the West.

In Vienna, Kati couldn't wait to show us off to her friends. We were ushered hither and thither. The opera, the palaces, the Vienna woods, cruises on the Danube. We were not allowed to miss a thing. My friend Juliana's father, sitting next to me in a coffeehouse one afternoon, nodded toward Don and whispered slyly to me, "I see how important your Jewish roots are to you and your family!"

One afternoon we met George, an old friend from my university days. Don told him how exciting it was for him to ride on the enormous Ferris wheel that Orson Welles had been filmed riding in *The Third Man,* and I prattled on about being lucky to have found an au pair to take back to New York. He eyed us with scarcely disguised scorn, took in Don's blond hair, wide shoulders, and open smile, my large belly and stylish American clothing, and I felt as if I were being dismissed forever. I could see that I had become worthless in his eyes. I had sold out to American vacuity and the worship of the Almighty Dollar. I was morally, ethically, and intellectually devalued if not bankrupt.

I became aware of the fact that many Europeans considered Americans to be poorly educated, uncultured, moneygrubbing, and without finesse. Indeed, as we drove west to Salzburg, we met the Ugly American. Dining one evening on exquisitely prepared food in the magnificent setting of a fourteenth-century castle, overlooking a fairy-tale-setting of lakes and mountains. We cringed as we heard a crude male voice from the next table, "Ah can't wait to get back home to mah Cheerios!"

Through the Austrian Alps and the wild gorges of the Vorarlberg, around the lakes and mountains of Bavaria, we progressed toward France. One afternoon, feeling heavier than usual, I asked to stop early, having spotted a charming inn by a lake, with swans lazily paddling along the shore and children running around on the grass. We were taken up to our room by the badly limping proprietor, who wanted to know where we were from.

"New York City, sir" announced Don proudly.

"I know New York. I vas dere for two years from 1937 to 1939, but den I come home to fight for de Vaterland," said the German, pointing proudly to his wooden leg. My face fell.

"We have to leave," I said as soon as he left the room.

"Why?" asked Don, bewildered.

"He's a Nazi!"

"How do you know?"

"He called Germany the 'Fatherland' and was proud of having fought!"

"So?"

"So I'm getting out of here."

Under the perplexed look of the owner and the disappointed faces of the children, we left to settle down for the night in a nondescript hostel by the side of the road.

Paris was beautiful, romantic, and I couldn't wait to show it to my husband. My cousin Claude loved Americans and America. He claimed he was a citizen of the world. He generously gave of his time and took us to all the hot spots.

I had always had a good relationship with Claude. Overlooking the nasty trick I had played on him when we were children, he always welcomed me to Paris and acted like a "big cousin." Sometimes, though, I had little pangs of guilt. Denis acted more like my father than his. Claude never showed signs of jealousy, and his mother, my aunt Eszter, who otherwise had nothing good to say of Denis, was pleased that he paid attention to me. Though Denis sent Claude vast sums of money when he had it, he spoke of him as though he didn't belong in "our" family, but in "his mother's." It seemed that made a crucial difference in Denis's eyes. Like that family, Claude could not be trusted! Like that family, Claude was not in touch with reality. Like that family, Claude would never amount to much. I felt disloyal toward Claude whenever Denis spoke of him to me. Then in Paris, Claude asked me whether it were true that Denis had lost all his money. I told him that as far as I knew he had lost most of it.

"But didn't that large apartment that he bought you cost a great deal of money?"

"What apartment?"

"The one on the West Side."

Don and I exchanged glances. Now what was Denis up to?

"Claude, Denis didn't buy us an apartment or anything else. As a matter or fact, I worked for him for nothing at the store." Claude sighed.

"I think he just said that to hurt me. He is so angry that I spent the money that he sent me from Caracas. But I have a family to support, and I needed equipment for the business. How was I to know that he was going to lose it all?"

"He told me that the money was in a joint account but that you spent it!"

"Joint account! You really think my father would put money in a joint account?"

No, of course Denis wouldn't. But I knew that Denis would never accept responsibility for anything that went wrong in his life. My family bewildered Don at least as much as his did me.

While in France, I wanted to visit the Château des Groux. In great anticipation, I directed Don up the road from the village. We drove up to the gate, but the Château was no longer there. Wealthy young people had bought the place and razed it. On the original foundation was a spacious swimming pool, and the stables had been turned into elegant living quarters. I explained to the owners why we were there, but they appeared completely indifferent. They were busy entertaining guests by the pool, but if I wanted to walk around the grounds, they said I could. I didn't. It was so different, it would only confuse my memories. Next we stopped at the school where Mme Salle had made my life so miserable. In the little playground where even the trees looked smaller than I remembered, my children played with the pebbles and said that it looked just like a real nice country school that they would love to go to. Don also thought that it looked charming.

While Don delighted over the trip, talking of castles and quaint villages, alpine scenery, and good food, I felt as though I was closing another chapter in my life. My life was no longer centered in Europe. I was tired and ready to go home. But I wondered whether Don and I understood each other better or less than before our trip.

•

We returned to New York ready to tackle the unpacking of boxes and the birth of a new baby. Don was delighted to be in his old home. He loved the elegant surroundings of his childhood. One of his disappointments with modern Europeans had been that they didn't know how to treasure their antiques, how to show them off to their best advantage, how to decorate with them. Apparently, "gracious living" had not yet become a priority among middle-class Europeans. Why, they didn't even have matching towels in their bathrooms! I, on the other hand, felt out of place in the enormous, ten-room apartment filled with my in-laws' antique furniture, with the gray silk Austrian shades covering the windows. I hated those shades. I thought that they looked funereal! I walked around, wondering whether I could change things and move things around to my liking.

"Why would you want to move anything?" asked Don. "It's beautiful the way it is!"

There was, however, something in that apartment that was important to me, but that I kept to myself. There was a back door! It opened onto a back staircase and a service elevator. Why that back door fascinated me, I couldn't tell. I never really thought about it, but it satisfied me and it was one of the reasons that I had agreed to move there.

The children were thrilled that their new home was big enough that they could ride their tricycles around. They took turns using different bathrooms and delighted in hiding from our new au pair, Hilda, and us in the dozen or so closets that seemed as big as rooms to them. But their glee was short-lived. As I returned home from the hospital with my new baby boy, my father-in-law also showed up. He took up residence as he felt he had every right to under our established "understanding" that he would use the apartment as his New York pied-à-terre. But evidently, he had not counted on the fact that children make noise and run around, that babies cry, or indeed that a whole new family had moved into his home. And I certainly had not counted on having my privacy invaded so soon after having a new baby. The atmosphere in the house became tense. The children kept out of their grandfather's way. He had nothing pleasant to say to them.

"Get a haircut! Only sissies wear long hair," he growled at six-year-old Nicky. Jennifer didn't even merit that much notice. She was usually ignored.

Don's father was angry. Angry that we had gone to Europe. Angry that Don had taken six weeks off. Angry that he had offered us his apartment. He was drinking heavily, staggering home late at night.

In the hospital, my milk had not come in and the baby had been put on the bottle, which he took to easily. But three days later, at home, the milk came and came and came. I was engorged. The baby didn't want the breast, and I was in pain and milking myself. I was told to drink a lot, bind my breasts, and wait for the milk to dry up. Hilda was as helpful as could be. But as she brought a cup of tea to my bedroom, she confided that she was terrified of my father-in-law whenever she came across him in the kitchen or a hallway, as she had just done. Don, who had just come home, laughed and told her that he was harmless. But I, suddenly feeling better, put on my robe, went to the kitchen and announced that I was ready to make dinner for the family. I had the big cast-iron frying pan on the stove, the one that I always lifted with difficulty. Within minutes the onions were sautéing nicely, and I was ready to make my special pasta when my father-in-law staggered into the kitchen. It was obvious that he had been drinking, and I immediately tensed up.

He leaned against the cabinets, pointed his finger at me and, slurring his words, shouted accusingly, "My mother had five children. She never had a servant bring her meals in bed, but you, YOU are different! Put a beggar on horseback and they'll ride you to hell!"

I stopped dead, then slowly turned to face him, rage engulfing me. This man was not only destroying the life I was trying to build, he had just insulted and degraded me to my face, and I lost all control. In one swoop, I lifted the heavy frying pan and went for him, ready to kill. For a man as inebriated as he was, his reaction was surprisingly quick. He took one look at me and ran, while I, gathering my robe around me and brandishing the heavy frying pan, went after him in hot pursuit.

"How dare you say that to me, you ignorant Irish peasant!" I shrieked. "I'm not the one who was a beggar. When you came here, you were still swinging from the trees!"

I couldn't believe I was saying the words that were coming out of my mouth. All restraint was gone. And he probably couldn't believe that a woman in a pink silk robe was chasing him in his own home with a cast-iron frying pan. He must have believed that I was bent on murder, though, because he was shouting for Don— "You better get here. Your wife's gone crazy!"—while rushing for the front door.

Don stuck his head out of the bedroom. And I heard him say, in an annoyed tone, "Will you two stop that!" And the bedroom door closed.

My father-in-law escaped through the front entrance, and fortunately the elevator was right there. He jumped in and the doors closed just as I reached it.

In the quiet that followed, the children and Hilda tiptoed down the hall anxiously toward me while I stood there, frying pan in hand, panting and crying from rage and humiliation. How could I have allowed myself to stoop to such a level of behavior?

Don finally emerged from the bedroom, looked at the little group at the front door and inquired, "What the hell happened?" What had happened was that war had been declared. And war it was—for the next two long years.

It was a terrible time. My father-in-law kept coming up from Florida, sometimes as much as two weeks out of every month. Neither one of us was particularly proud of the "frying-pan episode," and we avoided each other as much as possible. But even in the large apartment, it was impossible not to run into each other occasionally, and skirmish followed skirmish.

Jennifer and Nicky were enrolled in the local public school, where most of the students were children of color. They were doing well, had many friends, and were happy. My father-in-law, however, kept taunting them.

"Your mother sending you to school with aborigines and jigaboos, is she? What does she expect you to learn, Hottentot dancing?"

The children were afraid of him, and I seethed. We were never sure when he was coming or going. He would appear and disappear at will.

We had acquired a little weekend house on a lake in Connecticut, and we escaped there every weekend in order to avoid him. Often on our return, pieces of furniture were gone, shipped to Florida, even the antique porcelain lamp that had been our wedding present. We never knew what to expect. But the worst was the drinking. We heard him lurching through the door at all hours of the night, and sometimes Don found him on the floor in the morning.

I begged Don to leave and try to either get new a job or open his own office. By now he knew the business. But he couldn't leave his father, he said. He would have to go into competition with him. He just couldn't do it. Besides he felt that it was his business too, even if he had no say in the operations. Every now and then when his father sobered up, he thought that it was the end of his drinking. He refused to acknowledge that it was a chronic condition. The situation worsened till the day that, following an argument with Don, his father said, "If you don't like it, get out of my house!" Then he left for Florida.

Over the weekend, we moved into our dear friends' apartment; Erica and Tom were actors and, fortunately, away on location. Denis shrugged his shoulders and asked when he could come to dinner. He was becoming morose. He complained of shortness of breath, lamented over the loss of his money, and accused everyone in the family of contributing to his downfall. He totally ignored our situation. I was looking for an affordable apartment, Don was looking for another line of work. He decided that he wanted to join the New York City police force, even though he would probably have to start at entry level. I was horrified, outraged, frightened. No! I was not going to be married to a policeman! A rush of feelings overwhelmed me. A policeman? The butt of nasty jokes in every country in Europe. Those paid fascists! I didn't care that the police were different in this country; Don was too smart to be a policeman! All I could think was how in my childhood I heard my aunts repeating the Hungarian cliché "stupid like a policeman's boot." That wasn't enough for my mother. She embellished it: "stupid like the *sole* of a policeman's boot." It was visceral. It frightened me. Anything but a policeman! And what about waiting to see if he came home alive every night? I couldn't explain what part of the idea was the most repugnant or the most frightening, but to me it felt as though it would be the ultimate disgrace. I could just hear Denis: You came to America to marry a *policeman?* Ha ha ha. Don was flabbergasted by my violent reaction, but I wouldn't budge. When two detectives came to the house to interview Don, I told them that he had changed his mind about joining the force and closed the door in their faces.

For six weeks it was a standoff between Don and his father. My father-in-law blinked first. They met. They made peace. After all, Don was loathe to give up his stake in the business. He returned to the office, and my father-in-law got his own place. I was the only one who wasn't happy. I had hoped to sever all ties— yet I was the one who had prevented it.

We eventually bought the apartment, but it never became or felt like my home. It always carried my in-laws' imprint. Most of their furniture remained there, and though many of the pieces were priceless antiques, I still resented having to live with them.

For the next few years, I continued my secret struggle to create that Ideal Life, the kind that would protect me from . . . from what? I never answered this unspoken but powerful actual question. But "that life" was always eluding my grasp. Things never felt really safe. There was always something to fear. I was constantly jumping hurdles that were being thrown in the way. It was a frantic search down different paths and with varying levels of difficulties. During the Nixon years, the names in the White House were a constant threat. Ehrlichman, Haldeman, Kleindienst, Ziegler, all Germans! I was calculating how long it would take to pack for me and the children and get to Canada if . . . if what? I never thought that far. Would Don come with us? Would he want to? Would he realize that there was danger? Could he protect us if necessary? And what if Canada was not the right place? And then the thought: Is this what paranoia is? Is this what my cousin Pista is feeling?

On the surface I behaved as though I could handle anything. The consensus held among my family and our friends remained what it had always been: "Evi can handle anything. She's tough." Evi was also cheerful, capable, hardworking, funny, and bitingly sarcastic when she felt attacked.

Life did attack . . . several times. The time when Denis got so furious over a trifle that he flung a typewriter at me. I walked out, vowing that he would have to apologize before I would talk to him again. Six months later he hadn't called, but someone else did. Denis had suffered a heart attack and had died alone, in the little store on Herald Square. I wavered between despair and remorse, even anger. He hadn't bothered to say good-bye! It was his fault that we weren't speaking! But no matter how much anger I mustered up, the feeling remained—he, too, had abandoned me!

The time that Don, at thirty-nine, was diagnosed with cancer.

The time that Nicky fell out the twelfth-floor window, fortunately landing on a parapet.

On the day that Peter started kindergarten, I went back to work. My friend Ildi's career as a dress designer had taken off, and she helped me get a job in the Garment Center as an assistant designer interpreting the designer's sketch and making the first patterns. I had gone to school at night for several semesters, learning the technical side of the business. I followed the family mantra: Learn to do something with your hands that you can make a living at. That way, no matter where you end up, you'll be able to feed yourself!

I liked working. I liked bringing home my own paycheck, and I liked the fast-moving world of the Garment Center. I started out as a design assistant. Determined to move up in the ranks, I was always willing to put in extra hours. Don was very unhappy about that.

"For what they pay you, they can't expect you to put in overtime. Ask them for more money!"

"I just started. I can't do that!"

"All these people, they just take advantage!"

Nothing had really changed at his office. His father controlled every aspect of the business. The less Don fought him, the more contempt his father seemed to have for him. But Don had no heart for a fight. He was just putting in his time, working with indifference. Living for the weekends, for the evenings when he could just lie on the bed and lose himself in the fantasy world of the television, for the vacation trips—each one of which his father bitterly resented—and for the many lavish dinners and parties that we gave.

We entertained a great deal. The grand apartment was the perfect place for that. Each year we hosted a black-tie New Year's Eve party for about a hundred people. Don was always the perfect host, working as hard as I did with the planning and organizing. I always imagined my mother in the kitchen as I was giving the finishing touches to each food platter. "So did I learn to do it right?" I'd ask, waiting for her imaginary approval.

Each year we took pictures, and each subsequent year all the pictures were displayed. My in-laws had a beautiful enormous Meissen porcelain candelabra that was always on display behind glass. One year, Don proudly showed his parents the photographs from the party and pointed out how magnificent the candelabra looked, all ablaze and gracing the center of the heavily laden buffet table. The following day the candelabra was on its way to Florida!

When Don became sick and was diagnosed with cancer, his father hardly noticed. To him it was just another sign of weakness. "Real men" didn't get sick! While every day the hospital room thronged with friends and well-wishers, his father remained absent.

Don got well and went back to work, but his illness had changed him. There was a new defiance about him, a hardness that had not been there before. When I broached the subject of his going into his own business, his reasons for not doing it had also changed. It had nothing to do with leaving his father alone.

"Damn it, I've put in fifteen years. He owes it to me. I'll stick it out!"

Damn them all! I thought. Are we going to live our lives waiting for someone to die? I had removed myself completely from my in-laws. Don's life would always be influenced by his father. I had neither succeeded in wrenching him away, nor in joining him. We were not a unit. We never would be. We were two separate beings living side by side with different aims in life that we had never acknowledged to each other or ourselves. Neither of us knew what a real marriage was supposed to be. Neither of us had known the privilege of growing up within such a unit, and now I faced the fact that my children wouldn't either. I worried about them. I especially worried about my relationship with them. I didn't know how to talk to them. It was as though we spoke different languages. Their childhood and teenage years bore no resemblance to what mine had been. I didn't understand their problems, their worries, their freedom, their total trust in the future. Something was wrong in our house. We lived together in seeming peace, contentment, and plenty, but there was no cohesion. The essence of what I had wanted to build was missing. Don came home from work, retired to the bedroom, and watched television. The children lived their own lives with their friends. I shuttled between the two, but I didn't feel that my presence was essential to either side. I thought that we were a terrible example to them. There seemed to be no intellectual pursuit in the family. Don and I had become atrophied. This was not the life that I had envisioned. Something had gone wrong, but I didn't know what and I didn't know where. I was again questioning my identity, my place in life. How did I become an American wife? An American mother? Why didn't I celebrate Jewish holidays anymore? How did this family become mine? Is this it, for the rest of my life? The life that I smugly thought I had achieved was not at all what I wanted anymore. I had failed at forging a real family. I felt that the failure was mine alone. I thought that my father-in-law's influence was what had wrecked the marriage, and I had not been strong enough to fight it. The cohesive unit that I had envisioned never had a chance to knit together. Other than myself I blamed my father-in-law. Toward Don I only felt guilt. It never occurred to me at the time that he too might be to blame for our failed marriage. I didn't know what I wanted but I wanted what my life was supposed to be, my *real* life . . . but there was no such thing, only what *could have* been. It was time to think about how I wanted to start living the rest of my life.

The 1970s was a time when American women were critically reevaluating their lives. The women's movement had stirred widespread dissatisfaction among women with traditional roles. The women's voices got shrill, and the men were confused by all the accusations hurled at them. My own dissatisfaction and the temper of the times all blended into one. The only place I felt effective was at work. I loved that high-energy life, the quick decisions, the fast pace, the clever banter, the Jewish jokes and stories that flew across the desks and cutting tables. When I related them to Don in the evening, he looked at me wearily and asked, "Is that supposed to be funny?"

Of course it wasn't funny to him. How would Don know about the self-deprecating Jewish humor that developed in Europe over centuries of persecution? How could he understand the wry humor that told of the young Jewish mother pushing a stroller with her three year old and her one year old and introducing them as, "This is Jacob, the doctor, and his brother Marvin, the lawyer"? How could he understand the feeling of freedom that allowed the mother such ambitions for her children and the insecurities that drove her to the extremes with which she pursued them?

The executives were all Jewish men, the "Garmentos": the cocky, sometimes crude, witty, and charming skirt-chasers. Most lacked formal higher education, but were quick, bright, talented, and ambitious. Many of their parents still spoke with Yiddish accents and had grown up in Lower East Side tenements. Most had followed their fathers into businesses that had been painstakingly built up and proudly handed over to the younger, Americanized generation. This generation lived a fast life, made and spent a lot of money. They worked hard and enjoyed their successes. On occasion, a smutty joke or a lewd remark provoked a stony silence from me, but there was a humorous gallantry about them when they apologized that made it impossible to stay annoyed at them. I laughed a lot at work; I felt energized, and when I went home at night, I sighed. It felt good to be in the working environment. I felt in charge of something, competent. I was again looking for a place to belong. My marriage was no longer that place. I was lost again. What was I doing with Don? Who was this person that I had lived with for seventeen years, who didn't understand me at all? After all these years I didn't understand him or know who he really was anymore than he understood me or knew who I was. We each had a completely different frame of reference. Our values, our expectations of parents and children, the lifestyle that we wanted were all so different. How did we live together for so long ignoring these facts? Or were we just too frightened to acknowledge it? We rarely argued. It was just easier not to. Because of that, we thought we had a good marriage. And suddenly it came to me that for seventeen years I had lied to myself and to Don. I had squeezed and molded myself into a shape to become someone with a safe and secure life. But this life had never felt safe or secure, and the shape I had forcibly assumed was cracking. I still didn't know what was inside, but now I wanted to find out. I was almost forty. I had three children and I still didn't know who I was and where I belonged. I wanted to start all over again and repair the mistakes. For the first time in seventeen years, I spoke honestly to my husband. I needed time away from him. I needed to think about the rest of my life. I wasn't happy with the way we were living.

"Do you love me?" he asked. "Did you ever love me?"

"I don't know," I answered honestly. "I don't know that I know how to love, to really feel. I tried to be a good wife. I'm really sorry that I failed."

During the next few weeks that I was preparing to leave the marriage, we were closer than we had ever been. We pretended to ourselves that it was just a temporary arrangement. Don was going to take time to reevaluate what he wanted to do about his career, without the burden of having to support a family. I would move to smaller quarters and take care of the children. He even helped me find an apartment that I could afford, and I started my new life with three devastated and angry children. I found myself in the exact role that I struggled so hard against: my mother's role! And just as she had been, I was in sole charge of my own life.

The Storm Before the Calm

I dreamt of empty rooms every night. I didn't make plans for the future. I couldn't think beyond tomorrow. I went to work. I came home. I cooked for the children.

I took a few pieces of furniture from the large apartment, just a few. My new home was very small compared to the palatial apartment on the West Side. It was in the same neighborhood as Stuyvesant Town. I had taken three steps backward and planned to redirect my life in a new direction. The entire place probably would have fit into my old living room. I put up my own bookshelves; I hung my plants and did my best to make the place look like home. The rent was affordable, and it was within a half hour's walk from my place of work. In the morning, I got up early to have an extra twenty minutes to sip my coffee leisurely. I looked around my small living room, and a strange calm came over me. I didn't owe anyone anything. I didn't have to answer to anybody. I could arrange my furniture anyway I chose. I felt so free and unshackled. I thought, This is mine. Only mine. I didn't want to share anything. Not my life, not my home, not my children, not myself. I wanted to start all over again—without anyone telling me how to live my life. My mother was gone. Denis was gone. Kati was far away, and I had divorced my in-laws. Don could make his decisions without the consideration of having me or a family to support. Except for the children, nobody needed me, and I didn't want to need anyone. Money was going to be tight. In fact, we were going to have to live on what I earned, but I found some kind of comfort and familiarity in that. My mother's life and mine merged. I had regressed to a place where I knew I had been before.

The responsibility sometimes seemed overwhelming and I was aghast at the enormity of the action I had taken. Why couldn't I have at least held out till the children were grown? Why did I have to subject them to a fatherless home? Don was a good and kind man. What was wrong with me? Somewhere in my inner self there was a craving for a man totally devoted to me: to be my mentor, to console and protect me, to think of me first, to demand nothing in return. I knew that this was not a realistic expectation, but it had never occurred to me that I missed my father. I remember being a teenager and saying impatiently, "How can I miss my father? I never knew him!" But it seems that I did. This need was surfacing ever stronger as I was getting older. I deemed men weak, irresponsible, selfish, and faithless because they were not there for *me*. I didn't know what a husband's role was anymore than a father's. But the very word *father* brought on tears and a spasm in my stomach. That word *hurt*. And now I had taken away from my children that which I missed so much in my own life.

I wanted to create a calm and peaceful home for us, a place where the children would thrive and be happy. I wanted to do it by myself. I wanted to say, See, it can be done without interference from in-laws or a great deal of money. What I hadn't counted on was the children's anger. Nicky confronted me. "How dare you change all our lives, just because you wanted to change yours?"

Jennifer, at sixteen, was in the midst of a full-blown teenage rebellion against the world. We were either screaming at each other or she would retreat to her room and paint. Little Peter withdrew into himself and refused to learn to read or write.

But I was determined that we were going to be all right. I pushed hard at my job, took on freelance work, and tutored at night. We were just making it financially, but I knew that I was not spending enough time with my children. I was short with them. I was frightened. Things were happening without rhyme or reason, uncontrolled. We were being jostled and carried along by the turbulence of an as-of-yet-unorganized life. Nicky, my middle child, was having a hard time. The separation, the move, the confusion were taking their toll on him. He and his sister fought constantly. Peter was making demands on him that were meant for a father rather than a fourteen-year-old older brother.

But there were moments that were exactly right: that winter night when I was cooking dinner in the little galley kitchen, watching all three children sitting around the dining table, quietly doing their homework. Nicky helping Peter, Jennifer leafing through the *Encyclopedia Britannica,* the smell of dinner cooking on the stove. It was the picture of the family that I had imagined. All seemed right with the world. But there were too few of these perfect moments, and I wasn't prepared for how hard it would be.

Don was not doing well, either. Having finally left his father's business, he had sold the apartment and was living off the proceeds. He was feeling sorry for himself, and the children were impatient with him. I found myself defending him to the children. He fell into a depression, and I was so overcome with guilt that I agreed to live together again. We wanted the impossible: our lives to be made right, just because that was what we wanted. We had no idea how or what to do. We were just loathe to let go of each other. Don's depression was genuine, but I couldn't help him. I was barely keeping my own emotional head above water. It couldn't and didn't work, and Don decided to move to California and try something new. I drove him to the airport and cried all the way home. I felt as though I had abandoned one of my children. Nicky then decided that he wanted to go and stay with his father in California, and I persuaded myself that it would probably be good for both of them. As soon as the school year ended and all arrangements had been made, Don decided to move back east again. On this latest wave of chaos, Nicky went to live with a dear friend whose son was his best friend. There he gained the security of an intact family, went to high school, graduated, and eventually came home ready for college. Meanwhile I agonized over the fact that I had been unable to keep the family together. Peter, too, was struggling, a daily reminder of my failure as a mother. I couldn't seem to help any of my children. I cried every day, wondering aloud, "Oh, God! Doesn't the struggle ever go away? Do we just keep passing it on? Do these children realize that inside this so-called adult that they are looking to for help is also a helpless child?"

Jennifer's rebellion continued, compounded by the irrationality and confusion in our lives. We hardly communicated. Then one day she just announced that she wanted to go to Bennington College to paint and get her degree in fine arts. She asked whether I would pay for it. It was the most expensive undergraduate school in the country.

"You get in. I'll pay," was my terse answer.

She prepared her portfolio, filled out her application, went on her interview, and later announced that she had been accepted. For the first time in years I felt proud of both of us. Proud that I had raised a daughter who knew where she was headed and that, despite our endless skirmishes, I was right behind her.

The day before her first semester started, we drove to Vermont in almost total silence. She stared straight ahead, this tiny, wispy eighteen year old, trying to stifle her panic while pretending nonchalance. And I was stealing sidelong glances and smiling at my beautiful American daughter on her way to a prestigious college and the onset of her adult life.

Upon Don's return to New York, we finally gave up the pretense of our separation being temporary. We grew further and further apart until divorce became inevitable, and soon Don announced his plans to remarry. The day of his wedding was one of the saddest and loneliest in my life. I got the children all spruced up to go to their father's wedding and watched them go, unable to hide how I felt; and I knew that they could see it.

"Mom, are you OK?" they asked. "Would you rather we didn't go?"

"Don't be silly. Of course you must go. How else am I going to get all the gossip?"

I joked. But I felt so heavy and dull and bereft. There was no going back. I was a "divorced woman." I had entered the world of New York's working single mothers.

The dreams about empty rooms still continued. Sometimes my mother showed up unexpectedly, and I would rail at her, "How could you do this to me? How could you pretend to die and then reappear? How could you hurt me like this?" But on the surface, I was "holding it together." I had energy; I worked hard. I pushed the children with their studies. I had told them that they *had* to get into good colleges and also that I would pay for the best that they got into.

"Don't worry about how I'm going to pay for it. You get in. That's your job. Paying for it is mine."

I went into therapy for a short while and discussed my financial worries.

"You don't *have* to send children to college. That's a choice you make," said the therapist.

"Of course I have to send my children to college. I'm their mother. I owe it to them."

"No, you don't owe it. You are choosing to do it."

"No. As a parent I owe my children the very best education that I can possibly offer them. I owe them the best send-off for their future lives."

"Evi, you don't understand. This is a choice that you are making."

"It's not a choice!" I screamed at her. "Every parent owes his child!"

What did she understand, this southern WASP, about a European Jew brought up hearing, "*The only thing that can't be taken away from you is what's in your head! Knowledge is power, so learn! Learn to do something with your hands. That way, you can always earn a living. That way you can survive anywhere you end up.*" How could she understand that I feared for my children's future? We never got past the reasons for my divorce. She knew very little of my childhood. And when she started asking, I left.

I met other divorced women and formed new friendships. But again I was different. My role was not unfamiliar to me as it was to most of them. I had been here before, albeit in the role of the child. Most of the women were reliant on child support and alimony from their ex-husbands, and litigation over funds was a frequent subject of conversation. I was often asked, "Why don't you demand money for the children? He owes it to them."

"I'd rather put my energy into earning than fighting," I said. But the truth was I felt too guilty to ask. I felt that I had to pay because I was the one who had initiated the divorce. It was my fault. I had to deal with it. I was also proud of the fact that I was able to support the children by myself. Don did contribute now and again, but we hardly communicated. The children and his new wife did not get along, and soon we lost all contact.

I put a lot of energy into my work. There wasn't much time to think. Jobs came and jobs went, and the years blended into a blur of roguish, rough-hewn "Garmentos" carrying silver cocaine boxes; leggy models and vacant-eyed showroom girls looking as though they had just stepped off the pages of a glossy fashion magazine, playing sexual musical chairs with the bosses; legions of tired fabric salesmen tramping through my office with their heavy bags, begging for orders; color cards, fabric swatches, laces, buttons, and bows—all wrapped up in the frenetic pace of the Garment Center. There was always a sense of urgency as deadline followed deadline and emergency followed emergency. The fabric had come in on time—miracle of miracles! The shoulder pads came in the right size—God be thanked! The pattern fit—unbelievable! But then disaster struck—the buttons came in dyed the wrong shade! Those little plastic circles with the holes in the middle could make the sun stand still on Seventh Avenue. They could make grown men have childish tantrums. They could delay the shipment of thousands of dresses and cost the company hundreds of thousands of dollars. Little plastic circles, strips of vinyl with buckles, cardboard patterns, cheap printed fabrics became the things that my life revolved around. My stomach churned at every delay, every emergency, at every order that failed to come in. Nobody saw the insanity of it. We were so wrapped up in the effort of making a living that we either forgot or feared to laugh at the absurdities that were so much a part of the Garment Center.

At our weekly sales/production meetings, the CEO of one company went over every single lot in production, checking its progress with each division head, making sure that our pricing was correct, that all our trimmings had come in on time, that we were going to make shipping deadlines. At one such meeting, he called out the number "1812!" There were no takers.

"Whose lot is 1812?" he demanded.

No answer.

"WHAT IS 1812?" he screamed.

No answer.

"We are not moving from here till I find out what 1812 is," he declared, glaring at us.

Finally, irritated, I answered, "I'm pretty sure it's an overture by Tchaikovsky."

There was a sudden stifled guffaw, a surprised "Huh?" followed by an uneasy silence. The boss's volatile nature was unpredictable.

"Lucky you got that order last week, Missy . . . otherwise . . ." came the not-so-veiled threat. "Let's move on. We'll come back to 1812 later."

At another company, the diminutive owner with the Napoleonic complex was having a tantrum because J. C. Penney was returning several hundred dresses. The shoulder straps were a half-inch shorter than "spec."

"How did this happen?" he screamed. "What kind of quality control am I paying for? Whoever is responsible for this is fired!"

"But you're the one who ordered the dresses to be shipped without spec'ing them," the production manager protested.

"I don't want to hear any excuses!" screeched the little guy, stamping his foot so hard his toupee bounced. "Next time, heads are going to roll!"

Two weeks later the production manager came with the bad news.

"The dresses for Sears all came in with a half-inch hem, instead of a full inch. We'll have to send them back to the factory to rehem them."

"When's our shipping date?" asked the boss.

"Tomorrow!"

"Ship 'em out!" came the order.

The years were flying. The children became individuals. Jennifer became a "Bennington Girl," black-clad, intense, and driven in her art. Nicky, tall and blond, was cheering the Syracuse Orangemen. During one semester break, he came home and announced that he was taking a course in Holocaust studies, asking me for details about my childhood for a paper. He wrote down the alias that I had lived under, the name of the village where we had hidden, the exact dates. On his next visit home, he asked, "Mom, how come I didn't know that Jews were persecuted before the Second World War?!"

I was stunned. How could he not have known? Then again, how could he? It was not information one absorbs by osmosis. What could I say? I said nothing. Nothing at all. The words wouldn't come. Let him learn about it in class. Let it be academic. Let him not have to feel it. After all, that why I had married his father!

The various relationships that I formed with men over the next few years were, not surprisingly, unsuccessful. I was looking for the mentor that I never had, while they were looking for . . . for what? I never found out. I was too wrapped up in my own needs to pay attention to those of others. But I learned from each short alliance. I recognized the vulnerability of men. They needed me as much as I needed them! I remember resenting that. I didn't want to have to give anything. Besides, dividing up my energy among my children, my work, and myself didn't leave much for anyone else. But I tried, again and again, to find a mate for myself because I thought that was what I was supposed to do, totally unaware of what was lacking in each relationship. Until one day, a widower who I was dating was talking about his late wife and said, "There we were, just married, the two of us against the world. . . ." It was like a bolt of lightning! I had never thought of such a union, a team. I couldn't conceive of trusting or being trusted to that extent. So that's what a real marriage should be! I despaired of ever being able to form such a relationship.

Meanwhile, the society of women became more important to me. Very strong bonds were formed among those of us who were the first graduates of the women's movement. We worked hard, gloried in our independence, spread our wings, and strived to be the mythic "Superwomen." We were an aggressive bunch, jealously guarding our newfound freedoms and rights, and unaware of how intimidating and tough we must have seemed to men. We didn't give ourselves time to think about the direction that our lives were taking; we were rushing headlong into uncharted territory. Those of us who were raising our children alone were contemptuous of men. We took evening and Saturday courses in a variety of subjects—from art appreciation to Zen philosophy, from auto mechanics to zoology. We didn't talk about babies or recipes. . . . Oh no, not us! We were all Superwomen! Some of my fellow graduates of the consciousness-raising crowd bought it all, hook, line, and sinker. This was what was wrong with our lives: we had been victimized by men! And some indeed had been. But many of us bore self-inflicted wounds as well. Wounds of the times that we lived in and had lived through.

We formed strong support systems, often joking, "Of course we're not equal to men. We are superior!" We also wore T-shirts that proclaimed "A Woman Needs a Man Like a Fish Needs a Bicycle." There was, at times, sadness in our laughter, but we helped one another and stuck it out together, the childless career women often helping their beleaguered sisters.

Ildi, by now successful and childless, became my children's "Aunt Kati." She was the only one that I ever talked to about our childhood or that I could discuss my doubts with. We spent every Yom Kippur together and lit the memorial candles. Between both our families, we had enough candles to burn the house down. It was the only night of the year that we allowed ourselves to feel our grief and shed tears.

When Jennifer and then Nicky finished college, Ildi and I stood there awestruck at each graduation, watching, listening, unable to speak, filled with pride, as much for ourselves as for the children. My children, American college graduates! I had pulled it off! Their graduation presents were trips to Europe. My children were children of American pioneers who had freedom, fought and won from oppression, and now they were going to visit the lands of their forebears. They seemed like traveling princes to me!

Peter marched to his own drummer. He refused to mirror my fears, refused to walk the path that a frightened Jewish mother had laid out for him. And frightened I was. I thought that he would be helpless without our traditional weapons of scholastic achievements. But seemingly helpless children often find some inner strength to survive. The spirits of all those who came before them and became victims do not abandon them. They infiltrate their soul, they strengthen their psyche, they urge them to survive and make the dead immortal. Peter found his own way and one day I will forgive myself for all the obstacles that I put in my own and my children's lives.

Don and I met again on equal ground. I wasn't the only one who had matured. He had struggled out from under his father's formidable shadow and had successfully built up a rival business, to the latter's bitter chagrin. To have a father and yet not to have one was far worse than what I had experienced, I thought. What a tragically missed opportunity, what a sad and sinful deed by a parent to hurt a child by deliberately killing that child's love and respect for him. Though often misguided, I never really doubted that my eccentric and damaged relatives wanted what they thought was best for me, and I knew they would never have resented my triumphs. What a lonely journey it must have been for Don! And I had had no idea how comparable our early lives really were. We had both been robbed of our childhood. The realization that we could have helped each other came much too late. The damage had been done. How many more generations to come will inherit the failings of the former and pass them onto the next, robbing each of their potential for some measure of happiness for so much of their lives? Each generation guilty for the pain of the next.

Somehow we muddled through, weathering all the crises, never quite clear about the directions that we were taking. But one day, or so it seemed, the children were grown, and my life changed. It came into focus. I learned who I was. I took a step back and to the side, observing the previous fifty years as a flat plane—like those charts in the history books, where events are put into columns in relation to other events so one could see it all in context.

In the spring of 1991, my friend Edie Schiff handed me a magazine that carried a story about Jewish children in Europe who had survived the Holocaust by hiding. The Anti-Defamation League in New York City was organizing an international conference for these hitherto unknown "Hidden Children" to take place the following Memorial Day weekend. I stared at the article in amazement. *I* was one of these Hidden Children! How many of us were there? No one knew. The very fact that we had changed our identities and were never considered "survivors" made it impossible to know. Were there enough of us to have a conference, I wondered? And why bother? What could we possibly tell anyone that wasn't already known? Who were these others anyway? Were they like me? Was I like them? I called the number of the conference committee, and I registered.

New York City, May 1991

On a Sunday morning at the end of May, I walked into the Marriott Marquis Hotel and joined streams of people on the escalator going to the same place as I. We all looked solemn. Suddenly my throat was tight, and I was fighting to hold back sobs. It frightened and puzzled me. I wondered what was happening. I put myself on guard, detached myself from any thoughts, and walked up to the registration table, where I gave my name and handed in my ticket. While the volunteer was checking her list, I glanced around at the other attendees. There were so many! Where had they all come from? Where had they all been? We were mostly women, with just a sprinkling of men. Yes, I remembered, little Jewish boys were much harder to hide! All of us were middle-aged, between fifty and sixty. The volunteer behind the table handed me a blank label to be encased in a transparent plastic case adorned with a safety pin.

"You can write all your names on the card and all the countries that you are from. Welcome to the First International Conference of the Hidden Child!"

I was stunned. For the first time in my life, someone had taken as perfectly natural that I would have more than one name and country. Again I wanted to cry, but from relief. I felt a great sense of belonging that I had never felt before. All the people who were here would understand who I was because they were the same. We had all shared the same experience, one way or another, and forty-five years later we had been gathered together to finally be able to talk about it freely. It's not that I kept it a secret that I had been hidden during the war. It was just that talking about it in company, if it ever came up, became a momentary curiosity. I was someone with an interesting experience, a story to tell, and when the listener had heard enough, we changed the subject.

In the huge ballroom, I sat down in the last seat of a row and glanced at the woman next to me. She smiled. I noticed from her name tag that she was French; on mine she saw "French/Hungarian." She told me that the group that she was there with included a Hungarian woman.

"How did you get a group together?" I asked.

"Oh, we've been together for about four years. Don't you belong to a group?"

I explained that this was my first exposure to other Hidden Children and that I didn't know that groups existed. I was there alone. Within seconds she summoned several of her friends, and I was surrounded by and introduced to Hungarian, French, Polish, and Dutch women who immediately took me under their collective wing. There was a feeling of fellowship. No one was a stranger. We were all children of that terrible time.

The meeting started. One speaker after another got up and spoke about her or his childhood experiences. The yellow stars; the hiding; the fears; the false papers; the strange names; the sudden disappearance of parents, grandparents, friends; the love; the sacrifices; the cruelties of strangers; the religious conversions, the confusion, and finally the reconversions; the D.P. (displaced person) camps; the orphanages; the devastation. We sat and we listened, as rapid flashbacks appeared on the screen of our memory. Very few, if any, cheeks were dry. We all remembered things that had long been banished from our consciousness, things that hurt to think about. Mostly we remembered and relived our helplessness in the face of the most monumental evil that had swept Europe. We were not all prepared to open these wounds that had been exiled to the shadowy world of painful childhood memories. While struggling to stifle sobs, I felt my neighbor's hand on mine, giving and taking comfort. Tissues were quietly passed from hand to hand, and clear glasses were exchanged for dark ones. Silently we asked ourselves questions: Why have we been silent all these years about how much all this hurt? Why did we readily accept as fact the statement "You are the lucky one!"? And why, oh, why have we remained "in hiding" after all these years? Hiding our feelings from ourselves more than from anyone else? We had listened to concentration camp survivors tell their stories, and we had felt guilty. Anne Frank had been a Hidden Child, and she had recorded her feelings, her fears, and her trials—but she had been caught and had died in a camp. We had dared to stay alive, to escape. We had not earned the right to be "survivors." By our own standards, we had not suffered enough. We had survived without even a tattoo on our forearm. We felt ashamed for not having lived through what they had, for having been "lucky."

After the war, who had time to care about our confusion, our feelings of abandonment, alienation, fear of the future, the unknown, our nightmares of the horrors remembered? Once we were fed, we were going to be all right. How many times did we hear, "Children forget quickly, they're adaptable, they'll grow out of it. They're lucky"? We believed it. We perpetuated the myth. Until now. Now we cracked open the door to our childhood memories. They are not of carefree lazy summer days running in the grass, but stifling hot, crowded rooms because going out was not safe. They are not of scampering puppy dogs, but of rats and spiders in cellars and stables. Instead of the lilts of childish songs, we remember the dreaded sound of goose-stepping boots.

I spent the day going to workshops:

Fear of Abandonment
Who Am I, Christian or Jew?
Lost Childhood
Is Reconciliation with God Possible?
Hiding and the Problem of Identity
Learning to Trust and Feel Safe

I could say something about any of these subjects. They all related to me and to the Holocaust. Joining me were anywhere from a dozen to twenty-five people sitting in a circle. We started talking. I listened to some terrifying stories. Mine seemed so irrelevant, but as I attempted to talk, my voice broke and I started to cry. I couldn't understand why. It happened each time that I opened my mouth, and I couldn't stop myself.

A man said to me, "The only way to stop the pain is to go through it."

"It hurts too much," I heard myself say.

We cried together. What was it that was hurting so much? We all listened to one another. It was different than before. Nobody interrupted or changed the subject. We understood the meaning of certain phrases.

"My mother left me on the farm."

"I last saw him being herded onto the truck."

"We bought false papers."

"He asked me my name and I couldn't remember what I was supposed to answer."

We understood the volumes that those phrases spoke, the feelings that the speakers felt. We remembered their memories. We felt their pain and we shared their anger. Many of us had never spoken of our experiences the way we did in those two days. We didn't even know that they counted for anything special.

There are thousands of European Jewish women and men in their fifties and sixties. Where had we all been? How did we all survive? Some, of course, were in concentration camps, but of that age group relatively few remained alive. So where were the rest? There is no other answer: we all had to have been hidden. So why was everyone so surprised when we all came out of the woodwork? We were surprised, too. We didn't realize that there were so many of us. We all knew someone who had gone through similar experiences to ours. Yet all these years we didn't know where we belonged. We weren't allowed to classify ourselves as "survivors." Those were the people who had come back from concentration camps. Yet we weren't children of survivors, either; we were somewhere in limbo. Uncomfortable but uncomplaining because we didn't even consider that we had anything worthwhile to say about our own survival.

Between workshops, I scanned the five enormous bulletin boards set up in the lobby. Faded pictures of children from the 1930s and 1940s were haphazardly pinned up with notes under them. *Does anyone know me? I don't know who I am or where I was born. I was found at age three or four in a D.P. camp near Strasbourg. Please contact me. My name is now . . .*

This was my sister, Isabella, the last time I saw her. Does anyone know her? She was last seen in Warsaw in March 1943.

Under a serene family picture of a mother, father, and two children: *I was born Liesl B———. We lived at 32 Olzeltgasse, Vienna 3. I was separated from my brother Robert and parents, Rose and Albert B———, in December 1942. Has anyone ever heard of them?*

I cried so much that at one point I hid in the bathroom stalls so nobody could see me. I felt as though I had been turned inside out and left empty. It took a long time for me to get back to myself, and I haven't been the same since. I have a new understanding of myself, my vulnerabilities, my fears, my neurosis. But one thing astonished me and took a long time to emerge. For weeks after the conference, scenes from my childhood would pop up uninvited into my memory, and I was unable to stop myself from crying. It happened time after time, until finally I decided to confront what it was in my past that was causing me so much pain. I started writing down, pell-mell, anything that I remembered from my childhood. There was no chronology, just haphazard memories spilling out however they chose. And I cried.

Then one day, rereading what I had written I became aware of something that had been hovering in the back of my mind, but had not yet become a concrete thought. Nothing that I had written about had happened during the war. It all started directly after. My days in hiding, my fear of bombs, my changes of identity, visions of the yellow stars, all these things were indeed memories, bad memories, but they were not the ones that made me cry. Those came from a later date, when everything was supposed to have been made right.

It finally became clear to me that no matter what had happened during the terror of Nazi occupation, someone had always been with me. Someone who loved and protected me, be it my mother, my aunts, uncles, or even my "big brother" Peter, who was only five years my senior. Though I knew danger, I was too young to understand the real scope of what was happening, and I was among loved ones.

Once the war was over, everything changed. That's when the real trauma began for me and many others of the same age group. That's when I learned what it was to become a refugee, a foreigner, to feel lost and lonely, unloved and rootless. I became old enough to understand what it meant when, in the schoolyard, other girls walked away from me and I heard the word *Jew*. These were the memories that were festering. I was indeed a war child or a Hidden Child, but it was the end of the war that marked the beginning of my pain.

The end of the war? When did the war end? When the armistice was signed? When the guns stopped firing? When peace had been restored? Peace restored? Peace cannot be restored. *Restored* implies bringing it all back to its original condition, and that is just not possible. The armistice only ended armed conflict. It didn't give me back my father, my uncles, my grandmother, my home, my security, my former life. Nor did it reunite the remains of my scattered family. It didn't erase the memories of the nightmare and didn't stop those tentacles of fear that wrapped themselves around my being and held tight forever. A war does not end till the last survivor has died.

The 1991 conference was like an explosion. The Big Bang. Our watershed. We gave ourselves a name, an identity, an emotional sanctuary—and a place in history. It changed us all. We realized that we were not alone. We found solace in one another. We helped one another remember, and we helped one another to forget. We found out who we were and where we belonged. We belong here; we belong anywhere. We are the personification of this age, the mirror of the world, the ugly stain on the world's conscience. While we live, the Holocaust lives.

We are now a dwindling band of senior citizens, hiding the frightened child within us in our aging bodies. We watch, terrified, as our grandchildren proudly perform their songs and dances in the synagogue, while we are screaming silent warnings: NO! Don't let anyone know that you are Jewish. It's not safe!

But we cannot protect them anymore than we could protect ourselves. Has everyone already forgotten that of Europe's Jewish children alive between 1939 and 1945, only 11 percent survived? We will never be free of that terrible fact. We will always try to justify our physical survival. But our souls are imprisoned and frozen in that time, which will be known among the most shameful and darkest times in the history of the world. But soon it will be just history, and our stories will be forgotten.

With Denis. Caracas, 1960.

Caracas, 1960.

Donald Blaikie in U.S. Marine Corps,
1958.

Denis. New York City, 1960?

Wedding photo, Evi and Don. New York City, June 24, 1961.

Evi, Magda, and Jennifer. New York City, 1962.

Bob Blaikie's Granddaughter Kisses Voters

Instead of the usual political act where the candidate kisses babies, insurgent Robert Blaikie, running for the Democratic nomination for councilman - at - large, has a new wrinkle.

Blaikie sends out his 1-year-old granddaughter, Jennifer, to kiss the voters. Actually, Jennifer, daughter of Mr. and Mrs. Donald Blaikie, 277 Avenue C, is not quite one year old. That distinction occurs today which, by fortunate coincidence, is Primary Day.

Jennifer's mommy, Mrs. Donald Blaikie, a petite and charming French lady, has been wheeling the tot through this area in a carriage adorned with signs like:

"If I were only old enough, I'd vote for my grandpa Robert Blaikie."

T&V asked Jennifer for comment on the election. The 1-year-old replied:

"Goo."

And that's the most sensible thing we've heard in connection with today's voting countdown.

Bob Blaikie (author's father-in-law) and Jennifer. New York City, 1963.

From *Town & Village*, 1963.

Don, Evi, Jennifer, and Nicky. Stuyvesant Town (New York City), 1965.

Uncle Bandi. Vienna, 1975.

At work in the Garment Center, New York City.

Klari, Evi, and Peter. London, 1988.

Magda's grave with Herman's memorial,
London.

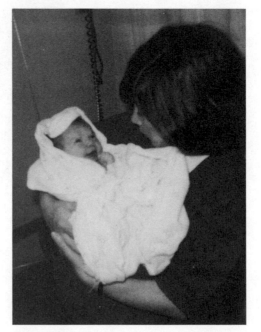

Evi with Magda Rachel (Maggie). New York
City, July 3, 1990.

Jennifer with husband Larry Robbins. New York City, 2002.

Peter. California, 2002.

Under the chuppa at Nicholas and Emily Lefkowitz's
wedding, 1995.

At the First International Conference of the
Hidden Child. New York City, 1991.

Some members of the Hungarian Hidden Children at a birthday celebration.
New York City, 2003. From left: Evi, Marielle Lang, Ildi Marshall, Erika
Hecht, Suzanne Nash.

Maggie, Jennifer, and Sophie. Connecticut summer camp, 2002.

Evi's grandson Joseph, 2002.

Evi's granddaughter Bailey, 2002.

Nicholas and son Henry at Shea Stadium, 2003.

Evi and Tomi. New York City, 2002.

Epilogue

Thus is justice defined:
  An eye for an eye. A tooth for a tooth. A life for a life.
  Six million lives for six million lives taken?
  Would justice then commit a worse crime than that which it is trying
to redress?
  Justice cannot be served where there is no punishment equal to the crime.
Nor can there be forgiveness for something out of the realm of the forgivable.

In the early spring of 1995, Kati died. From the window of her hospital room in the Bronx, the last things she saw were the skyscrapers of Manhattan, looking like gray ghosts in the distance. She is buried close to Denis, in a cemetery in New Jersey. My mother and Klari ended their lives in England. Like dust particles caught up in a malevolent wind, they were blown hither and thither. They had lived their lives like nomads, finally finding resting places thousands of miles from that little Central European town with the "unpronounceable" name where they were born, almost a century before. Upon their passing, I became a member of the "older generation." The next in line. Part of the generation who are now the Last Witnesses.

We meet once a month in one another's homes. We call ourselves Hidden Children, yet many of us are already grandparents. We have validated one another's memories and we have finally understood that we were part of a momentous piece of history, the Holocaust. This word, this event, this cursed time, which should only be written about in an evil language specially forged on Satan's anvil, has defined us, has redirected the course of our lives along paths that were unfathomable to our parents and grandparents. So we meet to talk. We talk of the country where we were children and occasionally slip into nostalgia, only to become aware of a frightening, if fleeting glimpse of that grinning, sneering demonic imp, the personification of the guilt, the feelings of disloyalty to those members of our families who never made it out of the country that we speak of in loving nostalgic terms. We feel shame for having any good memories of that place. "That country doesn't deserve it," we add hastily, superimposing the words on our feelings to chase away the demon. Yet we go back to visit, taking with us our children and grandchildren under the pretext of showing them their roots. Showing them where we grew up, where we went to school, where we hid, where we were liberated. We ride the trams and hear anti-Semitic remarks and don't translate them for our children, fearing that they would confront the speaker as they would at home, in New York. How could I explain that I didn't want anyone there to know that I'm Jewish? That I'm still afraid? What's the point, anyway? We'll go back home to America and meet in one another's living rooms and reaffirm the hatred that we want to feel but can't, because we are tired of it and we want to forget; yet we insist on meeting regularly and constantly inviting guest speakers to discourse on subjects that always, in someway, relate to that past.

This little group of Hidden Children is like a secret society that has its own initiation rites, though there are no new members to take the place of old ones. We are dying out. The Last Witnesses are fading. What is to be done with this fearsome legacy?

Half a century later, debates are still raging about the conditions that made the Holocaust possible. Psychologists are still questioning the methods developed and used in the treatment of the victims. Books and movies are proliferating, lectures are heavily attended, pilgrimages are made to the crematoriums. Half a century later, we are afraid that it can happen again—and indeed, it is happening—because we still can't fathom how human behavior can turn so inhumane.

I attend every meeting. I write the monthly newsletter.

I wonder how many, like me, sometimes stop, look around, and for an instant have a sense of confusion, a microsecond of memory lapse, of having the sense of being in foreign surroundings. When did I get here? What am I doing in this foreign land? Why am I speaking in a language that is not my mother tongue? Where is my extended family? The reality check takes but a moment. Of course I know how I got here. I know it only too well. I am here because I am a refugee. We came here, leaving behind us six million murdered corpses. And we are here because there was no honorable way to keep us out.

Am I ever going to get over the feeling that I am living in someone else's space, at someone else's sufferance, and that I am entitled to nothing? That I am a nomad, desperately trying to put down roots, to assimilate, pretending that I am part of the people whose land I have settled? I gave up bits and pieces of my religion, any customs and traditions that I remembered as "ours" to fit myself into the mold of my various unwilling hosts in order to blend in, to disappear, to become an invisible part of the whole. I only realized too late that I am never going to disappear, anymore than I am going to feel accepted. Maybe, at the very best, tolerated. My children, born in this country, feel at home and cannot understand my feelings of inferiority, my fears, my ambivalent reticence toward belonging, my reluctance to trust the future, all while I am impatient with their secure assurance that they are part of a society that I know can reject them at will. We spend our lives attempting to regain some measure of dignity that, as refugees, we feel we were never awarded.

We founded the group when we first met in 1991, hardly daring to believe that there were others just like us. Others who would understand us, who perhaps thought as we did, who had the same fears, the same hopes, the same memories, the same void in their memories. Memories that we weren't sure were *really* real, not when we were alone with them. Maybe it was all a nightmare. Who could we ask who wouldn't look at us as though we had a wild and suspect imagination? In the beginning, we sat in a circle, taking turns talking about ourselves, tentatively opening up hidden doors, watching the others' reactions—gradually coming to the realization that we had indeed shared the same nightmare. And this was the nightmare that we needed to talk about with others who had shared it. But there didn't exist a language for what we needed to express. The language that we spoke daily, we felt, would become polluted if we used it to talk about the events of the Holocaust. Does the language of every day have the words to describe the deeds, the events, the feelings that had been entombed somewhere beneath our consciousness? How can we, in human language, talk about that kind of inhumanity? We tried to describe the unutterable—not because we thought it was possible, but because we knew we had to try.

The language we speak every day, the one in which we best express ourselves, is one that we will always speak with a foreign accent. And our mother tongue, the one that the tongue in our mouths knows instinctively how to maneuver around faultlessly and that we on occasion use to summon up a word, a thought, a phrase, a concept that we can only describe in that language—that language has grown and developed beyond us. New words, idioms, slang have emerged that we do not understand when we go back and visit or read a newspaper. The language that we remember is no longer. It is the language of our stolen childhood, the childhood that we keep reliving instead of burying it, like all dead things should be.

A language learned in childhood becomes the "mother tongue" that expresses the first basic needs and emotions. And when that land, those people, even that language betrays one, it is the ultimate betrayal, like a parent turning her back. It is exile. To me, the word *Anyu* is the word that conjures up my mother's face, her voice, the feel of her cheek against mine, the trust that a child feels when holding the mother's hand. The words *mother, mère, mutter,* or *madre* are but pale translations. I don't call myself Hungarian. I have no wish to go back to Hungary, ever, or to live among Hungarians. I don't even find the language attractive. Yet when I speak of Hungary, I often, unconsciously, refer to it as *Otthon* (Home). When I hear of someone being Hungarian, I feel a resentful kinship. Yet when I speak the language, I have a feeling of intimacy, of recognition, of something that is in my very core, the oldest part of myself. It feels like *me*.

We bicker, in our small group. We resent the hold that the group has on us. We sometimes vow never to come again, but we do—saying that it was because the program sounded particularly interesting that evening. But in reality, it's because there is an invisible thread, steel strong, that holds us together. It is that common experience that gives us the feeling of security: we belong somewhere, we do indeed have roots, and though, with rational thinking, we cannot conceive that the unthinkable happened, through our collective memories we have proof that it did and that we survived it. By sharing the guilt of survival, we hope to dilute it, to water it down, make it bearable.

We are still trying to make peace with our dislocated lives. Otherwise, why would there be groups of us scattered around the world, getting together for our monthly meetings and yearly conventions? We were only children. Children robbed of childhood and family who became youths without homes, adults without a homeland.

For the last ten years, we have prepared a program for each month. And still there are surprises. Like when we found out that there are names given to those feelings and fears that we try to hide because we can't control them, and so had no idea that we shared them. There is "flooding," the psychoanalyst told us—the sudden bursting into uncontrollable sobbing, triggered by a seemingly mundane word, thought, or object. There is "the unexperienced experience" caused by the disassociation necessary for survival. We don't remember anything so terrible. So, what are we traumatized from? We didn't know that victims of trauma often suffer amnesia that leaves a void in the psyche even while certain experiences trigger nightmares or flashbacks (as Van Der Kolk and Fisher discuss in a 1995 study). Since finding that out, I still wonder: What is it that I don't remember and that hurts so much? Then there are those strange habits and compulsions that we also share and that we joke and laugh about, in an embarrassed way, because we know that they are irrational and the unmistakable signs of our early trauma.

"I have to have someone else clean out my refrigerator. I can't bear to throw anything away. I have little green things with fur on them running around in there already."

"I didn't let my husband sign the lease on that apartment. It didn't have a back door. I would have felt trapped. I just couldn't live there. He thinks I'm crazy."

"I had a fight with my wife. We were going on vacation by car, and since there was no luggage limitation, she didn't understand why I was insisting that she only bring the minimum. I never take more than a light handgrip. I still have the feeling that it might be necessary to suddenly pick up and run, and I only take what I can easily carry."

And the tearful confessions.

"Why do I still imagine such terrible things? If I don't hear from someone, in my mind's eye they are being tortured by some fiend and unable to call for help."

"No," says another, "I'm not afraid to die, but I'm terrified of living. Every day is a struggle or a burden, because all I do is worry. I worry that I'll end up in the streets alone and hungry. We know how fast things can be taken away from us and how in the blink of an eye our lives can change."

And another, who doesn't want to hold on to anything, so no one will be able to take it away.

In 1941, Abram Kardiner defined what is now called post-traumatic stress disorder (PTSD) as "a physioneurosis," a mental disorder that affects both the body and psyche, noting that sufferers from "the traumatic neuroses of war" continue to live in the emotional atmosphere of the traumatic event. He ascribed to them an enduring vigilance for and sensitivity to environmental threats. We share this condition with other traumatized children and young soldiers whose psyches could not absorb the horror that their eyes had seen. We attempt to hide a collective sigh of relief and tears when the visiting trauma specialist, Sylvia Mendel, tells us that psychotherapists are now learning to deal with trauma victims not on the basis of "What is wrong with you?" but "What happened to you?"

Then there are wonderful things within the group—the "reconnections." How many times have we listened to the delighted squeals of recognition: "Yes, I remember you! We were in the same second-grade class at the X school. Do you remember Miss Jozsef, our homeroom teacher? I think I still have a class picture. I'll bring it to the next meeting."

There are several in the group who belonged to the same Jewish Scout unit, founded when Jews were no longer allowed to belong to the "regular" scouts. And one woman was my cousin Peter's best friend's girl, who remembered Peter very well because he was always asked to chaperone them. She exclaimed, "Oh, then you must be 'little Evi,' his adopted sister!"

We seek these old connections and cherish them when we find them. That's all some of us have to compare to "normal" growing-up times. How I've always envied those who could introduce a friend with the words "We've known each all our lives"! Hearing of such permanence can create deep longing. The bonds that we develop in childhood with people, language, country are indelible. They are like a refuge that one always reaches out to in times of uncertainty. I need this connection with other Hidden Children probably more than the other members because I have less of a foothold. They remember a time when they had their own home, their own language, in which they learned the history, geography, literature, customs of "their" country.

When Tomi first came to a meeting, there was almost no need for introductions. I knew the street in the Budapest ghetto where he had spent his childhood, and he knew the toy store where my doll Ildiko had been purchased. He knew the same songs that I had sung as a child, and we both knew that the honey-loving yellow bear with the red shirt was really called Mici Macko and not Winnie the Pooh. We both interpreted the word *refugee* the same way. And we had both tried and failed to establish in our marriages those lines of communication that must be based on mutual trust in order to create a successful relationship. We are now settled together like two middle-aged people who have learned to communicate by means of a look, a smile, a frown, a touch. Our outdated mother tongue is a conspiracy between us against "the others," our hosts who, with the best of will, can never understand us. We speak the same language, emotionally and verbally, and we share the same history. We have finally found our home, but it is within each other, the only place it can be for us. Our other, more flamboyant ambitions we have passed on to the next generation. We still fear for them, even though they laugh at us. But we can't help it. We try and warn them—uselessly. They see us as relics of "that era," and maybe they are right. As the relics that we are, we are trotted out and exhibited on appropriate holidays in schools and synagogue, where we tell our stories and exhort the audience to be vigilant, to defend civil rights, to care for the freedom of others. We push our message desperately, knowing that we are the Last Witnesses to one of history's worst crimes and that time is running out. Someday we will become only a footnote in history books.

Some audiences shrink from our zeal, and occasionally I am hesitantly asked, "Could you please end your message on an upbeat note?" I sigh ruefully, nod, and swallow my rising indignation. (Just how "upbeat" can I paint the Holocaust?) We cannot allow the Holocaust to lapse into a "collective amnesia," which according to Dr. Judith Lewis Herman, in her essay "Trauma and Recovery," happens when a subject "provokes such intense controversy that it periodically becomes anathema." Sometimes, I just resign myself. I explain who we, the Hidden Children are, how we survived. The years it took us to get our lives back together. The cultures we passed through. The long, lone wanderings in search of a home.

"But now we have a home," I remind them. "It is called Eretz-Israel. Even if it is not the place where we live, it is our spiritual home to be defended fiercely. And generations to come must and will know how and why it came into existence. It is the final journey, but not a resting place . . . yet. We must still demonstrate to ourselves and the world that we *can* meet the challenge, that we *will* find a way to live in peace. It is our task, our charge, our assignment as a people to show the world that it can be done and we *will* do it!" There! I ended on an "upbeat" note. The rabbi and the congregation are satisfied.

I, however, feel that I betrayed the six million dead because I didn't talk about the horror. But that really isn't what *I* need to talk about. I just needed to tell the story of the one child who had her childhood stolen and whose prayer, when she can pray, is the following:

Please G-d, before I die, let me feel joy instead of fear when I hear my grandchildren sing the Hebrew songs on the Holidays. Allow me to revel in their childhood without thinking of mine. Let me believe that my children and their children are free citizens of the land where they were born and in no danger of ever losing that status. And maybe, G-d, maybe, just for a little while, you could allow me to feel free also. Free of fear, free of constant vigilance, of suspicion and insecurity. Just once, I would like to know what it feels like to belong, to feel at ease, to dance and sing with abandon, to feel alive and be able to believe that there is reason for hope.